Attacks on the Press
in 1994

330 Seventh Avenue, 12th Floor
New York, New York 10001
Phone: (212) 465-1004
Fax: (212) 465-9568
E-Mail: cpj@igc.apc.org

Begun in 1981, the Committee to Protect Journalists responds to attacks on the press everywhere in the world. CPJ investigates more than 2000 cases every year and takes action on behalf of journalists and their news organizations without regard to political ideology. Join CPJ and help promote press freedom by defending the people who report the news. To maintain its independence, CPJ accepts no government funding. We depend entirely on your support.

The Associated Press, LEXIS/NEXIS and Reuters provided electronic news services that were used to conduct research for this report.

ISBN: 0-944823-14-9

Preface

by John Seigenthaler

FOR THE U.S. JOURNALIST, the costly struggle for press freedom most often means little more than defending against libel and privacy suits, and pressing cases to open government records and meetings. After more than 40 years in that struggle, I came to a deeper understanding of it one night in mid-December—in Moscow, of all places.

I sat at dinner in a crowded hotel ballroom and looked up to a table where five delicate glass globes, awards symbolizing freedom of the press, glistened in a spotlight. Each of the globes was to be given later in the evening by the International Press Center to individuals and institutions who had made contributions to Russia's relatively newfound press freedom. I was there to accept one of the globes on behalf of The Freedom Forum, but another of the award winners could not be there to collect his.

Dmitry Kholodov, an investigative reporter for *Moskovski Komsomolets*, was killed when a briefcase-bomb exploded in his face at his newspaper's offices. This courageous young journalist had been investigating and exposing underworld connections with the Russian military. His killers, still unknown, had the briefcase delivered to him and had led him to believe that it contained papers that would assist him in documenting military corruption.

As a board member of the Committee to Protect Journalists, I have become sadly aware that the murder of reporters like Kholodov is all too common. Indeed, as this book documents, he was only one among 58 journalists in 1994 alone who were deliberately assassinated because of their work. And unfortunately, CPJ has strong reason to believe that 13 other deaths were political murders as well.

Another of the globes presented that evening was given to Erika Dailey, the Moscow Director of Human Rights Watch/Helsinki. She alerted us to the fact that as we sat there enjoying dinner, two journalists from Turkmenistan were being held in Lefortovo Prison, just across town.

Murad Esenov and Khalmurad Soyunov, whose reporting for Radio Liberty had been critical of Turkmen President Saparmurat Niyazov, were jailed by Russian Counterintelligence Service agents at the request of Turkmen authorities. They were described as "subversives" who were seeking to undermine the Turk-

---

John Seigenthaler, *a member of the board of directors of the Committee to Protect Journalists, is the chairman of The Freedom Forum First Amendment Center at Vanderbilt University in Nashville, Tenn.*

men government. Both of them had asked for asylum in Moscow, but instead were imprisoned to await extradition.

"If they are sent back to Turkmenistan, it is very likely that charges will be trumped up against them, and they will be executed," Dailey warned. She appealed for both Americans and Russians in the audience to demand their release.

The evening was a stark reminder that while fighting against chilling libel suits and for open government is neither unimportant nor unnecessary at home, the threats to a free press in other parts of the world are far more sinister and costly.

Nowhere are those threats spelled out with more complete clarity and current detail than in this book. Kholodov's name, of course, will be found in the section on Central Europe and the republics of the former Soviet Union, as one of four journalists killed in Russia and one of 72 who are known to have lost their lives around the world in 1994. And so, too, can Esenov and Soyunov's case be found on page 162.

For more than a decade, the Committee to Protect Journalists, through its actions and annual reports, has labored to bring to international attention the fact that there are governments that react brutally to journalistic criticism and that there are still others which are totally insensitive to the value of a free press.

The work of the Committee goes far beyond investigating, recording and publishing the cases of those who suffer from attacks on the press. CPJ is constantly at work exposing attacks on news media representatives and striving to bring help to journalists who are in prison or in danger.

Too often in the past, those who have lost their lives in the name of press freedom have been remembered only as statistics, often not accurately recorded. And those who lost their liberty for that cause languished in anonymity in prisons around the world.

But thanks to the vital and valuable work of the Committee to Protect Journalists, their contributions now are recorded and their suffering is recognized, appreciated and, in a significant number of cases, reduced.

Table of Contents

Introduction

by William A. Orme, Jr.

IN EARLY 1994, journalists in Albania called CPJ to tell us about the arrest of a reporter and editor in chief at a leading Tirana daily. They were charged with conspiring to reveal "state secrets"—in this case, the sensitive story they had published about government plans to take guns away from off-duty army officers. We quickly faxed a note to President Sali Berisha expressing our concern. Albanian press groups and human rights activists also vigorously protested the action.

The trials went ahead, however. The reporter was convicted and sentenced to 18 months in jail. The editor got five months.

We tried again, appealing to President Berisha's professed support of democracy and press freedom. In a detailed letter analyzing the two cases, we urged him to intervene. As always, our letter was copied to local media, the wire services, major international journalism and human rights organizations, the United Nations Human Rights Commission, the State Department, and other interested institutions and individuals. The letter was received on May 2. On May 3—World Press Freedom Day—President Berisha announced that in response to "international concern" he was pardoning both the reporter and editor. Since then, Albanian journalists tell us, there has been a marked decline in legal harassment of the country's increasingly independent news media.

It doesn't always work that way.

Despite our protests—and those of the other press freedom defense groups with whom we work around the world—there are more journalists in jail today than ever before. At the end of 1994, at least 173 reporters, editors, photographers and broadcasters were held in prison in 23 countries, all in direct retaliation for their work as journalists. One year ago, we had identified 126 cases of journalists jailed in 28 countries because of their profession. The huge increase is due to increased repression in much of the world, but also to CPJ's improved reporting in countries like Turkey and Peru where reporters are often jailed in remote provinces with little or no press coverage.

In Turkey alone, 74 journalists were serving prison terms at the end of 1994—the largest number we have recorded in one country. Our appeals helped free one

William A. Orme, Jr. *was appointed executive director of the Committee to Protect Journalists in August 1993. Previously he covered Latin America as a journalist for 15 years, based in Guatemala, Mexico City and Miami.*

Turkish journalist last year, but that was a rare exception in a systematic crackdown on independent and pro-Kurdish news reporting. Still, by carefully documenting and publicizing scores of press freedom violations in Turkey over the past year, CPJ called into question Turkey's claim to be an open, pluralistic democracy. Our reports received wide coverage in the local press and were often cited to Turkish leaders by visiting journalists and diplomats. The government's written responses to our letters, though conceding little, showed that such criticism is taken very seriously in Ankara.

Other countries are less sensitive about their image. The People's Republic of China appears utterly unmoved by the many appeals from CPJ and others to release 21 journalists from its jails. Yet international attention often results in improved living conditions and medical care for China's prisoners. And the imprisoned journalists know that they are not fighting their battle alone.

Most countries fall somewhere between Albania and China in their susceptibility to moral suasion. But almost everywhere, the prompt and accurate reporting of press freedom problems helps to make grievous violations less common—especially if that reporting leads to international censure, and if the country in question is at least ostensibly advancing toward democratization. While governments bitterly resent what they see as foreign intrusion into their domestic affairs, we always work closely with the local journalists we are defending. The best rebuttal to the charge that we are imposing anything-goes American free speech standards on culturally distinct Asians or Africans is to remind officials that we are echoing concerns already voiced by our Malaysian or Ethiopian colleagues.

THE GRAVEST PROBLEM facing reporters is the risk of political assassination. Homicide is now the leading cause of job-related death in the profession worldwide. This book documents 72 cases of journalists who were killed in 1994 as a direct consequence of their profession—the largest number since CPJ began systematically monitoring attacks against journalists a decade ago. At least 58 of these deaths were murders, with evidence strongly suggesting a deliberate attempt to suppress critical reporting.

What is most disturbing is that these crimes were carried out with apparent impunity. In none of the 18 countries where the murders took place has anyone been tried for these crimes; only two cases—one in Cambodia, one in Algeria—have yet led to arrests. In some countries (Afghanistan, Colombia), the failure to prosecute the murders of journalists is a symptom of a wider breakdown in the rule of law. In others (Tajikistan, Burundi), government unwillingness to investigate these murders strongly suggests complicity. And in nations embroiled in bloody civil conflict (Algeria, Bosnia, Rwanda) contending factions take advantage of the chaos of war to settle scores and muzzle critical reporting.

The most dangerous country in the world for journalists in 1994 was Algeria, where 19 reporters were assassinated by fundamentalist terror squads. This is the largest number of journalists deliberately killed in one country in one year since the assassination campaigns of Argentina's "Dirty War" in the 1970s. All but one of the victims were Algerian nationals; most were reporters for French-language newspapers, magazines and wire services. The Armed Islamic Group, which claimed responsibility for many of these killings, has now declared that it is imposing the "death penalty" on all radio and television journalists. Since May 1993, 33 journalists have been murdered by fundamentalist extremists in Algeria. CPJ has asked Algeria's government to investigate and prosecute these crimes, and has urged leaders of the Islamic Salvation Front, the main fundamentalist opposition group, to condemn these killings publicly and unequivocally.

Algeria was an extreme case in another regard: the absolute lack of ambiguity about the fact that these journalists were all deliberately targeted because they were journalists. In most countries with high numbers of press casualties, that causal link can be hard to establish.

In 1994, Rwanda was the most extreme example of this problem. At least 48 Rwandan journalists—reporters, photographers, editors and publishers—are known to have been among the nearly 800,000 victims of last year's genocidal massacres. Yet how many were killed because of their jobs, rather than because of their ethnicity, their political affiliations, or because they were at the tragically wrong place at the wrong time? Can such distinctions be meaningfully made in the vicious chaos of a situation like Rwanda? In a slaughter of such scale, journalists are obviously no more likely to be spared than any other group. Nor is the death of a journalist inherently more tragic or significant than the death of any other innocent victim. The issue for CPJ is whether there was a deliberate effort from the start to eliminate all independent reporting.

In the first days of this ruthlessly organized bloodletting, leading independent journalists—many of them members of the governing Hutu tribe—appear to have been systematically pursued and murdered by soldiers and Interahamwe militia. In the streets, reporters presenting press credentials to soldiers were killed on the spot. In at least 14 of these deaths, information gathered by human rights researchers and foreign journalists clearly indicates that the victims were targeted because of their profession. Investigations into the Rwanda massacres will undoubtedly reveal more such cases.

Even combat casualties cannot be assumed to be accidental tragedies. Fourteen correspondents were killed in 1995 while on assignment in battle zones—five in Bosnia, three in Somalia, two in Chechnya, two in South African townships, one in Angola and one in Rwanda. (Two of the victims were Americans, both

9

young free-lance photographers.) Most were killed by snipers' bullets. Did the gunmen know they were journalists? If so, is that why they pulled the trigger? In several instances the answers appear to have been yes, but the truth will never be known. Bosnian and Serbian insurgents certainly never disguised their contempt for the international press. It is a telling commentary on the risks facing journalists today that war reporters now fear the deliberate rifle shot more than they do the land mine or mortar blast.

We are still investigating 13 other murders in 1994 that may also have been targeted political killings. Our job is to ensure that these deaths are not forgotten, and not repeated. We always ask governments (including our own) to treat the premeditated murders of journalists not as common crimes, but as political assassinations. It may seem self-serving for journalists to describe the killing of journalists as crimes against society, but that is usually exactly what they are. The target, after all, is not the journalist as an individual, but the public who that journalist served.

CPJ's priority is the protection of local reporters in countries where press freedoms are routinely ignored or abused. We also come to the aid of foreign correspondents working on dangerous assignments abroad. Unsurprisingly, the places where foreign journalists get into trouble are usually places where the local press also faces severe problems.

We also take preventive measures. CPJ staffers and board members work behind the scenes to facilitate safe media access to zones of conflict. In 1994, after 18 months of intensive discussions, we persuaded the United Nations Protection Forces (UNPROFOR) to reverse its long-standing prohibition against the transportation of journalists on UNPROFOR aircraft—a policy change that immediately reduces the risks of covering Bosnia and other U.N. peacekeeping operations. Our newly revised field handbook for journalists in Bosnia provides up-to-date information on travel logistics, body armor, insurance and accreditation procedures, plus cautionary advice about professional behavior in battle zones.

THE COMMITTEE TO PROTECT JOURNALISTS is at heart a news organization, but one with a highly specialized brief. Virtually every working day, we receive a dozen or more reports of press freedom violations at our New York City office.

Much of this information comes from firsthand sources, but it still needs to be checked out. Our staff researchers must verify that the victims of the incidents we protest and publicize are legitimate journalists and news organizations, and that there is a direct relationship between these problems and their work. This constant monitoring requires extensive staff knowledge of the countries we cover and a wide network of journalists and other contacts in the field. Our annual

Attacks on the Press reports are evidence of this effort. This edition, chronicling more than 700 confirmed cases of harassment, censorship, imprisonment and physical attacks on journalists in 77 countries, is the most comprehensive published record anywhere of press freedom violations worldwide in 1994.

There are gaps in our coverage, however—some deliberate, some inadvertent. We do not monitor press freedom problems in the developed industrial democracies. This is not because there are no problems in those countries, but because we concentrate on regions where press problems are more severe, and where local journalists are most in need of international support.

In the United States, where journalists are protected by the Constitution and by strong domestic media organizations, CPJ limits its work to the most basic violation of press freedom: the murder of working journalists. These are cases that for reasons of consistency and international credibility we cannot ignore. We have worked especially hard to draw attention to the murders of immigrant reporters in our country: A CPJ report released in 1994 showed that 10 of the 12 journalists who were murdered in the United States in the past two decades were immigrants working for foreign-language media, and that most of these crimes remain unsolved. (The report is excerpted in the Americas section of this book.)

There are many cases we cannot confirm—and cases where we learn that a reported violation had little to do with either freedom or the press. Our reputation for accuracy is our most prized asset; we prefer sins of omission to sins of commission. Inevitably, then, given the difficulties of gathering information in many countries, our annual reports understate the frequency and severity of press freedom problems.

THE COUNTRIES PROFILED INSIDE span the spectrum from democracy to dictatorship, with those falling somewhere in between requiring the most intensive reporting. There are few specific press freedom violations in places like North Korea, Saudi Arabia and Cuba, which have no press freedom at all. Nations that are emerging from strict authoritarianism typically have the most problems: they have no tradition of independent journalism, but many suddenly have a lot of independent journalists. The fact that there are more countries in this category than ever before is the reason we have more cases of press freedom violations than ever before.

It is inspiring, and somewhat astonishing, to witness the spontaneous appearance of a combative, critical press in even the most repressive societies. Though this book records hundreds of harsh attacks against journalists and journalism, it also charts a more uplifting and ultimately more important story: the birth of a free press around the world.

—February 1995

How CPJ Investigates and Classifies Attacks on the Press

The cases of press freedom violations described in this volume were investigated and verified by CPJ's research staff. Each account was corroborated by more than one source for accuracy and for confirmation that the attacks were against journalists or news organizations and that their reporting was the probable motive. Additional information on individual cases is available from CPJ at (212) 465-1004. The cases in this report are classified as follows:

Killed
Killed or missing and believed dead with evidence of retribution for news coverage or commentary, including journalists killed unintentionally in the line of duty.

Imprisoned
Arrested or held against one's will, including kidnapped.

Attacked
Wounded; assaulted; a news facility physically attacked, raided, or searched; non-journalist employees attacked in any way because of news coverage or commentary.

Threatened
Threatened with physical harm or some other type of retribution.

Harassed
Access denied or limited; materials confiscated; materials damaged; entry or exit denied; family members attacked or threatened; fired or demoted (when it is clearly the result of political or outside pressure); harassed in some other way.

Legal Action
Credentials denied or suspended; fined; passage of a restrictive law; libel suit intended to inhibit coverage; sentenced to prison; visas denied or canceled.

Expelled
Expelled or forced to leave a country because of news coverage or commentary

Censored
Officially censored or banned; editions confiscated; news outlet closed.

Journalists are defined as people who cover news or write commentary on a regular basis. Only attacks that relate to the journalists' professional work are included in this report.

Africa

SENEGAL
GAMBIA
GUINEA BISSAU
SIERRA LEONE
LIBERIA
IVORY COAST
GHANA
TOGO
EQUATORIAL GUINEA
GABON
Cabinda (ANGOLA)
GUINEA
BURKINA FASO
MALI
NIGER
BENIN
NIGERIA
CAMEROON
CONGO
ZAIRE
CHAD
CENTRAL AFRICAN REPUBLIC
RWANDA
BURUNDI
TANZANIA
SUDAN
UGANDA
ERITREA
DJIBOUTI
ETHIOPIA
SOMALIA
KENYA
MADAGASCAR
ANGOLA
ZAMBIA
MALAWI
ZIMBABWE
NAMIBIA
BOTSWANA
MOZAMBIQUE
SWAZILAND
SOUTH AFRICA
LESOTHO

13

OVERVIEW
OF **Africa**

by Jennifer Pogrund

F IVE YEARS AFTER THE END OF THE COLD WAR, Africa's "democratic revolution" is struggling to create the kinds of civil society that have emerged elsewhere in the newly democratized world. The transitions in Africa have been slow and painful, with no quick fix for desperately ailing economies, massive underdevelopment or national debt. At best, a "democratic evolution" is taking place, as old-style one-party states reluctantly acknowledge that they cannot hold on to the reins of power indefinitely, nor accomplish democratization with half-measures. Perhaps the hardest lesson to learn has been that without freedom of expression, there can be no democracy; that the media's role is to check the abuse of power, fight the scourge of corruption, and keep elected governments accountable to their people. But while glasnost in Africa has allowed for an unprecedented mushrooming of independent and opposition publications and radio stations, political leaders, unaccustomed to strident criticism, still tend to lash out.

Any chronicle of press freedom in Africa must take into account the range of polities spanning the continent. At one extreme lie those in a near state of collapse, such as the failed states of Somalia and Liberia, and those recovering from civil wars, such as Rwanda and Angola. Next are the military dictatorships in Zaire, Nigeria, Sudan and other countries, where opposition voices are ruthlessly suppressed. Somewhat freer are the partial democracies, which include Mali,

Jennifer Pogrund is the program coordinator for Africa. A South African journalist and documentary filmmaker, she holds a master's degree in international affairs from Columbia University's School of International and Public Affairs.

From January to September 1994, the program coordinators for Africa were **Eleanor Bedford** and **Ahamat Omran. Avner Gidron,** CPJ's director of research and program coordinator for the Middle East and North Africa, wrote the Sudan section of the report. **Elizabeth Mermin,** a CPJ research assistant, contributed extensively to this chapter, in particular compiling the sections on West Africa. Also contributing to this report were **Maria Fadlelmula, Kelly David** and **Karin Lucke.** Special thanks to **Kim Brice.**

The research carried out for CPJ's Africa program in 1994 was made possible in part by a grant from The Menemsha Fund.

Togo, Gabon and Sierra Leone, where a semblance of tolerance persists. Then there are the newly democratized states—among them Kenya, Zambia and Cameroon—which have held elections in response to external pressure and where dissent is permitted within bounds. And finally, there are those with the most democratically representative governments—South Africa, Namibia and Botswana—where freedom of expression has become a norm, and where a free press is most likely to flourish.

The newly democratized countries have constitutions that guarantee freedoms of press and speech. Why, then, are these rights not upheld in practice? The underlying reason is that the guarantees cannot hold unless core institutions are overhauled. The African experience has shown that without all the other hallmarks of a democratic society—including a free and impartial judiciary, adherence to the rule of law, due process in the courts, and a free and unfettered press—a constitution will not be worth the paper it is written on, even where power-sharing arrangements are in place.

Indeed, one of the most marked shifts in Africa in 1994 was the means employed to control the press. Rather than using overt force, many governments sought recourse through the courts, in an attempt to criminalize the actions of journalists. In both Kenya and Zambia, for example, the governments relied largely on outmoded penal codes—the legacy of colonial and post-independence one-party rule—to curtail freedom of expression. In so doing, they illustrated how unreformed institutions can be used to perpetuate de facto one-party rule.

It is no coincidence that South Africa is hailed as a model for press freedom on the continent; the entirely new interim constitution and its bill of rights are upheld by a constitutional court as the supreme arbiter. The necessity of maintaining political goodwill remains, but as guarantees go, one probably could not hope for much better. The proposed Freedom of Information Act, drafted by the Independent Media Commission in May, would give individual citizens the right of access to government information, where relevance can be proved.

In the countries of West Africa, governments have used the courts to intimidate the media. But the greatest challenge to press pluralism there has been posed by economics. In January 1994, the currency of francophone West Africa was devalued by 50 percent. Consequently, many private newspapers, which depend on imported paper, ink, equipment and fuel, were forced out of business by sky-rocketing production costs, while inflation and higher newspaper prices reduced circulation for those that survived. Even official media felt the crunch; in Congo, for example, three state-owned newspapers were closed.

Angola

Angola's 19-year-long civil conflict became known as "the forgotten war" because it was largely an unreported war. Fighting and widespread violations of human rights continued in Angola throughout most of 1994. Both government and rebel forces kept journalists from the front lines, and information was tightly censored. Local press coverage reflected the battle lines of the conflict as the ruling Popular Movement for the Liberation of Angola (MPLA) and the rebel National Union for the Total Independence of Angola (UNITA) used the media as an integral part of their war effort. The MPLA government maintained control over state-run radio and television and its daily newspaper *Jornal de Angola;* UNITA used its clandestine shortwave radio station VORGAN (Voice of Resistance of the Black Cockerel) to convey its version of events.

Harassment and intimidation of Angolan journalists intensified throughout the year. Several journalists received death threats. The Angolan Journalists Union warned that the lives of Angolan journalists working for foreign media were in particular danger. Threats were repeatedly issued to the independent newsletter *Imparcial Fax,* as it grew bolder in its coverage of high-level corruption and the government's war effort. The threats appeared to come from factions within the military and security establishments. The pro-MPLA but semi-independent weekly newspaper *Correio de Semana* also received its share of harassment when it overstepped party political lines. And local journalists employed by state-run media variously lost their jobs or were demoted for being too critical.

On Nov. 20, after almost a year of U.N.-mediated talks, the MPLA and UNITA signed a peace accord—the Lusaka Protocol. But at year's end, tensions were still apparent and power-sharing and demobilization arrange-ments remained uncertain. It is too early to forecast to what extent the accord will improve conditions for the media.

May 6
Joao Mavinga, *Jornal de Angola,*
HARASSED,THREATENED
Francisco Fino, *Televisao Popular de Angola,*
HARASSED,THREATENED, ATTACKED
Police detained and questioned Mavinga, Cabinda correspondent for the government-owned daily, *Jornal de Angola,* following the publication of his article on plans by the Cabinda Liberation Front (FLEC) to open their own radio station in the area. Police reportedly warned Mavinga that he would be "in trouble" if he continued to pursue the story. He was released the same day. Fino, a journalist for the state television network, interviewed Mavinga after his release. The next day, police reportedly beat Fino and his cameraman, and destroyed their camera. Mavinga was subsequently detained for questioning again. FLEC is fighting for the independence of Cabinda, the northern Angolan enclave whose oil produces a large percentage of Angola's export earnings.

May 19
Leopoldo Baio, *Imparcial Fax,* HARASSED
Ricardo de Mello, *Imparcial Fax,* HARASSED
Police questioned Baio, editor of the independent newsletter *Imparcial Fax,* about his sources for an article exposing illicit police involvement in car sales. Four days later, police summoned *Imparcial Fax* director de Mello for questioning. He refused to reveal his sources.

May 19
Ric Kinayelako, *Batuque Amana,* ATTACKED
Kinayelako, editor of the opposition newspaper *Batuque Amana,* was attacked at his home by soldiers. The soldiers seized documents and money, and smashed a camera. Kinayelako was preparing to leave for Zaire to oversee *Batuque Amana*'s publication; the paper is printed in Zaire because all Angolan printing presses are

controlled by the ruling Popular Movement for the Liberation of Angola (MPLA).

June 12
Chris Simpson, *British Broadcasting Corporation (BBC),* IMPRISONED
Simpson, Angola correspondent for the BBC, was detained for two days after he talked his way past prison guards to interview imprisoned drug traffickers. The prisoners raised the alarm when they realized he was a journalist. Simpson was released on June 14, and appeared in court two days later to face charges of illegally entering a restricted area. He was found guilty and fined the equivalent of US$200.

June 16
Artur Gilela, *Radio Nacional de Angola* , KILLED
Gilela, a radio sound engineer for Angolan National Radio (RNA), was killed while covering heavy fighting around the central city of Kuito between government forces and those of the National Union for the Total Independence of Angola (UNITA).

September 4-6
Antonio Gouveia, *Sindicato dos Jornalistas Angolanos,* HARASSED, THREATENED
A family member of Gouveia, a member of the independent Journalists' Union, received a number of threatening phone calls meant for the journalist. Upon learning that Gouveia was out of the country, the callers said, "Tell him we want to kill him." A week earlier, Gouveia had reported on South African mercenaries fighting in Angola's civil war, in an article for the weekly independent newspaper *Correio Da Semana.*

September 20
Mariano Costa, *Imparcial Fax,*
IMPRISONED, HARASSED
Costa, a journalist for the privately owned newsletter *Imparcial Fax,* was held and interrogated for 28 hours by Home Affairs Ministry officials. The officials had stopped him at Luanda airport, as he was on his way home. They

tried to force Costa to reveal his sources for articles on the rebel National Union for the Total Independence of Angola (UNITA), and accused him of being a UNITA spy. He was warned upon his release "not to make a noise."

Cameroon

Journalists in Cameroon continued to suffer detentions, interrogations and threats in 1994, but the greatest danger to the independent print media was the constant invocation of censorship regulations to seize or suspend newspapers. Anglophone newspapers, often overlooked by mostly francophone censors, were censored less often than were the francophone papers. In particular, the francophone weekly *Le Messager* and its satiric supplement *Popoli* were routinely seized throughout the country. Financial losses incurred from such seizures, imposed at the whim of any federal or local official, can drive papers out of business. Since banned issues often sell on the black market for around five times their original price, and the government makes no effort to prevent such sales, many local observers see financial harassment rather than censorship as the primary motive behind the seizures.

Such tactics were made possible by the 1990 "laws on freedom" which, while establishing a multiparty system and allowing for the creation of over 50 private newspapers and magazines, prescribed mandatory censorship and granted the Ministry of Territorial Administration the power to suspend publication rights. At the beginning of 1994, there were around 80 newspapers and magazines, but many had to close during the year for economic reasons. Most of the remaining publications appear irregularly, and Cameroon's only daily is state owned. President Paul Biya, reelected in 1992 amidst widespread accusations of electoral fraud, consistently enacted liberalization policies in which statements of tolerance were countered by provisions for strict government control. He had been promising constitutional reform for two years, but postponed talks throughout 1994.

Despite provisions in the 1990 laws to open the airwaves, the government maintained control over television and radio. At a national forum on communication in September, the government announced that censorship regulations would be lifted, but by year's end nothing had changed. Escalating violence on the Nigerian border, nearly 50 percent inflation brought on by January's CFA devaluation, and an increasingly united and outspoken opposition added to Biya's insecurity about allowing freedom of the press; but privately owned publications, though financially feeble and constantly harassed, continued to be openly critical of the government.

January 7
Ndzana Seme, *Le Nouvel Indépendant,*
  IMPRISONED, CENSORED
Le Nouvel Indépendant, CENSORED
Police arrested Seme, publisher of the independent weekly *Le Nouvel Indépendant,* at his home/office and seized copies of the paper's recent editions. Police had earlier seized from the printers the Jan. 6 issue, which contained an interview with Joseph Owena, secretary general of the presidency. Seme had been publishing *Le Nouvel Indépendant* in defiance of a December 1993 suspension order from the government. He was released on Jan. 10, 1995, and allowed to resume publication of his paper in March.

January 10
Vincent t'Sas, *Reuters,* HARASSED
While interviewing teachers striking in Yaounde, Reuters reporter t'Sas was taken to the police station for questioning. After seizing his tape recorder, the police allowed t'Sas to leave for lunch. When he returned, they handed his tape recorder back to him, but retained the

cassette on which he had been recording his interviews. The cassette was returned a few days later with a note of apology.

February-March
Challenge Hebdo, CENSORED
The independent weekly *Challenge Hebdo* was temporarily suspended for publishing two interviews in which Ebale Angounou, a self-proclaimed associate of President Paul Biya, criticized members of the government and army. The official reason for the suspension was failure to submit the article to censors. The editors said that they had in fact submitted the article for review, and went ahead with publication only after receiving no response from the censors within the legal four-hour time limit.

March
Le Messager, CENSORED
Authorities banned an edition of *Le Messager* that dealt with the border conflict between Cameroon and Nigeria, as well as France's role in the dispute.

Late March
Perspectives Hebdo,
  CENSORED, LEGAL ACTION
The independent weekly *Perspectives Hebdo* was suspended for four months. Six days earlier, police had seized the paper's March 17 edition, which contained an article suggesting that President Paul Biya's fiancée was promiscuous. The fiancée's mother-in-law sued the paper, but dropped the case after the president's wedding. Shortly after the suspension, the government revived a 1992 case against *Perspectives Hebdo,* involving an article that accused certain government officials of confiscating funds for a national AIDS conference. The case was still being tried at year's end.

April 6
Le Messager, CENSORED
The Vice Prime Minister of Territorial Administration refused *Le Messager* permission to pub-

lish a special edition commemorating the tenth anniversary of the failed coup d'état of 1984.

June 30
Thomas Eyoum'a Noth, *Dikalo,*
  LEGAL ACTION, HARASSED
Eammanuel Nubissie Ngankam, *Dikalo,*
  LEGAL ACTION, HARASSED
Eyoum'a Noth, editor in chief, and Ngankam, publisher of the independent weekly *Dikalo,* were convicted of libel and sentenced respectively to six months in prison and a six-month suspended sentence. Both men were also fined. The charges arose from an April 18 article alleging that two ministers had smuggled a container of banknotes worth 17.5 million cfa. Eyoum'a Noth was called in for questioning on April 20 and again on May 5, when he was held overnight. He was interrogated on both occasions about his sources for the story. Despite the sentencing, Eyoum'a Noth was never imprisoned.

September
Popoli, CENSORED
Police seized a copy of the *Popoli,* a satiric supplement to *Le Messager.* The issue contained a piece about President Biya's security arrangements with Israel. The seizure took place the day after the Minister of Communication announced the end of official censorship.

October 14
Ndzana Seme, *Le Nouvel Indépendant,*
  LEGAL ACTION, IMPRISONED
Seme was arrested at his home/office. He was held for a week before being charged, on Oct. 21, with defaming the president. The arrest followed publication of articles in the paper's Oct. 12-19 issue about the arrest of Cameroon's special security forces head and the political maneuverings of other high-ranking officials. Seme was held in Yaounde's Central Prison. On Dec. 23, a court sentenced him to one year in prison, to be suspended for three years. He was released immediately thereafter.

November 11
Jean-Louis Kakmo Pideu, *La Nouvelle Expression,*
  HARASSED, THREATENED
Pideu, a reporter for the independent weekly *La Nouvelle Expression,* was arrested while covering an opposition demonstration in Yaounde. He was taken to the police station, interrogated, threatened, and held in a cell until late that night, when Reuters correspondent Vincent t'Sas came to inquire about his arrest. Police released Pideu, but kept his notes, tape recorder, and professional identification card.

Ethiopia

For the second year running, Ethiopia held more journalists in prison than any other country in Africa. A crackdown on independent and opposition publications, initiated in the fall of 1993, continued throughout 1994 and resulted in the imprisonment of 38 journalists during the course of the year.

The current "Transitional Government of Ethiopia" (TGE), is dominated by the Ethiopian People's Revolutionary Democratic Front (EPRDF), which overthrew the dictatorship of Mengistu Haile Mariam in May 1991. It substantially increased press freedom and improved the human rights situation shortly after coming to power. Independent and opposition papers flourished. But since the second half of 1993, the government has detained, imprisoned and fined dozens of journalists. The vague 1992 Press Proclamation has proven a useful tool for the TGE to silence critical reporting. It states that "press products" should be free from "any criminal offence against the safety of the State," "any defamation or false accusation against any individual, nation/nationality, people or organization," "any criminal instigation of one nationality against another," and "any agitation for war." Violators may be punished with one to three years' imprison-

ment and/or a fine of 10,000 birr
(US$1,600) to 50,000 birr.

Not only are these provisions ill defined,
but they can be interpreted to encompass
any criticism of the TGE's unilateral division
of the country into nine ethnically based
regions. This has been strongly opposed by
many Ethiopians, particularly ethnic Amha-
ras, and was a major factor in the boycott by
nearly all opposition parties of the June
1994 elections to the Constituent Assembly,
which would enact a controversial draft constitution in December.

The Press Proclamation also serves to
ban criticism of the proxy organizations
established by the EPRDF in the name of
other ethnic groups—a primary means by
which the EPRDF's ethnic Tigrean leadership
exerts control over the rest of the country.
Equally disturbing is the manner in which the
government has ridden roughshod over the
procedural requirements of the Press Proclamation, which provides that prosecutors
must present their cases before the appropriate court within 24 hours of filing charges.
The court in turn must issue its decision within 48 hours of receiving the case, and that
decision must be executed within 72 hours
barring a stay of execution order by the
appellate court. In practice, however, journalists charged under the Proclamation in 1994
were detained without trial for weeks, sometimes months, on end.

In light of the TGE's campaign against
the independent press and the opposition
complaints about unfair access to state-con-
trolled broadcast media, it seems doubtful
that coverage of the May 1995 parliamentary elections will be truly free or fair.

January
Ezedin Mohammed, *Ye Fikir Chawata,*
    IMPRISONED, LEGAL ACTION
Ezedin, editor of *Ye Fikir Chawata* (Love
Games), was arrested, and subsequently sen-
tenced to one year in prison on charges of

offending public morals. Ezedin is scheduled to
be released in February 1995.

January 15
Daniel Kifle, *Fendisha,*
    IMPRISONED, LEGAL ACTION
Police arrested *Fendisha* editor Daniel. CPJ
protested his arrest in a letter to President Meles
Zenawi. Daniel was sentenced to 18 months in
prison on June 1. His conviction stemmed from
articles that alleged corruption on the part of
Prime Minister Tamirat Layne, and claimed
Eritrean troops were deployed in Ethiopia.

Mid-January
Antensay Tafesse, *Mogad,*
    IMPRISONED, LEGAL ACTION
Kinfe Assefa, *Mogad,*
    IMPRISONED, LEGAL ACTION
Mogad editor Atensay and reporter Kinfe were
arrested on charges of spreading false news and
inciting public unrest. CPJ condemned their
arrests in a letter to the Ethiopian government.
The two were released in March.

January 22
Nayk Kassaye, *Beza,*
    IMPRISONED, LEGAL ACTION
Yohannes Abebe, *Beza,*
    IMPRISONED, LEGAL ACTION
Police arrested Nayk, editor in chief of *Beza,* and
Yohannes, the paper's deputy editor. CPJ
denounced the arrests in a letter to President
Meles Zenawi. The two journalists were released
on bail in March. Nayk disappeared on May 9
while on his way to the Central High Court. He
is believed to be in the state security service's custody. Yohannes was rearrested in October and
fined 10,000 birr on Dec. 12. He remained in
prison at the end of 1994. The grounds for his
fine and imprisonment are unclear.

January 22
Daniel Tadesse, *Waqt,*
    IMPRISONED, LEGAL ACTION
Daniel, editor of *Waqt,* was arrested for dissem-

inating false information. CPJ objected to his arrest in a letter to the Ethiopian government. He was fined between 10,000 and 20,000 birr, and released in mid-April.

January 24
Tamrat Bekel, *Addis Tribune* and *Addis Dimits*,
HARASSED
Tamrat, publisher and editor of *Addis Tribune* and *Addis Dimits*, was detained for questioning. He was released the same day on 10,000 birr bail.

Late January
Tesfaye Berehanu, *Muday*, IMPRISONED
Asrat Damtew, *Muday*, IMPRISONED
Tesfaye, editor of *Muday*, and Asrat, the paper's deputy editor, were arrested on charges of disseminating false information. The charges stemmed from articles published in the newspaper that were critical of the government. CPJ protested the arrests in a letter to President Meles Zenawi. The two journalists were released in March.

February
Kassa Kerega, *Ye Egziabeher Mengist*,
IMPRISONED, LEGAL ACTION
Kassa, editor of the Christian newspaper *Ye Egziabeher Mengist* (Kingdom of God), was fined 12,000 birr for insulting Islam. He was subsequently arrested and sentenced to two years in prison for failing to pay the fine. He was released in April.

February 8
Mesele Haddis, *Aimiro*, IMPRISONED
Netsanet Tesfaye, *Aimiro*, IMPRISONED
Kibret Makonnen, *Aimiro*, IMPRISONED
Police arrested three senior staff members of *Aimiro:* editor in chief Mesele, managing editor Netsanet, and editor Kibret. CPJ condemned the arrests in a letter to President Meles Zenawi. The editors were released on bail on March 3.

February 8
Befekadu Moroda, *Tomar*, IMPRISONED
Befekadu, editor in chief of *Tomar*, was arrested on charges of disseminating false news. CPJ protested his arrest in a letter to the Ethiopian government. He was released in early April.

February 9
Berehane Mewa, *Dewol*, IMPRISONED
Melaskatchew Amha, *Dewol*, IMPRISONED
Dewol publisher Berehane and editor Melaskatchew were arrested on charges of disseminating false news. CPJ denounced the arrests in a letter to President Meles Zenawi. The two were released on bail on March 16. However, they were immediately rearrested for having published a letter from an unknown armed group that had claimed responsibility for the attempted assassination of a USAID worker. The journalists were released in July on 20,000 birr bail.

February 22
Girmay Gebre-Tsadikm, *Muday*,
IMPRISONED, LEGAL ACTION
Mulugeta Gigo, *Muday*,
IMPRISONED, LEGAL ACTION
Authorities arrested *Muday* editor Girmay and reporter Mulugeta. CPJ objected to the arrests in a letter to the Ethiopian government. Girmay was released on bail in March, after being fined between 10,000 and 20,000 birr. Mulugeta was released on bail on March 7.

February 28
Biruk Tadesse, *Beza*,
IMPRISONED, LEGAL ACTION
Biruk, acting editor in chief of *Beza*, was arrested on charges of inciting public unrest. The charges stemmed from his publication of an article about conflict in southern Ethiopia. Biruk was released on bail on March 3.

March
Girma Lemma, *Aphrodite*,
LEGAL ACTION, IMPRISONED
Girma, editor in chief of *Aphrodite*, was sen-

tenced to one year in prison for publishing articles and photographs that "offended public morals." He had been arrested in January, and was released in October.

March 10

Tenker Tereda, *Mekdela*, IMPRISONED
Belanyneh Asegu, *Mekdela*, IMPRISONED
Feleke Alemu, *Mekdela*, IMPRISONED
Mekdela reporters Tenker, Belanyneh and Feleke were arrested on charges stemming from articles in the magazine's October 1992 edition. The three reporters were released in May.

March 17

Wolde Giorgis Wolde Mikael, *Free-lancer*,
  IMPRISONED
Police arrested Wolde Giorgis, an Awasa-based free-lance journalist who had been in hiding since Feb. 22. He was subsequently held incommunicado in an Awasa prison. Wolde Giorgis was released on 10,000 birr bail, after being detained for several months without charge.

Late March

Tefera Asmare, *Ethiopis*,
  LEGAL ACTION, IMPRISONED
Tefera, editor in chief of *Ethiopis*, was sentenced to two years in prison for "inciting people against the government" and disseminating "false rumours." The charges stemmed from an article about ethnic conflict in the Gondar region and an editorial entitled "The President Pretends Everything is O.K." Tefera was given an additional 18-month suspended sentence in late June for having published an editorial entitled "Fascism in Tigray" and an article about conflict in western Ethiopia. An appeal to the Supreme Court was pending at year's end. Tefera was arrested in November 1993, along with Iskander Nega, the paper's publisher. CPJ condemned their arrests in a letter to President Meles Zenawi. Nega was released in April 1994.

April 7

Kefale Mammo, *Ruh*,
  IMPRISONED, LEGAL ACTION
Authorities arrested Kefale, editor of *Ruh* and chairman of the Ethiopian Free Press Association. He was released the same month on 5,000 birr bail. On Oct. 27, he was fined 10,000 birr for publishing false information, inciting the public, and discrediting the government.

June 1

Mulugeta Lule, *Tobia*, LEGAL ACTION
Tobia editor Mulugeta was given a two-year suspended prison sentence and fined 10,000 birr. He had been charged with "publishing and disseminating false stories" about conflicts involving the army in the provinces of Gondar and Gojjam.

July

Habtamu Belete, *Ruhama*,
  LEGAL ACTION, IMPRISONED
Girma Endrias, *Ruhama*,
  LEGAL ACTION, IMPRISONED
Ruhama reporters Habtamu and Girma were sentenced to six months in prison each for contempt of court. Girma was reportedly released at the end of 1994. Habtamu remains in prison.

July

Melaku Tsegaye, *Muday*,
  LEGAL ACTION, IMPRISONED
Melaku, editor in chief of *Muday*, was sentenced to one year in prison after failing to pay a fine of 10,000 birr. He was released in November, after an appeal to the Supreme Court.

October 4

Kumsa Burayu, *Madda Walabu*, IMPRISONED
Tolera Tessema, *Madda Walabu*, IMPRISONED
Police arrested *Madda Walabu* editor Kumsa and deputy editor Tolera. The arrests were believed to stem from *Madda Walabu*'s publication of a communiqué by the exiled Oromo Liberation Front (OLF). Tolera was released in October. Kumsa was released on Dec. 12.

Mid-October
Tewodros Kebede, *Zog*, IMPRISONED
Keleme Bogale, *Zog*, IMPRISONED
Police detained Tewodros, editor in chief of *Zog*,
and Keleme, his deputy editor in chief. Tewodros
was released on bail the same month, without
ever being formally charged. Keleme, whose
detention stemmed from nonpayment of a
10,000 birr fine, was released in late November.

Late October
Goshu Mogues, *Tobia*,
　　LEGAL ACTION, IMPRISONED
Tobia editor Goshu was sentenced to a six-
month prison term. The charges against him
stemmed from the publication in *Tobia* of a letter written by Professor Asrat Woldeyes, jailed
leader of the All Amhara People's Organization
(AAPO). Goshu was released on Dec. 21.

December
Melaku Demisse, *Ingocha*, LEGAL ACTION
Melaku, editor in chief of *Ingocha*, was fined 4,000
birr and given a one-year suspended sentence.

December 14
Iyob Demeke, *Tarik*, IMPRISONED
Authorities briefly detained Iyob, manager of
Tarik. Shortly before Iyob's arrest, the weekly
Urji reportedly quoted him as saying that cer-
tain newspapers had published articles meant to
discredit the private press. Iyob was released on
10,000 birr bail.

December 19
Wondimeneh Negussie, *Beza*, IMPRISONED
Police arrested Wondimeneh, publisher and
distibutor of *Beza*, and released him a day later.

December 20
Bekele Makonnen, *Urji*, IMPRISONED
Tesfaye Deressa, *Urji*, IMPRISONED
Police arrested Bekele, publisher and manager
of the Oromo-language weekly *Urji*, and Tesfaye, the magazine's editor in chief. They were
released on bail in January 1995.

Gabon

In February 1994, the Gabonese government
stormed and destroyed the nation's last
remaining nongovernment radio station,
Radio Liberté, owned by the opposition party
Rassemblement National des Bûcherons
(RNB). President El Hadji Omar Bongo's government had closed down most private newspapers and destroyed the only other private
station, Radio Fréquence Libre, around the
time of the December 1993 presidential
elections. The closing of Radio Liberté came
amid a general strike and several days of violence in which opposition members were
arrested and killed.

Bongo's government has frequently
been accused of torture, arbitrary arrest and
other human rights violations. As 1994 progressed, the private and opposition press
reemerged to report on such government
abuses. Talks between the RNB and the government began in June, and in October
Bongo's Gabonese Democratic Party and a
united opposition signed an accord providing
for the creation of a transitional "Government for Democracy" to rule until the April
1996 elections. The main focus of the political accords has been on free, well-monitored
elections and on opposition participation in
the government. Little has been said, however, about the need to rebuild and protect the
independent media.

February 22
Radio Liberté, ATTACKED
The presidential guard attacked Radio Liberté,
a station owned by Gabon's largest opposition
party, Rassemblement National des Bûcherons
(RNB). Soldiers ransacked the offices, left the
station in flames, and destroyed the house of
Jules Mbah, the Bûcherons leader on whose
property the radio station was located. Authorities accused Radio Liberté, which had encouraged listeners to support an upcoming general

strike, of inciting violence. The station has not been reconstructed and is not broadcasting.

February 22
Vecka Brice Rostand Nang, *Radio Liberté,*
  IMPRISONED

Nang, a journalist, was in his office when the presidential guard attacked Radio Liberté. He was taken to a Libreville prison and held for several months. While in prison he was prevented from seeing his family, his failing health was ignored and, according to some reports, he was physically abused. CPJ wrote to the Gabon authorities, denouncing his detention on April 8. He was subsequently released.

April 7
Yves Jaumain, *Reporters Sans Frontières,*
  EXPELLED

Jaumain, director of the Africa desk at the French media rights group Reporters Sans Frontières (RSF), was expelled from Gabon. He had arrived on April 6 to investigate press freedom violations, including that of Vecka Brice Nang. The next day at lunch, he was detained and taken to a Defense Department office, where he was interrogated at length about his objectives and the people he had met with. His notes were photocopied, and that evening he was escorted to the airport and deported.

Gambia

On July 22, Lieutenant Yahya Jammeh led a bloodless military coup against the popularly elected president, Sir Dawda Kairaba Jawara. The coup ended 24 years of rule by a government that was often cited as a model for democracy in Africa. Although Jammeh and his Armed Forces Provisional Ruling Council (AFPRC) dissolved parliament and arrested former ministers and members of the security forces, the country remained peaceful, and the press reported freely on the coup. But on Aug. 4, the AFPRC passed a decree making engagement in any form of political activity, including the creation or distribution of anything that might appear to have been written "by or on behalf of or in the interest of any political party or its organ," an offense punishable by up to three years in prison or a 10,000 dalasi (US$1,000) fine. Two editors of an opposition party paper were arrested shortly thereafter for distributing their paper, and the decree stood as a threat to all journalists writing about domestic politics.

Instances of harassment and intimidation of journalists increased in October and November. Most attacks were aimed at the *Daily Observer,* an independent newspaper that employs a number of foreign journalists, and is owned by the internationally respected journalist and Liberian refugee Kenneth Best. Despite expressions of concern by CPJ and other human rights groups, Best was deported from Gambia in October. Soon after, three other *Observer* journalists fled the country to escape persecution by government forces.

August 19
Halifa Sallah, *Foroyaa,*
  LEGAL ACTION, IMPRISONED
Sidia Jatta, *Foroyaa,*
  LEGAL ACTION, IMPRISONED

Sallah and Jatta, leaders of the leftist People's Democratic Organization for Independence and Democracy (PDOID) and editors of the party paper *Foroyaa,* were arrested in Banjul while distributing their newspaper and accused of violating an Aug. 4 decree suspending political activity. The most recent issue of the paper had contained an open letter to Lieutenant Yahya Jammeh, calling on him to move peacefully towards democracy. On Aug. 22, they were released on bail. They were fined 1,000 dalasi on Oct. 12, and warned that they would have to refrain from political activity for the duration of the decree or face three years in prison.

October 10
Justice Fofanah, *Daily Observer*, HARASSED
Fofanah, a senior reporter at the *Daily Observer*, was detained by plainclothes policemen while covering a ports management conference. The police interrogated him about his sources for an article about the chief of protocol under the deposed President Sir Dawda Jawara. Fofanah refused to reveal his sources. He was released after several hours, and subsequently fled the country.

October 30
Kenneth Best, *Daily Observer*,
  EXPELLED, HARASSED, IMPRISONED
Best, managing director of the *Daily Observer* and a Liberian citizen, was seized at his Banjul home by an immigration officer, escorted to the airport, and deported to Monrovia.

He had been interrogated in early September about an *International Herald Tribune* article in which he had been quoted on the subject of the recent coup. He was questioned again on Oct. 3 about an issue of the *Observer* that contained an article quoting two MPs defending themselves against President Yahya Jammeh's accusations of corruption, and an interview with a German diplomat who maintained that the "army should defend and not rule." On Oct. 21, immigration officials arrested Best and took him to the Kartong police station. His wife attempted to follow him, but was ordered at gunpoint to turn around. That day, CPJ wrote to President Jammeh, expressing concern about the arrest. Best was held overnight and released the next day with a warning to be careful about what he published in his paper. The newspaper had recently published editorials demanding a timetable for a return to civilian rule.

October
Alie Badara Sheriff, *Daily Observer*,
  THREATENED, HARASSED
Rodney Sieh, *Daily Observer*, THREATENED
Sheriff, a *Daily Observer* reporter, was threatened and manhandled by soldiers who mistook him for Rodney Sieh, another *Daily Observer* reporter and a stringer for the BBC. Officials had been looking for Sieh since Oct. 21, when he dispatched a story to the BBC about the arrest of Kenneth Best, the *Daily Observer*'s managing director, Sieh, who was in hiding, fled the country shortly thereafter. Sheriff was interrogated again in November, this time about his own role as a journalist, and he, too, subsequently fled the country.

November 6
Abdullah Savage, *Daily Observer*, ATTACKED
Savage, a reporter for the *Daily Observer*, was severely beaten by soldiers. He had recently gone to the military base in Fajara to report on the repeated arrests of several former government ministers.

November 8
Ebrima Sankareh, *The Point* and *Deutsche Welle*,
  HARASSED
Sankareh, a reporter for the independent biweekly *The Point* and the German radio network Deutsche Welle, was detained for questioning. Local sources say that he was suspected of having written a letter, aired on a BBC program, about secret military killings and arms imports. He was released after 24 hours.

Guinea

On Jan. 29, 1994, following widespread vote-counting irregularities, Lansana Conte was inaugurated as the first elected president of Guinea's Third Republic. He immediately told the government newspaper *Horoya* that the Guinean press was henceforth free. Yet he did not do anything to change Guinea's highly restrictive press laws, which make libel a criminal offense and define sedition so broadly as to include chants. Under the laws, criticism of the president is prohibited, as are any statements that disturb the public peace. There was also little change in terms

of radio, Guinea's most important news medium, which remained firmly under government control throughout the year. Legislative elections, though promised for 1994, had not been scheduled by year's end.

March
Radio Fréquence Gandal, CENSORED
In early March, Guinean police shut down Radio Fréquence Gandal, Guinea's first and only independent radio station. For a few days prior to its closure, the station had been broadcasting music and test patterns. Shortly after the shutdown an official from the ministry of communication arrived at the station and demanded, but did not receive, the station's transmitter. Although Guinean law guarantees freedom of the press, it also reserves for the state exclusive power to grant broadcasting licenses. Radio Fréquence Gandal had been ready to begin broadcasts since January 1992, and was told several times by the National Council on Communication that it would be granted a license.

Ivory Coast

Press freedom declined considerably in Ivory Coast (Côte d'Ivoire) in 1994 under President Henri Konan Bedie, who constitutionally assumed the presidency after the death of President Felix Houphouet-Boigny in December 1993. Bedie spent the year consolidating his power in preparation for the October 1995 elections. Faced with the threat of an electoral challenge from within his own Democratic Party of Côte d'Ivoire, an urban economy devastated by the CFA's devaluation and a series of student protests, Bedie often tried to maintain order with censorship and force. Since the state maintained control over all television and radio stations, journalists for the opposition and independent press were the targets of most efforts to constrain free-

dom of expression. Abdou Dramane Sangaré, deputy secretary general of the Ivorian Popular Front (FPI) and director of publication for the FPI newspaper, was sentenced to three years in prison for insulting the head of state.

CPJ was able to confirm that seven journalists, four of whom worked for the FPI paper, were taken to court and convicted of either insulting the head of state, inciting revolt, or criminal libel. Though four of the sentences were suspended, prison terms ranged from one to three years. Bedie showed no signs of acknowledging domestic or international human rights protests until December, when he announced that he was releasing 2,000 out of a total of about 14,000 Ivorian prisoners in a decree of amnesty for the new year. Among these prisoners were three journalists, including Sangaré.

February 16
Hamed Bakayoko, *Le Patriote* and *Le Patriote Express*, IMPRISONED, LEGAL ACTION
Bakayoko, publisher of *Le Patriote* and *Le Patriote Express*, was arrested. On Feb. 24, he was convicted on a charge of insulting the dignity of the head of state, fined 200,000 CFA and sentenced to one year in prison. In addition, both of his papers were suspended for three months. The charge stemmed from an article in the Jan. 25 edition of *Le Patriote Express* titled "Letter from Kong to Ivorian Sisters and Brothers," which did not mention President Bedie by name but suggested that Prime Minister Alassane Dramane Ouattara was the proper successor to late President Houphouet-Boigny. CPJ condemned the sentencing and suspensions in a letter to the Ivorian government. After apologizing to Bedie, Bakayoko was granted a presidential pardon and released on July 3. Both of his newspapers were still out of print by year's end.

March 24
Abdou Draham Sangaré, *La Voie*,
  LEGAL ACTION
Souleymane Senn, *La Voie*, LEGAL ACTION
Freedom Neruda, *La Voie*, LEGAL ACTION
Jacques Prejean, *La Voie*, LEGAL ACTION
Cesar Etou, *La Voie*, LEGAL ACTION
An Abidjan court found Sangaré, managing editor of the Ivorian Popular Front (FPI) daily *La Voie*, and reporters Senn, Neruda, Prejean and Etou guilty of insulting the head of state. The charges arose from articles published on Jan. 22 that commented on a *Jeune Afrique* report that indicated President Bedie had asked France for $17 million to finance the funeral of late President Houphouet-Boigny. Each journalist was fined 200,000 CFA and sentenced to one year in prison. CPJ denounced the sentences in a letter to President Bedie. The journalists were never taken into custody. However, the case was upheld in an appeal hearing on May 31, and the defendants remain in danger of imprisonment.

April 13
Abdou Dramane Sangaré, *La Voie*,
  IMPRISONED, LEGAL ACTION
Souleymane T. Senn, *La Voie*,
  IMPRISONED, LEGAL ACTION
Managing editor Sangaré and journalist Senn were arrested for disturbing public order and inciting revolt. The charges followed the publication of an article by Senn in the April 5 edition of *La Voie* entitled, "The Balance of Terror," which listed legal methods of resistance available to the opposition, such as strikes, marches and civil disobedience. On April 21, after a week-long trial, the court sentenced each of the journalists to three years in prison. They appealed the verdict twice, in May and in November, without success. After each appeal, CPJ wrote to the Ivorian government to protest the journalists' convictions. And for eight months Bedie resisted considerable international and domestic pressures to free Sangaré, who is also the deputy secretary general of the opposition Ivorian Popular Front (FPI). On Dec. 16, the two were

released along with 2000 other prisoners under a presidential decree of amnesty.

May 24
David Deliwa Gogbe, *Le Changement*,
  IMPRISONED, LEGAL ACTION
An Abidjan court convicted Gogbe, editor of the weekly opposition newspaper *Le Changement*, of defamation and sentenced him to one year in prison. The case arose from an April 25 article implicating Germain Coffi-Gadeau, grand chancellor of the national order, in a murder. Under a presidential decree of amnesty that freed 2000 prisoners, Gogbe was released on Dec. 19.

September 18
Emmanuel Koré, *Soir Info*,
  IMPRISONED, LEGAL ACTION
Military officers arrested Koré, a journalist with the independent newspaper *Soir Info*, at a restaurant in Yamassoukro, the nation's official capital. He was writing an article on the future of the presidential guard, the personal guard of the late President Houphouet-Boigny. Police transferred Koré to Abidjan, and on Sept. 23, after five days in custody, he was charged with inciting social disorder. The charges against him were dropped, however, and he was released on Sept. 27. Koré had spent nearly a year in prison in 1991 for insulting the head of state.

Kenya

Since winning the December 1992 multiparty elections, President Daniel arap Moi's ruling party, the Kenya African National Union (KANU), has reneged on promises of full democratic reform. Despite numerous changes in the political system, state harassment of critics and political opponents steadily increased in 1994.

President Moi has set about silencing the independent press, opposition politicians and members of parliament, while maintain-

ing a public facade of legitimacy. Without relying exclusively on overt force, the government was able to coercively restrain freedom of expression through the judicial system throughout the year. Journalists and politicians intent on widening the national dialogue were often charged under the Penal Code with sedition—which carries a 10-year maximum sentence—or subversion, a penalty punishable by a maximum sentence of three years in prison.

More journalists were taken to court in 1994 than in any previous year. While most cases were not pursued for more than a few months, the looming threat of incarceration or massive financial penalties made the courts a powerful deterrent to independent reporting. Two journalists from the opposition paper *The People,* who published an article criticizing the lack of separation between the judiciary and executive branches, were, ironically, held up on charges of contempt of court. The journalists, Bedan Mbugua and David Makali, following the dictates of their consciences, chose to go to prison rather than apologize for their reporting.

As part of the general pattern of restraints on the press, journalists were prevented from entering "classified security zones," newspapers were impounded, and printing presses were shut down. After President Moi publicly complained that foreign correspondents were distorting Kenya's image abroad, Broadcasting and Information Minister Johnstone Makau warned that the government would withdraw accreditation from those who reported "lies" about Kenya.

In December, Makau announced that his ministry would not approve applications for licenses for private radio or television stations. The development came despite recommendations from the Press Review Task Force, appointed earlier in the year by Attorney General Amos Wako, to reform existing media laws and explore private licensing. Critics charged that the Task Force—estab-

lished under pressure from Western donors—had served its underlying function: to show that Kenya meant well. But in reality, they said, the ruling KANU party had no intention of relinquishing control of the airwaves. However, one pro-government cable TV station was granted a license.

March 5
Adam Bake Luko, *The Nation,*
IMPRISONED, LEGAL ACTION
Luko, a Moyale-based correspondent for *The Nation,* was arrested and detained without charge for 32 days at the Government of Kenya Prison in Moyale. He was brought before a Nairobi court on April 6, and charged with falsely reporting in *The Nation*'s Feb. 16 issue that an assistant chief had accepted bribes in return for national identity cards. Luko maintained that his report was accurate. He was released the same day.

March 16
Ngumo wa Kuria, *The Standard*
IMPRISONED, LEGAL ACTION
Peter Makori, *The Standard*
IMPRISONED, LEGAL ACTION
Kamau Kanyanga, *The Standard*
IMPRISONED, LEGAL ACTION
John Nyaosi, *The Standard,*
IMPRISONED, LEGAL ACTION
Kuria, Nakuru bureau chief for the privately owned daily *The Standard,* and Makori, a provincial correspondent based in Kisii, were arrested and charged with subversion. The charge stemmed from a report in *The Standard* stating that nine people had been killed and hundreds displaced in Molo in the Rift Valle—a site of violent ethnic strife. A week later, on March 23, managing editor Kanyanga and deputy chief sub-editor Nyaosi were charged with subversion for their roles in editing the article. All four were released March 31 on a KSh. 100,000 bail. On June 23, each subversion charge, which carries a maximum penalty of three years in prison, was replaced with the considerably more serious

charge of sedition—which carries a maximum 10-year prison sentence. The government described *The Standard*'s report as "total lies" and said that the authors would be dealt with firmly and ruthlessly. The case against the four journalists was dismissed on Aug. 16.

March 31
Bedan Mbugua, *The People,*
  LEGAL ACTION, IMPRISONED
David Makali, *The People,*
  LEGAL ACTION, IMPRISONED
Independent Media Services, LEGAL ACTION
The People editor in chief Mbugua, reporter Makali, lawyer G.B.M. Kariuki, and publisher Independent Media Services, were charged with criminal contempt of court. The charge stemmed from an article in the paper's March 6-12 edition that quoted Kariuki calling a recent Court of Appeals decision a "judicial lynching" that "reeked of state interference." Mbugua and Makali learned from a radio broadcast that the attorney general was pressing charges. When neither of the journalists appeared in the appeals court on March 31, a warrant was issued for their arrest. The first hearing was in the Court of Appeals, leaving no possibility for review by a higher court. The court found all four defendants guilty on June 2. Mbugua was fined KSh. 400,000, Makali KSh. 300,000, and Kariuki and the publisher KSh. 500,000 each. The fines totalled KSh. 1.7 million — the highest amount ever imposed in Kenya for contempt of court. The court also gave each defendant seven days to publish apologies in *The People* and three other dailies. Both the publisher and Kariuki, a prominent human rights lawyer, acceded to the order. Mbugua and Makali refused to do so as a matter of principle. They were arrested in *The People*'s offices on June 13, and sentenced to prison terms of five and four months respectively. Makali was released on Sept. 2 and Mbugua on Sept. 23. Mbugua was dismissed from his job on Nov. 24. CPJ denounced the journalists' trial and the detention in a letter to the Kenyan government.

April 5
Mutegi Njau, *The Nation,*
  LEGAL ACTION, IMPRISONED
Evans Kanini, *The Nation,*
  LEGAL ACTION, IMPRISONED
Nation news editor Njau was arrested, held overnight and charged with sedition in a Nakuru court. The charge stated that an article in the paper's April 4 edition was "calculated to promote feelings of hatred or enmity between different communities," and was written with "subversive intentions, prejudicial to the country's security." The article had dealt with the Burnt Forest, a "classified security zone" in the Rift Valley. Riven by ethnic strife, the Rift Valley is officially closed to the news media. *The Nation* had quoted a resident saying that attackers were transported to the area in helicopters. On April 5 police questioned Njau and Kanini, the paper's Eldoret correspondent. They asked Njau to drive to the Criminal Investigation Department (CID) offices in Nakuru, 200 kilometers from Nairobi. Njau was arrested upon his arrival. He was subsequently released on KSh. 300,000 bail, but had to report to the Nakuru police station weekly, until the case's June 24 dismissal. Although the charges have been withdrawn, they can be reinstated if police find further evidence.

July 11
John Lawrence, *The Nation,*
  HARASSED, EXPELLED
Lawrence, an Australian journalist who had been working as training editor for *The Nation* since 1985, was deported by immigration authorities on the grounds that his "continued stay in Kenya was contrary to the national interest." On the day of his deportation, Lawrence was taken from the newspaper's offices to the Immigration Department, where he was held incommunicado for eight hours. Authorities then escorted Lawrence to Jomo Kenyatta Airport and placed him on a flight to Australia. Lawrence's duties at *The Nation* did not involve actual writing. However, local

sources speculated that Lawrence was deported because of his role in compiling the paper's daily watchdog column, "The Cutting Edge," which commented on government corruption and bureaucratic incompetence. Other sources regarded the deportation as an attempt by the state to intimidate the paper. Two weeks after the deportation, government minister Moody Awori told Parliament that Lawrence's expulsion was related to matters touching on state security which could not be publicly discussed.

August 8
Odhiambo Orlale, *The Nation*,
LEGAL ACTION, IMPRISONED

Orlale, *The Nation*'s Kisumu bureau chief, was arrested and held overnight on charges of publishing false information. His arrest followed the July 1 publication of an article about health workers at a Kisumu clinic, who were planning to join a strike by doctors demanding better employment terms. Orlale denied the charges, and was released on KSh. 1000 bail. A hearing was held on Oct. 7, and the case is still pending.

September
Scott Peterson, *Daily Telegraph*,
LEGAL ACTION

The Ministry of Information and Broadcasting withdrew the accreditation of Peterson, an American correspondent for the *London Daily Telegraph*, after articles he had written were deemed "unacceptable." He had recently written an article about Nairobi's high crime rate, entitled "Nairobi is the New Mogadishu: Chaotic and Deadly." Also in September, Peterson's pregnant wife, a schoolteacher, was arrested and questioned on the grounds that she had violated her work permit. Under international pressure, the Kenyan government later restored Peterson's accreditation.

September 28
Nicholas Rukenya, *The Nation*, ATTACKED
Nation photographer Rukenya was assaulted by security officers of the Nairobi city council.

Rukenya had taken photographs of the officers while they were illegally demolishing a city slum. The officers damaged Rukenya's camera, slapped and kicked him, and shouted that he had "no business" taking their photographs.

October 13
Martin Matua, *The Standard*, HARASSED
Sheila Wambui, *The Standard*, HARASSED
Oscar King'ori, *The Standard*, HARASSED
Jacob Waweru, *The Standard*, HARASSED
Oliver Musembi, *The Nation*, HARASSED
Nicholas Rukenya, *The Nation*, HARASSED

All six journalists were detained for four hours at the local police station, after trying to report on a meeting between Kiambu district officer Bondo Ligawa and dissatisfied farmers from a local cooperative. Ligawa had ordered his administrative police to arrest *Standard* photographer Waweru, as the latter tried to take pictures of him addressing the farmers outside his office. Police confiscated Waweru's camera, threw him into a Land Rover, and drove him to the Gatundu Police Station. The other five journalists followed the vehicle in an effort to establish where Waweru was being taken. On arriving at the police station, the five were questioned by the commanding officer, while an armed officer guarded the doorway. They were then pushed by several officers into holding cells, where they remained until another police officer ordered their release.

December
The Nation, THREATENED
President Daniel arap Moi and Johnstone Makau, Kenya's minister for broadcasting and information, threatened to ban *The Nation* for subversion. "No paper is too big to be banned," said Moi. The government also said that they would not permit the establishment of private television and radio broadcasts. Nation Newspapers Limited had applied for permission to establish a television station.

Mali

Attacks against the radio and press in Mali increased sharply during 1994. After the 1991 coup that deposed the authoritarian Moussa Traoré, many independent and opposition newspapers appeared, as well as over 13 radio stations—a number unmatched elsewhere in West Africa. But as the popularity of Alpha Omar Konaré, Mali's first democratically elected president, has declined, his government has become less tolerant of criticism and has responded to public expressions of political frustration with a crackdown on the media.

In 1994, economic troubles, made worse by the devaluation of the CFA in January, gave rise to strikes for scholarship increases by high school and university students that often ended in clashes with the military. After Konaré ordered the closure of the nation's schools in February, a private radio station began broadcasting announcements for the striking Malian Students' Association (AEEM). The government cited the need for "preservation of national security" to shut the station down. Journalists were caught in clashes with the military in Bamako and assaulted by ruling party security guards. In addition, the state maintained tight control over information about Mali's most pressing political problem, the civil war with ethnic Tuaregs in the North.

Because Mali's literacy rate is only around 20 percent, radio is of great political significance, and many of the restraints on the media in 1994 were imposed on private radio stations. In particular, selective enforcement of previously disregarded licensing regulations kept several private radio stations off the air.

Lastly, no effort was made to reform the country's restrictive media laws. The National Assembly, under pressure from journalists and human rights organizations, had agreed to review its harsh new press laws in 1993, but by the end of 1994 no action had been taken.

February 17
Radio Kayira, CENSORED
Mali's prime minister invoked "conservation measures" to close the private Radio Kayira in Bamako for a week. Following the Feb. 15 student demonstrations and the government's subsequent closing of all schools, Radio Kayira began airing announcements for the Malian Students' Association (AEEM) and allowed students to broadcast from its studio. The station resumed broadcasting when the order expired, on Feb. 24.

February 26
Fousseiny Bengaly, *L'Observateur,* ATTACKED
Bengaly, a journalist for the independent weekly *L'Observateur,* was beaten by Malian police while covering a meeting of the Malian Students' Association (AEEM). The police had come to break up the meeting and had been beating students when they identified Bengaly as a journalist and beat him as well.

March 2
Les Echos, ATTACKED
Rioters ransacked the offices of the newspaper *Les Echos.* Although a number of people were arrested in connection with the attack, the case against them was dismissed several weeks later. *Les Echos* is part of the JAMANA media group, which is owned in part by President Alpha Omar Konaré.

May 3
Radio Kayira II, CENSORED
Radio Kayira II in Koutiala was closed by administrative order for allegedly disturbing the peace and inciting violence. The order expired after one week, and the station reopened only to be closed on the same day by order of the interior minister for lack of written authorization to broadcast. Though written authorizations are officially required, very few stations ever receive

them. The Kayira Group had been trying to get authorization for all of its stations since 1993. Radio Kayira II resumed broadcasts in the fall. In January 1995, official authorizations were granted for Kayira branches in Koulikoro, Koutiala and Sekou, but the station in Bamako continued to operate under a provisional license.

May 5
Radio Foko, CENSORED
Radio Foko in Koutiala was closed for lack of written authorization. The minister of communication reopened the station on May 9, reportedly after finding a written authorization in the archives. The station belongs to the media group JAMANA, of which President Alpha Omar Konaré is an owner.

May 12
Radio Kayira IV, CENSORED
The police commissioner closed Radio Kayira IV in Koulikoro because it lacked written authorization to broadcast. Like the other Kayira stations, Kayira IV continued to seek authorization throughout the year. The station resumed broadcasting in the fall.

May 28
Siaka Konate, *Radio Kayira II,* IMPRISONED
Adama Kone, *Radio Kayira II,* IMPRISONED
Adama Konate, *Radio Kayira II,* IMPRISONED
As they were checking station equipment after a flood, Kone and Adama Konate, program hosts at Radio Kayira II in Koutiala, and Siaka Konate, a technician, were arrested for violating a closure order imposed on the station. They were detained for two days.

June 13
Belco Tamboura, *L'Observateur,* HARASSED
Moussa Fofana, *L'Observateur,* HARASSED
Police interrogated Tamboura and Fofana, respectively publisher and editor in chief of the independent weekly *L'Observateur,* about the sources for an article by Fofana in the June 13 edition of the paper. The article, entitled "The

War Against Insecurity," dealt with plans to change the police force.

September 24
Ramata Dia, *Cigale Muselé,* HARASSED
Boubacoar Opa Kane, *Cigale Muselé,*
    HARASSED
Radio Liberté crew, HARASSED
Kane, Dia and a Radio Liberté crew were expelled from the opening of the congress of the ruling party, the Alliance for Democracy in Mali (ADEMA). They all claimed to have been invited. The crew from Radio Liberté was allowed to return to the meeting room after the opening discussions.

September 26
Issa Doumbia, *Le Républicain,* ATTACKED
Yero Dabo, *Radio Kledu,* ATTACKED
Security guards attacked Doumbia, a journalist for the independent newspaper *Le Républicain,* and Dabo, a reporter for the independent Radio Kledu, and then threw them out of the congress of the ruling party, the Alliance for Democracy in Mali (ADEMA). Doumbia's arm was wounded, his papers destroyed and his dictaphone broken; Dabo was assaulted as he was helping Doumbia.

October 25
Boubacar Touré, *Office de Radiodiffusion et Télévision (ORTM-TV),* ATTACKED
Modibo Gueye, *ORTM-TV,* ATTACKED
Bréhima Traoré, *ORTM-TV,* ATTACKED
Police trainees assaulted members of a team from the state television station, ORTM-TV. The trainees attacked journalist Touré, camera operator Gueye and crew member Traoré when they arrived to cover a fight between police and unlicensed taxi drivers in Bamako. The journalists suffered injuries, and some equipment was destroyed. The governor apologized publicly, as did the minister of territorial administration, who is in charge of the police. The ministry promised to pay for medical, psychological and material damages.

November 23
Sambi Touré, *Nouvel Horizon,*
 IMPRISONED, LEGAL ACTION
Touré, editor in chief of Mali's first independent daily, *Nouvel Horizon,* was arrested and charged with publishing false information detrimental to the national interest. The charges stemmed from the Nov. 18 publication of his article "Alpha Veut Demissioner?" (Does Alpha Want to Step Down?), which suggested that the president, fearing a coup, had tried to resign. Touré was released from prison on Dec. 2 to await trial, and was acquitted of all charges on Jan. 3. The public prosecutor began appealing the case soon after.

Nigeria

Simply citing the date "June 12" is a daring political act in Nigeria. Supporting or writing it, advocating or striking for it could land one in jail. On June 12, 1993, millionaire oil magnate and press baron Moshood K.O. Abiola won Nigeria's presidential election. But Gen. Ibrahim Babangida, the then ruling president, annulled the results. On the eve of the election's anniversary, as Abiola was preparing to declare himself Nigeria's legitimate president, Gen. Sani Abacha—who heads the junta that took power from Babangida in a November 1993 "military revolution"— banned Abiola's newspaper group and all other papers that supported him. Eleven days later, Abiola was under arrest, charged with treason. In failing health, he spent the rest of the year behind bars.

Abiola was the pivot around which the press's troubles turned. An intensive crackdown on all calls for Abiola's reinstatement as president resulted in the closure of three of the four largest media houses in Nigeria. This meant that 15 of Nigeria's leading independent publications ceased to exist, and thousands of journalists and related media workers found themselves without jobs.

Abiola's subsequent trial and a paralyzing nine-week oil workers' strike in support of him were especially sensitive subjects for the remaining media. Abacha proved intolerant of critical international reporting as well. Reporters from the *Wall Street Journal* and CNN were expelled. By September, Abacha had crushed the oil strike. Buoyed by success, Abacha's legal team came up with a legislative package of decrees that kept the newspapers shut, kept the regime's actions beyond the courts' jurisdiction, and provided for administrative detention of up to six months for voicing dissent.

Nigeria has one of Africa's oldest and most vibrant traditions of press freedom, and newspapers such as *Newswatch, The News, Tempo* and *PM News* continued to report critically. They did so despite repeated arrests, assaults, harassment and the constant threat of closure, and despite "letters of invitation" from State Security Service (SSS) officials to visit them and explain why certain stories had been published.

January 2
Tell, CENSORED
Police and State Security Service (SSS) agents stormed Academy Press, the printers of the weekly *Tell* magazine, and seized *Tell*'s entire print run of 50,000. The edition's cover story, titled "The Return of Tyranny: Abacha Bares His Fangs," reported on the decrees issued two weeks previously which had dismissed several matters before the court so as to favor the new military regime. The government subsequently issued a formal apology.

January 26
Femi Akintunde Johnson, *Fame,*
 IMPRISONED
Johnson, editor of *Fame* magazine, was arrested in Lagos. He was released 10 days later on Feb. 4.

March 14
Alhaji Hassan Sani Kontagora, *Hotline,*
HARASSED
Police briefly detained *Hotline* editor Kontagora and occupied the weekly magazine's offices.
The magazine had been publishing articles that
defended the ethnic interests of the country's
north, and supported ousted president
Babangida. The magazine's circulation was limited to Kaduna, and it stopped publishing on
March 24 due to what the editor called constant and persistent harassment, arrests and
intimidation.

April 4
Alex Kabba, *The News,* IMPRISONED
Kabba, bureau chief for *The News,* was arrested
in connection with an article alleging that a
government official was involved in an illicit
land deal. He was held for several weeks,
charged with extortion, and released. Two
weeks earlier he had been assaulted by a police
chief who complained that Kabba had once
written an article that resulted in his redeploy-
ment from a particlar station.

April 7
Dan Agbesse, *Newswatch,*
IMPRISONED, LEGAL ACTION
Ray Ekpu, *Newswatch,*
IMPRISONED, LEGAL ACTION
Yakubu Mohammed, *Newswatch,*
IMPRISONED, LEGAL ACTION
Agbesse, editor in chief of *Newswatch* magazine,
was arrested in Lagos. Over the weekend of
April 9, Ray Ekpu, former editor in chief of
Newswatch, was also arrested in Lagos and
Yakubu Mohammed, *Newswatch*'s former man-
aging editor, was arrested in his home state of
Lokoja. The arrests were made in connection
with a *Newswatch* report that military ruler Gen-
eral Sani Abacha planned to stay in power until
the year 2000. The journalists were charged
with publishing seditious material. They were
released on April 14. On April 28, a Chief Magistrate withdrew the four-count sedition charge

against them. CPJ condemned the detentions in
a letter to the Nigerian government.

April 9
Geraldine Brooks, *Wall Street Journal,*
IMPRISONED, EXPELLED
Wall Street Journal reporter Geraldine Brooks
was arrested in Port Harcourt, where she was
reporting on strife between ethnic Ogoni and oil
companies in Rivers State. Authorities held her
incommunicado for two days, confiscated her
notes, and deported her to the United States. In
a letter to the Nigerian government, CPJ
denounced Brooks' detention and deportation.

May 27
Wale Akin-Aina, *Newswatch,*
IMPRISONED, LEGAL ACTION
Soji Akinrinade, *Newswatch,*
IMPRISONED, LEGAL ACTION
Mike Akpan, *Newswatch,*
IMPRISONED, LEGAL ACTION
Tunde Asaju, *Newswatch,*
IMPRISONED, LEGAL ACTION
Ray Ekpu, *Newswatch,*
IMPRISONED, LEGAL ACTION
Sam Olukoya, *Newswatch,*
IMPRISONED, LEGAL ACTION
Judge Oni-Okpaku, head of the Miscellaneous
Offences Tribunal, issued a sweeping arrest
warrant for nine *Newswatch* reporters. The jour-
nalists had contributed to a March 7 *Newswatch*
cover story accusing her of impropriety in con-
nection with a drug scandal. Akin-Aina, Akinrinade, Akpan, Asaju, Ekpu, and Olukoya, were
detained for several days. Three other reporters
avoided detention, as they were away at the
time of the arrests. The journalists were
charged with libel and contempt of court. The
charges were later dismissed.

June 11
The Concord Group, CENSORED
The Punch Group, CENSORED
On June 11, State Security Service (SSS) offi-
cials sealed the offices of the Concord Group, a

media conglomerate owned by jailed president-elect Moshood Abiola. The same day, the offices of the Punch Group, another private pro-opposition publishing house, were sealed and then occupied by the military. *Punch* editor in chief Bola Bolawole was confined in his office for two days, until June 13. Both media groups sued for wrongful closure. Although the Concord group was unable to publish for the remainder of 1994, a court judgment ordered security agents to leave the premises, and awarded the Concord Group 1.5 million naira (US$60,000) in damages. The government, however, disregarded the judgment. On July 29, the Punch Group obtained a court judgment ordering the police to leave the publisher's premises, awarding damages of 25 million naira (approximately US$1 million), and permitting them to resume publication. *Punch* began publishing again in the first week of August, but on Sept. 7, the SSS returned to occupy and seal off *Punch*'s offices.

July 27-July 28
Shehu Kura, *Voice of America (VOA)*,
   ATTACKED, HARASSED
Five photographers, ATTACKED
Kura, a reporter for VOA's Hausa-language service, was among a group of journalists beaten by police outside the Abuja courthouse, where president-elect Moshood Abiola was being tried. The journalists were covering a demonstration in support of Abiola when police charged the group. The next day, confrontations between the police and demonstrators outside the courthouse intensified as Abiola appeared in court. Five photographers were assaulted by the security forces, and their cameras either confiscated or destroyed. The photographers were assaulted with horsewhips, batons and guns. Prior to Abiola's trial, Kura had been reporting from Abuja on the country's Constitutional Conference, and on alleged corruption among its delegates. State Security Service (SSS) agents had unsuccessfully attempted to stop his reporting by offering bribes, while

conference officials had threatened to withdraw his press credentials and told him his safety could not be guaranteed. CPJ protested the beatings, as well as the earlier attempts to harass and intimidate Kura, in a letter to the Nigerian government.

August 15
The Guardian Group, CENSORED
Hyacinth Onoh, *The Guardian*, HARASSED
Minet Ojodacen, *The Guardian*, HARASSED
Bola Odutan, *The Guardian*, HARASSED
Emmanuel Efeni, *The Guardian*, HARASSED
Police sealed the offices of The Guardian Group, one of Nigeria's most influential media conglomerates. The move effectively closed the group's flagship national daily newspaper, *The Guardian*. Police presented no written authorization for the closure, and the government offered no official explanation for its actions. Four staff members were arrested and later released without charge: reporter Efeni, computer operator Odutan, chief security officer Ojodacen, and production editor Onoh. CPJ condemned the closure in a letter to the Nigerian government.

August 23
Dapo Olorunyomi, *The News/Tempo/PM News*,
   IMPRISONED, ATTACKED, HARASSED
Olurunyomi, deputy editor in chief of *The News* and *Tempo*, was arrested and held overnight without charge in connection with a cover story entitled "Go Back to June 12, Babangida Tells Abacha." In another article, which dealt with the national constitutional conference in Abuja, he reported that President Sani Abacha's delegates had called for restoring the June 12, 1993, elections won by Moshood Abiola. Olurunyomi was arrested again on Sept. 8 or 9 by military intelligence agents, badly beaten, and released the next day. He was arrested a third time on Sept. 22, and again beaten when he refused to reveal his sources for an Aug. 11 article in *Tempo* entitled "The North Prepares for War." Olorunyomi's lawyers secured his release the following day.

August 26
Bob Cohen, *CNN*, EXPELLED
Amy Merz, *CNN*, EXPELLED
CNN reporter Cohen and camerawoman Merz were accosted in the lobby of their Lagos hotel by men claiming to be policemen. The men declined to show identification, and Cohen and Merz refused to go with them. U.S. Embassy officials, called to the hotel by the journalists, ascertained that the men were with the State Security Service (SSS), and that Cohen and Merz had to obey their instructions. The SSS agents then drove the two journalists, accompanied by United States officials, to the airport, where they were put on a flight to London. The Nigerian government offered no explanation for the expulsion. Cohen and Merz had arrived in Lagos on Aug. 22. They prepared a report, aired on CNN the morning of their expulsion, that included an interview with Gani Fawehinimi, a lawyer defending president-elect Moshood Abiola. Fawehinimi's offices had been attacked on the night of Aug. 25. The house of opposition leader Dan Suleiman, whom Cohen also interviewed, was firebombed the same night. CPJ protested the two reporters' expulsion in a letter to the Nigerian government.

September 5
The Concord Group, CENSORED
The Punch Group, CENSORED
The Guardian Group, CENSORED
General Abacha issued several decrees proscribing publication by the three leading media groups—Concord, Punch and Guardian—for six months. The offices of the publications were to remain sealed during this period. At least 15 publications were banned under the decrees, and thousands of journalists left unemployed. Decrees Nos. 6 and 7 banned all Concord and Punch publications, retroactively from June 10—the day before the offices of these groups were forcibly closed. Decree No. 8 closed the Guardian Group effective Aug. 14, the eve of the State Security Service (SSS) raid on the group's Lagos offices. All three media houses

had openly declared president-elect, and Concord Group owner, Moshood Abiola to be the country's legitimate leader. CPJ denounced the decrees and effective banning of the media groups in a letter to the Nigerian government.

September 7
Kunle Bakare, *Fame*,
HARASSED, IMPRISONED
Femi Akintunde Johnson, *Fame*,
HARASSED, IMPRISONED
Dayo Asaju, *Fame*, HARASSED, IMPRISONED
Managing editor Bakare, editor Johnson and senior staff reporter Dayo Asaju of the weekly *Fame* magazine were arrested, and subsequently released without charge.

September 26
Bayo Onanuga, *The News and Tempo*,
IMPRISONED
Onanuga, editor of *The News* and *Tempo*, was arrested and charged with libel. He was detained for two days and released on 10,000 naira bail. A trial date was set for Nov. 7.

December 12
Concord Group, CENSORED
Punch Group, CENSORED
Guardian Group, CENSORED
President Sani Abacha's Sept. 5 decrees banning publication by the three leading media groups, Concord, Punch and Guardian, were extended for a further six months. The extension came the same day that *Punch* resumed publication. Minister of Justice and Attorney General Michael Agbamuche warned the three media groups to desist from publication or circulation, and said that any attempt to oppose the decrees would meet with severe repression. The entrances to the newpaper offices remained sealed by armed forces. Although the ban on the Guardian Group was not due to expire until Feb. 14, the decrees' extension encompassed its publications as well.

Rwanda

Many of Rwanda's prominent journalists were among the first victims of the massacres that erupted after the presidents of Rwanda and Burundi were killed in a suspicious plane crash on April 6, 1994. Before that day, Rwanda's opposition and independent publications provided diverse perspectives on the political situation, the armed conflict with the Tutsi-dominated Rwandan Patriotic Front and human rights violations.

The systematic elimination of all forms of opposition and the ruthless silencing of all voices of reason and moderation by the Rwandan Armed Forces and Hutu militias were essential components in carrying out the genocide, which took the lives of nearly 800,000 people. Within the first few days of the massacres, critical journalists were either killed or were fleeing for their lives. This gave Radio-Television Libre de Milles Collines, a radio station owned by relatives of the late president, free reign to misinform the public and incite violence. Milles Collines instructed Hutus to slaughter Tutsis, and even gave the names and locations of individuals marked for death.

It is clear that ethnicity was not the sole motive for many of the killings. The Rwandan Armed Forces and Hutu militias took the opportunity to eliminate political opponents and independent journalists, among them Hutu critics of the regime. Based on information gathered by researchers with Reporters Sans Frontières (RSF) and African Rights, who conducted several fact-finding missions to Rwanda in the aftermath of the genocide, CPJ compiled a list of 14 journalists whose murders, a preponderance of circumstantial evidence suggests, are directly attributable to their work. CPJ had documented government attacks against many of these journalists during the previous three years. One other journalist, a cameraman with Rwanda

Television, was killed when the TV station was bombed. A further five assassinations are still under investigation.

April-June
André Kameya, *Rwanda Rushya*, KILLED
Kameya, editor in chief of the newspaper *Rwanda Rushya*, and an official of the opposition Liberal Party (PL), was killed along with his wife and son. Kameya had been imprisoned and threatened with death under the Habyarimana regime on several occasions since 1991.

April 7
Winifrida Mukamana, *Reba Videwo*, KILLED
Mukamana, an editor for the video production company Reba Videwo, was killed by the military in Remera, near Kigali's airport, on the first day of the massacres.

April 7
Eudès Nshimiryo, *TV Rwanda*, KILLED
Nshimiryo, a director of the state-run TV Rwanda, was killed at his home in Nyamirambo, Kigali on the first day of the massacres. Soldiers came to his home while he was entertaining guests, some of whom were Tutsi. The soldiers attacked the guests, and Nshimiryo attempted to come to their defense by showing the soldiers his press card. He was killed immediately.

April 7
Aloys Nyimbuzi, *L'Observateur*, KILLED
Nyimbuzi, a journalist with the opposition paper *L'Observateur*, was killed at his home in Gikondo, Kigali, on the first day of the massacres.

April 8
Gilbert Munana, *Le Flambeau*, KILLED
Munana, a journalist with the opposition newspaper *Le Flambeau*, was killed by militiamen in Kigali, on the second day of the massacres.

April 8 or 9
Tharcisse Rubwiriza, *Orinfor*, KILLED
Rubwiriza, a journalist with the radio section

of the official information department Orinfor, was killed at his home in Gikondo, on April 8 or 9. Rubwiriza ran a popular Sunday morning radio program during which he reviewed a cross section of the week's newspapers, and discussed opposition views. He had been demoted from a senior position because of his political openness.

April 9
Gratien Karambizi, *Imbaga*, KILLED
Karambizi, a journalist with the opposition paper *Imbaga*, was killed at his home in Kamisayara, Kigali, on the third day of the massacres. Two of his children were killed along with him. His wife, a Hutu, was spared, as was one of their children. Karambizi had been detained by the regime for six weeks in 1991.

April 10 to 12
Vincent Rwabukwizi, *Kanguku*, KILLED
Rwabukwizi, director of the opposition newspaper *Kanguku*, was shot dead by the military between April 10-12, in front of his home in Nyamirambo, Kigali. He was considered close to the rebel Rwandan Patriotic Front (FPR). Rwabukwizi had a long history of persecution by the government for his work as a journalist. In 1990, he was sentenced to a 15-year jail term for an interview with the last Tutsi king, in exile in Kenya. He was released after 10 months, but placed under house arrest. He was detained again three weeks later, and held for a further four months, on charges of inciting ethnic unrest and calling for the overthrow of the Habyarimana regime. After his release in September 1991, he was constantly harassed, and at times went into hiding.

April 11
Obed Bazimaziki, *Le Flambeau*, KILLED
Bazimaziki, a journalist with the opposition paper *Le Flambeau*, was killed near his home in Nyakabanda, Kigali. The government had detained him in 1991.

April 11
Charles Bideri-Munyangabe, *Le Messager*, KILLED
Le Messager reporter Bideri-Munyangabe was killed in Nyakabanda, at the same time as his colleague Obed Bazimaziki.

April 22
Marcellin Kayiranga, *Kanguka*, KILLED
Kayiranga, an editor of the opposition newspaper *Kanguka*, was thrown into the latrine at his cousin's home in Muhima and killed. Kayiranga had gone into hiding for several weeks in 1993, after learning that state security agents were searching for him.

April 24
Charles Karinganire, *Le Flambeau*, KILLED
Karinganire, a journalist with the opposition paper *Le Flambeau*, was killed at his home by soldiers who butchered him with machetes, and then cut him into pieces in front of his younger brother. Karinganire had been detained for over two months in 1991.

April 24
Emmanuel-Damien Rukondo, *Rubyiruko-Rubanda*, KILLED
Rukondo, a free-lance contributor to *Rubyiruko-Rubanda* and President of the Association of Newspaper Owners, was killed in Centre Saint-Paul, in Kiyovu, Kigali. He was forced to get into the back of a truck and was paraded naked around the neighborhood before being killed and cut into pieces.

April 29
Anastase Seruvumba, *Imbaga*, KILLED
Seruvumba, a journalist with the opposition paper *Imbaga*, was killed. He had returned to Rwanda in January 1994, after two years of study in Switzerland. He also worked for the newspaper *Kinyamateka*.

May 10
Vénant Ntawucikayenda, *TV Rwanda*, KILLED
Ntawucikayenda, a cameraman for state-run

TV Rwanda, was killed in a bomb blast at the television station, in Kigali.

April-June
Théotime Kamanayo, *Kiberinka,* KILLED
Kamanayo, a journalist with the opposition paper *Kiberinka,* was killed at his home in Mumena, Kigali, by militiamen. In 1992, Kamanayo and three colleagues had been harassed by the government and had temporarily gone into hiding.

April-June
Jeanne d'Arc Mukamusoni, *Le Soleil,* KILLED
Mukamusoni, director of the opposition newspaper *Le Soleil,* was killed by militiamen at a checkpoint in Nyakabanda as she tried to flee Kigali. *Le Soleil* was close to the Social Democrat Party (PSD).

April-June
Ignace Ruhatana, *Kanyarwanda,* KILLED
Ruhatana, editor in chief of the journal *Kanyarwanda* and an official of the human rights organization of the same name, was killed in his home district of Nyakabanda by a Rwandan Armed Forces soldier. Ruhatana had been attacked and injured in 1993 by armed men who tried to seize documents belonging to *Kanyarwanda.*

April-June
Alfonse Rutsindura, *Amakuruki i Butare,* KILLED
Rutsindura, editor in chief of *Amakuruki i Butare* and a contributor to the intellectual journal *Dialogue,* was killed by militiamen while he was returning to his home in Butare. His wife, children, and parents were also murdered. In 1990, Rutsindura had been detained for six months for reporting on the massacres of students in Butare, home of Rwanda's only university.

April-June
Vincent Shabakaka, *Kiberinka,* KILLED
Shabakaka, a journalist with the Kigali-based newspaper *Kiberinka,* was killed by militiamen

in Nyamirambo, at his neighbors' home. In 1992, he and several colleagues from the paper had been threatened, and fearing arrest, had gone into hiding.

Senegal

In 1994, for the first time in over a decade, the Senegalese courts officially banned a magazine. When President Abdou Diouf assumed office in 1980, after the resignation of Leopold Senghor, he allowed the establishment of an open multiparty system, and permitted the emergence of a private press. Particularly in the last few years, the Senegalese government has pointed to its flourishing free press, including two private dailies and a large number of private and opposition weeklies and periodicals, as evidence of the nation's democracy. The private press is very critical of the government, and in 1994 revealed many financial and human rights scandals, and criticized Diouf's handling of the economy and his jailing of opposition leaders. But while the government was tolerant of criticism from the domestic press, it cracked down unexpectedly on the French magazine *Jeune Afrique* **when it published an article linking an official's demotion to the highly political investigation of a 1993 murder.**

With Senegal's literacy hovering around 30 percent, radio has a far larger potential audience than the press. The year's most significant media development, then, was the licensing of Radio Sud, owned by the media collective that publishes Senegal's most popular daily and that for years has been trying to gain permission to start a private station. Radio Sud broadcasts largely in Wolof, the predominant local language.

June 2
Jeune Afrique, CENSORED
A Dakar court banned the Paris-based weekly *Jeune Afrique* for a year. Government Magistrate

Mansour Tall sued the magazine for defamation following an article published in October 1993 that suggested that Tall's demotion was linked to his sister's position in the opposition Senegalese Democratic Party (PDS) and to his expressed interest in the May 1993 assassination of the vice president of the Constitutional Council. Though Tall declined the magazine's offer to print his response and acknowledged that the author had no malicious intent, he proceeded with the case against the magazine's editor in chief, Bechir Ben Yahmed. Ben Yahmed, who could not travel to Dakar for health reasons, was tried in absentia, fined 50 million CFA in damages, and given a six-month suspended sentence. The year-long ban violated the Senegalese Press Law of 1991, which limits suspension of publications to three months. CPJ condemned the decision on July 28 in a letter to the Senegalese president. On Aug. 3, the government lifted the ban and dropped the charges.

September 18
West African Journalists Association, ATTACKED
Unidentified persons broke into the West African Journalists Association (WAJA) office in Dakar, where the press freedom monitoring branch of the association is based. The intruders forced the doors open, vandalized the office, and stole the fax machine and an annual report on press freedom in West Africa. No other valuable equipment was taken, and the office of the organization that shares the building with WAJA was left untouched.

Sierra Leone

Valentine Strasser and his National Provisional Ruling Council (NPRC), a group of young army officers who took power in a 1992 coup, showed no intention of allowing greater freedom of expression in 1994 as Sierra Leone moved towards multiparty elections scheduled for December 1995. New press laws passed by the NPRC in February essentially reaffirmed the restrictive measures introduced a year earlier. By laying out steep fees and strict guidelines for press registration, the 1993 laws had drastically reduced the number of newspapers from over 30 to around 10. Since Strasser had announced in April 1993 that he would repeal these laws to celebrate the first anniversary of the NPRC coup, their re-enactment reflected poorly upon his commitment to reform.

The prosecution of *The New Breed,* an independent weekly, continued throughout 1994, and remained underway at year's end. The threat of five-year prison sentences for the publication of opinions likely to cause "alarm or despondency" also kept journalists in check. In November, faced with the spread of Liberian-backed rebel insurgencies as well as an increasingly rebellious national army and rumors of another coup, the NPRC declared full censorship on military reporting.

March
Josie Sakedoh, *The Vision*, ATTACKED
Three soldiers in Bo, Sierra Leone's second largest city, attacked Sakedoh when he identified himself as a journalist. He was beaten, then detained for several hours.

August
Ibrahim Seaga Shaw, *Afro Times*,
    IMPRISONED, LEGAL ACTION
Abdul Abass Dumbuya, *Afro Times*,
    IMPRISONED, LEGAL ACTION
Shaw, editor in chief of the independent *Afro Times*, and Dumbuya, reporter for the paper, were arrested in Freetown in early August and charged with defamatory libel. They were held in Freetown for several days, transferred to Bo, and then released on bail. The charges arose from two articles printed the previous month implicating Charles Margai, a man with close ties to the government, in a financial scandal. The case was later dropped.

November 24
All Media, CENSORED
The military government announced that all information relating to military operations would be subject to censorship for four weeks. According to an order issued by the country's Secretary of State, the news blackout was intended to ensure the secrecy of a government operation against United Revolutionary Front (RUF) rebels in the east. The ban was still in effect at year's end.

December
Julius Spencer, *The New Breed,*
  IMPRISONED, LEGAL ACTION
Donald John, *The New Breed,*
  IMPRISONED, LEGAL ACTION
Mohamed Bangura, *The New Breed,*
  IMPRISONED, LEGAL ACTION
Alfred Payitie Conteh, *The New Breed,*
  IMPRISONED, LEGAL ACTION
Abdul Bashiru Alusine Kargbo, *The New Breed,*
  IMPRISONED, LEGAL ACTION
The High Court revoked the bail of the defendants in *The New Breed* case, returning managing editor Spencer, editor in chief John, reporter Bangura, sales director Conteh, and printer Kargbo to prison. The defendants' legal troubles began in October 1993, when *The New Breed* published an editorial asking the government to respond to an article in the Swedish newspaper *Expressen* that accused NPRC officials of corruption and reported that the chair of the NPRC, Captain Valentine Strasser, was making huge profits from the diamond trade. They were detained initially for 10 days, and then released on bail and charged with 10 counts of sedition. When the case came before the High Court in November 1993, the defendants' lawyers appealed to the Supreme Court in Freetown to consider questions of pre-trial publicity, freedom of expression and freedom of the press. In February 1994 the Supreme Court agreed to hear the case, but ruled against the defendants on Nov. 9, sending the case back to the High Court. On Dec. 1, the High Court

judge rejected a defense motion that the prosecutor, who had recently been appointed Attorney General and Minister of Justice, should be dismissed from the case for bias. In response, the defendants' lawyers withdrew from the High Court case. The judge in turn revoked the defendants' bail and continued to hear the case for a week with no defense counsel present. On Dec. 20, charges against Bangura were dropped due to his illness. On Jan. 6, 1995, the Supreme Court rejected the defense's second case, that the judge and prosecutor were biased against the defendants. On Jan. 16 the defense lawyers agreed to return to the High Court to represent their clients, and the defendants were released on bail.

Somalia

Even before the withdrawal of the U.S. Marines in March 1994, Somalia was an extremely difficult and dangerous place to work. Journalists and international aid workers had been caught in the crossfire between warring clans, and at times deliberately targeted as part of an unwelcome foreign occupying force. The phased withdrawal of the rest of the United Nations Operation in Somalia (UNOSOM), and a rapidly deteriorating security situation, raised the risks of covering a story that by year's end the rest of the world increasingly seemed indifferent to.

Major news organizations no longer have permanent full-time staffers based in Somalia, and most foreign correspondents assigned to the country are based in neighboring Nairobi, Kenya, 600 miles from the Somali capital Mogadishu. Many editors acknowledge that the obvious dangers of working Mogadishu are a significant factor in their reluctance to send their journalists to cover the story. But throughout 1994, Somalia still made news, and a steady stream of coverage was maintained largely by freelancers and local Somali stringers.

Gunmen deliberately shot and killed

three journalists during the year, and an AP correspondent was kidnapped at gunpoint and held for US$300,000 ransom. After three weeks of negotiation, the journalist was released unharmed.

The danger is expected to increase when the last of the peacekeepers leave Somalia in March 1995, but at least some journalists and aid workers are determined to remain behind despite the risks.

March 20
Ilaria Alpi, *RAI-3 television*, KILLED
Miran Krovatin, *RAI-3 television*, KILLED
Alpi, an Italian journalist, and Krovatin, a Slovakian cameraman, on assigment for Italy's RAI-3 television, were shot and killed by a group of Somali gunmen in Mogadishu. The gunmen stopped the reporters near the Italian Embassy and opened fire into their pickup truck. Alpi and Krovatin were the sixth and seventh journalists killed in Somalia since the U.N. operation began.

June 18
Tina Susman, *Associated Press (AP)*, ATTACKED
Susman, AP correspondent and news editor of the Johannesburg bureau, was kidnapped by Somali gunmen on a main road in Mogadishu. She was travelling with Kenyan AP photographer Sayyid Abdul Azim, and several security guards. The gunmen forced them to a stop, pulled them out of their car, hit Azim with their rifle butts, and drove Susman away at gunpoint. They demanded a $300,000 ransom, which they later dropped to $60,000. After 20 days of negotiations between AP, Somali intermediaries, the U.S. government, and the kidnappers, Susman was released unharmed. No ransom was paid, according to AP. The international press agreed not to report on the kidnapping until Susman was released.

August 31
Pierre Anceaux, *CARITAS-Switzerland*, KILLED
Anceaux, a Swiss journalist on assignment with the charity group CARITAS-Switzerland, was shot and killed in a CARITAS-run refugee camp in Baidoa, southwest of Mogadishu. Armed men in a jeep fired at Anceaux as he was interviewing a Somali woman. CARITAS shut down its operations in Somalia after Anceaux was killed.

South Africa

South Africa's monumental transition to democracy gave birth to the government of national unity (GNU), where, for the first time in the country's history, the black majority was democratically represented and accorded equal rights before the law. Several years of intense dialogue and negotiation between representatives from across the political spectrum resulted in consensus power-sharing arrangements, an interim constitution and an enshrined bill of rights.

As a reflection of the process of transformation, the evolving relationship between the media and the new government was for the most part harmonious. Editors across the board reveled in the newfound freedoms, the openness of the parliamentary process, and far greater access to the political leadership. But there were glitches, most often brought about by the legacy of apartheid: a lack of a culture of democracy, a lack of trained and skilled journalists, and the vastly unequal proportion of white-owned versus black-owned media. In the name of "nation building" and "reconstruction and development," some officials in the new government railed against what they saw as misrepresentation of their positions and policies, accusing the media at one point of sensational and irresponsible journalism.

To a seasoned press corps, on the lookout for any infringements on their newfound freedoms, the alarm was sounded. President Nelson Mandela stepped in and averted a "dogfight" between the media and the government by reaffirming the ANC's commitment to freedoms of speech and press. There was, however, one incident: Defense Minister Joe Modise's attempt to block *The Weekly Mail and Guardian* newspaper from publishing a follow-up to a story that certain ANC officials had spied for the now-defunct white regime. Modise threatened to use old apartheid security laws to prevent the revelations, but again the ANC interceded, and condemned the minister's actions, reiterating that the new government stood for openness and accountability.

The pattern of attacks against the press in 1994 tells what happened in South Africa with remarkable clarity. All occurred before the elections of April 26-29. Two journalists were killed in crossfire in violence-wracked townships shortly before the elections; one of them was most likely the hapless victim of an Inkatha Freedom Party (IFP) bullet. Although there were incidents or skirmishes after the elections, the press was generally able to operate freely. The major exception was the still violence-prone Kwazulu/Natal region, which, in a continuing climate of intimidation and fear, remained underreported.

It bears mention that many of the cases detailed in this report happened in the then independent homeland of Bophuthatswana, prior to the elections. In early March, in the midst of strikes and civil unrest to oust President Lucas Mangope, thousands of white South African right-wingers entered Bophuthatswana to prop up Mangope's reign. As the confrontation intensified, two right-wingers were executed by the homeland security forces, after which the right wing retreated to South Africa. Journalists covering the five days of civil strife said this story was one of the most difficult to get out to the world since the South African states of emergency and news blackouts in the mid- to late 1980s. In the course of the week, numerous journalists were attacked by the right wing, by the homeland police and by disaffected youth.

The major shift in the media was that of democratic representation. Zwelakhe Sisulu,

former editor of the alternative weekly, *New Nation,* who at the height of the state of emergency was imprisoned for two years for his activities as a journalist, was appointed to the top executive position in the South African Broadcasting Corporation (SABC). Attempts at more balanced TV and radio news coverage were still in their infancy, as the SABC grappled with affirmative action, training journalists, and making the old guard work with the new. Issues of opening up the airwaves will be further determined in 1995. But in 1994, with few exceptions, they remained firmly under state control.

The greatest loss for the print media was the demise of the alternative press, largely for financial reasons. The Afrikaans weekly *Vrye Weekblad* was forced to close, while *Work in Progress* folded with the drying up of foreign funds. *South* was in bad financial shape at year's end, as was *New Nation.* And many journalists expressed concern that the takeover of the English-language press by Irish newspaper tycoon Tony O'Reilly will undermine press freedom in South Africa.

January 8
Joe Louw, *Sunday Star,* THREATENED
Joe Louw, a reporter with the *Sunday Star,* was threatened at gunpoint by right-wingers demolishing a squatter camp at Nooitgedacht, outside Johannesburg. The men demanded that Louw hand over his camera. When Louw asked if they were policemen, and asked to see their identification, one of the men threatened to kill him. The men backed off when a large group of squatters came to Louw's defense.

January 9
Abdul Shariff, *Free-lancer,* KILLED
Charles Moikanyang, *South African Broadcasting Corporation (SABC),* ATTACKED
Anthea Warner, *SABC,* ATTACKED
Shariff, a free-lance photographer on assignment for the Associated Press (AP), was killed in cross fire while covering an African National

Congress (ANC) peace initiative tour in the township of Katlehong. He died of a bullet wound in the chest, after shots were fired at the group led by ANC General Secretary Cyril Ramaphosa and South African Communist Party chairman Joe Slovo. The shots were fired from a nearby hostel. Two other journalists were wounded in the shooting: SABC television news journalist Moikanyang was hospitalized with a bullet wound to the hip, and SABC radio reporter Warner received a flesh wound.

January 17
Vrye Weekblad, LEGAL ACTION

It was announced that the Afrikaans alternative weekly newspaper, *Vrye Weekblad*, was to cease publication in February. The paper had been bankrupted by the continuing costs of a legal battle dating back to November 1989, when the *Weekblad* had published an exposé that former forensics chief and deputy commissioner of police, General Lothar Neethling, had provided poison to "third force" agents for the purposes of assassinating ANC operatives. The cover story was part of an ongoing investigation into state-sponsored death squads. Neethling sued *Weekblad* and *The Weekly Mail* for defamation. In November 1993, the Supreme Court ruled in favor of the two papers, but the ruling was overturned a month later by the Appeals Court. Neethling's legal expenses were paid by the state—an arrangement that the new South African government has had to uphold and maintain. But *Weekblad*'s legal costs of over 1 million rand, and payment of damages to Neethling of a million rand, bankrupted the paper, making it technically illegal to continue publishing. The paper was forced to close, with the final edition published in February.

February 18
Modise, *Bop-TV,* HARASSED

Modise, a cameraman for the homeland government-controlled Bop-TV, was arrested while attempting to film Bophuthatswana police violently dispersing a picket called by the ANC Mafikeng branch in Mafikeng town square. As a crowd gathered to present demands for free political activity, police armed with tear gas, whips and shotguns began to assault people randomly. Modise was released later the same day without having been charged.

February 24
Lucie Hoyos, *German television network,*
ATTACKED

Youths in Soweto robbed a German television crew of their car and equipment. Two youths armed with a gun and a knife dragged reporter Hoyos from the car. The crew were producing a program about street children.

February 27
White journalists covering funeral,
THREATENED

White journalists attending the funeral of Sabelo Phama, commander of the Azanian People's Liberation Army (APLA), at Umtata in the Transkei were threatened by Pan Africanist Congress (PAC) supporters, who urged APLA cadres to shoot them. The APLA soldiers gathered a short distance from the grave and fired random shots in the air. Earlier, at the funeral rally, PAC officials had offered to provide marshals to accompany white journalists who wanted to move in and out of the stadium, or out of the VIP area and into the crowd. After the incident, a PAC media officer responded by saying, "we don't want people to intimidate journalists," and that steps would be taken to provide protection. On Feb. 17, the PAC Youth Wing had called a press conference to complain that the SABC was conducting a campaign against them by not covering PAC events, and asked if the Youth Wing had to kill a journalist or threaten civil war to ensure fair media coverage.

February 28
Benny Gool, *Cape Times,* HARASSED
John Christopher, *Free-lancer,* HARASSED
Fanie Jason, *Free-lancer,* HARASSED

Photographer Gool of the *Cape Times*, and freelancers Christopher and Jason were forced out of the Cape Town City Hall by armed right-wingers. Afrikaner Resistance Movement (AWB) leader Eugene Terre'Blanche was due to speak at the hall, and the AWB said the black photographers were evicted "for their own safety."

March 9

Bop-TV, HARASSED

Lucas Mangope, president of the Bophuthatswana homeland, closed the public radio and television broadcaster, Bop-TV, after the staff went on strike. He fired all striking workers, who were then evicted from the building. The staff had gone on strike demanding a 50 percent pay increase. On March 13, Mangope was ousted, and an administrator was appointed to take his place. Fired workers were all reinstated.

March 9

James Brittan, *Independent Television News (ITN),* ATTACKED
Sky News crew, ATTACKED

ITN reporter Brittan, travelling with a Sky News crew, was stopped at a roadblock in Mmabatho, where youths threatened to shoot them if they did not leave their car. Brittan and the crew told the youths they were members of the press. They escaped unharmed, but shots were fired at the car as they drove away, and the car windows shattered.

March 9-10

Nan Roux, *South African Broadcasting Corporation (SABC),* HARASSED, ATTACKED

An SABC crew, headed by Nan Roux, were assaulted by youths outside Mmabatho, the capital of Bophuthatswana, on March 9. At a makeshift roadblock, the youths tried to pull Roux out of her car, and failing to do so, stoned the car. The next day, the crew were stopped by members of the right-wing Afrikaner Resistance Movement (AWB). AWB members pulled Roux from her car, took her keys, and threw them away. The crew's footage was destroyed, and they were left stranded on the road.

March 9-10

Phineas Biphopo, *South African Broadcasting Corporation (SABC),* ATTACKED, THREATENED

SABC radio correspondent Biphopo was stopped by Bophuthatswana police on the Mmabatho airport road, severely beaten, and told he would be shot if he was seen on the roads again. Biphopo had been assaulted at the same spot the previous night, by youths who had blocked the road with stones and burning tires.

March 10

Mark Chisholm, *Reuters TV,* ATTACKED
Paul Arubicek, *Reuters TV,* ATTACKED
Frank Kgolane, *Reuters TV,* ATTACKED

Bophuthatswana police stopped Chisholm, Arubicek and Kgolane, of Reuters TV. They forced them out of their car, ripped off their bulletproof vests, and beat them with batons and whips. After the assault they were ordered to leave. The police accused them of littering the streets with stones.

March 10

James Brittan, *Independent Television News (ITN),* HARASSED, THREATENED
Mark Austin, *ITN,* HARASSED, THREATENED
Andy Rex, *ITN,* HARASSED, THREATENED
Nicodemus Mphalele, *ITN,* HARASSED, THREATENED

ITN news crew Brittan, Austin, Rex and Mphalele were pulled from their car by a group of right-wing militants outside the University of Bophuthatswana. The militants took the crew members' bulletproof vests and video cameras. They marched Brittan and Austin across an open field at gunpoint, held a gun to Brittan's head, and threatened to shoot him.

March 11

Agence France-Presse (AFP), HARASSED
South African Broadcasting Corporation (SABC), HARASSED

An AFP news team was surrounded and ordered to leave upon arriving at Mmabtho's air base by right-wing militants encamped there. The same day, a SABC aerial camera crew was surrounded by heavily armed khaki-clad right-wingers when they landed at the air base to refuel.

March 11
John Battersby, *Christian Science Monitor,*
ATTACKED
Paul Taylor, *Washington Post,* ATTACKED
Christian Science Monitor correspondent Battersby and *Washington Post* correspondent Taylor were assaulted by members of the right-wing Afrikaner Resistance Movement (AWB) three times on the same day. The journalists had attempted to speak with a group at the tail end of an AWB convoy retreating from its encampent at Mafikeng's air base. Four of the AWB members cursed and threatened the journalists, and two men beat them. Taylor sustained several blows to his head. After reaching their car, the correspondents drove away. Farther along the road, however, the AWB members stopped them, dragged them out of their car and beat them severely. Battersby and Taylor managed to drive away, heading toward Mafikeng, but the AWB members followed the journalists, blocked their car, and pointed rifles at them. The correspondents were again pulled out of their car and assaulted. Battersby suffered a cracked rib.

March 11
Sandile Nchunu, *Worldwide Television News*
(WTN), ATTACKED
Brian Green, *WTN,* ATTACKED
WTN news correspondents Nchunu and Green were beaten with whips by Bophuthatswana police in Mafikeng, and ordered to leave the area.

April 18
Ken Oosterbroek, *The Star,* KILLED
Juda Ngwenya, *Reuters,* ATTACKED
Greg Marinovich, *Free-lancer,* ATTACKED
Star photographer Oosterbroek, Reuters correspondent Ngwenya, and Marinovich, a free-lance reporter on assignment for *Newsweek,*

were caught in crossfire while covering a battle between the National Peacekeeping Force (NPKF) and pro-Inkatha hostel-dwellers in Thokoza township. Oosterbroek was killed by a bullet allegedly fired by the NPKF. The wounded photographers were taken to a hospital, where Oosterbroek was pronounced dead on arrival.

April 28
Michael Allen, *New York Daily News,* ATTACKED
Allen, an African-American reporter with New York's *Daily News,* was kicked and beaten by members of the Afrikaner Resistance Movement (AWB), while covering an anti-election rally the group was holding in Rustenberg. The police did not come to his aid. Two African-American women working with Allen were verbally harassed.

June 3
Weekly Mail and Guardian, LEGAL ACTION
Defense Minister Joe Modise obtained an interdict from the state attorney forbidding the *Weekly Mail and Guardian* from printing follow-up reports to its June 3 article, "Spies Want Jobs Back." The article said that 23 former military intelligence agents fired in 1992 were asking for amnesty and reinstatement. The article also named intelligence operatives who had been dismissed for illegal activities and then rehired. According to the *Sunday Times,* the *Weekly Mail and Guardian*'s sources planned to reveal the names of top ANC officials who had leaked information to the government of former President F.W. de Klerk. The ANC publicly condemned Modise's action, and on June 13 he withdrew the order.

September 25
South African Broadcasting Corporation (SABC),
HARASSED
Mangosuthu Buthelezi, home affairs minister and president of the Inkatha Freedom Party (IFP), interrupted a live SABC studio broadcast of an interview with Prince Sifiso Zulu, spokesperson

for Zulu King Goodwill Zwelithini. After Buthelezi and his bodyguards burst into the SABC television studios in Durban, an on-camera scuffle ensued. A gun was drawn, although it was not clear to whom it belonged. Prince Sifiso had just commented that the Zulu King did not consider Buthelezi his rightful advisor. Buthelezi was censured by his fellow cabinet members, and on Sept. 28 he offered an unconditional apology, which the cabinet accepted. Buthelezi was appointed minister of home affairs in South Africa's government of national unity, after the April elections. A power struggle between Buthelezi and the King emerged after the King distanced himself from Buthelezi and the IFP—the major opponent of the majority ANC.

Sudan

Independent newspapers have been forbidden in Sudan since the 1989 coup that brought a Muslim fundamentalist-backed military regime to power. A press law introduced in 1993 lifted the ban on privately owned papers. _Al-Sudani al-Doulia,_ established in January 1994, was the first new paper to publish under the law. It was granted a license because its owner was a member of the ruling National Islamic Front (NIF). But the paper soon proved too independent, addressing sensitive subjects such as government corruption and food shortages. It also covered the long-standing war against the Sudanese People's Liberation Army (SPLA), which has resisted the Khartoum government's attempts to impose Islamic law on the largely Christian and animist population of southern Sudan. In April, the government permanently closed _Al-Sudani al-Doulia,_ arresting the publisher and several journalists from the paper.

In 1994, at least six journalists were held in "ghost houses"—clandestine detention centers where prisoners are routinely tortured. None were ever formally charged.

February 24
Mutasim Mahmoud, _Al-Sudani al-Doulia,_
IMPRISONED
Security forces raided the offices of _Al-Sudani al-Doulia,_ the country's only independent daily, and arrested reporter Mahmoud. Mahmoud is also the Khartoum bureau chief of the Cairo-based _Al-Khartoum_ newspaper. He was held at first in a "ghost house," or clandestine detention center. After going on a hunger strike, he was reportedly moved to a military hospital in Omdurman. Friends and family were denied permission to visit him. He was released on April 19.

March 12
Al-Sudani al-Doulia, CENSORED
Al-Sudani al-Doulia, the country's only independent daily, was temporarily suspended by the government-appointed press and publications committee. The paper had previously operated out of Beirut, and did not publish out of Khartoum until January 1994, when it was licensed by the Sudanese government.

April 4
Mahjoub Erwa, _Al-Sudani al-Doulia,_
IMPRISONED
Ahmad al-Baggadi, _Al-Sudani al-Doulia,_
IMPRISONED
Mutawakel Abd al-Daafieh, _Al-Sudani al-Doulia,_
IMPRISONED
Nour al-Dine Madani, _Al-Sudani al-Doulia,_
IMPRISONED
Al-Sudani al-Doulia, CENSORED
Al-Sudani al-Doulia, Sudan's only independent daily, was shut down by the government. Security forces detained owner and editor in chief Erwa and reporters al-Baggadi and Abd al-Daafieh. Another journalist with the paper, Nour al-Dine Madani, was detained the same day. Among the items cited as possible catalysts for the closure of _Al-Sudani al-Doulia_ are articles about corruption among goverment officials, food shortages, a call for self-determination for southern Sudanese, and a plea for expanding

press freedom. Justice Minister Abd al-Aziz Shiddo claimed that the paper served "hostile foreign circles and countries." In addition, Culture and Information Minister Abd al-Basit Sabdrat accused Erwa of soliciting funding for the paper from a hostile foreign government. CPJ wrote to the government urging the immediate release of the journalists and requesting that *Al-Sudani al-Doulia* be allowed to resume publishing. Abd al-Daafieh, al-Baggadi, and Madani were released after about two weeks. Erwa was freed on June 30 in a gesture commemorating the fifth anniversary of the coup that brought the al-Bashir regime to power.

June 23

Mohamed Abd al-Seed, *Al-Khartoum,*
   ATTACKED, IMPRISONED

Abd al-Seed, a journalist with *Al-Khartoum,* a Sudanese opposition paper based in Cairo, was arrested when security forces entered the newspaper's Khartoum offices. After beating and kicking Abd al-Seed, the officers took him into custody. They accused him of involvement in a conspiracy, allegedly led by former prime minister Sadiq al-Mahdi, to assassinate Hassan al-Turabi, leader of the National Islamic Front (NIF). Abd al-Seed had recently interviewed Ummah Party leader al-Mahdi for *Al-Khartoum.* Al-Mahdi was arrested earlier in the week. CPJ wrote to Gen. al-Bashir in June and September, urging Abd al-Seed's immediate release. Abd al-Seed was held in a "ghost house," a clandestine detention center where prisoners are routinely tortured. He was released in October or November. He had been arrested and held for nearly two months in a "ghost house" in 1993, when he was Khartoum bureau chief for the Saudi-owned daily newspaper *Asharq al-Awsat.*

September 11

Mohamed Mahmoud Rajih, *Al-Khartoum,*
   LEGAL ACTION

Mutasim Mahmoud, *Al-Khartoum,*
   LEGAL ACTION

Nafisa al-Hadj, *Al-Khartoum,* LEGAL ACTION

Murtada al-Ghali, *Al-Khartoum,*
   LEGAL ACTION

Najib Nourredine, *Al-Khartoum,*
   LEGAL ACTION

Al-Khartoum, CENSORED

Members of the security forces raided and closed the Khartoum office of the independent Cairo-based newspaper *Al-Khartoum.* A day earlier the office had received a warning from the international section of the Ministry of Culture and Information that the bureau would be closed. Officials confiscated the press cards of all five journalists who worked in the bureau: Rajih, Mahmoud (who had been imprisoned earlier in the year), al-Haj, al-Ghali and Nourredine. Sudanese authorities have given no official explanation for the closure. Security officials claim that *Al-Khartoum*'s office was a "party headquarters" being used to arrange clandestine opposition meetings. This has been emphatically denied by the paper.

November 8

Sawt al-Ummah, HARASSED

Security authorities detained four members of the opposition Al-Ummah party and interrogated them about the editing and publishing site of its clandestine paper, *Sawt-al-Ummah.* The party had been publishing the underground paper for several weeks. The four officials were released later that evening, but were requested to return for further questioning the next day.

November 17

James Schofield, *Australian Broadcasting*
   Corporation, ATTACKED

Schofield, Nairobi correspondent for the Australian Broadcasting Corporation, was hit in the leg with shrapnel from a tank shell. The injury occurred as he was covering a battle between government troops and forces of the Sudan People's Liberation Army (SPLA) in southern Sudan, near the Ugandan border.

Togo

Although there appeared to be fewer physical attacks against journalists than in previous years, Togo imposed the harshest prison sentences on journalists anywhere on the continent during 1994. Three journalists were sentenced to five years in prison each for "slandering" President Gnassingbe Eyadema. The convictions stemmed from articles that charged the president's military government with corruption.

Eyadema assumed power 27 years ago, in a 1967 military coup, and his 1993 electoral victory was generally considered fraudulent. He claims to have weathered a number of coup attempts, and has used the specter of such incidents to justify his intolerance of political opposition and domestic criticism. February's National Assembly elections were violent and contested, and the date for by-elections continued to be postponed while the opposition demanded better monitoring.

Harassment by authorities, and the threat of harsh sentences in dangerous, unsanitary prisons, drove many journalists into exile. According to some local observers, the government harasses journalists accused of slander so that they will flee before their trials, as was the case for at least four journalists in 1994.

May 6
Martin Dossou Gbenouga, *La Tribune des Democrates,* IMPRISONED, LEGAL ACTION
Gbenouga, editor and publisher of the independent biweekly *Tribune des Democrates,* was sentenced to five years in prison and fined five million CFA for slandering President Gnassingbe Eyadema. He had been arrested on April 26, four days after the *Tribune* published an article in which France's minister of cooperation was quoted reproaching Eyadema for his delay in appointing a new prime minister. That same issue also carried an editorial by Gbenouga that criticized the president for his military rule, for his falsification of facts and for his exploitation of ethnic politics. CPJ denounced Gbenouga's arrest in a letter to the Togolese government. Gbenouga was held in the Civil Prison in Lome until May 18 and then transferred to a prison in the remote town of Mango. On Jan. 12, 1995, an appeals court reduced his sentence to one year and his fine to one million CFA.

July 25
Lucien Hounkanli, *La Sentinelle,*
    LEGAL ACTION
Theo Woboube, *La Sentinelle,*
    LEGAL ACTION
La Sentinelle, CENSORED
Woudoube, editor of the independent weekly *La Sentinelle,* and Hounkanli, the newspaper's director of publication, were each sentenced in absentia to five years in prison and fined 3 million CFA for defaming the head of state. The charges arose from an article by Wodoube in the paper's July 25 edition, which reported that President Gnassingbe Eyadema had bought a 300-million-CFA Mercedes-Benz with state funds. The issue was seized, as was the following week's. The two men fled the country in mid-August. In addition to their sentences, the judge imposed a six-month ban on the newspaper. By the end of the year, Hounkanli and Woboube were still in exile and *La Sentinelle* had ceased publication.

Zaire

In the latter half of 1994, President Mobutu Sese Seko earned a reprieve from international ostracism by working with the humanitarian aid community to mediate the Rwandan refugee crisis. But at the same time, his regime continued to inflict serious human rights violations on many Zairians and rescind in practice freedoms of speech and press guaranteed in the country's constitution and the 1993 Transition Act. In January, Mobutu combined the two governmental bodies that had vied for power since March 1993—his own High Council of the Republic and the Transitional Parliament, led by Prime Minister Etienne Tshisekedi of the opposition Union for Democracy and Social Progress (UDPS)—to form a new, more pliant transitional government, the HCR-TP. But Mobutu maintained control of the army, the security forces and the national treasury, thereby effectively holding onto power. His commitment to democratic reform was further belied by his refusal to relinquish state control of radio and television. Opposition and independent journalists were routinely subjected to threats, beatings, detention and, at times, torture, most often at the hands of Mobutu's Special Presidential Division (DSP) and the Military Action and Intelligence Service (SARM). Two journalists were killed, one of whom was the editor-owner of an opposition newspaper and a member of the UDPS.

Zaire is in a state of chaos and near collapse. The actions of what is, in effect, Mobutu's shadow state and a continuing reign of terror have given rise to a situation in which people are afraid to speak openly. In conjunction with the desperate economic conditions and barely functional infrastructure, this means that many human rights violations and attacks on the press go unreported, and unprosecuted.

March 4
Thierry Michel, EXPELLED
Authorities expelled Michel, an independent Belgian filmmaker preparing a documentary on Belgian expatriates in Zaire. He had been in the country for less than two weeks when he was arrested on March 3. He was interrogated and held overnight, and his cameras, notes, and personal effects were seized. The military escorted him to the airport the following day and put him on a flight to Brussels. Michel had previously made a documentary that was critical of President Mobutu's regime.

March 12
Kalala-Mbenga Kalao, *La Tempête des Tropiques,*
HARASSED
Security agents detained Kalao, a columnist for *La Tempête des Tropiques,* as he was getting on a ferry to cross the Congo River to Brazzaville. They held him for 18 hours, and seized his camera, luggage, and watch. The agents released him when he paid a bribe of several hundred dollars. At the time of his detention, Kalao was on his way to Washington, D.C., to receive the National Press Club's International Press Freedom Award. Kalao had spent 27 days in prison in 1993 for writing an article about the Zairian armed forces, and had been in hiding since his release in September. Kalao was subsequently granted political asylum in the United States in May.

April
Leon Moukanda Lunyama, *Umoja* and *Renaissance,*
THREATENED
Moukanda, editor and owner of the newspapers *Umoja* and *Renaissance,* received death threats throughout April. The threats followed the publication in *Umoja* of an article entitled "Prima-Curia," about the policies of President Mobutu and Prime Minister Kengo.

June 8
Pierre Kabeya, *Kin-Matin,* KILLED
Kabeya, a reporter for the opposition weekly *Kin-Matin,* was found dead on June 9 near Loana military camp in the Kintambo district of Kinshasa. A copy of *Kin-Matin* had been placed near his body. His death may have been related to an article he had written about a 1991 trial that implicated security forces in an attack a year earlier on the Lumbumbashi University campus. Several students lost their lives in that attack.

Late June

Wilifried Owandjankoi, *La Tempête des Tropiques,*
HARASSED

Owandjankoi, director of publication for *La Tempête des Tropiques,* was arrested by members of the Special Presidential Division (DSP) and detained for several hours. The arrest followed the June 21 publication of an unsigned article by Owandjankoi entitled "Mobutu and Eyadema Gain a Modest Diplomatic Success," which exposed nepotism in the civil service. Interrogators demanded to know who had written the article. Owandjankoi was released that afternoon after assuring his interrogators that he was not the author.

October 10

Ipakala Abeiye Mobiko, *La Référence Plus,*
THREATENED

Members of the military intelligence service (SARM) came to the office of the privately owned daily *La Référence Plus* looking for editor in chief Mobiko and the paper's directors. Finding no journalists present, they took an accounting intern into custody and demanded a list of editors' addresses and the license-plate numbers of the paper's directors. The visit followed publication of articles on Oct. 8 and Oct. 10 about counterfeit currency.

October 28

Adolphe Missamba Ndengi Kavula, *Nsemo,*
KILLED

Kavula, editor in chief and owner of the opposition newspaper *Nsemo* and a member of the National Committee of the main opposition party, Union for Democracy and Social Progress (UDPS), was kidnapped by a group of men believed to be Presidential militia members. He had been repeatedly harassed and threatened for his activities as a journalist. He was found 10 days later in critical condition in a field on his farm outside Kasangulu, 30 kilometers from Kinshasa, on Nov. 6. He appeared to have been badly tortured, and was unable to speak. He was taken to a clinic in Kinshasa and

died on Nov. 12, while awaiting permission from the Zairian authorities to be transferred to South Africa for further medical care. An autopsy was not performed, but medical tests suggested that he may have been injected with a toxic substance. Zairian authorities said that he suffered from "nervous depression" and had committed suicide. Kavula died without regaining consciousness.

Zambia

At the center of Zambia's once pace-setting transition to democracy is a growing conflict between President Frederick Chiluba's government and Zambia's leading independent newspaper, *The Post*—a champion of exposing high-level abuses of office, controversial government policies, corruption and drug-trafficking.

Chiluba's Movement for Multiparty Democracy (MMD) came to power in a landslide victory in the October 1991 elections. But the early strides toward establishing an open society and accountability have been hampered by the government's taste for the "sweetness of power," and its reluctance to relinquish the laws of old that help maintain it. Significantly, no institutional or media law reform was drafted in 1994. While the vast majority of Zambians are caught between structural adjustment, massive unemployment and declining standards of living, members of the ruling elite have found ways to make life more comfortable for themselves. *The Post* sees the exposure of rampant corruption and government unaccountability as flip sides of the same coin, and central to its mission of maintaining checks and balances in the public arena.

The vitriolic nature of the legal attacks against *The Post* intensified as the year progressed. *Post* staff members have lost count of the numerous criminal charges against them, which include over 24 counts of criminal libel, several counts of sedition and an alleged violation of the State Security Act that is punishable by up to 15 years' imprisonment. The state surpassed itself in late December by threatening to file two separate charges of treason—both carrying life terms—against editor in chief Fred M'membe and a 21-year-old *Post* reporter.

As elsewhere on the continent, the battle is in the courtroom. But what makes *The Post* stand out is its intention to test the boundaries and limits of reform by challenging the constitutionality of outmoded and oppressive laws still on the statute books. Despite the presence of a new constitution, recourse is still made to Penal Code statutes that date back to the colonial and post-independence periods. A case in point is Section 69, proscribing "ridicule of the President"—a crime for which truth affords no defense.

Most alarmingly, there were more, rather than fewer, laws on the books at year's end. The controversial Parliamentary and Ministerial Code of Ethics Act, signed into law in September, empowers ministers and parliament members to summon journalists before a tribunal, where they must testify about articles criticizing the aggrieved officials' conduct and reveal the sources for the offending reports.

January 29-February 2
Sheik Chifuwe, *Weekly Post,* HARASSED
Bright Mwape, *Weekly Post,* HARASSED
Weekly Post photographer Chifuwe was briefly detained and his film confiscated after he photographed police officers beating a suspect. His film was returned when the newspaper's lawyers intervened. Four days later, officers threatened to detain *Weekly Post* reporter Mwape, who had gone to the Kafue police station to report on the shooting of a suspect who was in police custody. CPJ, in a letter to the Zambian government, expressed its alarm at the intimidation of the *Post* reporters.

April 29
Fred M'membe, *The Post*,
LEGAL ACTION, HARASSED
Bright Mwape, *The Post,*
LEGAL ACTION, HARASSED
Post editor in chief M'membe and reporter Mwape were arrested and charged with publishing an article insulting President Frederick Chiluba. The March 29 piece was entitled "Nakathindi Declares from the Dock: Chiluba is a Twit"—a reference to a comment made in court by Princess Nakathindi Wina, former Minister for Community Development, during her trial for alleged drug trafficking. The former Minister had muttered the comment as she was listening to testimony against herself. M'membe and Mwape were released later the same day, and charged with violating Section 69 of the Penal Code. Section 69 prohibits the publication of comments deemed insulting to the head of state. *The Post* challenged Section 69's legality in a May 6 hearing, citing the right to press freedom under Article 20 of the Constitution. The case was referred to the High Court for determination of the constitutionality of the charge. On May 11, CPJ protested the ongoing legal proceedings against M'membe and Mwape.

* *The Weekly Post* changed its title to *The Post* when it became a biweekly on March 29.

May 26
Fred M'membe, *The Post,* HARASSED
Police summoned M'membe, *The Post*'s editor in chief, for questioning about a 1993 article on government housing policy. M'membe did not respond to the summons. "The police know where to find me. I have nothing to fear as I am not a criminal," *The Post*'s May 27 edition quoted M'membe as saying. He was formally charged under the State Security Act three months later.

August 23
Fred M'membe, *The Post,*
  LEGAL ACTION, HARASSED
Bright Mwape, *The Post,*
  LEGAL ACTION, HARASSED
Goliath Mungonge, *The Post,*
  LEGAL ACTION, HARASSED
Nkonkomalimba Kafunda, *The Post,*
  LEGAL ACTION, HARASSED
Masoutso Phiri, *The Post,*
  LEGAL ACTION, HARASSED
Dingi Chirwa, *The Post,*
  LEGAL ACTION, HARASSED
Lowrie Mwinga, *The Post,*
  LEGAL ACTION, HARASSED
Magayo Mambo, *The Post,*
  LEGAL ACTION, HARASSED
Peter Chilambwe, *The Post,*
  LEGAL ACTION, HARASSED
Post editor in chief M'membe, and reporters Mwape, Mungonge, and Kafunda were arrested and charged with various counts of criminal libel and with contravention of the State Security Act. M'membe was charged on all counts. The three reporters were collectively charged with five counts of criminal libel against President Chiluba's Press Attache, Richard Sakala. The latter charge stemmed from a profile that referred to Sakala as "Trickey Dickey." The maximum sentence for these offenses is two years' imprisonment. In addition, all four were charged with criminal libel against President Chiluba for reporting a former minister's allegations that the president smoked marijuana and was involved in drug trafficking. This charge carries a maximum prison term of three-years. The most serious charge—publishing classified documents in contravention of the State Security Act—stemmed from a March 1993 article about government housing policy. The article had included a cabinet memorandum. The maximum sentence for this offense is 15 years in prison. The final charge against the journalists— publishing a "false report...intended to alarm the public"—was related to a report that the United Nations had accused Zambia of assisting

UNITA rebels in neighboring Angola. The journalists were detained for several hours, and ordered to appear in court later that week. Five present and former *Post* journalists—Phiri, Chirwa, Mwinga, Mambo and Chilambwe—were summoned to the police station the day before the court date to face similar charges; however, those charges have not been pursued. In October, *The Post* refused to appear before Zambia's Media Ethics Committee to answer complaints related to the charges, on the grounds that the state was trying to use the committee to elicit information that would bolster the prosecution's case.

September
All media, THREATENED, LEGAL ACTION
The Parliamentary and Ministerial Code of Ethics Act was passed by parliament and signed into law by President Chiluba. A highly controversial clause in the act allows ministers and parliament members to lodge complaints with the chief justice against journalists who have written articles alleging that they have breached the Ethics Code. The chief justice may then convene a tribunal, before which the journalists must justify their allegations. Such justification may include disclosing their sources of information. If the tribunal rules that a report is false, the journalist faces a prison term of up to two years. Critics of the act point out that it undermines press freedom by using the threat of prolonged imprisonment to coerce journalists into revealing their sources. Journalists roundly condemned the bill as breaching the ethical requirements of their profession. Vice President Godfrey Miyanda attempted to justify the bill by claiming it would protect ministers and parliament members from unfair criticism.

December
Fred M'membe, *The Post,* THREATENED
Bright Mwape, *The Post,* THREATENED
Nkonkomalimba Kafunda, *The Post,*
  THREATENED
Post editors M'membe and Mwape, and reporter Kafunda, faced charges under the Drug Act for

refusing to identify government sources quoted in articles published between October and November. According to the sources, the Drug Enforcement Commission (DEC) had given President Chiluba a report confirming that his son Castro was a drug user. The DEC admitted authoring the report, but denied having leaked the information. If convicted of refusing to reveal sources under the Drug Act, the three journalists could be sentenced to 10 years in prison.

December 8

The Post, ATTACKED

Heavily armed paramilitary police stormed *The Post*'s offices in a midday raid, as the paper was about to go to press. During a five-hour siege, police rummaged through documents and computer files. They confiscated a reader's letter criticizing the inspector-general of police, a statement by a Malawian politician recently deported from Zambia, and an article about a visit by President Chiluba to Sweden. Police in Ndola stopped presses and delayed printing of *The Post* for three hours while they conducted a simultaneous raid. Local sources speculated that an article in the delayed edition implicating the defense minister in by-election vote-rigging may have prompted the raid. In the following week's edition, however, *The Post* said the raid was apparently prompted by rumors that the paper had received compromising photographs of the President and his personal secretary. An article in the previous week's edition about the personal secretary's luxurious lifestyle may have fuelled such fears.

December 13

Stewart Mwila, *Crime News,*
   IMPRISONED, LEGAL ACTION
George Malunga, *Crime News,*
   IMPRISONED, LEGAL ACTION

Mwila, managing editor of *Crime News*, and his deputy, Malunga, were arrested, refused bail, and held for several days. Their detention is believed to have stemmed from an article, published two weeks earlier, that accused the President's wife, Vera Chiluba, of involvement in drug trafficking. The journalists face criminal libel charges.

Dec 19-28

Fred M'membe, *The Post,*
   LEGAL ACTION, HARASSED
Mulenga Chomba, *The Post,*
   LEGAL ACTION, HARASSED

Post editor in chief M'membe and reporter Chomba were summoned to police headquarters, interrogated for several hours, and warned that they would be charged with two treasonable offenses, both punishable by life imprisonment. The police had conducted a five-day search for Chomba, including an early-morning search at his parent's home in Kitwe. During the interrogation, Chomba was asked to reveal his sources for an article that had appeared in the paper's Dec. 2 edition. The article had quoted a Zambia Opposition Front (ZOFRO) official as saying he feared extremists might take advantage of a power vacuum in the country, leading to a mutiny in the army. The police also wanted to know if Chomba was involved in a coup plot, who the coup plotters were, and what their sources of funding were. Chomba denied knowledge of a coup plot. He and M'membe were warned that they faced charges of inciting mutiny and withholding information related to a treasonable offense. Plans to charge them with the latter crime were apparently dropped on Dec. 28, following a second interrogation. Instead, police told the two journalists that besides inciting the army to mutiny, they would be charged with sedition.

Zimbabwe

1994 started well for Zimbabwe's media, with the settlement of long-standing libel and contempt-of-court cases against journalist Geoff Nyarota, formerly with the government-controlled *Bulawayo Chronicle*. Though the judge ruled against Nyarota in the libel

54

case, he held that Nyarota could not be held in contempt of court for refusing to reveal his sources, and declared that forcing jour nalists to reveal their sources would be detrimental to the public interest. This would have been a major victory for press freedom if suitable forums for a critical and independent media existed. But the government still had control over television and radio broadcasting, and on Dec. 25, the country's only independent daily, the *Daily Gazette,* closed for financial reasons.

The closing of the *Gazette* is particularly troubling because of the presidential and parliamentary elections due to be held in the spring of 1995. The government-owned *Daily Herald* has become more objective and critical of the government since the creation of the *Gazette* in 1992, and many fear that the paper will revert to its former role as a mouthpiece for the Zimbabwe African National Union-Patriotic Front (ZANU-PF), the party of President Robert Mugabe. The *Gazette* was continually subjected to expensive libel suits and, according to one editor, investigations and harassment by the Zimbabwean secret service. The elections—the nation's third since independence from Britain in 1980—are likely to be contentious, and without a free press many feel that it is unlikely that the opposition will be fairly represented.

February 5
Brian Latham, *Daily Gazette,*
LEGAL ACTION, HARASSED
Basildon Peta, *Daily Gazette,*
LEGAL ACTION, HARASSED
Detectives interrogated Latham, editor of the *Daily Gazette,* and reporter Peta for several days after the newspaper—Zimbabwe's only independent daily—ran an article by Peta exposing massive tax evasion by companies that the ruling ZANU-PF party owned. Police seized Peta's notes, letters and diaries, and returned them about three months later with pages miss-

ing. In early March, Latham and Peta were charged under the Official Secrets Act with refusing to reveal sources. The case was still pending at year's end.

March 12
Rex Maphisa, *Daily Herald,* IMPRISONED
Beitbridge police arrested Maphisa, a reporter for the government-owned *Daily Herald,* on charges of criminal defamation in connection with an article he wrote entitled, "Beitbridge Court Resembles Drama Club." Maphisa was released on March 14. Although his case remained open, no charges had been pressed by year's end.

The Americas

OVERVIEW
OF **The Americas**

by Ana Arana

The Americas

CONTINUING THE TREND OF RECENT YEARS, restrictions on press freedom in the Americas were imposed by governments in more subtle ways than a decade ago. Few journalists were killed in the hemisphere in 1994, and only a small number were put in jail because of their work. But governments continued to mistrust and misunderstand the role of a free and robust press. Censorship laws and mandatory licensing for journalists were used by some governments to rein in the profession. Venezuela became the worst offender when its Congress passed a new law that will impose three- to six-month prison sentences on journalists who work without licenses. Strict libel and defamation laws were introduced in other countries. In Argentina, Congress ended the year on the verge of passing a new law proposal that would send journalists to prison for up to 10 years for dishonoring the name of a politician—a higher penalty than that given to corrupt politicians charged with illicit enrichment.

Peru, Cuba, Mexico and Colombia exhibited some of the most egregious violations against the press. Peru has the highest number of imprisoned journalists. Ten are serving prison terms under draconian anti-terrorism laws. These cases are included in the "Imprisoned" section of this book for the first time. CPJ had omitted their names in previous years because of incomplete data. Prosecu-

Ana Arana, *program coordinator for the Americas, is a former foreign correspondent who covered Latin America for six years. She was a senior correspondent for the Ft. Lauderdale* Sun-Sentinel, *staff reporter for the* San Jose Mercury News *and a news writer for CBS News and KCET (PBS) in Los Angeles. She was also a free-lance correspondent for the* Miami Herald, *the* Baltimore Sun *and* U.S. News & World Report *in Bogota and San Salvador. Arana, a native speaker of Spanish, has an M.S. in journalism from Columbia University's Graduate School of Journalism.*

 Mira Gajević, *a CPJ research associate, contributed extensively to this report.*

The research carried out by CPJ's Americas program in 1994 was made possible in part by a grant from the Robert McCormick Tribune Foundation.

tors and government officials agree that the journalists are innocent of the charges, but they are destined to remain in jail, trapped by a law that allows false testimony to be heard as truth.

In Cuba, journalists face the rigors of a new order imposed by the cash-strapped government. Many were forced out of their jobs for reasons of "ideological incompatibility"; others opted for defection. Three journalists asked for asylum in the United States and Europe during state-sponsored trips.

The Mexican press was surprised with many crises that made great copy. How ever, self-imposed controls prevented most journalists from challenging the status quo. And Mexican television remained among the least independent broadcast news services in the hemisphere.

Colombian journalists faced the most danger in the Americas. Two were killed for reasons related to their work. In the last 15 years, violence from paramilitary and guerrilla groups and drug traffickers has killed up to 50 journalists, ending Colombia's tradition of powerful investigative journalism.

Brazil is an example of a country in which local state governments were more powerful than the central government in Brasilia. Journalists in the major metropolises enjoyed total freedom, but those working for provincial newspapers faced limitations.

In Haiti, the military government had crushed the free press, but with the restoration of democracy, radio stations and newspapers were again operating openly. In the English-speaking Caribbean, where most nations enjoy a tradition of a free if conservative press, there were no violations reported.

A positive new trend in the region is the appearance of national press moni-toring groups that work closely with CPJ and other regional and international press freedom organizations. An example of this new trend is the Instituto Prensa y Sociedad (IPYS), founded this year in Lima. It accomplished the great task of uniting representatives from the conservative and liberal sectors of journalism. In Central America, the Journalists' Center for Freedom of Expression (CEPEX) has been organizing local press-defense workshops. Journalists in other countries have expressed the desire to set up similar groups.

In the United States, CPJ continues to press for Justice Department action on the unsolved murders of immigrant journalists over the past decade. A CPJ inves-tigative report on these cases—"Silenced," published in December 1994—is excerpted within (see p. 89).

Argentina

Press freedom in Argentina took a jolt in late 1994, with the introduction in Congress of a new press bill, supported by President Carlos Menem, that would amend the penal code, disproportionately increase penalties for defamation and libel, and require newspapers to obtain libel insurance of $500,000. The proposal would prescribe prison terms of up to 10 years for journalists convicted of libel and defamation—as harsh as those given for criminal offenses such as manslaughter. Under the law proposals, journalists would also be liable for soiling the "good name" of the dead. The courts would apply the penalties regardless of the existence of malice, and would lay all burden of proof on the reporter and the newspaper.

Because of the Argentine press's traumatic experience of censorship under past military regimes, the new press law sent shock waves through the news media, which, despite the anti-press sentiments of President Menem, has flourished under his leadership. Menem is particularly irritated about scandalous reports in the press on his family, his government aides and his own lifestyle. President Menem continued his personal battle with the independent left-wing daily *Página 12,* introducing his fourth lawsuit against the newspaper.

Violent attacks against journalists in provincial cities also escalated in 1994. Journalists reported death threats, assaults and harassment. Many reporters accuse local provincial government officials who were reacting to critical press accounts of instigating the attacks.

February 2
Various journalists, ATTACKED, THREATENED
Soccer star Diego Maradona shouted obscenities at reporters and fired at least five shots at them with an air gun, injuring several journal-ists who had gathered near his country home. He threatened reporters with real bullets if they didn't leave. During a live report, TV crews were doused with water from a hose. Maradona now faces charges of bodily harm and minor injuries brought by four journalists.

February 3
Julio Torres Cabanillas, *La Razón,*
ATTACKED, THREATENED
Cabanillas, a reporter with *La Razón,* was severely beaten by eight unknown assailants when his car was intercepted by three vehicles in downtown Buenos Aires. He was threatened with future beatings if he refused to halt his investigations. In December 1993, Cabanillas had published critical reports on street protests in La Rioja. In another article, he wrote about the 1993 beating death of Italian Mafia personality Valeriano Forzatti, who died under suspicious circumstances in a prison in Buenos Aires.

February 6
Julio Sanders, *Revista Caras,*
ATTACKED, THREATENED
Sanders, a journalist with the magazine *Caras,* was attacked and threatened by the bodyguards of first lady Zulema Menem as he attempted to photograph her.

February 11
Alberto Carlos Vila Ortiz, *La Capital,*
THREATENED
Ortiz, editor of the daily *La Capital* in Santa Fé province, was intercepted by three individuals who threatened to kill him and his family if he did not stop his political reporting.

February 17
Rodolfo Irineo Ceballos, *Diario El Pregón* ,
ATTACKED
Ceballos, a journalist with the *Diario El Pregón* in Jujuy province, was severely beaten by unknown individuals because of his investigations into local political corruption.

February 23
Carlos González, *FM Makakos,*
ATTACKED, HARASSED
González, a radio journalist in Machagai, Chaco
province, suffered broken bones after he was
beaten by a nightclub owner in Machagai.
González reported that the club had contami-
nated several clients with cholera.

February 27
Francisco Ramírez, *Agencia Telam,*
THREATENED
Ramírez, a reporter with the news agency
Telam, received telephone death threats, warn-
ing him against continuing an investigation into
police abuses.

March 2
Alberto Carlos Vila Ortiz, *La Capital,*
THREATENED
Unknown individuals threatened Ortiz, saying
they would kill his son if he did not resign from
his job as editor in chief of the daily *La Capital*
in Rosario, Santa Fé province. It was the second
threat against Ortiz in less than four weeks.

March 21
Alfredo Zacarias, *El Clarin,* THREATENED
Zacarias, the correspondent of the Buenos Aires
daily *El Clarín* in Corrientes province, received
several anonymous telephone death threats
while he was investigating the trafficking of
children for adoption in the city of Goya.

April 4
Daniel Perazzo, *FM Metrópoli,* HARASSED
Perazzo, a radio journalist with FM Metrópoli
in Rosario, Santa Fé province, was threatened
by an unidentified individual when he left his
office. The person threatened to kill him if he
would not stop his investigation into the disappearance of a child.

July 1
Julio Humberto Bravo, *FM La Cocha-Tucumán,*
ATTACKED, THREATENED, HARASSED
Bravo, director of the FM radio station in the
town of La Cocha-Tucumán, was assaulted and
threatened with death by a town councilman,
who was offended because Bravo criticized him
in his radio programs.

July 1
Henry Von Wartenberg, *Revista Gente,*
ATTACKED
Inés Hernández, *Revista Gente,* ATTACKED
Photojournalist Von Wartenberg and reporter
Hernández, both with the magazine *Gente*, were
beaten by bodyguards protecting Carlos Facun-
do Menem, President Carlos Menem's son, as
they attempted to photograph him and his girlfriend. Photographic equipment and film were
taken from the journalists.

September 12
Agencia Diarios y Noticias, THREATENED
The news agency received two anonymous calls,
falsely claiming there were three bombs in the
building.

November 1, 1994
Página 12, LEGAL ACTION
President Menem sued the newspaper *Página
12* for an Oct. 30 article that questioned the
veracity of the president's claims that he was
tortured under the military dictatorship.
Menem accused the daily and local human
rights groups of plotting together to undermine
his leadership. This is the fourth libel suit initiated by Menem against the paper. The daily
also has six pending lawsuits from members of
Menem's government. In a letter to the president, CPJ criticized his continued legal harassment of the newspaper.

The Americas

Bolivia

As in the rest of Latin America, the Bolivian press works free of official government censorship. But reporters who investigate local corruption and other abuses such as environmental pollution and drug trafficking are persecuted—especially journalists who scrutinize alleged ties between traffickers and army officials. In late 1994, several journalists were attacked because of their reporting on charges against former President Luis García Meza, who is accused of receiving drug money during his presidential term.

February 1
Gilmer Zambrana, *Radio Yungas,*
   IMPRISONED, HARASSED
Zambrana, a reporter with Radio Yungas in the city of Chulumani, was arrested by local officials and held for two weeks after he reported on the misappropriation of state money and the construction of a road that crosses known pre-Columbian archaeological sites. He was released after filing a habeas corpus petition but has been warned against continuing his investigation.

April 16
Judith Muñoz, *Radio Nueva América,*
   HARASSED, LEGAL ACTION
David García, *Primera Plana,*
   HARASSED, LEGAL ACTION
Muñoz, a reporter with Radio Nueva América, and García, a photographer with the daily *Primera Plana,* were both in the capital of La Paz when they were arrested by police, held for three days and accused of having belonged to a terrorist group in 1989. During their detention, they were handcuffed and blindfolded, and their personal belongings were confiscated. Both were set free after a habeas corpus petition was filed on their behalf. A previous investigation into the charges of terrorism had turned up no evidence supporting those charges.

August
Radio Pio XII, HARASSED
The highlands station Radio Pio XII has come under attack for speaking out against toxic mineral waste dumping in the mining villages of Patacamaya and Siglo XX. Since a protest in August, which was suppressed by the government, Radio Pio XII has faced abuse and harassment by officials in a barrage of letters, phone calls and denunciations in the media.

August 25
Wilson García Mérida, *Los Tiempos,*
   LEGAL ACTION
The Supreme Court overturned a libel conviction against Mérida, a reporter with *Los Tiempos,* a daily in the province of Cochabamba. Mérida had been sued by two local politicians for criminal libel and convicted. García still faces charges that he was involved in drug trafficking. In 1993, García was stabbed by unidentified individuals and says he was attacked because of charges he made that there were ties between drug traffickers and members of the Bolivian police.

October 6
Carlos Arce, *Radio 11 de Octubre,* HARASSED
Ramiro Irusta, *Radio 11 de Octubre,* HARASSED
Arce, the director of Radio 11 de Octubre in the Amazonian town of Cobija, and Irusta, a reporter for the station, were verbally threatened by a local government official who is suspected of having ties to drug traffickers in the area. The radio station had been doing stories on local corruption. The journalists attempted to file charges, but no lawyer would accept the case, for fear of retaliation.

October 29
Carlos Mesa, *Canal 7,*
   ATTACKED, THREATENED
Postal workers discovered a bomb in a package addressed to veteran journalist Mesa, producer of a television newsmagazine broadcast on Canal 7 in La Paz. Mesa, who had accused

friends of former President Luis García Meza of planting the bomb, had received threats before and after airing a program that was critical of Gen. Meza.

October 30
Luis Soruco Barba, *Canal 2*, ATTACKED
Three unidentified men shot several times at Barba, owner of the Canal 2 television station in Santa Cruz, but wounded a 15-year-old neighbor instead. Local sources said the attacks came after the television channel reported that Brazil had accepted Bolivia's extradition request of former President Luis García Meza. Meza was convicted and sentenced in absentia to 30 years in prison in Bolivia for crimes committed while he was in power in the 1980s.

Brazil

The Brazilian media continued to face a rash of legal proceedings in 1994, as politicians and influential citizens unhappy with aggressive reporting used the 1967 Press Law to muzzle journalists. Private citizens who feel their moral standing was damaged by a press report use the legislation to take journalists to court. Journalists convicted under this law face prison terms and fines. It also affords the successful plaintiff the right to reply. The law was more widely abused in Brazil's interior, where conservative judges ruled mostly against the press. Violence against reporters continued to be a problem in regions far from the central government.

A law left over from the military dictatorship of the 1960s requires licenses for journalists, but most Brazilians ignore the requirement. In the state of Belem, though, the local journalists *colegio*, which in Latin America functions as a licensing body, took to court a number of journalists who did not have university journalism degrees. A judge presiding over the case ruled that the law is unconstitutional.

January 4
Folha de Sao Paulo, LEGAL ACTION
Presidential candidate Luiz Inacio Lula da Silva of the Workers' Party (Partido dos Trabalhadores) sued *Folha de Sao Paulo* for "moral damage" and defamation. Lula objected to a November 1993 *Folha* report on the alleged illegal transfer of a local union's money to Lula's party and used the 1967 Press Law to bring the charges. Lula also accused *Folha* and other mainstream media of partiality in favor of then presidential candidate Enrique Cardoso, who won the presidential elections. He used the 1967 Press Law to bring the charges.

January 13
Lúcio Flávio Pinto, *Jornal Pessoal,* LEGAL ACTION
Pinto, editor and publisher of the daily *Jornal Pessoal,* in the state of Belem, was sentenced to three months in prison and fined the equivalent of five months pay for defamation and libel against the administrator of the state agency Sistema Romulo Maiorana de Comunicaçao. The charges were filed after Flávio's newspaper published two reports describing ongoing disputes between the state agency's administrator and another top agency official. Flávio is appealing the sentence.

February 19
Joao Alberto Ferreira Souto, *Jornal do Estado,* KILLED
Souto, owner of *Jornal do Estado* in Vitoria da Conquista, was shot dead by a group of unidentified men who ambushed him when he arrived home. He was an outspoken critic of politicians and government officials.

June 14
Roberto Romano, *Folha de Sao Paulo,* LEGAL ACTION
Romano, a guest columnist for *Folha de Sao Paulo,* was sued for defamation and libel by Congressman Roberto Cardoso Alves for a 1993 article in which Romano accused Con-

gress of acting like prostitutes. He was especially critical of Cong. Cardoso Alves. Romano was sued under the 1967 Press Law on defamation and libel. Action was still pending at year's end. The Eighth Chamber of the Criminal Court of Sao Paulo denied his petition for habeas corpus.

July 6
Nelson de Sá, *Folha de Sao Paulo,*
LEGAL ACTION
De Sá, columnist with the daily *Folha de Sao Paulo,* was sued by Nilo Batista, Rio de Janeiro's governor, for punitive damages. Batista was unhappy with a column in which de Sá commented on an appearance by Batista on a TV show to raise funds for the Associacion Brasileira Interdisciplinar da SIDA, an AIDS research group. Batista objected to the derisive language used by de Sá.

July 27
José Henrique Mariante, *Folha de Sao Paulo,*
LEGAL ACTION
Mariante, journalist with *Folha de Sao Paulo,* was sued for defamation by Kalunga Comercio e Industria Grafica, the main sponsor of soccer tournaments. Mariante wrote an opinion column that criticized the introduction of business commercials in sports.

August 5
"25a Hora," *TV Record,* LEGAL ACTION
25a Hora, a program at TV Record, was forced to suspend broadcasting for two hours due to a decision by Sao Paulo's Regional Electoral Court. The program director was accused of not being impartial in the presidential election process and of favoring President-elect Fernando Henrique Cardoso.

August 29
Carlos Carvalho, *Free-lancer,*
THREATENED, HARASSED
Carvalho, a free-lance journalist, was detained by Brazilian police while he was covering a protest by rubber tappers against loggers who

were hired by a rancher in Xapuri, in the state of Amazonas. He was released several hours later. Local officials then recommended that he leave the city, as they could not guarantee his security. Carvalho is known to be a supporter of the rubber tapper movement in the area.

September 14
Marcos Cardoso, *Cinform,*
THREATENED, HARASSED
Cesar Gomes Gama, *Cinform,*
THREATENED, HARASSED
Jose Antonio Moura Bonfim, *Cinform,*
THREATENED, HARASSED
Eenaldo dos Santos Santana, *Cinform,*
THREATENED, HARASSED
Cardoso, Gama, Bonfim and Santana, all reporters with the newspaper *Cinform* (Clasificados e Informaçoes), published in Aracaju, Sergipe state, were threatened and stalked by armed men after they wrote stories on a shadowy death squad that operates in their region. The reporters were warned that there is a contract out on their lives. Their report mentioned that several army officers and policemen participate in the death squad, which eliminates prostitutes, beggars and other people considered "anti-socials."

September 23
IstoÉ, LEGAL ACTION
The Superior Electoral Court ordered the newsweekly *IstoÉ* to publish a five-page text of the leftist Partido Trabajador as a response to a magazine report on alleged ties between the party and former President Fernando Collor, who was impeached for corruption.

September 26
Leonel Julio Farah, *Esquema Oeste,*
LEGAL ACTION
Farah, director and owner of the magazine *Esquema Oeste,* was detained for one day because he rejected a prior restraint order issued by a local judge against his magazine. The order was requested by two candidates for the Legislative

Assembly, who wanted to stop the distribution of an issue of the magazine that featured a report on alleged corrupt practices by both politicians. Farah was released after he filed a habeas corpus petition but was ordered to delay publication for five more days until another judge allowed the magazine to be distributed.

September 26
Folha de Sao Paulo, CENSORED, HARASSED
Reporters for *Folha de Sao Paulo* were denied entry into Sao Paulo jails despite a judge's permission. The reporters wanted to interview inmates about the upcoming presidential election.

Chile

In 1994, Chile succumbed to the trend of licensing journalists, which has recently come back in vogue in Latin American nations. Newly elected President Eduardo Frei introduced some changes to a press law that originated under the government of Patricio Aylwin. The bill would modify freedom of the press and institute mandatory licensing of journalists. Under the revised proposal, a journalist is defined as an individual who graduated from a university that has been accepted by the Chilean Journalists *Colegio*. All those who do not have such a degree must register with the *colegio* in order to work as reporters.

The armed forces continued to muzzle the free debate over military issues. Capt. Humberto Palamara, a retired navy intelligence officer who wrote a book on military ethics, was sentenced in October to 541 days in prison for noncompliance with military duties, to three years for one charge of disobedience and to 541 days for a second charge of disobedience. Palamara's book, *Ethics and Intelligence Services,* argues that torture and killings are never justifiable and that intelligence officers should be fully

trained professionals. According to his lawyer, the book did not violate national security nor leak classified information. But its subject matter is extremely sensitive since hundreds of suspected Chilean leftists were tortured and killed by the armed forces during the period leading to the military coup against President Salvador Allende. Palamara was warned by former superiors not to write the book. He is appealing his sentence.

January 13
Francisco Herreros Mardones, *Pluma y Pincel*
Juan Andrés Lagos, *El Siglo,*
    LEGAL ACTION, CENSORED
Journalists Mardones and Lagos were sentenced to 300 days in jail for publishing an articles critical of the Supreme Court. They initially were charged in January 1993, under State Security Law, with offending the judiciary after they criticized the court's decision to transfer investigations on political disappearances to military courts. Both had at least one other defamation case pending at the time but were set free on bail pending appeals. *El Siglo,* the newspaper for which Lagos worked and which was published by the Chilean Communist Party, has since ceased publication.

Colombia

Colombian journalists continued to face violence from leftist guerrilla groups, drug traffickers and paramilitary groups in 1994. Two journalists were killed for reasons connected to their profession, according to colleagues. Investigations by CPJ concluded that the murders of two others were probably not related to their work. Abuses by local army commanders continued to be a problem, especially in areas beset by rebel activity and drug trafficking.

The press had difficulty handling the emergence of a set of audiocassettes that described alleged connections between newly elected President Ernesto Samper and the Cali drug cartel. President Samper used Decree 1812, which prohibits the broadcast or publication of interviews with guerrilla groups and drug traffickers, to ban the broadcast of a second and third cassette that made further accusations against him. Most leading newspapers dealt with the issue gently, afraid of the origins of the cassettes and the validity of the charges. It is said that President Samper himself asked for gentle treatment from the press.

Colombia's *Tutela* law, a 'right of reply' statute adopted by the 1991 constitutional assembly, continued to create havoc for reporters. Editors and journalists complained they had to censor themselves for fear of being dragged to court. Under the law, citizens have the right to ask a court of law to order the publication of a rebuttal or a retraction if they can show that they've been "injured" by a news report. But the journalistic community is not in agreement about the effect of the *Tutela* statute. Some leading journalists believe it is necessary because many in the Colombian press lack the discipline to be ethical and fair.

Violence against journalists from drug traffickers subsided after the dismantling of the Medellín Cartel. But interviews with journalists in the provinces revealed that threats are numerous and self-censorship is rampant. Provincial journalists in zones with a strong guerrilla presence run the double risk of being accused of being subversives by the army, or army informants by the guerrillas.

January 28
Jesús Medina Parra, *"El Fogonazo,"* KILLED
Parra, a Cucuta province radio host, was killed on his way to work. An unidentified gunman shot him three times in the head before escaping on a motorcycle. The area is conflict-ridden, with guerrillas from the Colombian Revolutionary Armed Forces and the National Liberation Army fighting against government forces.

Parra hosted "El Fogonazo," a morning show during which listeners would call in to complain about government corruption.

March 18
Alvaro Martínez Pinzón, *Colmundo,* HARASSED
Pinzón, news director for the radio station Colmundo in Ibague, broadcast eyewitness accounts that contradicted the official army version of the killing of an 8-year-old child. According to the witnesses, the child was killed in cold blood by soldiers. The army maintained that the child died during an armed confrontation between the army and leftist guerrillas. The day of the broadcast, a brigade commander demanded copies of the taped interviews with the witnesses, and afterwards, local army officials continued a campaign of intimidation against the station.

June 14
Radio Cadena Nacional, ATTACKED
Radio Caracol, ATTACKED
Leftist terrorists blew up the transmission towers of Radio Caracol and Radio Cadena Nacional during the Fourth Ibero-American Summit in Cartagena. No group has claimed responsibility.

June 15
Various journalists, ATTACKED
Bodyguards of Cuban President Fidel Castro assaulted a group of reporters. The journalists were trying to film and interview the bodyguards after they attacked a group of cameramen who tried to talk with Castro during the Fourth Ibero-American Summit in Cartagena.

September 3
Martín Eduardo Munera, *Radio Reloj,* KILLED
Munera, a broadcaster with Radio Reloj, a subsidiary of Radio Caracol Network, and vice president of the network's Workers' Union, was killed under suspicious circumstances in the city of Medellín. The killer approached Munera as he walked to the bus station and thrust a syringe

apparently containing cyanide into Munera's neck. The murder occurred as the union was negotiating a new contract. The case remains under investigation by CPJ.

December 13
All television networks, LEGAL ACTION
The Colombian Senate passed a law that will force television news programs to retract a news story if a citizen or institution objects to it and claims the news story damaged the citizen's good name or the institution's reputation and interests. According to the new law, a news program can be permanently suspended if it is forced to retract three times. News directors for the country's 10 news networks protested this attempt to institute censorship in TV news.

Costa Rica

For the Costa Rican press, 1994 will be remembered as the year when the simple remark "pigheaded" earned a journalist a harsh sentence and fine. The sentence and fine against Bosco Valverde of *La Nación,* because of statements he made in a column against justices of the Supreme Court, revived the use of a contempt law that had not been applied in many years. Journalists then had to worry about damaging the honor or decorum of public officials, as described in Article 307 of the Penal Code.

Another incident that challenged the independent status earned by the Costa Rican media in recent years was the firing of a number of reporters from Channel 7, on charges of partisan reporting in the most recent presidential elections. Channel 7 officials said the firings were the result of a simple labor dispute. The Journalists *Colegio,* which operates as a licensing body similar to a bar or medical association, investigated the dismissals, but many journalists said the investigation was biased from the start. The

colegio ruled against the journalists and accused them of partial coverage during the presidential elections. The decision has split the professional journalistic community.

The power of the *colegio* is also a sore point for many Costa Rican journalists. The *colegio* determines who can practice journalism in Costa Rica, and in 1994, it began lobbying for passage of a constitutional amendment to permanently ensure its ability to do so. In order for the amendment to pass, it would require presidential support. And some journalists see a connection between this lobbying effort and the Channel 7 *colegio* decision. A constitutional amendment also would protect the *colegio* from international criticism, such as that issued by the Inter-American Human Rights Court, which ruled the licensing practice a violation of press freedom. Journalists may practice in Costa Rica only after the *colegio* rules that they graduated from an acceptable journalism school.

One bright note for the Costa Rican press in 1994 was the decision to reopen the media market to foreign investment. The government revoked a law that reserved ownership of the media to native Costa Ricans.

January 7
Pilar Cisneros, *Telenoticias Channel 7,* CENSORED
Isabel Ovares, *Telenoticias Channel 7,* CENSORED
Humberto Arce, *Telenoticias Channel 7,* CENSORED
Guillermo Fernández, *Telenoticias Channel 7,* CENSORED
Laffite Fernández, *Telenoticias Channel 7,* CENSORED
Julio Rodríguez, *Telenoticias Channel 7,* CENSORED
Javier Solís, *Telenoticias Channel 7,* CENSORED
Cisneros, director of Telenoticias, Ovares, her assistant, and the other five people, all reporters, were fired. Cisneros claimed that the

firings were the result of political pressure from President José María Figueres because the television journalists were critical of his presidential campaign. On May 5, a special investigative commission from the Costa Rican Journalists *Colegio* ruled against the seven people and accused them of conspiring "to broadcast information against Figueres." The seven were not allowed the opportunity to defend themselves before the association, and Cisneros said the *colegio* was not a fair judge of the case because most of its members were not working journalists and because the group had political connections to Figueres' party. Some say the firing was for internal reasons and not because of the journalists' reporting.

July 8
Bosco Valverde, *La Nación*, LEGAL ACTION
Valverde, a columnist for the daily *La Nación*, was given a three-year suspended sentence and fined $10,000 for "offending the honor and decorum of a public employee" in a column in which he questioned the competence of certain judges. His lawyer said this was the first time anyone had been convicted of such an offense.

Cuba

The Cuban press continued to suffer the effects of the ongoing fiscal crisis. Pressure on journalists to remain loyal to the government and the Communist Party increased, especially as cutbacks in newspapers and shrinking news hours in radio and television left many journalists without work.

Cuba has been attempting to modernize its economy, moving away from state control and encouraging foreign investment. But liberalizing the state's monopoly over the media is not on the agenda. President Fidel Castro and other government officials continue to see the media as a propaganda tool to convey to the Cuban public the government's perspective.

Scores of journalists were "laid off" in the past two years. They receive their monthly salaries but are banned from journalism. The actions targeted journalists identified by the government as discontented and exhibiting "ideological incompatibility" with the government. Their economic situation will worsen under a new decree expected to become law in 1995. The law will make amendments to current labor codes, allowing the government to terminate people's employment without full pensions or salaries.

Three journalists defected to the United States and Europe in 1994. The most important defector was Gretchen Galindo, Cuba's best-known television host. She asked for political asylum with her son in Rome in early 1994, complaining of severe controls on the media. In August, a second journalist, Luis Hernandez Iglesias of the newspaper *Trabajadores,* defected while covering a baseball tournament in Tennessee. At the December Summit of the Americas held in Miami, Fla., Carlos Santana of Radio Rebelde defected. Said one journalist in Havana, "No one is surprised by the defections—the surprise was that Santana pretended to be pro-government so well, the government felt comfortable sending him abroad."

Government controls over radio and television news have grown more intensive, according to Cuban journalists. In times of crises, such as the August 1994 exodus of up to 30,000 people who left Cuba on rafts, television and radio showed the government in control. The Cuban government, though, does not have an effective monopoly over the airwaves. With the island's proximity to the United States, anti-Castro radio stations in Miami beam news reports detailing events the government has kept secret, and some broadcast anti-Communist tirades. Cuban citizens have began to listen openly to the Miami radio stations. The most popular are Radio Martí, funded by the U.S. government, and La Voz de la Fundación, run by the anti-

Castro Cuban-American National Foundation. Radio Martí and La Voz recruit Cubans living on the island to phone in reports on political events or disturbances. During the Havana riots last summer, some of these special correspondents working for both radio stations were at the scene first and told their listeners what they saw. The U.S. press was able to get visas to travel to Cuba within the next few days, but the riots had been squelched by then.

The Cuban government equates working for the Miami radio stations with treason. In early 1994, a court convicted Radio Martí's special correspondent Rodolfo Gonzalez to seven years in prison for his reports. CPJ is including these kinds of cases in the Cuba section for the first time. Although the special correspondents are not full-time journalists, they often provide the only independent accounts of the news, which otherwise would not be broadcast in Cuba.

CPJ has started two other important campaigns related to Cuba. Last July, it initiated a media campaign to lift a 25-year-old ban on the free flow of information between the United States and Cuba. The restrictions, a legacy of the Cold War, not only have proven disadvantageous to U.S. news operations in their coverage of Cuba, but also have kept Cuban journalists from working freely in the United States. The campaign already led to the U.S. Treasury Department's lifting restrictions on expenditures in Cuba for U.S. news-gathering operations. CPJ has asked the Clinton administration to unilaterally lift the ban on Cuban news operations in the United States. CPJ also wrote to President Fidel Castro, asking him to reciprocate, once the United States eliminates the restrictions, and allow American news bureaus back into Cuba.

In addition, CPJ started a campaign to gain the freedom of Yndamiro Restano, a former radio reporter who is now serving a 12-year prison sentence for rebellion. Restano was fired by Radio Rebelde in 1985 for criticizing Cuban government policies, and was permanently banned from working in journalism in Cuba in 1986. Founder of the Cuban Association of Independent Journalists, which was established for journalists fired for political reasons, Restano was jailed in 1992 after he founded the nonviolent political organization known as Harmony Movement (MAR). The Cuban government has offered Restano his freedom if he leaves Cuba. He has refused the offer of exile, arguing he is not guilty of any crime. He wants to continue his journalistic and political work in Cuba. Restano was a recipient of the 1994 International Press Freedom Award. CPJ organized a letter-writing campaign asking for Restano's freedom and hopes to secure his unconditional release in 1995.

January
Joel Mesa Morales, *La Voz de la Fundación,*
IMPRISONED
Morales, a contributor to La Voz de la Fundación, the shortwave radio station based in Miami and run by the Cuban-American National Foundation, was arrested in January. He was charged with spreading "enemy propaganda" in early 1994, because of his collaboration with the radio station. The station provides daily news for Cubans on the island who otherwise would be able to listen only to the censored Cuban state-owned media. The station uses citizens as special correspondents who report by phone on political news events that transpire on the island.

April 16
Rodolfo González, *Radio Martí,* IMPRISONED
González, a Cuban dissident who telephoned news reports to the U.S.-funded Radio Martí, was sentenced to seven years in jail for disseminating enemy propaganda and spreading false news with the purpose of giving a chaotic image of Cuban society. The Cuban authorities consider Radio Martí an enemy radio station.

The Americas

69

April 28
"MacNeil/Lehrer NewsHour" crew, HARASSED
A five-person crew with the "MacNeil/Lehrer NewsHour" was stopped on its way to an interview with Elizardo Sánchez, a political dissident in Havana. According to one of the journalists, three armed men identified themselves as police and ordered the journalists out of their car. The men seized $50,000 worth of equipment and fled in the journalists' vehicle. Members of the crew said they suspected the thieves were state policemen, but officers at the police station in Havana, where the journalists filed a complaint, reported the incident as an armed robbery and insisted that the armed men could not have been Cuban police. CPJ wrote to President Fidel Castro, urging that an investigation of the case be conducted.

May 15
Alexis Castañeda Pérez, *Vanguardia*,
IMPRISONED
Pérez, a journalist, art critic, essayist and poet, was sentenced to five years in prison for spreading "enemy propaganda." He was on the editorial board of the newspapers *Vanguardia* and *Huella*. The Cuban government is reported to have denied medical treatment to the journalist, who suffers from asthma.

August
Eugenio Rodriguez Chaple, *La Voz de la Fundación*,
HARASSED, THREATENED
Chaple, a contributor to the anti-Castro shortwave radio station La Voz de la Fundación, was arrested, held for 11 days and given a warning by state security not to file reports on disturbances and political events in Cuba. He was detained because of his reports on the Havana riots that preceded a mass migration of Cubans on rafts and because of a telephone interview he gave to the U.S.-based Spanish-language Telemundo Network.

September/October
Migdalia Rosado Hernández, *La Voz de la Fundación*,
HARASSED, THREATENED
In early September, Hernández, a frequent contributor to the anti-Castro shortwave radio station La Voz de la Fundación, was called in twice for questioning by state security and warned not to continue her broadcasts for the station. The Cuban government deems all contributors to this radio station as engaging in the spread of enemy propaganda.

1994
Iliana Curra Lusson, *La Voz de la Fundación*,
IMPRISONED
Lusson was sentenced to three years in prison on charges of spreading enemy propaganda in 1994. She was one of many Cubans who contributed reports the daily news show of La Voz de la Fundación, a shortwave radio station beamed from Miami to Cuba by the anti-Castro group the Cuban-American National Foundation. Lusson had been warned numerous times to discontinue her work with the station.

1994
Abel Jesús Acosta-Ameneiro,
La Voz de la Fundación, THREATENED
Amado Núñez Daniel, *La Voz de la Fundación*,
THREATENED
Acosta-Ameneiro and Daniel were warned by state security to stop their reports to La Voz de la Fundación, considered an enemy radio station by the government, or they would be arrested for spreading enemy propaganda.

Dominican Republic

As claims of widespread electoral fraud spread after the May presidential elections, there were a few incidents that threatened freedom of expression in the Dominican

Republic in 1994. Foreign journalists who covered the elections came under attack from government ministers after they pointed out irregularities in the electoral process. Dominican correspondents for international news agencies were also targeted by some government officials who felt the foreign coverage was damaging to the country's image. In the end, after U.S. election observers also challenged the election results, President Joaquin Balaguer himself agreed to hold new general elections within two years to resolve claims of widespread voting fraud.

The disappearance during the period preceding presidential elections of Narciso González, a political activist, professor and columnist for a university paper, was of concern to CPJ, although his case was not taken because his principal occupation is not that of a journalist.

May 19
Foreign media, CENSORED
The Dominican Foreign Ministry released a communiqué, which was widely published, accusing foreign journalists of participating in an international conspiracy against the Dominican government. According to the communiqué, the foreign press is working towards the unification of the Dominican Republic and Haiti. The government was angered specifically by foreign press reports that detailed alleged electoral fraud during the recent presidential elections. CPJ wrote a letter to the government denouncing its intimidation campaign.

Ecuador

Several rural radio stations were taken over by the army in 1994, following peasant revolts against new agrarian legislation that reassigns indigenous lands. Radio Latacunga, a church-funded radio station, and two other smaller stations were occupied temporarily by army troops. Their directors were arrested and released only after international protests. CPJ was especially concerned about the attack since it was directed against a community-based news outlet. At a UNESCO meeting in May, Ecuadorean journalists signed a declaration agreeing to promote rural radio stations.

June 22
Radio Emisora Latacunga, ATTACKED
About 50 government soldiers raided Radio Emisora Latacunga, an indigenous radio station south of Quito, and held two workers inside the building for about five hours. The station's director, Sister Alma Delia Montoya, was taken to a nearby military post and forced to sign a statement saying the station would not broadcast any opinion programs. The station has since limited its programs to music and religious shows. Radio Latacunga broadcasts in the indigenous language of Quechua and serves the large indigenous populations in the Riobamba and Canar areas. Many of the communities rely on radio because of high illiteracy rates and lack of electricity in their villages. CPJ wrote the government and protested the raid. The Ecuadorean government replied, saying the station was stirring agitation and contributing to the peasant uprisings. The letter also said the station was run by a church group led by foreigners, including its director, a Colombian-born missionary.

El Salvador

The criminal defamation lawsuit won by right-wing businessman Orlando de Sola against former guerrilla leader Joaquín Villalobos was the media event of 1994. Instead of charging Villalobos, who accused de Sola of financing death squads during the country's civil war, the judge directed the defamation charges to the daily *El Latino,* which printed Villalobos' remarks. De Sola successfully appealed the ruling and the Superior Court convicted Villalobos.

The Americas

In general, however, the independent media continued to flourish in El Salvador. A new center-left weekly, *Primera Plana,* began circulating nationally in late 1994, challenging the traditional dominance of three major conservative dailies.

September 19
El Latino, LEGAL ACTION
A judge ruled that the daily *El Latino* had slandered businessman Orlando de Sola by printing statements made to the newspaper by former Farabundo Martí National Liberation Front (FMLN) commander Joaquín Villalobos in November 1993. Villalobos accused businessman Orlando de Sola of financing death squads that killed tens of thousands of people during the Salvadoran civil war. After 10 months in court, the judge ruled that "there does not exist sufficient proof that (the businessman) would have financed the death squads, nor that he ordered anyone killed." However, the court decided that the charge of slander should fall on *El Latino* for publishing Villalobos' accusations and not Villalobos himself. On Oct. 7, El Salvador's superior court reversed its decision regarding *El Latino.*

Guatemala

Next to Peru and Cuba, Guatemala holds the worst press freedom record in the hemisphere. Anonymous death threats against journalists multiplied in 1994. President Ramiro de León Carpio continued to speak in favor of a free press. But extreme right-wing groups and thugs with connections to the most conservative sectors of the Guatemalan army continued a vendetta against the press. There were kidnappings and bomb attacks, and one reporter was forced to flee the country with his family. Because of past persecution of journalists, most of the Guatemalan press is still reticent about reporting government corruption, drug trafficking and military abuses.

The brutal attack by an angry mob in the Guatemalan highlands against American journalist June Weinstock in early 1994 was of concern to foreign journalists based in the country. Weinstock was targeted because she was a foreigner, not because of her work. But much of the reporting in this country takes journalists to the highlands, which is where many refugees who fled during the civil war are returning to since peace negotiations between the guerrillas and the army are expected to continue.

The family of Jorge Carpio, the late publisher of the daily *El Gráfico,* who was killed in 1993, was harassed for insisting on a thorough investigation into his murder. Carpio was also the leader and founder of the National Centrist Union Party. Army officers threatened his family after it had charged top military officers with ordering Carpio's murder.

February 25
La Hora, ATTACKED
At various points in Guatemala City, heavily armed men in vehicles with tinted windows threatened distributors of the Guatemalan daily *La Hora,* in an apparent attempt to impede circulation of the paper. The paper's headline on the day of the incidents announced that President Ramiro de León Carpio was accused by the political opposition of ordering members of the Civil Self-Defense Patrols to vote in favor of a recent referendum.

March 1
Adolfo Barrera, *ACEN-SIAG News,*
    ATTACKED, HARASSED
Unidentified individuals threw a bomb late at night at the home of Barrera, director of the ACEN-SIAG news agency. Barrera, his four children and a domestic worker were in the house, but the bomb exploded near the garage and no one was injured. Neighbors said the attackers fled in a pickup truck. Barrera's brother, Byron, is director of CEPEX, a freedom of expression group in Central America. He was

director of ACEN-SIAG until 1989, when he fled to Costa Rica after being ambushed by armed men. His wife was killed in the attack. On March 9, Adolfo Barrera and his family went into exile in Canada, where they were still living by year's end. CPJ wrote to President Ramiro de León Carpio, urging a full investigation into this attack.

March 18
Gabriel Espinozo Gonzalez, *Radio Stereo Amistad,*
    ATTACKED
Radio Stereo Amistad, ATTACKED
Several armed men raided the offices of Stereo Amistad, a radio station in El Cerro El Ingeniero, Chiquimula. The men threatened station operator Gonzalez, then tied him up and shut him in a room. They also destroyed the station's equipment.

April
Foreign reporters, THREATENED
Anti-foreigner sentiment, fanned in Guatemala by conservative groups, hampered foreign correspondents' ability to travel throughout the country. CPJ wrote to President Ramiro de León Carpio, expressing concern about the situation.

April 14
Rafael Aragon Ortiz, *Prensa Libre*, ATTACKED
Ortiz, marketing director for the daily *Prensa Libre*, reported that he was kidnapped for a few hours by a group of heavily armed men. The men, Ortiz said, took him to another city and forced him to write down a message criticizing the government, which he was then forced to distribute to the press in Guatemala City. CPJ wrote to President Ramiro de León Carpio, calling for a full investigation of this case.

April 26
La República, ATTACKED
The offices of the daily were sprayed with bullets at night. No one was injured. The director of the newspaper, Gonzalo Marroquín Godoy, attributed the attack to extreme right-wing

groups. *La República* had recently begun publishing reports on social issues and human rights violations.

May 17
José Ruben Zamora, *Siglo Veintiuno,* HARASSED
Zamora, director of the newspaper *Siglo Veintiuno*, was questioned by the Congressional Human Rights Commission, at the request of two senators who accused the daily of attacking their honor.

May 31
Fernando Quezada Toruño, *Crónica*, ATTACKED
Unidentified men bombed the home of Toruño, a member of the editorial board of the weekly magazine *Crónica*. CPJ wrote to President Ramiro de León Carpio, requesting a complete investigation into the bombing.

June 23
Tinamit, ATTACKED
Unidentified individuals threw a hand grenade at the offices of *Tinamit* magazine in Guatemala City. No injuries were reported. The opposition weekly often lampoons military officials and has been the target of several attacks from right-wing groups, according to its publisher. CPJ wrote to President Ramiro de León Carpio, urging him to investigate the case promptly.

September 8
Association of Guatemalan Journalists (APG),
    ATTACKED
Unidentified men in a car in Guatemala City sprayed the building housing the APG with bullets. The attack occurred as the group was holding a seminar on the civil war and displaced Indian populations. Representatives of various popular organizations that work with the displaced were participating. The topic of the seminar was the accord on the return of refugees signed on July 17 by the government and the group known as Guatemalan National Revolutionary Unity.

September 8
Radio Cobán, ATTACKED
Unidentified men in cars and on motorcycles opened fire on the studios of Radio Cobán, in Alta Verapaz province, strafing the office of the radio news program "Día a Día." No one was injured in the attack.

September 12
Victor Hugo López Escóbar, *Radio Progreso,* KILLED
Escóbar, director of the radio news program "Nuevo Diario del Aire" on Radio Progreso, was gunned down by unidentified assailants as he emerged from his car in downtown Guatemala City. Guatemalan journalists believe the motive for the murder was Escóbar's journalistic work.

September 13
Gerson López, *La Hora,* ATTACKED
Unidentified assailants shot at López, a reporter-editor with the daily *La Hora,* when he was getting out of his car in the vicinity of his office in south Guatemala City. He escaped unhurt after he threw himself on the ground to avoid the bullets. López did not know who was responsible for the attack, and he said that he had never had problems before. The incident came one day after the murder of journalist Victor Hugo López Escobar. CPJ wrote to President Ramiro de León Carpio to express its concern about these and a series of other violent attacks against the press.

Haiti

The media in Haiti, both domestic and foreign, came under increasing fire in 1994 during the last months of military rule in the country. The de facto government escalated attacks against journalists as it faced increasing pressure to cede power to democratically elected President Jean-Bertrand Aristide.
On Aug. 5, CPJ called on the United

Nations and the Organization of American States to take all necessary steps to protect the free flow of information within Haiti and the rest of the world.
President Aristide returned to power Oct. 15, more than three years after he was deposed in a military coup. With his return, there were expectations that the Haitian media will again flourish.

January 1
Guerard Vilton, *Radio Plus,* HARASSED
Vilton, a correspondent for Radio Plus in Gonaives, was detained by army soldiers and attachés (paramilitary thugs). Soldiers confiscated Vilton's press card, tape recorder and two notebooks. At the time of his arrest, he was at the Cathedral of Gonaives to cover a religious ceremony to be attended by the Armed Forces commander, Gen. Raoul Cedras. Vilton was accused of wanting to clandestinely record the sermon and Gen. Cedras' speech. He was released after a few days and fled to Port-au-Prince.

February 4
Jean Jacobe, *Radio Caraibes,* ATTACKED
Jacobe, a reporter with Radio Caraibes, was beaten by supporters of the Front for the Advancement and the Progress of Haiti (FRAPH), a neo-Duvalierist group.

April
All journalists, HARASSED
For several weeks, the army barred press access to the northern town of Bassin Caiman, a stronghold of supporters of President Jean-Bertrand Aristide. On April 10, army soldiers and armed civilians reportedly invaded Bassin Caiman, firing weapons, breaking down doors, stealing livestock, torching fields and burning down as many as 100 homes.

June
All foreign journalists, HARASSED
The Haitian military authorities required spe-

cial permits from foreign journalists to travel outside Port-au-Prince and urged hotel owners to inform the police of the identity of foreigners, especially journalists, staying at their hotels.

June 13
NBC crew, HARASSED

An NBC crew was detained and their equipment was confiscated for a few days after military authorities accused the network of using sophisticated microwave satellite dishes (used for their feeds) to eavesdrop on Haitian military communications. NBC had obtained official permission to use the equipment.

August 1
Haitian journalists, CENSORED, HARASSED

The Haitian Information Ministry advised local journalists that, given the state of siege, it was their duty to maintain peace and calm by refraining from any alarmist or tendentious broadcasts, and to resist being used as tools for foreign propaganda. Two weeks earlier, de facto Foreign Minister Charles David met local media owners and news directors to pressure them for more airtime for government and official commentary. The de facto government also warned Haitians working for foreigners that they would be accused of cooperating with the enemy if it were proven that they encouraged the invasion of the national territory.

August 4
Elizabeth Farnsworth, *"MacNeil/Lehrer NewsHour,"*
    EXPELLED, HARASSED

"MacNeil/Lehrer NewsHour" correspondent Farnsworth and her crew were expelled and escorted by the Haitian military to the Dominican border. Farnsworth and crew had been in detention since July 31, when Haitian police arrested them for filming near Haiti's international airport. A Haitian driver and a Haitian interpreter were kept in jail several days after Farnsworth's expulsion.

August 8
Radio Lakansyel,
    THREATENED, CENSORED, HARASSED
Radio Citadelle,
    THREATENED, CENSORED, HARASSED

Radio Lakansyel and Radio Citadelle were forced to stop broadcasts of the Creole-language programming syndicated by Voice of America, after receiving warnings from the de facto government. Radio Lakansyel stayed off the air for several weeks in August and September, after unidentified armed men threatened its staff. In another related case, members of Gen. Raoul Cedras' personal security corps warned at least two radio directors in the first two weeks of August to observe press restrictions and not to criticize the government.

August 12
All media, HARASSED

The Information Ministry reminded journalists and accredited foreign correspondents that they are barred from strategic areas such as police stations, airports, military barracks and other locations.

August 13
Local news media, CENSORED

The government banned local news media from broadcasting communiqués or information from foreign embassies or international groups.

August 24
Planeload of foreign reporters, HARASSED

Haitian military authorities refused to permit a press shuttle plane to land in Port-au-Prince airport. Commercial flights to and from Haiti had been banned by a worldwide embargo, but with this action military authorities also banned any further access to planes chartered by the news media to enter or leave Haiti.

September 9
Ernst Ocean, *Radio Tropic FM,*
    THREATENED, HARASSED

Ocean, a reporter for Radio Tropic FM in St.

The Americas

75

Marc province, went into hiding when the military came looking for him after he had reported on alleged human sacrifices at a local military base. He had served a short prison term in 1993 after he was detained for allegedly distributing pamphlets supporting President Jean-Bertrand Aristide.

September 9
Peter Arnett, *CNN*, HARASSED, ATTACKED
Lorescu Voirel, *Newsday*,
    HARASSED, ATTACKED
CNN correspondent Arnett was assaulted by government supporters as he reported on an anti-American demonstration in front of the U.S. embassy. Lorescu Voirel, a *Newsday* photographer, was nearly strangled with an American flag during the demonstration.

September 12
Jean-Michel Caroit, *Le Monde, Radio France Internationale*, LEGAL ACTION, HARASSED
Haitian authorities denied Caroit, Caribbean correspondent for *Le Monde* and Radio France Internationale, entry to the country. Under new state-of-emergency measures, all reporters must enter the country by land through the border with the Dominican Republic, and the Army High Command must approve each visa application. The process takes days, even weeks for some reporters.

September 30
Unidentified Haitian, KILLED
U.S. TV crew, ATTACKED
Lee Celano, *Reuters*, ATTACKED
John Bowner, *Associated Press*, ATTACKED
Bahram Molise, *CBS News*, ATTACKED
Mario Delatour, *Free-lancer*, ATTACKED
Maurice Roper, *NBC News*, ATTACKED
Five U.S. journalists were wounded and a Haitian driver for a U.S. television crew was killed when army supporters attacked them with guns, machetes and clubs during a pro-democracy march marking the third anniversary of the 1991 military coup. Reuters photographer

Celano was grazed on the head by a bullet. AP photographer Bowner was hit on the back of the head with the blunt side of a machete. CBS News cameraman Molise was hit with a club by an army supporter. Free-lancer Delatour, on assignment for CBS News, was wounded on the knee by a rock, and NBC News cameraman Roper was hit over the head with a club. An unidentified Haitian driver for a U.S. television crew was shot in the head and killed by a paramilitary gunman.

September 30
State-owned media, LEGAL ACTION
U.S. troops led a predawn occupation of state radio and television headquarters, and ordered employees not to return to work. U.S. officials in Haiti accused the radio and television station of criticizing the United States and inciting Haitians to violence against the return of President Jean-Bertrand Aristide. Control of the stations was given back to Aristide's government when he was reinstalled in power.

October 4
Dan Coughlin, *Inter Press Service (IPS)*,
    HARASSED
Pastor Vásquez, *Hoy*, HARASSED
Unidentified reporter, *Notimex*, HARASSED
Coughlin, an IPS reporter, Vásquez, a reporter for the Dominican Republic daily *Hoy*, and an unidentified journalist for the Mexican news service Notimex were detained by Haitian soldiers for several hours six miles from the border between Haiti and the Dominican Republic. The reporters had attempted to cross into Haiti without permission after waiting for several days for a visa. During the journalists' detention, the soldiers stole several thousand dollars from them. Coughlin later received permission to enter Haiti.

November 8
Ceramy Duquene, *Signal FM*,
    THREATENED, HARASSED
Several soldiers and armed civilians came look-

ing for Duquene at his cousin's home. They fired machine-gun shots at the front door and then ran away. Duquene, a correspondent in Gonaives for the private radio station Radio Signal FM, was reportedly hiding in his cousin's house at the time. Six days later, armed men fired shots near Duquene's home. He remained in hiding during most of 1994, until President Jean-Bertrand Aristide returned to power.

Mexico

The Chiapas uprising, the murder of a presidential candidate and other calamities in Mexico challenged the role of the press in the country in 1994. In some cases the press shone, as in its efforts to cover the Zapatista rebellion in Chiapas. But television news and much of the print press continued to present a skewed pro-government view of events. This media bias was widely considered the critical factor in the ruling party's victory in the August 1994 general election.

Three journalists were murdered in the state of Morelos under suspicious circumstances. Government investigators argued the murders were not connected to the victims' work, but circumstantial evidence in all three cases was enough to raise concern. No one was charged or prosecuted for any of the crimes. The murders occurred within six weeks and involved two journalists who worked for the same daily. The other victim was a known government critic. Two of the suspected killers of two of the victims reportedly fled to the United States. Rumors about these unsolved murders have contributed to an atmosphere of fear and have had a chilling effect on journalism in the area. Morelos journalists published an open letter in major newspapers calling for an exhaustive investigation. But there was little follow-through in the press, and the three journalists' murders were forgotten.

In November, the independent Mexico City daily *Reforma* had a showdown with the government-affiliated Newspaper Vendors' Union. The union hit the newspaper with a distribution strike, which came after labor negotiations broke down over the daily's decision to publish an edition during all legal holidays in Mexico. The union also opposed the daily's plans to start distributing newspapers independently. The current labor contract denies both options. The government and the ruling party remained surprisingly quiet as the conflict broke out, although the union has ties to both. *Reforma* criticized the union's strike as a strong-arm tactic that goes against Mexico's new ideology of free enterprise and free trade. Few papers covered the boycott and its effects on *Reforma*. Ruy Pérez Tamayo, a columnist for *La Jornada*, saw the conflict as "extremely grave" and an attempt to restrict freedom of expression.

Despite the international scrutiny of the presidential elections, Televisa, the country's largest television network, owned by financier and pro-ruling party stalwart Emilio Azcarraga, gave government candidates far more extensive and favorable news coverage.

Reporting on the Chiapas uprising showed much journalistic enterprise. But here the rebels themselves exercised censorship of the press. Rebel leaders banned Televisa and any other news media suspected of collaborating with that network from attending a national convention they convened in the summer.

January
El Tiempo, HARASSED
El Tiempo, a local newspaper in San Cristobal de Las Casas, was harassed because of its detailed reporting on the rebel uprising in Chiapas. Shortly after the uprising began, government officials and soldiers confiscated the newspaper or bought it in bulk from newspaper vendors.

The Americas

January 5
Ricardo Flores, *Univisión,*
   THREATENED, ATTACKED
Bruno López, *Univisión,*
   THREATENED, ATTACKED
Porfirio Patiño, *Univisión,*
   THREATENED, ATTACKED
Gerardo Tena, *Agence France-Presse,*
   THREATENED, ATTACKED
Flores, López and Patiño, all reporters with
Univisión, and Tena, a reporter with AFP, were
shot at by military planes as they attempted to
interview residents of a hillside area during the
rebel uprising in Chiapas state. The planes
strafed the ground a few meters from the journalists, who had entered the area with the military's knowledge. The journalists said the planes
singled them out even though they were traveling in vehicles that had signs reading "Press"
and "TV." The journalists also waved a white
flag at the oncoming aircraft. CPJ wrote to the
government criticizing the lack of access given
to the media. In a memo to CPJ, the Mexican
government quoted a statement López made to
the *New York Times,* in which he said that he did
not believe the planes had singled them out on
purpose. But in private conversations with CPJ
after the *Times* article appeared, López said that
in fact he did think they were targeted.

January 11
**Centro Nacional de Comunicación Social
   (CENCOS),** ATTACKED, HARASSED
CENCOS offices were raided on Jan. 11, 14, 15
and 17 by unidentified people who took about
$6,000 worth of video materials and typewrit-
ers. Director José Alvarez Icaza said that among
the items taken was the cassette of the answering machine. Icaza thinks the thieves were hired
to find a video produced by Canal 6 de Julio, an
independent video group associated with the
leftist Revolutionary Democratic Party. The
video in question was called "Barbaridades," the
group's documentary on events in the state of
Chiapas.

January 19
Raul Ortega, *La Jornada,* THREATENED
Ortega, a correspondent for *La Jornada* who
was on assignment in Chiapas, received a
threatening phone call at his hotel. The unidentified caller warned him to soften his coverage,
which had been very critical of governmental
abuses during the Chiapas uprising.

January 28
Carlos Ramírez, *El Financiero,* HARASSED
Well-known political columnist Ramírez complained in one of his columns that the government began tapping his phone after he
criticized the government's handling of the Chiapas uprising.

February 2
Elio Henríquez, *La Jornada,* THREATENED
Carmen Lira, *La Jornada,* THREATENED
Gaspar Morquecho, *La Jornada,* THREATENED
Carlos Payan Velver, *La Jornada,* THREATENED
Blanche Petrich, *La Jornada,* THREATENED
Josexto Zaldua, *La Jornada,* THREATENED
Staffers with *La Jornada* received death threats
from the Mexican Anticommunist Front. The
group accused the paper of being the mouth-
piece for the National Zapatista Liberation
Army, otherwise known as the Chiapas rebels.

June 6
Jorge Martín Dorantes, *El Crucero,* KILLED
Unknown assailants shot and killed Dorantes, a
known critic of local government officials and
editor of the weekly *El Crucero,* which is published in Cuernavaca, Morelos. CPJ wrote to
President Carlos Salinas de Gortari, urging a
prompt and serious investigation. The Morelos
prosecutor's office said an investigation of the
murder indicated Dorantes was killed for reasons other than his work. CPJ is keeping this
case under investigation because nobody has
been arrested for the murder. Dorantes was the
first of three journalists mysteriously murdered
in the state of Morelos within a six-week period.
Two other journalists were killed in July.

July 6
Enrique Peralta Torres, *La Unión de Morelos,*
  KILLED
Torres, a reporter with *La Unión de Morelos,* was
murdered. Investigators claim that before he
died of multiple bullet wounds, Torres identified his assassin as Fidencio Muñoz Malpica, a
business associate. The alleged murderer is
reported to have fled to the United States. CPJ
believes the investigation into the murder was
too superficial, especially since another journalist was mysteriously killed a few weeks earlier,
and because Morelos state had not been particularly dangerous for journalists in previous
years.

July 11
José Luis Rojas, *La Unión de Morelos,* KILLED
Rojas, a prominent reporter for *La Unión de
Morelos,* was found strangled to death on July 13.
Seven days earlier, Enrique Peralta Torres from
the same daily was also killed under suspicious
circumstances. Rojas was not known for critical
or controversial writing, but he was one of the
most famous journalists in Morelos state.
Authorities have identified the alleged murderer
as Israel Lavín Rios, a friend who lived with
Rojas during the weeks before the murder. Rios
is reported to have fled to the United States. CPJ
is keeping this case under investigation because
no one has been charged or tried for the murder.

September 6
Juan Solis, *Televisa,* HARASSED
Bruno López, *Univisión,* HARASSED
Ricardo Castillo, *The News,* HARASSED
Other news media, HARASSED
The Zapatista National Liberation Army
(EZLN) banned various news media organiza-
tions from attending the National Democratic
Convention, a conference sponsored by the
EZLN in Chiapas. The EZLN denied access to
those journalists who worked for outlets con-
nected to the Mexican television network Tele-
visa and to news media the EZLN considers
critical of its movement and its goals.

September 9
Tele Verdad, CENSORED, LEGAL ACTION
Tele Verdad, an unlicensed private radio station,
was closed down by Mexican authorities and the
station's equipment was confiscated. Tele Verdad staff claimed they were forced to operate
illegally because the government refused to give
them a license.

September 29
Gunther Dietz, EXPELLED
German Gunther Dietz, a representative of the
indigenous press organization AIPIN (Agencia
Internacional de Prensa Indigena), and a fellow
at the German Social-Democratic foundation
Friedrich-Ebert-Stiftung, was detained by Mexican police in the state of Morelos and expelled
from the country within 48 hours. Authorities
detained him for working as a journalist on a
tourist visa. But Dietz claimed he was targeted
because of his association with AIPIN. The
state of Morelos has had many conflicts over
the issue of land rights for indigenous groups.

November 7
Reforma, HARASSED
The independent Mexican daily *Reforma* faced a
crippling distribution boycott organized by the
government-affiliated Newspaper Vendors'
Union. The boycott forced the daily's reporters,
editors and other workers to go out on the
streets and sell the newspaper. The daily had
run into problems because it attempted to begin
an alternative distribution network that would
compete with the government union. Newspaper officials also had wanted to publish the
newspaper on holidays, a practice that is prohibited under the union's contract. CPJ wrote
to President Carlos Salinas de Gortari, urging
him to issue a statement repudiating the union's
boycott and condemning its strong-arm tactics
that threaten freedom of expression.

Nicaragua

The Nicaraguan media encountered problems in 1994 because of the fact that every news outlet is somehow linked or openly affiliated with a political party. For instance, the editor and some of the reporters for the daily *Barricada,* the former party organ of the Sandinista National Liberation Front (FSLN), were fired after they supported a reformist candidate within the splintered FSLN Party.

Also common throughout the year were incidents of physical abuse by police against reporters covering demonstrations or other public disturbances.

June 29
Melba Sánchez, *La Tribuna,*
ATTACKED, HARASSED
Sánchez, a correspondent for *La Tribuna* newspaper, was attacked by a police lieutenant and three policemen in the town of Chinandega, where she was reporting on the peasant occupation of the Agrarian Reform Institute. Sánchez suffered injuries to her arms, back and neck, and her photo equipment was destroyed.

September
All newspapers, HARASSED
Managuan municipal authorities had been ignoring a March presidential ruling that removed a municipal tax on the sale of newspapers. City Hall had continued to forcibly collect the tax from newspaper publishers. The dispute was settled in favor of the newspapers through a public statement by the Finance Ministry in September.

September 13
Carlos Fernando Chamorro, *Barricada,*
CENSORED
16 staff journalists, *Barricada,* CENSORED
Internal conflict between radicals and reformers erupted at *Barricada,* which used to be the organ of the Sandinista National Liberation Front

Party (FSLN). Sixteen reporters at the daily and Chamorro, its editor in chief, were fired by FSLN Secretary-General Daniel Ortega for their alleged support of Sergio Ramírez, the reformist politician within the FSLN. Upon being fired, the 16 journalists were not allowed to negotiate their labor demands. Barricada was the official newspaper of the FSLN but became more independent in the last two years as splits within the party developed. The FSLN infighting has become a media war with Ortega's side in control of three radio stations and one television channel, and the reformists in control of two dailies and one weekly newspaper.

Paraguay

There is no government-sanctioned censorship of the press in Paraguay. But journalists who write about the burgeoning drug and arms trade and its connections to some government officials face retaliation. In 1994, there were several instances in Ciudad del Este, a strategic town that borders Brazil and Argentina, where corrupt government officials sued journalists for libel and defamation.

Journalists also continued to be wary of writing critical accounts of the still-powerful military. Even though Paraguay's strongman, Gen. Alfredo Stroessner, was overthrown in 1989, the military has since maintained its taste for politics and was displeased by a law passed in 1994 that forbids military officers from making political statements. The passage of this law created problems for President Juan Carlos Wasmosy, as rumors of a possible military coup spread.

March 23
Hector Guerín, *ABC Color,* LEGAL ACTION
Osvaldo Cáceres, *ABC Color,* LEGAL ACTION
Guerín, a correspondent with the Asunción daily ABC Color, and Cáceres, a photographer for the paper, were indicted for defamation and

libel by Criminal Court Judge Porfirio Zacarías León in Ciudad del Este. Guerín is an investigative journalist who covers corruption.

March 25
Dolly Galeano, *Ultima Hora,* LEGAL ACTION
Galeano, a reporter for *Última Hora,* was sued for defamation and libel by Social Security Director Luciano Perrera.

May 2
Mariano Godoy, *ABC Color,* ATTACKED
During a demonstration by farmers in Tacuara, Godoy, a special correspondent with the Asunción daily *ABC Color* was struck by a bullet in the lower back. The bullet had been fired by police who were repressing a farmers' demonstration. One farmer was killed by police during the confrontation.

May 2
César Palacios, *ABC Color,* ATTACKED
Blas Ceferino Peña, *ABC Color,* ATTACKED
Gualberto Arcco, *Noticias,* ATTACKED
Juan Carlos Salinas, *Noticias and Red Privada de Comunicación,* ATTACKED
Dolly Galeano, *Ultima Hora,* ATTACKED
Celseo Salcedo, *Canal 13,* ATTACKED
The six journalists were beaten with batons by police while they were covering a demonstration in Ciudad del Este, on the Brazilian border.

July 28
Juan Carlos Salinas, *Noticias and Red Privada de Comunicación,* LEGAL ACTION
Hector Guerín, *ABC Color,* LEGAL ACTION
Both Salinas and Guerín, correspondents in Ciudad del Este, were charged with contempt and defamation by Criminal Court Judge Justo Salvador Reyes, who had been accused of corruption by the journalists. In another incident two months later, officials from the customs and ports administration offered both journalists bribes in return for not writing about corruption in that department.

August 1
Red Privada de Comunicación, LEGAL ACTION
Judge Marcelino Arevalos issued a prior-restraint order against a news program prepared by the television station Red Privada de Comunicación that was going to focus on drug trafficking. The judge's order came down only hours before the broadcast was supposed to air, after individuals implicated in the trade by the news account made appeals to the judge. The program aired without editing two weeks later.

September 19
Mercedes Barriocanal, *"El Ojo,"*
   LEGAL ACTION
Barriocanal, a television anchor for the news program "El Ojo," was summoned by a criminal court to testify on her sources for a news report she aired that linked military officers and drug traffickers.

Peru

Journalists in Peru suffered the highest number of attacks in the hemisphere for 1994. Jailing, harassment, bombings and lawsuits were common, with many of the attacks taking place in provincial areas. Several journalists had to flee their hometowns because of death threats or harassment from drug traffickers, paramilitary groups and the military. Many of the attacks involved local government officials who reacted violently against unflattering press accounts. And in one instance, the terrorist group Shining Path bombed the home of a Lima-based journalist who had been critical of the organization.

The government released 12 journalists who had been in jail on terrorist charges since 1992. But a study by a new Lima-based press monitoring office, Instituto Prensa y Sociedad, has documented 13 other cases of journalists in jail, serving sentences of up to 20 years for terrorism. Most of them were jailed in 1992 on trumped-up charges,

according to the Lima group, and the study found that anti-terrorist legislation was used by corrupt local officials to send reporters to jail. Three of the cases included in the new report demonstrated this trend.

Reporting on drug trafficking is still the most dangerous and difficult assignment for Peruvian journalists. In the interior, dozens of journalists received threats and faced lawsuits for publishing or broadcasting reports on alleged connections between civilian and military officials and drug traffickers.

The central government continued to use the threat of property confiscation (for back taxes on sales and newsprint) to intimidate certain independent news outlets.

On the positive side, Congress disallowed the application of the constitutional guarantee of *Habeas Data,* which was used repeatedly by individuals demanding reparations for alleged defamation and libel.

January 15
Alberto Mortola Aburto, *El Heraldo,* HARASSED,
    LEGAL ACTION, THREATENED
Aburto, a reporter at the newspaper *El Heraldo,* was accused of defamation by José Navarro, mayor of the city of Chincha. Aburto was convicted and sentenced to one year of probation, fined and suspended from journalistic activity for one year. The case remains under appeal, and Aburto has been threatened with death if he continues to publish stories about Navarro.

Early February
Hermes Rivera Guerrero, *Radio Oriental,*
    HARASSED, LEGAL ACTION,
    IMPRISONED
Guerrero, a reporter for Radio Oriental, in the province of Jaen in the Andean department of Cajamarca, was sentenced to 20 years in prison for alleged terrorist activity. In his defense, Guerrero said policeman Idelfonso Ugarte arrested him arbitrarily on May 8, 1992, and brought the false charges against him. Guerrero's wife, Dilsia Miranda, also accused the

policeman of demanding $500 for the release of her husband and making uninvited sexual advances. When she refused to cooperate, Miranda said, Ugarte apparently falsified evidence to show Rivera's participation in terrorist attacks in the area. By year's end, Rivera was being held at the Picsi prison.

March 14
Patricio Ricketts, *Expreso,* ATTACKED
A bomb went off in front of Ricketts' house at 9:45 a.m., killing two women and wounding six other people. The journalist, a former minister who writes for the conservative daily *Expreso,* was not home, but his daughter Monica was injured in the blast. Two people, believed to be associated with the Shining Path, masqueraded as banana sellers and left a pushcart filled with explosives in front of the journalist's home. A week before the bombing, Ricketts had written an article critical of Shining Path. In September, the National Direction for Counterterrorism arrested 18 Shining Path members responsible for several terrorist attacks, including the bombing of Ricketts' home. CPJ wrote a letter commending the arrest of those responsible for the attack against the journalist.

March 15
Linne Torres, *Radio Palmera,*
    THREATENED, CENSORED
Sí, THREATENED, CENSORED
Torres, news director for Radio Palmera in Bellavista, was threatened with death by a local drug kingpin known as "El Barón." The drug trafficker suspected Torres of providing incriminating evidence on his operations in Bellavista for an article published in *Sí* magazine on Feb. 28, 1994. Torres said he was not a source for the story, which reported on alleged links between the army and the drug traffickers. Issues of *Sí* were confiscated by the trafficker's henchmen, who burned the magazine in the main plaza in Bellavista, and Torres was forced to flee his home and move to the nearby town of Tarapoto. CPJ condemned the threats against Torres

in a letter to President Alberto Fujimori and Defense Minister Gen. Victor Malca Villanueva.

March 16
Caretas, HARASSED
Oiga, HARASSED
La República, HARASSED
Sí, HARASSED
In a document released by the Office of Military Information, the Peruvian army criticized the media for abusing freedom of expression. It accused the newsweeklies *Sí, Oiga, Caretas* and the daily *La República* of purposefully printing damaging information on the alleged links between drug traffickers and army officers in the Huallaga region. The army believes that a campaign to tarnish its image is being orchestrated through the national and international media.

March 25
Mariano Paliza Mendoza, *Radio Cadena,*
THREATENED
Mendoza, the host of "Urgent Action," a call-in radio program funded by human rights organizations, received telephone threats between March 25 and March 28. Mendoza also reported seeing unfamiliar cars parked outside the station when he was broadcasting the program, which focuses on human rights violations. CPJ asked President Alberto Fujimori to investigate the case.

April 11
El Comercio, LEGAL ACTION
La República, LEGAL ACTION
Expreso, LEGAL ACTION
Santiago Sanguinetti, a close friend of President Alberto Fujimori, launched several *Habeas Data* cases in criminal court against publishers of *El Comercio, La República* and *Expreso* newspapers. He sued after the newspapers wrote about his lawsuits against the mayors of eight Lima boroughs for charging excessive parking rates. After Superior Court threw out the cases against the mayors because they were not filed in a civil court, Sanguinetti filed the *Habeas*

Data case alleging that the newspapers' reporting had "damaged his honor and reputation" by not having published a letter he wrote protesting the court decision. The directors of the newspapers published a joint press release protesting Sanguinetti's abuse of the clause.

April 12
Rossana Cueva, *Channel 4,* LEGAL ACTION
Nicolas Lucar, *Channel 4,* LEGAL ACTION
Lawyer and university professor Vladimir Paz de la Barra brought a *Habeas Data* action against Cueva and Lucar, journalists with Channel 4's Sunday show "La Revista Dominical." Paz brought the action after the program broadcast a story on his alleged misappropriation of state funds. The court dismissed the action. Paz maintains that he attempted to clarify the information carried on the program but that Lucar refused to accept his calls. This was the first attempt to apply the controversial *Habeas Data* law, a constitutional guarantee that gives any person the right to demand reparations for defamation or libel. Its application was banned by Congress on Aug. 18.

April 13
Mariella Balbi, *Channel 9,* LEGAL ACTION
Balbi was summoned to appear before a military panel because of a television interview she conducted with Gen. Salidad Sedo, who led a coup attempt in 1992 and is serving a prison sentence. The court was investigating charges that Salidad Sedo defamed the armed forces and made derogatory comments against the army chief of staff during an interview broadcast on the program "Crossfire" on Channel 9.

April 25
All media, THREATENED
Ricardo Z, the leader of a Shining Path splinter group that refused to honor a government truce with other factions of the movement, warned that journalists who reported critically on the Shining Path "will be punished, attacked, annihilated."

The Americas

May 2
Raul Celis López, *Radio Arpegio*, HARASSED
Journalist López was detained in Iquitos for
contempt for two days before being released. It
is believed that his detention was linked to a
media campaign conducted by him and other
journalists to publicize the poor administration
of justice in the province of Maynas.

May 10
César Flores Gonzáles, *Radio Estudio Cinco*
and *Radio Huanta 2000*,
THREATENED, HARASSED
Saúl Montero Villanueva, *Radio Estudio Cinco*
and *Radio Huanta 2000*,
THREATENED, HARASSED
Gonzáles and Villanueva, both journalists with
Radio Estudio Cinco and Radio Huanta 2000,
fled to Lima from the city of Huanta for security reasons. Both had received death threats after
exposing wrongdoings by members of the army,
the National Police and public officials.

May 12
Emilio Carrasco Moreno, *Radio Sensación*,
IMPRISONED, LEGAL ACTION
Moreno, owner of Radio Sensación, who had
been in prison since Dec. 2, 1993, was found not
guilty of charges of membership in the terrorist
group Shining Path. The verdict was reached
after a former member of the organization who
had first implicated Moreno testified that he had
made the charges after being tortured by anti-
terrorist police. However, in accordance with
anti-terrorist legislation, the case was referred
for a second opinion to the Superior Court of
Lambayeque, where the anonymous public
prosecutor recommended a sentence of 30 years
in jail. Since Nov. 15, 1994, Carrasco has been
held in the Picsi jail in Chiclayo.

Radio Sensación, which broadcasts a mix-
ture of music and community news, is located in
Huancabamba, Piura, an area of known Shining
Path activity. Carrasco is an illiterate farmer
who has owned the station for seven years.

May 15
Luis Velásquez Tagle, *Global Televisión and La*
República, ATTACKED, HARASSED
Tagle, news director of Global Televisión's
regional news program and a correspondent of
the daily *La República*, was brutally beaten by
two policemen in Huanuco. Peru's Journalists
Colegio said the beating was related to Tagle's
critical reports on Channel 13. Tagle is a local
officer for the *colegio* in Huanuco.

May 16
Oiga, LEGAL ACTION
The opposition magazine *Oiga* was served with
a restraining order by the government, which
ordered the magazine to bring all its tax payments up to date. Publisher Francisco Igartua
said the measure will bankrupt the magazine
and that the publication is being discriminated
against because it is an opposition forum. He
also said that *Oiga*'s debt is small compared to
that of other media outlets.

May 18
Guido Falcón Nivín, *Moquegua al Día*,
LEGAL ACTION
Wilfredo Mendoza Flores, *Moquegua al Día*,
LEGAL ACTION
Rony Flor Coayla, *Radio Minería*,
LEGAL ACTION
Nivín and Flores, reporters for the weekly
Moquegua al Día, and Coayla, a reporter with
Radio Minería, were each sentenced to six
months in prison for defamation of government
employee Guillermo Meza Beteta. The journal-
ists wrote and aired stories accusing Beteta of
tax fraud, corruption and extortion in his job as
manager of Moquegua City's sanitation services.
The journalists said the official had attempted
to bribe the owner of Radio Mineria by paying
US$5,000 not to run the stories. In his ruling,
the judge prohibited the journalists from presenting information that backed up the stories.
The journalists were released on bail and were
ordered by the court not to report on local government officials.

July 11
Pedro Salazar Angulo, *El Oriente,*
LEGAL ACTION
Santiago Gonzáles Coronado, *La República and*
Radio Programas del Perú, LEGAL ACTION
Angulo, director of the daily newspaper *El Oriente,* and Coronado, local correspondent for the
Lima newspaper *La República* and for Radio
Programas del Perú, were charged with contempt of court by the provincial prosecutor in
Maznas. The accusation was prompted by news
reports filed by the journalists a few months
earlier that questioned a judge's decision to
release a suspected drug trafficker from prison.

July 11
Nicolás Prokopiuk, *Radio Atlántida,*
THREATENED, HARASSED
Prokopiuk, a journalist with Radio Atlántida, was
threatened by members of the National Police in
the department of Loreto in eastern Peru for
reporting that police officers had raped two
women. The women made the accusation on the
Atlantid program "El Patrullero Atlántida."

July 17
Oscar Tercero Cardenas Bartra, *Selva,*
IMPRISONED, HARASSED,
LEGAL ACTION
Bartra, director of the regional weekly *Selva,*
was arrested by police on charges of contempt.
On April 23, police had raided the studios of
the Cumbaza radio and television station in the
belief that he was hiding there. One day after
his detention Bartra expressed concern for his
physical safety because of his strong criticisms
of corrupt public officials. By year's end he was
being held in the judicial prison in Lima.

July 20
José Romani Pérez, *Free-lancer,* IMPRISONED
Pérez, a photojournalist, was arrested and
charged with collaboration with the Shining
Path. Romani worked for five months in 1988
at the newspaper *El Diario,* which is considered
to be the terrorist group's propaganda organ.

August 16
Nicolás Lúcar, *Channel 4,* LEGAL ACTION
A lawyer representing former President Alan
García filed a *Habeas Data* motion against Lúcar
after he reported on telephone conversations
between García and a prominent businessman
who is on the lam for fraud. Lúcar is director of
the political program "La Revista Dominical"
broadcast by Channel 4. The intent of the
motion was to prevent Lúcar from disclosing
more information about García's conversations
with the businessman.

August 19
Jesus Alfonso Castiglione Mendoza, *Radio*
Amistad, IMPRISONED
Castiglione, owner of radio station Amistad in
the highlands town of Huacho, was given a 20-
year prison sentence for terrorism, despite overwhelming evidence supporting his innocence.
On April 29, 1993, he was arrested and accused
of having participated in a Shining Path attack
in the town of Huaraz. CPJ wrote several letters
urging the special anti-terrorism court to carefully evaluate all the evidence presented in Castiglione's favor.

September 6
Reynero Guerra, *La República,* HARASSED
Guerra, a photographer with the Lima-based
daily *La República,* was forced by the head of the
First Military Region, Gen. Howard Rodríguez
Málaga, to turn over a roll of film Guerra shot
during a visit by President Alberto Fujimori to
Piura. Guerra had photographed the general
passing out election pamphlets supporting Fujimori. Peruvian law prevents military personnel
from taking part in political activities. CPJ
wrote to Defense Minister Victor Malca
requesting an investigation of the matter. On
Sept. 14, the defense minister told Congress
that Gen. Rodríguez was not handing out the
almanacs to the general public but passing one
out to an elderly woman who had difficulty
reaching the table where they were located. He
blamed an unidentified soldier for confiscating

the film. In an Oct. 12 letter to CPJ, the Peruvian embassy stated that the soldier had no orders to confiscate the roll and that he had already been disciplined.

September 8
Carlos Valdéz, *Reuters Television*, CENSORED
Valdéz, a Peruvian photojournalist working for Reuters Television, was ordered by President Alberto Fujimori to erase videos he shot during a press visit by the president to a high-security prison in the town of Puno.

September 12
All media, HARASSED
The Military Information Office circulated a communiqué criticizing the news media. The document accuses the national and international media of orchestrating a campaign to tarnish the image of the Peruvian army by representing it as an institution that systematically violates human rights.

September 19
César Flores, *Antena 1*
Eduardo Piñeda Gamboa, *Antena 1*, ATTACKED
Flores and Gamboa, correspondents in Huanta for the radio station Antena 1, were attacked and beaten by police and military officers after they started a radio campaign against the use by the military of a brothel located in the middle of the city. Flores subsequently moved to Lima.

October 3
Clemente Quincho Pánez, *La República*,
    LEGAL ACTION, THREATENED
Pánez, a correspondent for the Lima daily *La República* in the city of La Oroya, was sentenced to a one-year conditional arrest—which forbids him from leaving the country—and a fine for contempt against a public employee. Pánez had reported corruption, nepotism and abuse of authority by the manager of the main state-owned metallurgic company. His lawyer has appealed the decision. On Dec. 12, Pánez's home was burglarized. The thieves left a mes-

sage saying that journalists "can get killed for talking too much."

October 31
José Reyes Cespedes, *JSV Radio*, HARASSED
Cespedes, news director at the JSV radio station in Huanuco, was warned that he may be charged with supporting terrorism and obstructing investigations of terrorism. The threat came from Huanuco Political-Military Command headquarters. In an earlier radio news broadcast, Cespedes had reported on irregularities in the arrest of the rector of the National University of Huanuco.

November 1
Jorge Zavaleta, *Cambio 16*,
    HARASSED, CENSORED, THREATENED
Cambio 16, HARASSED, CENSORED,
    THREATENED
Issue number 1166 of the Latin American edition of the Spanish magazine *Cambio 16* was seized by Peruvian authorities. The magazine claims that the decision to seize it was made by the Peruvian Foreign Ministry and was prompted by a map that illustrated an article on the border region between Ecuador and Peru. The authorities acted on the basis of Law 26291, which prohibits the "importation, commercialization, printing or distribution of maps, historical texts, books or any other related material which distorts national territory." The article in question analyzes the border dispute between Ecuador and Peru, and highlights the issue of the land claimed by each but granted to Peru under the Rio de Janeiro agreement. Zavaleta, a correspondent with *Cambio 16*, subsequently received a number of veiled threats by telephone at his home and office and a summons to appear before judicial officials.

November 7
Javier Tuanama Valera, *Hechos*, IMPRISONED
Valera, editor in chief of the magazine *Hechos*, was sentenced to 10 years in prison by an anonymous judge from the Superior Court of Lambayeque. He was first detained on Oct. 16, 1990, and

charged with having links to the terrorist group Revolutionary Movement Tupac Amaru (MRTA). He was found not guilty of the charges in two trials held in 1994. He was subsequently released but arrested again soon after. Under the Repentance Law, which allows terrorists to turn themselves in and inform on former comrades, a former member of the MRTA confessed that Tuanama had recruited him into the MRTA. The same individual later recanted, but by year's end, Tuanama was still being held at the Picsi prison.

November 8
Rubén Valdéz Alvarado, *ANP-FNTCS,*
   THREATENED
Andrés Gonzáles Prada, *Radio Studio 5,*
   THREATENED
The political-military head of the city of Huanuco, Col. EP. Eduardo Negrón Montestrugue, had spearheaded an intimidation campaign in 1994 against journalists in the eastern-central Peruvian city. He threatened to jail them if they spread information that, in his view, sympathized with terrorism. The first journalist to face such threats was José Reyes Cespedes, news director for the JSV radio station, on Oct. 31 (see case above). On Nov. 8, the colonel indicated two other journalists that were "on his list" to clarify remarks regarding information deemed supportive of terrorism: Alvarado, national head of a Peruvian journalists' association (ANP-FNTCS) and executive committee member of the Brussels-based International Federation of Journalists (IFJ), and Prada from Radio Studio 5. All three journalists are known for their opposition to the terrorist movement. These actions have induced great fear among journalists in the region because the city of Huanuco is a focal point for terrorist activities, drug trafficking and military repression.

November 16
Alfredo Loza, *Radio Cultura and Canal 4 TV,*
   IMPRISONED, LEGAL ACTION
Loza, a journalist with Radio Cultura in Puno and a correspondent for Lima's Canal 4 televi-

sion station, was detained by police. He is accused of collaborating with the terrorist group Revolutionary Movement Tupac Amaru (MRTA) after he was identified as a member by a convicted terrorist. Under the "Repentance Law," imprisoned terrorists can often reduce their jail terms by naming other "terrorist" collaborators. Loza is being implicated in the MRTA attack against a police station in the city of Sandia. He had been visiting his father during the attack and reported on the story. He interviewed the head of the MRTA unit and filmed part of the attack, which was aired later on Canal 4. The report allowed police to identify and capture the MRTA leaders in the zone.

December 21
Felipe Paucar, *Channel 4*
José Claudio Torres, *Channel 4,* HARASSED
Paucar, a correspondent for Channel 4 in the city of Tingo María, and Torres, his cameraman, had their credentials taken on orders of Tito Celis, commander of the Army of Engineers Batallion. Paucar and Torres were filming the return of soldiers, wounded in a battle with a Shining Path unit, to the batallion headquarters in Tingo María. Both journalists need their credentials to work in the area, which is a center of drug trafficking and terrorist activities. Paucar believes his credentials were taken because he had recently reported about the return of Shining Path to the area.

United States

In its recent report "Silenced: The Unsolved Murders of Immigrant Journalists in the United States," CPJ documents how immigrant journalists working for non-English-language media run the risk of being killed for doing their jobs (see Special Report: United States, p. 89). The murder of a journalist working in an ethnic minority community is often accompanied by a spate of other incidents of harassment. **In 1994, several reporters working for the ethnic press reported violations. From a firebombing against an African-American newspaper that published a controversial article on Muslims to a Cuban-American magazine that endorses renewed relations between the United States and Cuba, the attacks against minority news media continued to deprive these vital U.S. communities of a free and robust dialogue on national and international issues.**

January 24

Community Focus, ATTACKED
Community Focus, a Latino weekly newspaper that crusaded against drug dealers and police brutality, was firebombed in Philadelphia, causing an estimated $10,000 in damages. The newspaper is in the same building as the National Congress of Puerto Rican Rights, which had received threatening phone calls from unidentified sources the week before.

March 29

Cincinnati Herald, ATTACKED
Unidentified people threw a firebomb through a window of the building that houses the *Cincinnati Herald* newspaper, which serves the African-American community in Cincinnati, Ohio. The firebomb attack came days after the newspaper published an article by a guest columnist who wrote that blacks should not support Muslims because they were the first to enslave Africans and were known pillagers in past centuries. CPJ wrote a letter to Ohio Gov. George Voinovich, requesting a full investigation of the attack. Gov. Voinovich replied to CPJ, saying that he was troubled by the bombing and that the case was being thoroughly investigated.

July 18

Diep Ly, *Angkor Borei News*, THREATENED
Ly, editor and publisher of the Californian weekly *Angkor Borei News*, received a telephone death threat from an individual who identified himself as Gen. Por Bun Sur. Sur returned to Cambodia in 1994 to work for the Ministry of the Interior. Ly said he received the death threats apparently because his paper had published articles that criticized corruption by current Cambodian government officials.

August 26

Free-lancers, CENSORED
The Treasury Department issued new sanctions that could affect the work of journalists wishing to cover Cuba. Under new regulations, "journalists regularly employed in such capacity by a news reporting organization" may travel to Cuba. But free-lance journalists, book writers and others who are not regularly employed by news organizations must apply to the Treasury Department for a onetime license. CPJ wrote to the White House, urging President Clinton to eliminate the new restrictions.

September 4

Replica, ATTACKED
Unidentified persons threw Molotov cocktails into the offices of the weekly magazine *Replica* in Miami. Max Lesnik, editor of *Replica*, believes the attack was due to the magazine's editorial stance in favor of an open dialogue between the United States and Cuba.

October 11

Franz Israel, *Haiti Observateur*,
     LEGAL ACTION, CENSORED, HARASSED
Israel, a reporter for the conservative New York-based *Haiti Observateur*, was denied access to a U.N. press conference with President Jean-Bertrand Aristide, even though he was duly accredited to cover U.N. events. Israel's newspaper had actively opposed Aristide's return to Haiti. The move to exclude Israel was protested by the U.N. Correspondents Association, which threatened to delay the press conference until he was allowed to participate, which he finally was. CPJ wrote to Aristide to complain about the attempt to exclude Israel.

—*continued on p. 102*

SILENCED:
The Unsolved Murders of Immigrant Journalists in the United States

by Ana Arana

IN 1976, Don Bolles, a reporter for the *Arizona Republic*, drove to a hotel to get information from a source about fraudulent land deals. His car exploded, destroyed by a bomb. Bolles had to have both legs and an arm amputated. He died 11 days later.

Reporters from newspapers, TV stations and radio outlets descended on Arizona to pursue Bolles' investigation. They exposed massive corruption. They unearthed information about Bolles' killers. They established the principle that, if all Americans were to be able to speak and write freely, reporters in America could not be murdered with impunity.

In 1994, that principle still holds—unless the journalist is a member of an ethnic minority who works in the non-English press. Since 1981, 10 immigrant journalists—five Vietnamese, three Haitians, one Chinese-American and a Cuban-American—have been assassinated in the United States, and only two of the cases have been solved. If 10 American reporters working for the mainstream press—10 Don Bolleses—had been murdered on U.S. soil over the past 13 years, the shock waves would have galvanized the media and law enforcement. Yet the assassinations of 10 immigrant journalists*—assassinations specifically intended to smother fact-finding and to silence dissent—have rarely produced more than ripples of protest.

DE DIOS CASE SPURS CPJ INVESTIGATION

It was the cold-blooded execution of Manuel de Dios Unanue in 1992 that prompted CPJ to turn its attention to attacks against jour-

---

Ana Arana is the Americas program coordinator for the Committee to Protect Journalists and a former foreign correspondent in Latin America. This special report is an excerpt from a longer report by the same title that was published by CPJ in December 1994.

*For a listing and summary of these cases, see p. 99.

nalists in the United States. De Dios had been editor in chief of *El Diario-La Prensa*, New York City's leading Spanish-language daily, and was renowned for his muckraking exposés of drug traffickers in two upstart magazines he distributed in Queens. His assassination shocked Latinos and journalists in New York City. The killing of a reporter or editor in the United States was thought to be a rare event. The only recent cases that came quickly to mind were the murders in 1976 of Don Bolles and in 1984 of Denver radio host Alan Berg.

Many people, including some of de Dios's colleagues, initially tried to attribute his death to petty criminal motives. From the beginning, however, police suspected that drug traffickers were involved. Pressure from Latino leaders and leading New York journalists, as well as the federal government's interest in pinning a U.S. homicide on Colombia's Cali cocaine cartel, forced an all-out investigation.

A task force of 30 was assigned to the de Dios case with officers from the federal Drug Enforcement Administration and drug experts from police departments in New York, Baltimore and Miami. Two years later, the assassin and five Colombian conspirators—all said to have been working for the Cali cartel—were arrested and charged. Five pleaded guilty, and one was convicted and sentenced to life in prison.

The de Dios murder investigation was solved. CPJ's was just beginning. We were soon startled to learn that immigrant journalists like de Dios have been murdered almost routinely in this country. As we dug deeper, we discovered these disturbing patterns:
• Most of the murders remain unsolved and have received little attention by law enforcement agencies or national news media.
• Violence was aimed not only at the victims, but also at the communities they served in order to conceal information about criminal activities, silence dissent and discourage open debate.
• Each murder was only a small part of a larger campaign of intimidation, terror and harassment carried out by military, government or criminal organizations.
• Despite strong evidence that these organizations operated across state and national boundaries, the murders were usually treated by authorities and the press as local crimes.
• Law enforcement sources who have followed leads for years

believe that many of these crimes still could be solved and successfully prosecuted if the Justice Department were willing to give
investigators sufficient resources.

VIETNAMESE AND HAITIAN CASES REMAIN UNSOLVED
The Don Bolles murder was one of four cases that received substantial attention from both prosecutors and the press. The sweeping
follow-up investigation conducted by news organizations exposed
widespread corruption in Arizona, led to the founding of Investigative Reporters and Editors, Inc. and spurred a thorough prosecutor-
ial effort. Suspects were identified quickly. A conviction, however,
was not won until 1994, when Max Dunlap, a Phoenix contractor
with mob ties, was sent to prison for orchestrating the murder.

In 1984, the fatal shooting by neo-Nazis of Denver radio host
Alan Berg also gained national attention and prompted an intensive
FBI investigation. David Lane and Bruce Pierce, members of the
white supremacist group "The Order," were arrested in 1987. The
two men are serving 150-year prison sentences. The case received
further publicity when Eric Bogosian used the Berg murder as the
basis for his play and subsequent film, "Talk Radio."

Also in 1984, San Francisco writer Henry Liu was killed by
assassins working for the Taiwanese military. His case attracted considerable coverage, especially on the West Coast and in Asia. Liu
had long disparaged the repressive Kuomintang regime in Taiwan,
and a short time before his death he had published a critical biography of Taiwan President Chiang Ching-kuo. Several military intelligence and organized crime figures were convicted for Liu's murder
in Taiwan, but either received light sentences or were released from
jail after serving only six years of life prison terms. One was extradited to the United States, where he was convicted of the murder and
sentenced to 27 years in jail, but was killed in a prison fight three
years after his conviction.

In each of these cases, timely and aggressive responses by local and
federal authorities led quickly to suspects and eventually to convictions, although questions remain in the Henry Liu case as to whether
the conspirators have all been prosecuted or adequately punished.

Unfortunately, federal law enforcement authorities never gave
such attention to the murders of eight other immigrant journalists
killed between 1981 and 1993—five of them of Vietnamese origin,

three of them Haitians living in Miami. These journalists had fled repression and turmoil in their native countries only to find death in the United States for openly expressing their political views. Their killers have not been found. Informed investigators believe that timely and forceful investigations could have produced successful prosecutions and that a sustained effort now might still do so.

Why did the Vietnamese and Haitian cases draw less attention from law enforcement authorities and the media than the others?
• Berg and Bolles were white journalists working for mainstream English-language news media—and their accused assassins were linked to Mafia and right-wing groups already targeted by FBI task forces.
• The de Dios case also involved a criminal organization already under attack by U.S. law enforcement—the Cali drug cartel.
• Both the Liu and de Dios cases involved ethnic communities too large and politically significant to ignore: the Chinese-American population of the San Francisco Bay area and the Latino community of greater New York.
• The Vietnamese and Haitian cases involved smaller communities, made up mostly of first-generation immigrants who had a history of conflict in their homelands. Vietnamese-Americans are often loath to call attention to their internal conflicts, fearful of retaliation. Haitian-Americans in Miami are wary of a local Duvalierist criminal underground that appears to operate with impunity.

THE ETHNIC PRESS IS SILENCED

The non-English-language press has always been an integral part of American journalism, just as immigration is the quintessential American experience. For two centuries, new arrivals have relied on newspapers in their own languages—and, today, on radio and television programs—as their primary sources of information. These news outlets also are essential to mainstream media as sources for stories about changing immigrant life and American society.

Violence against immigrant journalists has robbed ethnic communities and society at large of robust and engaged dialogue about national and international issues. These new Americans cannot enjoy the fundamental American right to freedom of expression. Haitian and Vietnamese journalists, in particular, must fear for their lives if they expose crime or corruption among right-wing exile groups or simply voice a different political viewpoint.

Upon arrival in the United States, many immigrant journalists report stories or take political positions that they would not consider publicizing in their homelands for fear of retaliation. They believe that the U.S. government will ensure their rights under the U.S. Constitution. Yet some have been killed, and many have suffered physical attack, vandalism and threats against their lives. Some have reported such incidents to the police, and sometimes—not often— suspects have been brought to justice. Others have lowered their profiles. Often, out of fear, these incidents are not reported at all. The chilling effect is palpable:

• Haitian radio commentators in Miami scaled back their criticism of the Haitian military and of people in the community with alleged ties to the military regime in Haiti.

• Vietnamese-language journalists across the country avoid clear positions on the re-establishment of U.S. trade and diplomatic relations with Vietnam, even after the Clinton administration lifted the embargo.

• Latino journalists in Queens do not report on drug trafficking or corruption.

CPJ SEEKS FBI AND MEDIA INVESTIGATIONS

CPJ has appealed repeatedly to the Federal Bureau of Investigation and the Justice Department to launch a coordinated investigation of the unsolved murders of Haitian and Vietnamese journalists. We have spoken about the cases personally with Attorney General Janet Reno. Yet no serious investigation is underway. The Committee has found understaffed local law enforcement officials frustrated by the failure of federal authorities to treat the cases seriously.

With its modest resources, CPJ has been able to identify new leads and details in many of these cases—and we have been able to document in almost all instances that local and national law enforcement authorities are not vigorously pursuing these leads.

Absent adequate law enforcement action, it would require the talents and resources of a professional news organization to unearth the truth about the murders of these eight American journalists. Neglected by federal authorities, these cases are likely to remain unsolved unless the media itself spotlights the apparent unwillingness of law enforcement officials to devote their resources to these attacks on immigrant journalists and the communities they serve.

Targeted by Terrorists

SILENCE IN LITTLE SAIGON:

FIVE VIETNAMESE-AMERICAN JOURNALISTS KILLED

In 1994, newscasters at a Vietnamese radio station in Southern California's Little Saigon received death threats when they broadcast BBC interviews with Vietnamese leaders. The station's owners played down the incident, but the newscasters became cautious and selective about what they aired. The incident brought back troubling memories for Vietnamese-American journalists.

Five Vietnamese-American journalists were murdered between 1981 and 1990 during a right-wing wave of terror that left the Vietnamese community quiet and fearful. In five separate incidents across three states, right-wing exile groups claimed credit for, or were suspected of, the murders in 1981 of publisher Lam Trang Duong of San Francisco; in 1982 of publisher Nguyen Dam Phong of Houston; in 1987 of magazine editor Tap Van Pham of Garden Grove, Calif.; and, in 1989 and 1990 respectively, of layout designer Nhan Trong Do and columnist Triet Le, both from a Vietnamese-American magazine based in Fairfax County, Va. All the murders remain unsolved. The attacks on the Vietnamese-American press also included at least four attempted murders, numerous beatings and death threats, and countless acts of vandalism against journalists and news organizations.

The murders and other acts of violence intimidated the Vietnamese-language press, which had become a vibrant and influential voice in Vietnamese-American communities. Reporters and editors began to avoid controversial topics involving their homeland, such as the potential for normalized diplomatic relations between the United States and Vietnam. They also shied away from covering corruption and organized crime, which reportedly were often sponsored by the same extreme-right exile groups.

The five journalists were murdered during a decade when many newly arrived Vietnamese refugees still believed it was possible to end communist rule in Vietnam through organized resistance. Detractors have said the journalists were killed because they were communist sympathizers in a heavily anti-Communist refugee community, but only one of the victims supported the communist government of Vietnam. The others were anti-Communists who became targets because they or their publications favored some relaxation in U.S. policy toward Vietnam or criticized powerful paramilitary exile groups, according to law enforcement sources and Vietnamese community members. Different factions led by former South Vietnamese army and navy officials fought for control of these groups during the 1980s. Many of these groups were trying to raise money among refugees for an alleged invasion of Vietnam. Journalists and other critics charged that some of these funds were being raised to finance private business ventures, both legal and illicit.

Sources in law enforcement and in the Vietnamese-American community charge that most—and perhaps all—of the victims were killed in a well-orchestrated conspiracy carried out by a shadowy death squad: the self-appointed Vietnamese Organization to Exterminate Communists and Restore the Nation (VOECRN). The suspected masterminds were influential members of the Vietnamese community and former members of the South Vietnamese government and armed forces, law enforcement sources say. Many of VOECRN's members were also active in legal anti-Communist exile groups that organized political activities around the country and lobbied U.S. policy makers against making peace overtures to Vietnam, according to investigators.

There has never been a thorough federal investigation into the possible links among these murders. However, law enforcement sources told CPJ that there is strong circumstantial evidence indicating that some of the murders were contracted out to professional hit men working for Vietnamese criminal gangs, while others were carried out directly by VOECRN.

VOECRN has not struck since 1990, but authorities say it is only dormant and could strike again. "We have begun to look at the group again because there is a lot of unhappiness about the new relations between the U.S. and Vietnam," said an investigator with the Garden Grove police department in Orange County, Calif., who has tracked Vietnamese crime for 10 years. (Most police sources requested anonymity because the cases remain open.) Some California law enforcement agencies went on alert in 1994 after violent demonstrations were organized against visiting communist Vietnamese performers and politicians.

No suspects have been arrested or charged in any of the murders or acts of harassment against journalists and news outlets. They occurred in a larger context of intimidation and violence that affected the entire Vietnamese community, and police have had a difficult time persuading Vietnamese-American witnesses to provide testimony, one investigator told CPJ. Hard-line elements in the community exert power at the grassroots level. "It is difficult for me to push some of the people who I know can help our case against the killers, because I can't protect them from retaliation. The killers live in their communities," said another law enforcement source in California. Fear is compounded by the language barrier, and by a long-standing distrust of authorities that émigrés brought with them from Vietnam.

Jim Badey, a retired Virginia police investigator and a specialist on Asian crime, told CPJ that U.S. authorities often fail to solve political crimes in Vietnamese communities because they ignore or do not understand Vietnamese political feuds. "What law enforcement fails to understand is that these people are different . . . If they threaten to kill someone, they will get them," Badey said.

"They might sometimes kill their enemies in a home invasion or a robbery, but the underlying reason will be political. Police departments don't look beyond the evidence at hand." Some of the suspected conspirators in the murders have connections to the National United Front for the Liberation of Vietnam, also known simply as the Front, an exile group founded in San Jose, Calif., in 1981, investigators tell CPJ. The Front spearheaded rallies and demonstrations against any leniency in U.S. policy toward Vietnam throughout the 1980s. It promoted a military overthrow of the Vietnamese government and raised money to form an army of resistance in the Vietnamese-American community. It was active in California, Texas and Virginia. In many communities, refugees were threatened with being labeled pro-Communist unless they contributed money. Its leaders were Hoang Co Minh, a former admiral in the South Vietnamese navy, and Pham Van Lieu, a former colonel. Its membership includes other former high-level members of the South Vietnamese army and navy. By 1984, the Front falsely claimed that it had grown from several hundred men to several thousand uniformed troops based in Thailand and Vietnam, according to law enforcement and Vietnamese sources.

Taking their cue from the U.S.-funded Contra war in Nicaragua, Minh and others in the group hoped that the U.S. government might support them if officials believed they already had soldiers in the field ready to fight. Their claims brought in thousands of dollars each month from the Vietnamese community, but no U.S. aid. The Front set up a massive public relations organization, its own magazine, a fishing fleet and a worldwide chain of restaurants. By 1985, the group split as Lieu accused Minh and his followers of pocketing Front funds. Lieu also revealed that there was no truth to the claims that the Front had stationed thousands of freedom fighters inside Vietnam. Support in the Vietnamese community plummeted. In 1987, Minh attempted to lead a group of freedom fighters into Vietnam, but they were ambushed and he was reportedly killed. Twenty men who survived the attack were tried and executed in Vietnam. (Front leaders contend that Minh survived the attack and is in hiding in Vietnam.)

In 1991, a federal grand jury in San Jose indicted five top members of the Front, accusing them of conspiring to divert funds from the organization, which had nonprofit status, for their own use. Lawyers for the Front filed repeated motions, delaying a trial for the last four years. In January 1995, a federal judge dismissed the case, on grounds that a defendant has the right to a speedy trial. The Front contended that its activities were sanctioned by the U.S. government. They delayed the trial by issuing subpoenas to officials from several U.S. agencies, including the Central Intelligence Agency and the Department of Defense. Preliminary inquiries that led to the indictment show that the Front had collected millions of dollars in the 1980s, but that its leaders used most of the money for personal gain and to finance its restaurants. Once the Front members were indicted, one investigator said, law enforcement agencies noticed an immediate drop in the number of politically motivated attacks and acts of harassment. "They were too busy preparing their defense," he said.

THE MURDER INVESTIGATIONS

VOECRN operated across state and national boundaries, providing ample justification for a sweeping federal investigation into their activities.

That has not happened. Local police departments conducted reasonably thorough investigations of several of the murders, but cooperation among different law enforcement agencies has been lacking. Evidence in the earlier cases was mishandled; some was lost. Many of the local investigators who took an interest in solving the cases have retired. FBI investigations of some of the murders have been inconclusive and short-term. No overarching federal and local task force has been set up with the resources and authority to pull together the evidence in all the cases, despite the existence of special FBI units specifically devoted to tracking domestic terrorism. VOE-CRN was not even listed among terrorist organizations targeted by the FBI until 1987, when newspapers reported that the FBI hadn't considered the group a terrorist organization even though VOE-CRN claimed responsibility for terrorist acts.

RECOMMENDED ACTION

The murders of Vietnamese journalists could be solved within a year if the following steps are taken, according to law enforcement sources and Asian crime experts:

• The FBI should set up a national task force, which would work in conjunction with local law enforcement agencies in the cities where the killings occurred or where paramilitary exile groups were known to be organized. The task force would need to share information across state lines. According to one investigator, any investigation that does not include an interstate component will fail, because the gangs hired to carry out the murders are mobile and operate across state lines.

The task force must include a sufficient number of agents who speak Vietnamese or are Asian crime experts. The murder of Alan Berg in Denver was solved within a year because the FBI deployed up to 50 agents, many of them experts on white-supremacist groups. The Manuel de Dios murder was solved after 30 experts on drug trafficking from the Drug Enforcement Administration and local drug enforcement agencies from New York, Miami and Baltimore worked together for a year.

Previous FBI attempts to investigate Vietnamese murders were headed by small contingents of agents with little background on Asian crime. These investigations were not afforded the same priority in the FBI infrastructure. FBI investigations were often short-lived. In many cases, federal agents ended all inquiries a couple of months after each incident.

Previous FBI investigations also failed because they did not effectively share information with local investigators. Much of what has been unearthed by local law enforcement agents in each city can be used to decipher the overall pattern used by the assassins, according to Asian crime experts.

Journalists Murdered
in the United States
1976-1993

Dona St. Plite

October 24, 1993

Miami

St. Plite was killed while attending a benefit concert for the widow and children of his colleague, Fritz Dor. St. Plite's name had appeared on a death list circulated in Miami's Little Haiti by supporters of the Haitian military regime. One Bahamian-Haitian man has been indicted in connection with the murder; his trial is pending.

Manuel de Dios Unanue

March 11, 1992

New York

De Dios, 49, was shot twice in the head at point-blank range, reportedly on orders of the Cali cocaine cartel in retaliation for his coverage of its drug trafficking and money-laundering operations. A gunman was convicted and five co-conspirators pleaded guilty. Investigators are pursuing ties between the murder and members of the cartel.

Fritz Dor

March 15, 1991

Miami

Dor, 33, fled Haiti after becoming a target of the notorious security police of the former Duvalier regime. A radio broadcaster, he was shot and killed probably because of his political views in support of then exiled Haitian President Jean-Bertrand Aristide. One Bahamian-Haitian pleaded guilty to manslaughter for his role as the lookout and was sentenced to 25 years in prison. The accused gunman in the murders of both Dor and Jean-Claude Olivier was arrested in November 1994 in a South Florida prison, where he is serving a life sentence for an unrelated murder.

Jean-Claude Olivier

February 18, 1991

Miami

Olivier, 47, a popular radio personality in Miami's Haitian community, was shot and killed outside a Miami nightclub. It is widely believed that Olivier also was killed because of his opposition to the former Haitian military regime. The driver of the getaway car was convicted of manslaughter and sentenced to 25 years in prison. The alleged triggerman was arrested in November 1994 and faces trial in 1995 (see Dor case above).

Triet Le
September 22, 1990
Baileys Crossroads, Va.
A controversial columnist for the Vietnamese-language magazine *Van Nghe Tien Phong* (Art and Culture Vanguard), Le, 61, and his wife, Tuyet Thi Dangtran, were gunned down in their car in front of their home. Le had received many threats on his life because of his views. It is believed that an anti-Communist refugee group was responsible. In late 1990, the newspaper accused three top members of a paramilitary group of ordering Le's murder. The members sued for libel, but lost their case on Dec. 5, 1994. The murder case remains unsolved.

Nhan Trong Do
November 22, 1989
Fairfax County, Va.
Do, layout editor for the Vietnamese-language magazine *Van Nghe Tien Phong*, was found dead of gunshot wounds in his car outside his Virginia home. No one claimed responsibility. It is believed that an anti-Communist refugee group was responsible. The murder case remains unsolved.

Tap Vam Pham
August 7, 1987
Garden Grove, Calif.
Pham, editor and publisher of the weekly Vietnamese-language magazine *Mai* (Morning) in Orange County, Calif., was killed when his offices were set on fire. Pham had been receiving threats from anti-Communist organizations. The murder case remains unsolved.

Henry Liu
October 15, 1984
Daly City, Calif.
Liu, who had written many books and articles in which he criticized the Taiwanese government, was shot by several gunmen as he sat in his car in his garage. Several military intelligence and organized crime figures were convicted of the murder in Taiwan; two, however, were released from prison after serving only six years of life sentences, two others were sentenced to only two and a half years in prison and one was placed under house arrest. One conspirator was extradited to the United States, convicted of Liu's murder in 1988 and sentenced to 27 years in prison. In 1991, he was stabbed to death in a prison fight.

Alan Berg
June 19, 1984
Denver
Berg, a popular Denver talk-show host whose call-in show incited heated debates on controversial issues, was gunned down outside his home. Two white supremacists were convicted.

Nguyen Dam Phong

Aug. 24, 1982

Houston

Phong, 48, founder of the newspaper *Tu Do* (Freedom) was shot to death outside his home. Phong had received numerous threats on his life, apparently as a result of the many articles he wrote about local groups that claimed to be raising money to overthrow the Hanoi government. The case remains unsolved.

Lam Trong Duong

July 21, 1981

San Francisco

Lam Trong Duong, editor of a Vietnamese newspaper in San Francisco sympathetic to the Hanoi government, was shot to death on a busy San Francisco street. A group calling itself the Anti-Communist Viets Organization claimed credit. The case remains unsolved.

Don Bolles

June 2, 1976

Phoenix

Bolles, 47, a reporter for the *Arizona Republic*, died of injuries caused by a car bomb that exploded in a hotel parking lot where he had gone to receive information on allegedly fraudulent land deals involving Arizona's top politicians. A Phoenix contractor with mob ties was convicted for orchestrating the murder.

—continued from p. 88

In its letter, CPJ said this was the second time the Haitian U.N. Mission attempted to stop Israel from carrying out his work. The last incident, according to Israel and U.N. colleagues, occurred in August, when he was summoned to the New York Police Department, after a Haiti U.N. Mission official called the police to report harassment.

November 2
CNN, LEGAL ACTION
U.S. District Judge William Hoeveler found CNN guilty of contempt of court for willfully violating his 1990 order against broadcasting the jail-house phone conversation between former Panamanian dictator Manuel Noriega and his attorney. CNN, which is facing a possible $100,000 fine, argued during the trial in September that it was legally entitled to broadcast the tapes and that it had a journalistic responsibility to show what it called government misconduct for taping the calls in the first place. In December, in a public statement, the network apologized for violating the court ruling.

Venezuela

In late 1994, this country introduced the hemisphere's harshest law on licensing for journalists. It imposes prison terms of three-to-six months on those who do not abide by the law. Under the measure only those journalists who have a university degree and are members of the Venezuelan Journalists *Colegio* may work as journalists in the country. Publishers have opposed the law, but the measure has substantial support among Venezuelan journalists.

Several smaller newspapers and radio stations are foundering, following the government takeover of most of the private banking system, which had been rocked by financial scandals. Journalists said many of these smaller stations and newspapers are not able to pay the principal or interest on their loans, and indeed, several media outlets began to lay off journalists because of the new financial crisis.

January 6
Saúl Gómez Vásquez, *Omnivisión*, HARASSED
Oscar Vigas, *Omnivisión*, HARASSED
Vásquez and Vigas, crew members from Omnivisión, were detained at the San Carlos Fort when they attempted to film the front of the building. The fort houses a group of military officers who led one of two failed coups carried out in 1992. Both journalists were harassed by military police and forced to give up their film.

February 2
Mairbot Petit, *El Carabobeno*
Sotero Bandez, *El Nuevo País*,
    ATTACKED, HARASSED
On the day President Rafael Caldera took office, Petit, a journalist with *El Carabobeno*, was beaten and Bandez, a journalist with *El Nuevo País*, was beaten, teargassed and had her camera broken.

December 22
All media, LEGAL ACTION
Venezuelan President Rafael Caldera signed a media law that established jail sentences of three to six months for working journalists who are not members of the National Journalists *Colegio*. The *colegio* had pushed for this law since February, when the group first proposed it to Congress. The "Journalistic Practice Law" imposes mandatory licensing and makes it illegal for nonjournalists to work for the media. Mandatory licensing of journalists has existed in Venezuela since Caldera's first presidential term, which began in 1972. In April 1994, the Venezuelan Press Group, which represents newspapers and magazines, appealed for the revocation of that law. President Caldera refused, asserting that the current reform does not threaten freedom of the press.

Asia

OVERVIEW
OF **Asia**

by Vikram Parekh

THROUGHOUT MUCH OF ASIA, the exchange of ideas and information continued to take a backseat to the exchange of goods in 1994. Of the 12 Asian countries represented at the November summit of the Asia-Pacific Economic Conference (APEC), at least half saw significant press freedom violations during the year.

Among the worst offenders was the summit's host, Indonesia. In midsummer, President Suharto's regime abruptly ended a two-year experiment with press freedom and banned three leading weeklies that had reported on political scandals, separatist movements and labor unrest. Nationwide demonstrations against the bans were suppressed as well—in many cases brutally so. The government furthermore attempted to rein in the country's only free journalists union—the Alliance of Independent Journalists (AJI)—by pressuring editors to either fire AJI members on their staffs or reassign them to marginal posts.

Two of Indonesia's neighbors, Malaysia and Singapore, retaliated harshly during the year against critical reporting by the foreign media. Malaysia temporarily banned all new contracts with British firms after the London *Sunday Times* accused senior Malaysian officials of accepting bribes from a British contractor. The move, which was quickly followed by diplomatic overtures from Britain, underscored the growing economic clout of Southeast Asia's so-called "tiger cub." Singapore, taking another tack, filed contempt of court charges against Christopher Lingle, an American academic at the city-state's National University, after he

Vikram Parekh *is the program coordinator for Asia. He holds a J.D. from Rutgers Law School and is fluent in Gujarati. Before coming to CPJ, he was a Ford Foundation fellow at New York's International Center for Law in Development, and worked both for the International Human Rights Law Group in Washington, D.C., and the International Institute of New Jersey.*

Shanthy Nambiar, *a CPJ research assistant, contributed extensively to this report.*

The research carried out for CPJ's Asia program in 1994 was made possible in part by a grant from The Freedom Forum.

Asia

104

published an opinion piece in the *International Herald Tribune*, criticizing the "compliant judiciaries" of unspecified Asian countries.

China similarly attempted to curb the foreign press in Beijing, detaining and interrogating several correspondents who had variously attempted to contact prominent dissidents or report on the anniversary of the Tiananmen Square massacre. But its most severe measures were reserved for journalists writing for the Hong Kong press. Two mainland-born journalists, Xi Yang and Gao Yu, received stiff prison terms this year for allegedly disclosing state secrets in economic and political news articles published in Hong Kong. The sentences alarmed many of their colleagues in the British colony, who were understandably concerned about their own future following China's assumption of sovereignty over Hong Kong in 1997.

Journalists in countries lying outside the APEC community faced a decidedly different set of issues. Gripped by a paroxysm of ethnic, religious and caste conflicts, South Asian societies have seen press freedoms restricted by both state and non-state actors. Working under these conditions, four journalists in South Asia lost their lives during the year. In the North Indian state of Jammu and Kashmir, Ghulam Mohammed Lone—a correspondent for several Kashmiri newspapers—was killed in August, allegedly by an Indian Border Security Forces officer for his reporting of troop movements in the area. Newspapers in the state also faced repeated attempts to shut them down by feuding separatist groups seeking to block coverage of their rivals. In Pakistan's strife-torn city of Karachi, prominent magazine editor Mohammed Salahuddin was killed by suspected activists of the Muhajir Quami Movement (MQM), an ethnic party for which he had reserved strong criticism. Two days, later, in a seemingly retaliatory move, gunmen shot the business manager of the pro-MQM paper *Parcham*. And just outside the Afghan capital of Kabul—an area bitterly contested by government forces and those of renegade Prime Minister Gulbuddin Hekmatyar—masked gunmen abducted and killed BBC correspondent Mirwais Jalil, very likely the country's sole independent reporter.

Perched at unenviable crossroads between anarchy and repression was the Cambodian press. The first full year under a fractious "government of national unity" saw three journalists—Tou Chhom Mongkol, Nun Chan and Chan Dara—killed in apparent retaliation for their work, the drafting of a repressive press law, and the jailing on two occasions of an outspoken editor, Nguon Nonn.

Afghanistan

Of the 72 killings of journalists documented in this report, few resonated as strongly in 1994 as the assassination of Mirwais Jalil in July in eastern Afghanistan. Five masked gunmen abducted the 25-year-old BBC correspondent as he was returning from an interview with renegade Prime Minister Gulbuddin Hekmatyar in Charasyab, south of Kabul. When his bullet-riddled body was discovered the next day, the warring mujahideen factions in the area quickly intimated each other's culpability. In many ways, Jalil *was* Afghanistan's independent press, and his death not only dealt a severe blow to the news service that most Afghans rely on for nonpartisan reporting, but also threatened to deter other Afghan reporters from following his courageous lead. Aside from the BBC and Voice of America, very little reporting is available to Afghan citizens on a regular basis. Newspapers, crippled by chronic shortages of almost all essential supplies, publish only intermittently, and their circulation is limited even in the best of times by the country's low level of literacy. Radio stations operated by various mujahideen factions reach a larger audience, although these can scarcely be termed reliable sources of information.

Reporting in Afghanistan continued to be severely constrained in 1994 by the country's political fragmentation. Nine major mujahideen groups controlled different regions, with several areas bitterly contested. In Kabul, the nominal government was hard pressed to maintain its hold on the capital amid military challenges from Hekmatyar and his newfound ally, northern warlord Gen. Abdul Rashid Dostam. For foreign journalists, negotiating the frequently shifting fault lines was a risky proposition. A free-lance reporter was captured while on assignment in northern Afghanistan and detained in the hotly contested town of Kunduz by the Jamiat-e-Islami forces of President Burhanuddin Rabbani. She was later released unharmed. And in March, Canadian free-lance journalist Tyler Brule was shot and wounded by snipers while taking photographs in a front-line area of Kabul.

Mid-January
BBC World Service, ATTACKED

An unidentified Afghan mujahideen faction fired rocket-propelled grenades at the BBC's Kabul offices. There were no reported casualties. In early February, President Burhanuddin Rabbani's Jamiat-e-Islami party accused the news service of biased reporting in its coverage of fighting in Kabul, and charged it with favoring Rabbani's opponent, Prime Minister Gulbuddin Hekmatyar, in its broadcasts. BBC reporters had also received death threats in the past from Hekmatyar's forces.

March 5
Tyler Brule, *Free-lancer,* ATTACKED
Zed Nelson, *Free-lancer,* ATTACKED
Unidentified Interpreter, ATTACKED

Canadian free-lance journalist Brule and British photographer Nelson were shot at while taking photographs of government militias in Kabul's Microrayon district, near the front line between three of Afghanistan's warring Islamic factions. Brule was hit in both arms, and his Afghan interpreter was shot in the neck. Nelson was not injured. Brule was on assignment for the Brtish magazine *Sky* and the German magazine *Focus*, for an article about the French medical aid group, Medecins Sans Frontières (MSF). All three were travelling in a car marked as an MSF vehicle. It was not known with certainty who was responsible for the attack. However, Brule said the shots appeared to have been fired from the direction of territory controlled by Uzbek warlord Abdul Rashid Dostam.

Bangladesh

Avowedly secular journalists came under fire during 1994 from both religious extremists and the government of Prime Minister Begum Khaleda Zia. Although unlikely candidates for mass appeal because of their pro-Pakistan stance during the 1971 war for independence, radical Islamic parties were assiduously courted by Zia in a bid to regain her parliamentary majority. Nongovernmental organizations (NGOs) working in rural areas were a particular target of fundamentalist ire, frequently earning religious injunctions for their grassroots development work with village women. Copies of the daily newspaper *Janakantha*, which has been outspoken in criticizing extremist clerics and supporting the work of rural NGOs, were burned en masse in various parts of the country in May. And in early June, the paper's Dhaka offices were attacked following a rally at a leading mosque. Rather than grant police protection to the newspaper, however, the government capitulated to fundamentalist political pressure and charged four of its editors with insulting Islam and the religious sensibilities of Muslims in violation of the country's civil code. The same charges were leveled against the popular feminist novelist and newspaper columnist Taslima Nasreen, after she allegedly advocated revising the Koran in an interview with Calcutta's *Statesman* newspaper. Nasreen was forced into hiding, but eventually found asylum in Sweden. The four editors of *Janakantha* were jailed, and then released on bail. At year's end, charges were still pending in each case.

April 21
Motiur Rahman Chowdhury, *Bangla Bazar Patrika*, LEGAL ACTION, IMPRISONED
Zakaria Khan, *Bangla Bazar Patrika*, LEGAL ACTION
Chowdhury, the editor of Bengali-language

May 1
Maria Korolov, *Free-lancer*, IMPRISONED
Korolov, an American free lance correspondent on assignment for Britain's Sky TV, was detained for several days in Kunduz by government forces. Korolov had entered northeastern Afghanistan in late April from Tajikistan's Gorno-Badakhshan region to report on Tajik refugees and opposition figures living in Afghanistan. Jamiat-e-Islami militiamen detained her as she was leaving a Tajik refugee camp near Kunduz. Korolov, who did not have a visa from the Afghan government, was held for several days in a walled compound. The local Jamiat-e-Islami commander authorized Korolov's release upon being notified that she was in his forces' custody, and apologized for her detention. Korolov was turned over unharmed to Red Cross authorities in Kabul on May 7.

July 29
Mirwais Jalil, *BBC World Service*, KILLED
Jalil, a 25-year-old reporter for the Pashto and Persian-language sections of the BBC World Service, was kidnapped and murdered while returning from an interview with renegade Prime Minister Gulbuddin Hekmatyar at the latter's base in Charasyab, south of Kabul. Five masked militiamen stopped Jalil's taxi and abducted him at gunpoint. The assailants released the taxi driver and an Italian journalist who was traveling with Jalil. Jalil's body was discovered the following morning in Chelsitoon, on the outskirts of Kabul. He had been shot at least 20 times in the head and chest. Jalil had received threats during the year from several of Afghanistan's warring mujahideen factions. He had aggressively covered the country's internecine civil war for the BBC, and his reports were widely recognized as authoritative in Afghanistan. CPJ condemned the murder and requested an independent investigation by a team of international observers.

Asia

daily *Bangla Bazar Patrika*, was arrested at his office by police and charged with defaming a top government envoy in an April 10 article. The defamation case was filed by Morshed Khan, the chairman of a private bank who was recently appointed a special envoy of Prime Minister Begum Khaleda Zia. The article alleged that top financial officials, including Morshed Khan, had misappropriated thousands of dollars in funds. Zakaria Khan, the newspaper's publisher, went into hiding after a complaint was lodged against him. Police reportedly searched the newspaper's offices and Chowdhury's home, seizing several documents. On April 23, Chowdhury was released on bail. Khan, who had surrendered on April 22, was also released on bail.

June 3

Janakantha, ATTACKED

A rally after Friday prayers at Dhaka's Baitul Mukaram National Mosque was followed by a mass procession of up to 3,000 persons in which bricks were hurled at the offices of the daily newspaper *Janakantha*. The attack was preceded by demonstrations in late May in Bogura and Jamalpur against *Janakantha* and the daily *Bhorer Khagoj*. The BBC reported that copies of the two papers were burned at the demonstrations. *Janakantha*'s editors have openly criticized religious extremists for demanding the banning of nongovernmental organizations involved in women's development activities. CPJ called on the government of Bangladesh to grant *Janakantha* police protection.

June 4

Taslima Nasreen, *Writer*,

LEGAL ACTION, THREATENED

Dhaka's chief metropolitan magistrate issued a warrant for the arrest of Taslima Nasreen—a novelist and newspaper columnist—on charges of breaching section 295A of the Penal Code, which criminalizes "deliberate and malicious acts intended to outrage the religious feelings of any class of citizens by insulting its religion or religious beliefs." The charges stemmed from a

May 10 interview with Nasreen in *The States-man*, a Calcutta newspaper that quoted her as saying the Koran should be "thoroughly revised." Nasreen said the interviewer misquoted her, and that she had called for changes in Islamic or Shari'a law to ensure gender equality. Nasreen could be sentenced to up to two years of hard labor if found guilty of violating the statute. She spent two months in hiding after the government ordered her arrest and militant Islamic groups offered cash rewards of up to US$5,000 to anyone who killed her. CPJ urged the government to drop the criminal charges against Nasreen and to protect her from death threats made by fundamentalist groups. Nasreen fled to Sweden on Aug. 9, where she was granted asylum. On Jan. 10, 1995, the Bangladesh High Court rejected an appeal by Nasreen's lawyers to drop the charges and ordered a lower court to proceed with her trial.

June 8

Borhan Ahmed, *Janakantha*,

IMPRISONED, LEGAL ACTION

Toab Khan, *Janakantha*,

IMPRISONED, LEGAL ACTION

Mohammad Atiqullah Khan Masud, *Janakantha*,

IMPRISONED, LEGAL ACTION

Shamsuddin Ahmed, *Janakantha*,

IMPRISONED, LEGAL ACTION

Four editors of the Bengali-language newpaper *Janakantha* were arrested in early June, and charged by the government under section 295A of the Penal Code with deliberately insulting Islam and the religious sentiments of Muslims. The charges stemmed from a May 12 *Janakantha* editorial that said fundamentalist clerics had misled the public by distorting the meaning of a verse in the Koran. Executive Editor Borhan Ahmed and Advisory Editor Toab Khan were arrested June 8 and held at a high-security jail in Dhaka. The other editors charged under the act, Shamsuddin Ahmed and Atiqullah Khan Masud, went into hiding but surrendered a few days later. Each of the four editors was released on bail after spending about two weeks in jail.

Cambodia

The first full year under Cambodia's U.N.–brokered coalition government saw a severe testing of the country's newly emergent free press. The most alarming events were the assassinations of three journalists—Tou Chhom Mongkol, editor of *Antarakum,* Nun Chan, editor of *Samleng Yuvachun Khmer,* and Chan Dara, a reporter for *Koh Santepheap.* An army colonel was arrested and charged with Dara's murder—a good-faith effort by the government, and also a clear example of the danger Cambodian journalists face from the military. Beyond the arrest, however, there was little reason to laud the authorities. Tou Chhom Mongkol's death received only a cursory investigation—a disturbing development in light of a grenade attack on his newspaper's offices two and a half months earlier. And Nun Chan's case remained similarly unresolved. Moreover, the government often adopted a directly adversarial stance toward the press, twice jailing *Morning News* Editor Nguon Nonn, temporarily closing the newspaper *Sakol,* and frequently issuing warnings to the press. These developments threatened to undo the gains for press freedom under the United Nations' two-year transitional administration of Cambodia—a period marked by a remarkable proliferation of Khmer-language newspapers.

Much of the difficulty facing the press in 1994 stemmed from the fractious nature of the government and the highly partisan character of many newspapers. Investigations of threats or attacks on the media were easily compromised by their potential effect on the delicate balance of power. And unfortunately, the only legal remedies in sight for aggrieved parties were ones that stood to inhibit the growth of a truly independent press. At year's end, a revised draft of a press law—strongly opposed by local press and human rights groups—awaited debate and approval by the National Assembly. Key provisions criminalized the breach of national security—a term so broadly defined that most political reporting could fall within its reach—rendered the king inviolate, granted the government the power to shut down publications, and criminalized libel and "humiliation."

March 23
Nguon Nonn, *Dom Ning Pel Prek,* IMPRISONED
Nguon, editor of Phnom Penh's *Dom Ning Pel Prek* (Morning News), was arrested and charged with libel for stories alleging corruption by government officials. The articles accused Hok Long Dy, governor of Svay Rieng Province, and Yuth Phou Thang, deputy governor of Prey Veng province, of stealing and selling U.N. vehicles. Nguon had reportedly ignored several court summonses requesting him to account for the stories. He was released March 25.

March 24
Antarakum, ATTACKED
Two unidentified men hurled grenades into the office of the Khmer-language newspaper *Antarakum* (Intervention) in Phnom Penh. The explosion wounded five people, including two reporters. The biweekly had reportedly published articles accusing politicians and generals belonging to Prince Norodom Ranariddh's FUNCINPEC party and Second Prime Minister Hun Sen's Cambodian People's Party of involvement in crime and corruption.

May 16
Sokal, CENSORED
The Cambodian government banned the publication of *Sokal* (Universal) for publishing articles and cartoons criticizing King Norodom Sihanouk and his past ties with the Khmer Rouge. Police also seized about 17,000 copies of *Sokal* when they raided its offices. No one was arrested. The paper was charged with violating the constitution for having insulted King Sihanouk. In late May, the charges were dropped and *Sokal* was permitted to resume publishing.

Asia

June 10

Tou Chhom Mongkol, *Antarakum,* KILLED

Mongkol, editor in chief of the biweekly *Antarakum* (Intervention), died of a head injury June 11, a day after police found him lying unconscious on Monivong Boulevard in Phnom Penh. Mongkol was last seen by his staff members at 9 p.m., on June 10, leaving for his home on a motorcycle. In a "preliminary conclusion" following a hasty police investigation, authorities attributed his death to a traffic accident. According to local human rights workers, however, Mongkol's body bore no sign of lacerations, and his motorcycle was similarly unscathed. Prior to Mongkol's death, *Antarakum* had carried a number of articles charging individual government and military officials with corruption. It was also targeted in an unsolved March 24 grenade attack. CPJ requested the government to fully investigate the circumstances surrounding Mongkol's death on June 17, and asked that the findings be made public. On June 25, Information Minister Ieng Mouly reiterated the government's "preliminary" findings and said it was continuing to investigate the case—a claim that local human rights workers disputed.

July 8

Nguon Nonn, *Dom Ning Pel Prek,* IMPRISONED

Nguon, editor of *Dom Ning Pel Prek* (Morning News), was arrested for breaching national security laws after publishing articles linking several high-ranking government officials from the Cambodian People's Party to the failed July 2 military coup. The paper was also temporarily shut down. Those implicated in the plot to topple the government included Interior Minister Sar Kheng and president of the National Assembly, Chea Sim. The government said it found no evidence linking Kheng to the coup attempt, and arrested 14 Thais and several senior security officials. Nguon was released on Aug. 6 after serving one month in prison. As of October, the government had yet to dismiss all criminal charges against Nguon.

September 6

Nun Chan, *Samleng Yuvachun Khmer,* KILLED

Nun Chan, editor in chief of *Samleng Yuvachun Khmer* (Voice of Khmer Youth), was shot and killed by two unidentified gunmen on a motorcycle near Wat Phnom, in central Phnom Penh. The newspaper was reportedly critical of Second Prime Minister Hun Sen and the Cambodian People's Party (CPP), and had alleged government corruption. According to human rights workers in Phnom Penh the paper had recently printed articles accusing several generals of selling state property for personal gain. Nun had received several official warnings and anonymous death threats earlier in the year. CPJ denounced the murder and called for an investigation. On Sept. 10, King Norodom Sihanouk requested that the government conduct a public investigation into the killing.

October 30

Romain Franklin, *Libération,*
    LEGAL ACTION, THREATENED

Alain Lebas, *Libération,*
    LEGAL ACTION, THREATENED

Franklin and Lebas, Paris- and Bangkok-based reporters for the French daily *Libération*, were banned from entering Cambodia because of an Oct. 19 article, "Paris in the Cambodian Trap," which dealt with French policy in Cambodia, foreign military assistance to Phnom Penh and government corruption. It also referred to acts of cannibalism by Cambodian army troops. Prime Minister Prince Norodom Ranariddh threatened to file a government suit against *Libération* for slandering the Ministry of Defense and the Cambodian army.

December 8

Chan Dara, *Koh Santepheap,* KILLED

Dara, a reporter for the Khmer-language newspaper *Koh Santepheap* (Island of Peace), was fatally shot in the northeastern province of Kompong Cham, about 100 kilometers from Phnom Penh. According to local sources, gunmen ambushed Dara as he was leaving a restaurant. Two days earlier, Dara reportedly said local officials threatened him and warned him against writing for *Preap Norm Sar*, a recently launched opposition newspaper directed by a former *Koh Santepheap* staff member. Among the articles published in *Preap Norm Sar*'s first five issues were several implicating the province's governor in illegal logging operations, and the governor's son in a murder. Dara denied writing any articles for *Preap Norm Sar*. CPJ condemned the murder and called for a full investigation. On Dec. 11, Lt. Col. Sath Soeun, a high ranking army officer, was arrested and a day later charged with the murder.

China

China took a great leap backwards in 1994, doling out severe prison sentences to reporters in the Hong Kong press, cracking down on private publishers and distributors, and stepping up its vigilance over foreign correspondents. With social unrest growing in the cities and a power struggle looming ahead in the capital, the increased repression may well have been intended to remind observers—at home, in Hong Kong and overseas—of the regime's authority.

For Hong Kong journalists, in particular, the year's developments provided an alarming indication of what they are likely to face when China assumes sovereignty over the colony in 1997. Xi Yang, a mainland-born correspondent for the Hong Kong daily *Ming Pao*, was sentenced to 12 years in prison on March 28 for allegedly leaking state secrets—a reference to his reporting on changes in interest rates at the People's Bank of China, and plans to liquidate some of the bank's gold reserves. Xi's arrest sparked prolonged demonstrations in Hong Kong by his colleagues, as well as condemnations by CPJ and press freedom groups worldwide. In another closely monitored case, dissident journalist Gao Yu was sentenced to six years

in prison in early November for allegedly leaking state secrets—ironically, in an article published by the pro-China Hong Kong magazine *Monthly Mirror*. The vagueness of the state secrecy law, and the rather arbitrary manner in which the two journalists were singled out, led some observers to conclude that the regime's underlying goal was to heighten insecurity in Hong Kong over the acceptable boundaries of press freedom, and thereby stifle critical scrutiny of China's politics and economy.

On the home front, the government excluded independent publishers from the ambit of market reform. Amid directives that broadly indicted distributors of pornography and "reactionary" materials alike, Chinese authorities last October launched a massive raid on an underground publishing house in Beijing, seizing 4,000 books and journals and arresting 14 persons allegedly involved in the operation. Authorized publications were reined in as well, notably the legal newspaper *Fazhi Ribao*, which was censured in September for having published articles advocating an independent judiciary and increased monitoring of the government by the media.

Chen Ziming and Wang Juntao—publishers of the now-banned *Economics Weekly* and the so-called "Black Hands" of the 1989 democracy movement—were released early in the year, apparently as part of a bid to secure the United States' renewal of China's most-favored-nation (MFN) trading status. However, China did little else to encourage the Clinton administration's eventual delinking of MFN and human rights. Wei Jingsheng—China's most prominent dissident, released in September 1993 after 14 and a half years in prison—was rearrested on April 1, following official warnings for articles that he had published abroad and for his late February meeting with John Shattuck, U.S. assistant secretary of state for human rights and humanitarian affairs.

Foreign reporters were interrogated on several occasions during the spring for attempting to contact prominent dissidents, and a number were detained on the fifth anniversary of the Tiananmen Square massacre—which the reporters said was marked by a boosted security presence.

March 11
Nick Driver, *United Press International (UPI),* HARASSED
Matthew Forney, *Newsweek,* HARASSED
Driver and Forney, UPI and *Newsweek* correspondents, respectively, were detained by police while leaving dissident Liu Nianchun's home. They were interrogated separately about their relationship with Liu and his wife. Forney was released six hours later after he signed a statement acknowledging that he had intended to speak with Liu, and that he was not carrying a residence permit. Driver was told he had been detained for causing a traffic accident, failing to carry proper identification, and interviewing Liu without permission from local authorities. He was released when he signed a statement admitting he had violated local rules and promising not to report his conversations at Liu's home. Both reporters were prevented from making any phone calls during their detention—including a call to the U.S. Embassy requested by Forney. CPJ condemned the detentions and urged Chinese authorities to allow foreign journalists in China to pursue their work unhindered.

March 12
Caroline Straathof, *De Volkskrant,* HARASSED
Beijing police detained Straathof, a correspondent for the Dutch newspaper *De Volkskrant,* after she met with Chinese dissident Xin Hong. Straathof was attempting to contact dissident and labor activist Liu Nianchun, with Xin's help. She was released five hours later after a police interrogation. Police refused to let her speak with her husband, who had called during the interrogation. Xin was arrested March 12, and released the following day. CPJ protested

Straathof's detention on March 24 and urged the government to respect the rights of foreign journalists in the country.

March 13
Carrie Gracie, *BBC,* HARASSED
Gracie, a BBC reporter, was detained by police while leaving a party with several Chinese friends in western Beijing. Gracie and her friends were interrogated separately and released four hours later. Police forced her to sign a statement promising not to report her conversations at the party and admitting to having violated the law by not carrying her residence permit. None of the people attending the party were known to be dissidents. CPJ condemned Gracie's detention in a letter to the Chinese government.

March 28
Xi Yang, *Ming Pao,* IMPRISONED
Xi, a mainland-born Beijing correspondent for the Hong Kong daily *Ming Pao,* was sentenced to 12 years in prison for allegedly stealing and publishing state secrets. He is also to be denied political rights for two years after his jail term. The secrets, according to the official Xinhua News Agency, were unpublished interest rate adjustments and plans for international gold transactions by the People's Bank of China. Xi, who had published a series of reports on China's economy in *Ming Pao* in June and July of 1993, was arrested on Sept. 27 of that year and—barring one brief visit from his father—was held incommunicado pending his trial. Tian Ye, a bank official, was sentenced to 15 years for leaking the information to Xi. Xi had no legal representation during his closed trial, and officials did not disclose the court's decision to Xi's family or employers until four days after the ruling. In an April 5 letter to the Chinese government, CPJ condemned Xi's sentencing and demanded his unconditional release. The sentence also drew massive protest demonstrations by journalists in Hong Kong. Subsequently, on April 13, Xinhua issued a lengthy statement of the

case against Xi—an extremely rare development in political trials. It indicated, however, that the regime had no intention of yielding on the matter; the following day, Xi's sentence was upheld on appeal by the Beijing Higher People's Court.

March 31
Chen Ji, *Beijing Youth News,* CENSORED
Chen, editor in chief of the *Beijing Youth News,* was fired from his job for allegedly having "independent views." Chen, who was editor for six years, had published articles on previously taboo subjects such as worker disputes, murder and rape cases, criminal trials and political corruption. The newspaper's colorful layout attracted a wide audience. Vice Minister Xu Weicheng of the Communist Party Central Propaganda Department said newspapers must step up the battle against "extreme individualism." Xiao Pei, a conservative official, replaced Chen as chief editor.

April 1
Wei Jingsheng, *Tansuo,*
HARASSED, IMPRISONED
Wei, a prominent dissident and former co-editor of the pro-democracy journal *Tansuo* (Explorations), was arrested while trying to re-enter Beijing from a forced exile in Tianjin. His arrest is believed to stem in part from a Feb. 27 meeting with John Shattuck, U.S. assistant secretary of state for human rights. Wei reportedly asked that the United States continue to exercise economic leverage as a means of pressuring China to release political prisoners and improve its human rights record. He had been released on parole Sept. 14, 1993, after serving 14 and a half years of a 15-year prison sentence. In March, several days before U.S. Secretary of State Warren Christopher's visit to China, police detained Wei for 30 hours, for alleged violations of his parole terms. Earlier in the year, Wei received several warnings for contributing an essay to the Op-Ed page of the *New York Times,* giving interviews to foreign journalists and signing a contract to write his prison memoir.

April 2
Lena Sun, *Washington Post,* HARASSED
Sun, Beijing correspondent for the *Washington Post,* was detained for two hours by Chinese police for taking photographs in a public cemetery in Peking, where some of the victims of the 1989 Tiananmen Square massacre were buried. Sun was questioned by six security officials about the photographs and was told she needed advance permission to visit the cemetery. Police officers said Sun had not "gone through the necessary procedures" for taking photos in the Wan An graveyard.

April 4
The Express, HARASSED
Two journalists from *The Express,* a Chinese-language daily in Hong Kong, were harassed by police for carrying a book about the culture and politics of Wenzhou that was marked for "internal circulation." Police confiscated the book, medical documents and other printed materials after they searched the journalists' hotel room in Wenzhou, Zhejiang province. The journalists, who do not want to be identified, were on assignment in Wenzhou to cover a Hong Kong medical team performing voluntary work in the region. They reportedly purchased the book from a local bookstore and obtained the medical documents with the city hospital's consent. According to local media sources, police accused them of violating China's State Secrets Law.

April 4
Ricky Lee, *China Television (CTV),* CENSORED
Taiwanese television reporter Lee was detained for two hours while reporting on the murder of 24 Taiwanese tourists on board a ferry on Zhejiang province's Qiandiao Lake. Security officers told Lee that his coverage was not legal, and asked him to delete his videotape. According to press reports, journalists were denied access to the crime scene. The tourists were apparently robbed, and then burned to death in the ferry's lower cabin during the March 31 incident. After protests by Taiwan's National

Press Council, 40 Taiwanese reporters were allowed to cover the May 10 trial of the four criminal defendants in the case.

April 7
Xu Wenli, IMPRISONED

Xu, leader of the 1978-79 democracy movement, was on parole from prison when he was rearrested for allegedly violating his parole terms, which precluded him from giving interviews to foreign journalists or writing articles for publication abroad. He was released after five days of detention and police interrogation. He had been released on parole in May 1993 after serving 12 years of a 15-year prison sentence for "counterrevolutionary crimes." Xu had helped edit an underground journal during the Democracy Wall movement in the late 1970s. Police continued to guard Xu's apartment after his release and barred foreign journalists from entering the premises or interviewing him.

April 8
Geoffrey Crothall, *South China Morning Post,* HARASSED
Barbara Alighiero, *ANSA (Italy),* HARASSED
David Schlesinger, *Reuters,* HARASSED
Henrik Bork, *Frankfurter Rundshau,* HARASSED
Andreas Landwehr, *DPA (Germany),* HARASSED

Crothall, Alighiero, Schlesinger, Bork and Landwehr were detained and questioned by police when they tried to visit Kang Tong, wife of dissident Xu Wenli, at her home in Beijing. About a dozen policemen stopped the five journalists as they arrived at Kang's home and briefly confiscated their press passes. The reporters were released within an hour.

May
Jingpin, CENSORED

Beijing stopped the publication of *Jingpin* (Elite), a liberal Chinese-language monthly journal, by refusing to grant it an official registration number to publish its third edition. The two previous editions were published using a temporary registration number. Local media sources said the authorities' refusal reflected a nationwide effort to control the number of registration permits granted to new publications, particularly magazines that publish articles critical of the government and the Communist Party. Jingpin was launched in late 1993 in Beijing, and its editors and contributors include former *People's Daily* Editor Qin Chuan, former Culture Minister Wang Meng, and liberal economist Yu Guangyuan. Officials were reportedly concerned that *Jingpin's* "liberal" writers would support the underground dissident movement.

May 11
12 Hong Kong journalists, HARASSED

China's Hong Kong and Macao Affairs Office banned 12 Hong Kong business journalists from covering an international securities conference in Beijing. Officials stated that reporters who were not fully accredited through the Xinhua News Agency were "unwelcome guests." The journalists were invited by the China Securities and Regulatory Commission to attend the symposium, but Chinese officials later claimed that foreign journalists had not been formally invited to report on the event. In response, Hong Kong press agencies and publications recalled their reporters.

May 17
Lucky Severson, *NBC*, HARASSED
Crew members, *NBC*, HARASSED

Reporter Lucky Severson and four NBC crew members were detained for two hours by police after they interviewed prominent Chinese dissident Wang Dan in Beijing. Police reportedly raided Wang's home during the interview and asked the journalists for proof that they had been granted official permission to carry out the interview. When they failed to produce any authorization documents, the journalists were taken to a police station, where the their passports, press cards and videotapes were temporarily confiscated. Wang was held for an hour

—continued on p. 123

Endangered Species:
Press Freedom in Hong Kong

by Daisy Li Yuet-wah

LET ME START OFF with a story about a truly "endangered species"—the rhinoceros. The story was written by the late avant-garde playwright Eugene Ionesco. I was introduced to his masterpiece, "Rhinoceros," by a good friend of mine who is a very experienced journalist.

Ionesco's story tells about a man who becomes disturbed and frightened when the people around him turn into rhinos. Initially, only a few people suffer the transformation, but gradually his friends, neighbors and colleagues—even his girlfriend—join up with the rhinos, and he is left alone.

At first, people are opposed to the idea of turning into rhinoceroses, and regard it as a disgrace to the human soul. But as more and more people change, the idea is no longer absurd and unacceptable. Rhinos become good-looking and their voices take on a musical tone. Even those initially horrified by the idea join the trend, voluntarily or reluctantly. Their last words as humans are: "We must move with the times."

Although the work was written in the late 1950s by a European playwright, there are parallels with Hong Kong today and the fate of press freedom in the territory. As 1997 approaches, pressures are growing for the journalistic profession to transform, to fit in with the new system under Chinese sovereignty.

The press freedom report card in Hong Kong has not been encouraging over the past year, and journalists are now in a much more precarious position than a few months ago. But in recent weeks, the issue of press freedom has been pushed to the forefront of the Sino-British political dispute. The latest politicization of journalists' difficulties was prompted by the remarks made by Hong Kong's Chief Secretary, Anson Chan, when she was speaking at a

Daisy Li Yuet-wah *is the vice chair of the Hong Kong Journalists Association's executive committee. This article was originally delivered as the 1994 Harry W. Anderson Lecture at the National Press Club in Washington, D.C. It is reprinted with permission from the World Press Freedom Committee.*

U.S.-Hong Kong business seminar in New York on Oct. 18, 1994.

Answering a question from the floor, Mrs. Chan echoed the concerns of journalists that in recent years there had been a tendency on the part of some sections of the media to exercise self-censorship. She further reiterated that the Hong Kong government was committed to removing those laws that inhibited press freedom.

To those who have been campaigning for several years to repeal those draconian measures, Mrs. Chan's remarks sounded hollow. They also drew immediate criticism from a Chinese official based in Hong Kong with the New China (Xinhua) News Agency, Beijing's de facto embassy in the territory. Without naming Mrs. Chan, the agency's propaganda chief, Sun Nansheng, accused senior Hong Kong government officials of misleading outsiders into believing Hong Kong would not have press freedom after 1997.

Mr. Sun questioned the motives of those who "exaggerated" the issue, and implied that Hong Kong government officials wanted to incite anti-Beijing feelings and stir up mistrust over the principle of "one country, two systems," under which Hong Kong is meant to retain its separate identity after 1997.

Mr. Sun further warned that if the government wanted to amend laws to create trouble for the post-1997 administration, its plan would fail because the future legislature would repeal any such law.

Self-censorship was a form of social responsibility and a manifestation of journalistic ethics, Mr. Sun said, adding that news executives had the freedom to decide which articles should be included in a publication and which should not.

Two days later, the Communist Party newspaper in Hong Kong, *Wen Wei Po*, in an editorial, linked the remarks of the Chief Secretary with the work of the Hong Kong Journalists Association (HKJA). The editorial alleged that the publication of the Association's 1994 Annual Report on Freedom of Expression in Hong Kong was intended to provide a base for the British administration to use "defending press freedom" as an excuse to change laws before the change of sovereignty. It further alleged that the report was written under the orders of the British administration by two or three people who worked for pro-British media organizations in Hong Kong.

Both the New China News Agency propaganda chief and the editorial writer for *Wen Wei Po* tried to rationalize self-censorship as responsible media behavior. To them, any resistance to self-censorship would be regarded as a lack of responsibility to readers, society and professional ethics.

The HKJA strongly rejects these assertions. Perhaps the best way to explain the problems facing Hong Kong journalists is to describe some of the events of the past year.

The first incident was the arrest and jailing of my colleague, Xi Yang. The 12-year sentence imposed on him not only shocked the journalistic community in Hong Kong, it also cast a long shadow over press freedom in the run-up to 1997 and beyond.

Hong Kong journalists were deeply disturbed when Xi, a correspondent for *Ming Pao*, was detained in Beijing on Sept. 27, 1993. His formal arrest was announced on Oct. 7, along with that of Tian Ye, a deputy director of the foreign affairs department of the People's Bank of China.

Both Xi and Tian were charged under the provisions of the State Security Law. Xi was accused of "spying and stealing state financial secrets," and Tian of passing on the information to Xi. According to the official New China News Agency, the information included unpublished interest rate changes and the bank's plans for international gold transactions.

The agency said, without elaboration, that the theft of this information had "caused serious consequences" and that both Xi and Tian had "candidly confessed" to the charges leveled against them.

The journalistic profession was disturbed not only by the seriousness of the charges, but also by the way the Chinese authorities handled the case. The HKJA and many leading advocates of freedom of expression—among them the International Federation of Journalists, the Committee to Protect Journalists, Article 19 and the World Press Freedom Committee—called on the Chinese authorities to substantiate the charges against Xi and ensure that he would be tried in an open and fair manner.

Despite these calls, no further details of his charges were disclosed, and Xi was held incommunicado for six months after his arrest. He was denied access to legal representation and to his employer, and allowed to see his father only once.

Xi was tried in camera by the Beijing People's Intermediate Court on March 28, 1994. He was sentenced to 12 years in prison, and he will be further deprived of his political rights, which include public speaking, for two years after that. The ruling reached Xi's family verbally four days after the sentencing, in the early morning of April Fool's Day, and the court refused to confirm the ruling publicly until April 4. The written judgment has never been made public, which itself is a violation of China's Criminal Proceedings Law.

Two Chinese lawyers had the courage to take on Xi's case on appeal. They argued for his innocence on the grounds that there was inadequate evidence, a lack of clarity in the facts and improper application of the law when the intermediate court reached its verdict. They argued that Xi had not committed what the law defined as stealing, nor did he consciously try to "spy" on state secrets.

It came as no surprise, however, when the Beijing Supreme Court upheld the original verdict. The harsh sentence provoked an unprecedented reaction from the journalistic profession and the community at large. Hundreds of journalists joined a spontaneous march to the New China News Agency headquarters, and 1,300 of them—some from Taiwan—signed a petition letter to the Chinese leadership, protesting the conviction and heavy sentence. The general public also reacted strongly, with more than 2,000 people taking part in a march after Xi's appeal was rejected.

To people in Hong Kong, Xi's case is not only about justice. It also has wider implications for the future of press freedom in Hong Kong, which is regarded as one of the cornerstones for the territory's success.

The underlying message is clear—Hong Kong journalists should not cross the line of what is and is not permissible in the eyes of the Chinese authorities. Yet the danger is that one can never tell for sure where that line is drawn. Together with the ambiguities involved in Chinese law, the Beijing authorities tend to interpret their laws freely to suit a particular political need.

This worry is not unfounded or exaggerated. Take, for example, Hong Kong's post-1997 constitution, the Basic Law. Article 23 of that document stipulates that the post-1997 legislature must enact laws to prohibit any act of treason, secession, sedition or subversion against the Central People's Government, or theft of state secrets. With the final interpretation of this part of the Basic Law lying firmly in the hands of the Standing Committee of China's National People's Congress—which is not known for its political flexibility—post-1997 press freedom is in serious doubt.

Another incident of serious concern to Hong Kong journalists is the arrest in Beijing of Gao Yu, a mainland journalist who has contributed articles to a pro-China magazine in Hong Kong. Gao was detained on Oct. 2, 1993, two days before her scheduled departure for Hong Kong. She was due to travel on to the United States to take up a fellowship at Columbia University's Graduate School of Journalism.

She was subsequently charged with revealing state secrets to people outside mainland China. Like Xi, Gao was kept incommunicado. She was tried in camera in April this year, but the Beijing Intermediate Court returned the case to the prosecutor for more evidence. [*Editor's note:* In November 1994, Gao was sentenced to six years in prison. Her lawyers were never informed that she was being brought to trial.]

Gao was the deputy editor of the now defunct *Economics Weekly*, which was run by Wang Juntao, a famous dissident who was sentenced to 13 years in jail following the crushing of the 1989 pro-democracy movement. Wang was released early in 1994, apparently as part of China's efforts to secure American renewal of its most-favored-nation trading status. He is, of course, now in the United States.

Many people see Gao's case as an example of China's "revolving door" system: When one prominent dissident is released, another is detained. This ensures that there is another victim for the next round of trade concessions. To journalists in Hong Kong, Gao has become another victim of the ambiguous nature of Chinese law, in this case on state secrets.

WHILE THE DETENTION and arrest of journalists is a visible threat to press freedom in Hong Kong, an even more disturbing and invisible threat is that of self-censorship.

A 1990 survey conducted by the Chinese University of Hong Kong asked journalists about their attitude towards self-censorship. It found that 23 percent of some 500 respondents were apprehensive about criticizing the Chinese government. Roughly 55 percent said they were not. The HKJA is now in the process of finding out whether this trend has worsened.

There is no doubt that acts of self-censorship are difficult to substantiate with hard evidence. However, we recorded the largest number of documented cases over the past year. Let me cite a few examples.

• The leading television station in Hong Kong, TVB, refused to air two BBC documentaries on China, even though it had the rights to do so. The reluctance of TVB to air these programs— "Chairman Mao, The Last Emperor" and "The Laogai," which reports on Chinese labor camps—was clearly aimed at avoiding embarrassment for China, which had in particular attacked the Mao documentary on the grounds that it had "seriously hurt the feelings of the Chinese people."

• The management of the territory's other terrestrial broadcaster, ATV, intervened in an editorial decision to broadcast parts of a Spanish documentary on the Beijing massacre in June 1989 to mark the fifth anniversary of the crushing of the pro-democracy movement. Management backed down and aired segments of the documentary after six senior journalists from the station's News and Public Affairs Department made a public protest. But the journalists eventually decided to resign, citing a loss of confidence in management.

• In April 1994, Rupert Murdoch's satellite broadcasting station, Star TV, dropped BBC World Service Television from its northern beam, which covers China and Hong Kong. Mr. Murdoch subsequently admitted in an interview that he had dropped the BBC in the hope of easing tensions with China. He also admitted in the same interview that the sale of his shares in a major Hong Kong newspaper group, the *South China Morning Post*, was likewise aimed at avoiding conflict with China.

Although these examples all relate to the broadcast media, it does not mean that the print media are immune from self-censorship. It merely indicates that self-censorship in the print media is more discreet and difficult to prove.

Self-censorship highlights another problem: the desire of media proprietors to maintain good relations with Beijing, or at least not to be seen as anti-Beijing. The desire to seek business opportunities in China is a major factor in this trend. So much about the future sovereign state.

LET US NOW TURN to the record of the present administration. The Hong Kong government has recently put forward a bill to strengthen the protection of all endangered species covered in international covenants. However, for press freedom, another "endangered species," greater protection has yet to materialize.

Although Hong Kong enjoys a relatively high degree of press freedom, its foundation is very fragile. Our statute book contains numerous draconian laws that could suppress the media overnight, if used to the full.

In September 1992, we submitted to the Hong Kong government a list of 17 existing laws that could be used against the media. Topping the list are security-related laws, including the Official Secrets Act, the Emergency Regulations Ordinance—and its sub sidiary legislation, the Police Force Ordinance—the Crimes Ordinance, the Prevention of Bribery Ordinance and the Public Order Ordinance.

Those who attended the World Press Freedom Committee conference in Hong Kong in 1993 will probably recall the pledge made by the governor, Chris Patten, to review and amend suspect laws to secure the protection of press freedom in Hong Kong. Gov. Patten and senior government officials have restated this pledge many times. But one year later not a single law—I repeat, not a single law—has yet been changed.

We are deeply concerned about the continual slippage in this law-reform exercise, particularly the delay in bringing forward changes to security-related legislation.

It appears that the government may lack the political will to amend many of these suspect laws, either because of resistance from within the civil service or because of fear of an adverse reaction from China.

I should mention here that the government is now prepared to consider changes to some laws that it previously refused to touch, for example on criminal libel. There have also been indications that it will not oppose moves to scrap a political censorship provision in the Film Censorship Ordinance.

The reality, however, is that time is fast running out. There are only three legislative sessions left before the handover in 1997, and possibly only two, if the final one is devoted to transitional matters.

To make the situation worse, the Independent Commission Against Corruption recently charged three senior journalists from the *Ming Pao* newspaper—again my colleagues—for violating a provision in the Prevention of Bribery Ordinance, which bars the disclosure of anti-corruption investigations without lawful authority or reasonable excuse before an arrest is made.

The only "crime" committed by the *"Ming Pao* Three" was to report that the Independent Commission Against Corruption was investigating a controversial land auction. They did not name names, nor did they provide any details of the investigation, apart from the fact that the probe was taking place.

This case sets a very bad example for the future government. It also clearly demonstrates that if a particular power exists, then the government—however tolerant it may be—may use it against the media. It goes without saying that the HKJA is lobbying vigorously for the repeal of the relevant provision used against the *"Ming Pao* Three."

There is a clear and urgent need to bring forward meaningful changes to suspect laws in the very near future to ensure that the law-reform process can be completed well before 1997. The British government cannot shake off its moral responsibility if the future administration uses existing powers to gag the press after 1997. It is now time for Gov. Patten, as the last governor of the colonial government, to demonstrate his commitment to the people of Hong Kong.

But what do the people of Hong Kong think? The HKJA and Radio Television Hong Kong are sponsoring a series of public opinion surveys to monitor media performance and freedom of speech in Hong Kong in the run-up to 1997. The first survey was conducted in June 1994. Of the 538 respondents surveyed, 46 percent felt that press freedom had increased over the past three years, while 31 percent felt it had decreased. Their views on the future, on the other hand, were bleak. Sixty percent thought there would be a decline in press freedom in the coming three years, while only 11 percent thought there would be an increase.

To many people, Hong Kong is an oasis of press freedom in the region. We do not want this oasis to turn into a mirage, which will disappear as 1997 approaches. Press freedom in Hong Kong may be an endangered species, but it is never too late to preserve and protect it from extinction.

At the end of Ionesco's play, the main character says, "Now I will never become a rhinoceros.... I'll put up a fight against the lot of them, the whole lot of them! I'm the last man left, and I'm staying that way until the end. I'm not capitulating."

Fortunately, I am not the only one left. There are still many journalists in Hong Kong fighting this battle for press freedom with the support of the public and the international community.

—continued from p. 114

and interrogated about the journalists and the interview. Following their release, Wang and Severson separately stated that the interview had dealt with human rights and the U.S. renewal of China's most-favored-nation trading status.

May 27

Kwon Heung-Soon, *Munhwa Broadcasting Company (MBC),* EXPELLED

Crew Members, *MBC,* EXPELLED

Kwon, a television correspondent for the South Korea-based MBC, was expelled from China for reporting in the country without government permission. The journalist had come to Jiangsu in Nanjing province with a camera operator and audio technician to cover a May 30 ceremony inaugurating Nanjing as sister-city to Taejon, South Korea. Chinese officials said Kwon had not reported his travel plans to the city and had failed to secure permission to cover the Nanjing celebration. The MBC crew members were stripped of their visas and sent back to Seoul. According to sources at MBC, the crew had legally entered China on May 21 to cover South Korean investment in Yantai, Shandong province, but had not notified Chinese officials when they changed their travel itinerary and flew from Yantai to Jiangsu.

May 31

Kathy Chen, *Wall Street Journal,* HARASSED

Chen, a *Wall Street Journal* correspondent, was stopped at Beijing University's campus and detained by security officials for over four hours after she interviewed Chinese students at the university without registering at the campus gate. Police accused Chen of violating local regulations and she was forced to apologize for the incident. CPJ protested Chen's detention in a June 3 letter to the Chinese government.

June 2

CNN, CENSORED

Chinese police suspended CNN transmissions into hotels in Beijing for five days. Officers sent a fax to hotels ordering them to switch off CNN transmission a day before the June 3-4 anniversary of the Tiananmen Square massacre. A local hotel manager, quoted in a Reuters report, said he received a follow-up call notifying him that CNN transmissions would not be allowed to resume until June 6. CNN is transmitted via satellite into rooms at the capital's major hotels. CPJ denounced the government's action and urged it to lift the ban placed on CNN news coverage in China.

June 3

James Hattori, *CBS,* HARASSED

Joan Gilbertson, *CBS,* HARASSED

Brad Simpson, *CBS,* HARASSED

CBS, HARASSED

Police detained a CBS news crew while they were filming in Tiananmen Square. CBS correspondent James Hattori, producer Joan Gilbertson, cameraman Brad Simpson and a Chinese staff member were taken to a local police station, where they were questioned for two hours. They were released only after they agreed to sign a statement apologizing for breaking local rules, including filming a police officer without permission. Later that day, Chinese television officials informed CBS that because of alleged personnel shortages, they would be unable to feed a CBS transmission from Beijing until the next morning—a development that effectively barred any coverage from Beijing on the network's evening news broadcast. Police confiscated the crew's videotape. The crew said the officer they filmed was a plainclothes policeman, and that they had been unaware of his identity. CPJ criticized the detention of the CBS crew and urged the government to respect the rights of foreign journalists to report in China.

June 4

Nick Driver, *United Press International (UPI),* ATTACKED, HARASSED

Driver, the UPI Beijing bureau chief, was assaulted and then detained for about four hours by police for allegedly causing a "traffic acci-

Asia

dent" in the university district of northwest Beijing. Five undercover police officers in a car and motorcycle reportedly followed Driver from his home. In a suspicious accident, the motorcyle collided with Driver's car as he was making a right turn. After the collision, the officers punched him and dragged him from his car, and traffic police then detained him for allegedly causing the accident. In March, Driver had been detained for six hours for visiting the home of a Chinese dissident, during a visit to China by U.S. Secretary of State Warren Christopher.

July 6
Hong Kong journalists, THREATENED
Ma Cheng-kun, *Eastern Express,* THREATENED
During an informal gathering of reporters for the Lizhi Festival in Shenzhen, Huang Xinhua, deputy director of the city's propaganda department, declared that Hong Kong journalists should "be wise" and "act in line with the circumstances." He then turned to a reporter for Hong Kong's *Tung Fang Jih Pao* (Oriental Daily News), and asked him to tell Ma Cheng-kun, owner of the Hong Kong-based *Eastern Express*, to "watch out." Shortly after the incident, Shenzhen city officials apologized for the remarks, saying they were Huang's personal views and did not represent the Chinese government's position.

September
Fazhi Ribao, THREATENED
Communist Party officials warned the Chinese daily *Fazhi Ribao* (Legal Daily) not to continue publishing articles calling for an independent judiciary and asking the media to play a bigger role in supervising the government. The paper had reportedly stated that there was a need for new legislation to protect the media from lawsuits and censorship. Central Propaganda Department head Ding Guangen and other officials demanded that the journalists who wrote the commentaries practice "self-criticism" and said the articles contained "wrong opinions, strong bias and bad influence."

October
Tian Qi, CENSORED
Yu Yan, CENSORED
Lian Yinze, CENSORED
Hu Shuwei, CENSORED
Beijing police raided an underground publishing house in the Yuetan District and seized about 4,000 copies of books and journals, which were banned by the government. Police claimed that of the nine types of publications seized, five were "reactionary" materials, and many of the books contained "defamatory" phrases about state leaders and the Communist Party. Police arrested 14 people believed to be involved in the publication and distribution of the materials, including Qi, Yan, Yinze and Shuwei.

October 5
Hu Jiwei, HARASSED
Hu, a dissident and former editor of the *People's Daily*, was banned from attending the inauguration of a journalism awards foundation in Taiwan on the grounds of "poor" relations between Beijing and Taipei. Beijing officials rejected Hu's application to attend the Oct. 15 event. Hu was to serve on the foundation's panel of judges, which included journalists and scholars from China, Taiwan and Hong Kong. Several news reports said the ban on Hu was imposed because of a series of articles he wrote criticizing press freedom in China shortly after his return from the United States. Hu, a former member of the National People's Congress Standing Committee, had been removed as the *Daily*'s editor due to his involvement in the 1989 pro-democracy movement.

Early November
Gao Yu, IMPRISONED
Dissident journalist Gao, the former deputy chief editor of the defunct *Economics Weekly*, was sentenced to six years in prison for "leaking state secrets." Gao's lawyers had not been informed that the journalist was being brought to trial. She had been held incommunicado by state security officials since her detention on

Oct. 2, 1993, just two days before she was to depart for the United States to start a one-year research fellowship at Columbia University's Graduate School of Journalism. Gao was initially tried on April 20, at which time the court held that evidence against her was insufficient. Instead of acquitting her, however, the court ordered the prosecutor's office to find additional evidence for its case. According to court papers obtained by Reuters, Gao was charged with having obtained classified documents about China's structural reforms from Gao Chao, a Communist Party official and a former university acquaintance. She allegedly used the information therein for political and economic stories published in the *Mirror Monthly*, a pro-Beijing Chinese-language magazine in Hong Kong. Gao Chao was given a 13-year prison term for accepting bribes and providing state secrets to Gao and others. Gao was jailed for 14 months following the June 1989 Tiananmen Square demonstrations and released in August 1990, after showing symptoms of a heart condition.

November 15
Ming Pao, CENSORED
The China Press and Publications Administration announced measures to curtail the distribution and sale of the Hong Kong daily *Ming Pao* in China. Officials said they would no longer process requests to subscribe to the newspaper because of the allegedly "negative" effect of the daily's "strong political leanings in recent reports."

India

Press freedom in India in 1994 increasingly came to reflect the social and economic diversity of the country itself. Despite incidents such as the July 1 beating of two reporters for *The Statesman* by aides to the Punjab police chief, the English-language print media—serving elites in the major

cities—were largely unfettered by government censorship or violent assaults on their reporters. The rest of the press, however, had to operate under markedly different conditions. This was not so much a reflection of official policy as an apparent desire by regional and local politicians to shape coverage in what is often the only print media accessible to their constituents. The most egregious example came in November, when the elected leader of India's most populous state exhorted his followers to attack the state's two leading Hindi-language dailies. In the wake of his call, hawkers for the two papers were assaulted in several areas, and thousands of copies of the papers were burned.

Elsewhere in the country, regionally powerful political parties brazenly carried out similar tactics. In the western town of Aurangabad, reporters for an Urdu-language newspaper were assaulted at a press conference held by Bal Thackeray, leader of the Hindu nationalist Shiv Sena Party; the two papers had offended Thackeray by reporting that a Shiv Sena rally in the area had been poorly attended. Perhaps the most disturbing element of these attacks—which were widely reported by Indian newspapers—was the Indian government's reluctance to press criminal charges against the offending parties.

Journalists in Kashmir continued to face censorship and intimidation by both the Indian Border Security Forces (BSF) and armed separatist movements. Kashmiri stringer Ghulam Mohammed Lone was assassinated in his home in late August, just days after he reported having received death threats from a local BSF commander for disclosing Indian troop movements in the area. Aggravating the danger to Kashmiri journalists was the increasingly fractious separatist movement, which was divided between groups favoring independence for the state and those advocating its union with Pakistan. In October and November, several separatist organizations ordered the closure of Kashmiri newspapers that had printed news—even in the form of advertisements—of their rivals' activities. Their demands prompted a temporary "strike" by all of the state's newspapers, and the closure of three publications.

Despite the tensions caused by the separatist movement, two unifying trends within the Indian press emerged during the year. The first of these was mounting opposition to the Parliamentary Privilege Act, which permits members of parliament or state legislatures to sue newspapers for virtually any critical reporting about them. The second was the emergence of an open debate—in government and the national press—over the Terrorist and Disruptive Activities (Prevention) Act [TADA], under which journalists in Punjab, Assam and Kashmir have frequently been jailed for extended periods of time without charge.

January 11

Gurdip Singh, *Aaj di Awaz*, IMPRISONED
Jasbir Singh, *Aaj di Awaz*, IMPRISONED
Jasbir Singh Rode, *Aaj di Awaz*, IMPRISONED
Malkiat Singh, *Aaj di Awaz*, IMPRISONED
State police raided the offices of the Punjabi daily *Aaj di Awaz*, in Jullundur, and arrested four staff members as well as three other persons present. The detained staff members—managing editor Gurdip Singh, proofreader Jasbir Singh, managing trustee Jasbir Singh Rode, and receptionist Malkiat Singh—were charged with violating the Terrorist and Disruptive Activities (Prevention) Act (TADA). The charges stemmed from testimony by Nisar Ahmed, a Kashmiri separtist who had been in custody for two years, that allegedly implicated the daily as a meeting place and weapons storage site for Kashmiri militants. Indian officials had also reportedly warned Gurdip Singh 10 days earlier against printing "objectionable matter." All of the detainees were subsequently released on bail, with the exception of Gurdip Singh, who remained in custody at year's end.

February 19

Mustafa Alam, *Dainik Citizen*, ATTACKED
Eight other journalists, ATTACKED
Shiv Sena activists assaulted nine journalists during a press conference held by Sena leader Bal Thackeray in Aurangabad, Maharashtra. Thackeray ordered Alam, executive editor of *Dainik Citizen*, evicted from the conference because his paper had reported earlier that a Shiv Sena rally in the surrounding Marathwada region was poorly attended. As Alam and eight other journalists left the hotel where the conference was being held, they were attacked and beaten by members of the Hindu nationalist party. Two of the journalists were hospitalized. Thackeray issued a limited apology on Feb. 21, but did not extend it to Alam, who filed a criminal complaint the same day. Police subsequently registered a case against Thackeray, charging him with manhandling, deliberately humiliating, and insulting an individual. Thackeray was apprehended, but not arrested in connection with the charges. Journalists in Bombay and Aurangabad, meanwhile, called for a news blackout on the Shiv Sena pending an unconditional apology by its leader.

March 3

S. Arumughasamy, *Dinamalar*, ATTACKED
Arumughasamy, a reporter for the Tamil-languauge daily *Dinamalar*, was stripped and beaten by several men at a bus station in Kamuthi, near the city of Madurai. The attack reportedly stemmed from articles in *Dinamalar* that alleged corruption among local officials of Tamil Nadu's governing All-India Anna Dravida Munatra Kazhagam (AIADMK) party. Police arrested four AIADMK members on charges of assault.

April 22

Nikhil Wagle, *Mahanagar*, IMPRISONED
Wagle, editor of the Bombay daily *Mahanagar*, was jailed for four days after the Maharashtra Legislative Assembly found him guilty of breaching legislative privilege. The assembly

had passed a resolution on April 21 ordering Wagle's detention in connection with his March 1992 article in which he had accused several lawmakers of hypocrisy for paying tribute to the late Vithal Chavan, a Shiv Sena member of the legislative assembly. According to Wagle, Chavan had strong ties to the Bombay underworld and a criminal record of his own. Wagle had also written that other legislative assembly members had criminal ties as well. Under the Privilege Law—a vestige of the British colonial era—journalists can be summoned before a special committee of parliament or the state legislative assembly if legislators have accused them of defamation. Wagle, who had refused to appear before the committee, was released on April 26.

June 3
Far Eastern Economic Review, CENSORED
Indian customs seized copies of the June 2 issue of the *Far Eastern Economic Review* because the weekly magazine contained an "objectionable" photograph of Muslim separatists burning the Indian flag in Kashmir. Distributors were asked to black out the photographs.

June 23
Hind Samachar, THREATENED
Unidentified separatists ordered *Hind Samachar*, an Urdu-language Kashmiri daily, to cease distribution because of its anti-separatist editorial stance and publication of allegedly obscene pictures on the front page. Its Hindi-language sister publication, *Punjab Kesari*, was ordered closed in Srinagar on July 4 by the pro-Pakistan separatist group Jamiat-ul-Mojahedin. Both newspapers are published by The Hind Samachar, Ltd.

July 1
Abhijit Das, *Statesman,*
    ATTACKED, THREATENED
Rahul Banerjee, *Statesman,*
    ATTACKED, THREATENED
Statesman sports reporter Das and deputy sports

editor Banerjee were assaulted and abducted in retaliation for questions put to Punjab Police Chief K.P.S. Gill at a Delhi press conference. The two had asked Gill, recently elected chief of the Indian Hockey Federation, about his record of support for the sport and the last-minute withdrawal by his rival in the campaign for Gill's newly won post. Supporters of Gill assaulted both journalists, who were then forced into a vehicle by several armed men (reportedly Gill's personal guards), driven from the hotel and threatened with death. Das and Banerjee were released later that evening outside a Delhi police station. Following the assault, a local human rights group, the Lawyers' Forum for Civil Liberties, filed a writ petition against Gill and his guards in the New Delhi High Court. In a letter to the Indian government, CPJ called for an independent parliamentary investigation into the attack. The Indian Embassy replied two weeks later that Gill had personally apologized to *The Statesman* on July 8, and had accepted "moral responsibility" for the assaults. It also noted that the Delhi police were investigating the case, pursuant to a July 3 order by the Home Ministry.

July 5
Ajit Kumar Bhuyan, *Sadin,* IMPRISONED
Bhuyan, editor of the Assamese weekly *Sadin*, was arrested at his home in Guwahati and charged under the Terrorist and Disruptive Activities (Prevention) Act (TADA) for allegedly instigating the kidnapping of Hema Ram Keot, Assam state tax commissioner. He was hospitalized five days later for internal bleeding, high blood pressure and asthma following his interrogation. According to local human rights groups, Bhuyan was never questioned about the abduction but was interrogated about sources for articles he had published in May that alleged corruption on the part of state government officials, including Keot and the chief minister and his family. Bhuyan, who is also coordinator of Guwahati-based Human Rights Struggle Committee, was released on Sept. 25.

August 29

Ghulam Muhammad Lone, *Free-lance*, KILLED
A group of masked gunmen fatally shot Lone
and his seven-year-old son in their home in
Kangan, Kashmir. Lone, 35, was a newspaper
salesmen and a free-lance journalist for several
publications, including the English-language
Srinagar paper, *Greater Kashmir.* Several days
before the killing, Lone had allegedly received
death threats from an Indian security officer for
stories on troop movements in Kashmir. His
home was also searched. Before completing
their investigation into the slayings, Srinagar
police issued a statement charging Kashmiri
separatists with responsibility. CPJ condemned
the murders in an Aug. 31 letter to Indian
Prime Minister P.V. Narasimha Rao, and
requested a parliamentary investigation.

October-November

Dainik Jagran,
   HARASSED, ATTACKED, CENSORED
Amar Ujala,
   HARASSED, ATTACKED, CENSORED
Uttar Pradesh Chief Minister Mulyam Singh
Yadav called on his supporters to attack the
state's two leading Hindi dailies at the national
convention of the state's ruling Samajwadi Party
in mid-October. In the weeks following Yadav's
call, Samajwadi Party activists throughout the
state assaulted hawkers selling *Dainik Jagran*
and *Amar Ujala*, and burned thousands of
copies of the newspapers. Yadav also imposed a
ban on government advertisements in the two
dailies, denying them what is normally a principal source of revenue. Both *Dainik Jagran* and
Amar Ujala had strongly criticized Yadav's
recent crackdown on residents of the state's hill
districts, who were protesting a stepped-up
affirmative action policy and demanding state-
hood for their upper-caste-dominated region.
Yadav, who defended his call to attack the two
dailies as an offensive against an oppressive
social elite, draws his political support primarily
from lower-caste Hindus.

October-November

All Kashmiri newspapers,
   ATTACKED, THREATENED
Separatist groups fired shots outside the offices
of the *Daily Aftab* in Srinagar, Kashmir. Two
days later, the separatist group Hizbol Momi-
neem ordered *Aftab* shut after it printed an
advertisement for a meeting of the rival Shia
Association. These attacks and other threats
forced the Urdu-language daily to shut down
indefinitely. The *Srinagar Times* and the *Al-Safa
News* were also forced to close by separatist
groups. On Oct. 18, newspapers launched a
one-week strike protesting the threats and
attacks against journalists. On Nov. 7, however,
the Jammu and Kashmir Freedom Front issued
a statement accusing all Kashmiri newspapers of
pro-government views and "banning" their distribution in the Kashmir Valley. The same day
editors started a second strike. Then on Nov.
11, several militant organizations issued another
statement requesting all newspapers to resume
publication and vowing to uphold freedom of
the press. Newspapers began publishing again
on Nov. 13.

December 23

All India Radio, ATTACKED
A rocket was fired at the office complex of the
state-owned All India Radio in Srinagar, Kashmir. The rocket hit the building's upper story,
smashing windows and damaging the station's
roof. No one was injured in the attack, which is
believed to have been the work of Kashmiri
separatists.

Indonesia

**For Indonesian journalists, 1994 was the
year of living dangerously. Reversing a policy
of greater press freedom that had been in
effect during the previous two years, the
government in June revoked the publishing
licenses of three popular and distinctive**

weeklies—*Tempo, Detik* and *Editor.* The publications had carried dissenting commentaries, covered political scandals—including a controversial warship purchase—and reported on labor and ethnic unrest. The closures drew condemnation from CPJ and human rights groups worldwide, and prompted demonstrations throughout Indonesia that were brutally suppressed by security forces. The government also threatened to bring legal action against *Sinar* magazine and issued warnings to others, including the *Jakarta Post,* for publishing articles on the demonstrations. By year's end, the government had issued publishing licenses to two weeklies that it regarded as replacements for *Tempo* and *Editor. Gatra, Tempo's* "successor," is co-owned by President Suharto's crony Muhammad "Bob" Hassan, while *Pro Aktif Weekly,* composed largely of *Editor* staff members, is owned by Minister of Manpower Abdul Latif. As if to complete its media makeover, the government announced it would not issue any additional publishing licenses to newspapers or news magazines during 1995.

The one positive development during the year was the formation in August of the Alliance of Independent Journalists (AJI). Indonesia's only independent journalists association, AJI is explicitly committed to upholding press freedom and includes among its members a large number who had worked for the banned weeklies. Amid an increasingly repressive climate, AJI daringly took the offensive, producing a short book in the Bahasa Indonesia language about the bans and holding a press conference about media freedom during the November Asia-Pacific Economic Conference (APEC) in Jakarta. Its efforts quickly incurred the wrath of the state-sponsored Indonesian Journalists Association (PWI), which pressured leading editors to dismiss or marginalize reporters on their staffs who had joined AJI. With CPJ's encouragement, however, the International Federation of Journalists recognized AJI as its sole affiliate union in Indonesia—a development that will hopefully strengthen AJI's position at home.

While foreign journalists were officially free to cover the APEC summit, the open door policy was limited by the regime's acute sensitivity to media scrutiny of its rule in the former Portuguese colony of East Timor. Between mid-November and early December, 10 reporters attempting to cover protests on the third anniversary of a massacre in Dili, East Timor, were expelled from the island for not having the required work permits. Police also accused the foreign media of fueling the pro-independence demonstrations, which started on Nov. 12 and swept through East Timor for 10 days afterward.

June 21
Tempo, CENSORED
Detik, CENSORED
Editor, CENSORED
The Ministry of Information revoked the licenses of three leading Indonesian news weeklies that had reported extensively on government scandals and a controversial naval warship purchase. Prior to the bannings, all three publications had received several verbal and written warnings for "potentially" violating the government's code of conduct for journalists. *Tempo's* publishing license was revoked because its articles about political corruption were declared incompatible with a "healthy" and "responsible press"; the government also accused it of failing to adhere to national press guidelines and of disregarding prior government warnings. The magazine, briefly suspended in 1982, was criticized for covering labor unrest and a corruption scandal involving a Bapindo bank official. *Detik* was banned for reports on government corruption, and its editor was cited for license violations. Originally licensed in 1986 to publish crime news, the magazine relaunched itself in 1993 with daring reporting and commentary on

Asia

Indonesian politics and quickly became the country's largest circulation news weekly. In revoking *Editor*'s publishing permit, the Ministry of Information said the magazine was licensed to editors who were no longer on staff. Indonesian press sources said the government had refused to authorize the change in editorship in 1993. CPJ protested the closure of the weeklies and requested that the government rescind the ban. Two weeks later, the Indonesian Embassy in Washington reiterated the government's position in a letter to CPJ and said the publications had violated the code of conduct, and exercised their responsibility and freedom to operate in a questionable manner. On Oct. 7, *Tempo* founding editor Goenawan Mohamad and other employees filed two lawsuits against Information Minister Harmoko for banning the weekly.

June 27
Demonstrating Journalists,
ATTACKED, HARASSED
Soldiers and riot police wielding rattan clubs broke up a demonstration against the closure of *Tempo, Detik* and *Editor* by about 350 unarmed protestors outside the Department of Information in central Jakarta. The protestors included journalists, students and human rights activists. Several suffered broken bones and head injuries. About 60 people were arrested during the protests, and 20 were later fined or sentenced to up to five days in jail on charges of participating in an illegal demonstration. Journalists resumed protests on July 5—this time outside the Jakarta offices of the state-sponsored Indonesian Journalists Association (PWI)—calling for an end to the media ban.

July 27
Sinar, THREATENED
Kompas, THREATENED
Sinar Pagi, THREATENED
Jakarta Post, THREATENED
Indonesia Business Weekly, THREATENED
Ministry of Information officials threatened legal action against *Sinar* magazine and issued

verbal warnings to dailies *Kompas* and *Sinar Pagi* for publishing stories about demonstrations against the June 21 ban on *Tempo, Detik* and *Editor.* Subrata, director-general for press and graphics, issued a letter on July 27 criticizing Sinar for an editorial supporting Indonesians' right to demonstrate. Other publications, including the English-language daily *Jakarta Post* and *Indonesia Business Weekly* magazine, received warnings for covering the demonstrations and the unrest in East Timor.

September 13
Mitra Media, CENSORED
Mitra Media, a 12-page Indonesian-language newsletter, was banned by the Ministry of Information for allegedly lacking a license to publish. *Mitra Media*, which focuses on women's issues, is published by Yayasan Kalyanamitra, a leading women's rights non-governmental organization.

October 5
Syamsu Hadi, *Simponi*, CENSORED
The state-sponsored Indonesian Journalists Association (PWI) withdrew its endorsement of Hadi, the chief editor of *Simponi.* The weekly tabloid had been purchased and relaunched on Oct. 4 by the publishers of *Detik*, one of the three news weeklies banned by the government on June 21. For all Indonesian publications, PWI's support is vital to the granting of a publishing license. According to PWI, Hadi had employed journalists who were not PWI members for *Simponi*'s Oct. 4-10 issue. PWI, which recommended Hadi for the post in 1985, said he had failed to carry out the terms of the association's recommendation. On Oct. 7, *Simponi* reached a compromise with the government, agreeing not to publish until it met all official requirements. The tabloid agreed to resubmit names for a new editorial board and to formally reapply to publish.

October 8
Alliance of Independent Journalists (AJI),
HARASSED

The state-sponsored Indonesian Journalists Association (PWI) convened a meeting of Indonesia's leading news editors and demanded that they "reeducate" reporters on their staffs who had joined the Alliance of Independent Journalists (AJI). AJI—established Aug. 7 in Sirnagalih, West Java, as an alternative to PWI—had been described as "unjustified" by Information Minister Harmoko during a September parliamentary hearing. According to AJI, the PWI had also threatened to prevent AJI members from covering official events in the country, including the Nov. 15 Asia-Pacific Economic Conference (APEC) in Jakarta. On Oct. 11, CPJ urged President Clinton—who was attending the APEC summit—to support AJI's right to organize by requesting and ensuring equal access for AJI members to all press conferences and speeches in Indonesia by U.S. government officials. CPJ also wrote to the International Federation of Journalists (IFJ) on Oct. 12, asking that it admit AJI as an affiliate union, which IFJ subsequently did. AJI is the only union in Indonesia to be accorded that status.

Late October
Andreas Harsono, *Jakarta Post,* CENSORED
Harsono, a prominent member of the Alliance of Independent Journalists (AJI), was fired from his job at the English-language daily *Jakarta Post* under apparent pressure from the state-sponsored Indonesian Journalists Association (PWI). Harsono was told that his work contract, which expired at the end of October, would not be renewed because he was considered "unsuitable" for the job. According to Harsono, *Jakarta Post* editor in chief Santoso Pudjomartono said that while his skills as a journalist were not in doubt, his reporting tended to be "unbalanced." Harsono's dismissal came two weeks after a PWI-sponsored meeting of editors in which Pudjomartono reportedly pledged to take firm measures against AJI

members on his staff. *Jakarta Post* editors also reportedly removed all AJI-member journalists from a team of reporters sent to cover APEC.

November 12
Amy Goodman, *WBAI Radio,* EXPELLED
Allan Nairn, *Free-lancer,* EXPELLED
Goodman, a reporter with WBAI Radio, and Nairn, a journalist on assignment for *Vanity Fair,* were detained while trying to enter East Timor. They were held overnight in West Timor and later flown to Jakarta. The reporters were traveling to East Timor to report on the third anniversary of the shooting of pro-independence East Timorese protestors by government troops in Dili. CPJ protested the journalists' detention. In its Nov. 23 reply, the Indonesian Embassy said the two journalists had not sought government permission to travel to East Timor. Both Goodman and Nairn had been beaten by Indonesian soldiers while covering the Nov. 12, 1991, demonstration; Nairn had suffered a fractured skull.

November 19
Andrew McNaughtan, *Free-lancer,* EXPELLED
McNaughtan, an Australian journalist, was expelled from the East Timor capital of Dili, for working as a journalist without government authorization. He had entered the Indonesian-held territory on a tourist visa. Government officials also accused him of being involved in local politics and taking part in a Nov. 18 pro-independence protest outside a cathedral in Dili.

November 21
Jeff Widener, *Associated Press (AP),* EXPELLED
Craig Fuji, *Associated Press (AP),* EXPELLED
Simon Beardsell, *Worldwide Television News (WTN),* EXPELLED
Jonathan Drake, *Reuters,* EXPELLED
Widener, Fuji, Beardsell and Drake, who were covering pro-independence demonstrations in Dili, were ordered to leave the disputed province. Immigration officials said the journal-

ists were expelled because they had not obtained the work permits and accreditation required to report from East Timor.

November 22
Francois Touron, *Associated Press Television,* EXPELLED

Touron, a senior producer with Associated Press Television, was expelled from the East Timor capital of Dili, for not having the required work permit and proper press accreditation. He was ordered to leave less than 24 hours after arriving in the city.

December 2
Jill Jolliffe, *Free-lancer,* EXPELLED
Irene Slegt, *Free-lacer,* EXPELLED

Australian journalist Jolliffe and Dutch journalist Slegt were expelled from East Timor because they did not have the required work permits and press accreditation. Officials said Jolliffe and Slegt had entered the province on Nov. 28 with tourist visas, but had proceeded to work as journalists. They were arrested two days later in Baucau, interrogated and then flown to Bali.

December 7
Suara Timor Timur, ATTACKED

Six members of Pemuda Pancasila, a pro-government youth group, attacked and vandalized the office of *Suara Timor Timur* (Voice of East Timor), an independent daily in Dili, East Timor. They were reportedly angered by an article published in the newspaper about an assault on the group's leader, Ahmed Alkatiri, several days earlier by a group of East Timorese in Dili. Previously, on July 23, unidentified assailants had set fire to the car of the deputy chief editor, Agus Yohanes. The attack on Yohanes was reportedly linked to the daily's coverage of a series of pro-independence demonstrations in East Timor.

Malaysia

With Prime Minister Mahathir Mohamad required to call general elections in 1995, press freedom has emerged as a major opposition concern. An acerbic critic of the West and a self-styled spokesman for Asia, Mahathir has pledged to review the Internal Security Act, which permits detention without trial, and to deregulate the tightly controlled media—a promise foreshadowed during 1994 by an increased willingness to grant new magazines and newspapers publishing permits. But Mahathir's incipient policy of tolerance did not guarantee more autonomy for editors.

Foreign journalists' reportage on "sensitive" subjects—including corruption, politics, and racial and ethnic issues—was a target of the government's ire. In early 1994, Inter Press Service correspondent Leah Makabenta was expelled from Malaysia for writing articles that the government said threatened national security. The expulsion came in the wake of a simmering trade row with Britain over British press reports alleging bribery and corruption among Malaysian politicians. The London *Sunday Times* reported that Malaysian officials, including Mahathir, received bribes from a British construction company to secure a building contract. In retaliation, the government imposed a ban against awarding new contracts for any British firms, and threatened to bar foreign reporters who wrote what authorities considered to be negative and false reports about the country.

While Malaysia's constitution guarantees free speech and expression, journalists there were confined in 1994 to rigid boundaries set by the government, and many hesitated to pursue sensitive stories for fear of retaliation. The Official Secrets Act effectively discourages investigative journalism, and many of the major English and Bahasa

Malaysia dailies are owned by political parties in the government's National Front coalition. The government retained the right to revoke publishing licenses, ban publications and censor journalists. And throughout the year, controversial articles and news broadcasts about member countries of the Association of Southeast Asian Nations (ASEAN) continued to be censored and prohibited because of the six-nation agreement to maintain security and stability in the region.

February 25
Sunday Times (London), CENSORED
Foreign journalists, CENSORED
The government of Malaysia banned all new contracts with British firms in retaliation for an article that appeared in the Feb. 20 edition of the London *Sunday Times*. The article in question claimed that British contractor George Wimpey International had made "special payments" totalling $50,000 to Malaysian politicians "at the highest level," while bidding for a contract to build an aluminum smelter. On March 6, the deputy home affairs minister announced that Malaysia would henceforth ban all foreign journalists who wrote what the government considered to be negative reports about the country, and that an investigation would be undertaken to determine whether Malaysian citizens had collaborated with British journalists in compiling the *Sunday Times* report. On April 11, CPJ called on the Malaysian government to lift the ban on contracts with British firms, cease investigations of local press contacts and rescind its policy of banning foreign journalists for their allegedly unfavorable press coverage. The government lifted the ban on contracts with British firms on Sept. 8.

March 8
Sunday Telegraph, HARASSED
Canberra Times, HARASSED
The Malaysian government asked Australian Interpol to assist it in questioning journalists from the *Sunday Telegraph* and the *Canberra Times*. The request was made in connection with articles alleging that Australian spies had bribed Malaysian politicians in the late 1980s. On Jan. 16, the *Sunday Telegraph* charged that former agents of the Australian Secret Intelligence Service (ASIS) had bribed opposition politicians in Malaysia for years without the knowledge or consent of the Australian government. Then, on Feb. 3, the *Canberra Times* published a story alleging that politicians belonging to the ruling United Malays National Organization had received bribes from ASIS. In May, the Australian government denied Malaysian police permission to interview the newspapers' editors and reporters about the allegations.

April 1
Leah Makabenta, *Inter Press Service (IPS),*
EXPELLED
Malaysian immigration officials revoked the press pass of Leah Makabenta, an IPS correspondent, and gave her 48 hours to leave the country. The government said her work permit was cancelled because of an August 1993 story comparing Malaysia's 1969 race riots to the civil strife and mass expulsions in Bosnia, and for what it termed a "very negative" article about Malaysia's mistreatment of migrant laborers and immigrants. Government officials warned Makabenta on March 25 of their intent to revoke her press pass and gave her seven days to respond. However, they neglected to specify which articles had caused offense, and Makabenta's request for clarification went unanswered. Makabenta, who had covered Malaysia for two years for IPS, left the country on April 3 without having had a chance to appeal her case. CPJ condemned the expulsion on April 11, and urged the government to restore Makabenta's press pass.

May 4
BBC, CENSORED
Radio Television Malaysia (RTM) cancelled the BBC World News Service following a dispute

Asia

over RTM's editing of the British-produced news programs. In April, the state-run channel had cut several scenes from a BBC report about a labor riot in Medan, Indonesia, in which a Chinese businessman was killed, and factories and Chinese-owned shops were damaged. The BBC warned on May 2 that it would stop providing news programs to RTM if the latter continued to censor its news bulletins. Malaysian officials defended their actions, pointing to an agreement among member countries of the Association of Southeast Asian Nations (ASEAN) to refrain from broadcasting news sensitive to member countries. The Information Ministry said further that the government maintained the right to censor certain news items.

June 21
Thoothan, CENSORED
The Malaysian Home Ministry banned the publication of the Tamil-language biweekly *Thoothan* for printing several articles it considered embarrassing to Datuk Sri S. Samy Velu, president of the Malaysian Indian Congress (MIC). In the preceding three months, *Thoothan* had published interviews with V. Subramaniam Barat Maniam, former MIC public relations committee chairman, who admitted he was part of a political and financial scandal involving Maika Telekom shares.

Maldives

An island country with perhaps the most repressive press policies in South Asia, Maldives is governed by the absolute authority of President Maumoon Abdul Gayoom. Under Gayoom, political parties have been banned, and thus candidates must contend as individuals for election to the rubber-stamp legislature. This prohibition on organized opposition to the government was a source of trouble for the Maldivian media in 1994. Two leading dissident journalists, Mohammed Nasheed and

Mohammed Shafeeq, were detained in late November as part of a crackdown on opposition figures prior to the Dec. 2 parliamentary elections. Nasheed was charged with spreading "false and derogatory" information about Maldives; and Shafeeq was detained while returning from a journalists' conference in Nepal. Both men, who were formerly editors at the banned newspaper *Sangu,* had been jailed previously on what human rights activists believe were spurious charges of terrorism. In mid-October, the government also arrested journalist Mohammed Saeed Moosa Wajdee, after he reportedly criticized the "strong-arm tactics" of leading officials.

October 19
Mohamed Saeed Moosa Wajdee,
Free-lancer, IMPRISONED
Free-lance journalist Wajdee was arrested in connection with an article he wrote for the daily *Haveeru* alleging that government officials regularly bought votes and used "strong-arm tactics" to influence voters during presidential and general elections. Wajdee had been detained several times in 1990 for articles published in *Hukuru,* a weekly newspaper he edited that was banned the same year.

November 30
Mohammed Nasheed, *Free-lancer,*
IMPRISONED, LEGAL ACTION
Nasheed, a free-lance dissident journalist and former assistant editor of the banned newspaper *Sangu,* was arrested in Male, the capital of Maldives. On Dec. 5, he was charged with spreading "false and derogatory" information about the Maldives. The charges are believed to have stemmed from an article he wrote about government sales of fishing rights. He was released on Dec. 6, pending his trial. Nasheed had been released from prison in 1993, after serving three years on charges of withholding information about an alleged terrorist act by *Sangu* editor Mohammed Shafeeq.

November 30
Mohammed Shafeeq, *Free-lancer,* HARASSED
Shafeeq, a free-lance journalist and former editor of the banned newspaper *Sangu,* was detained in the Maldivian capital of Male for several hours. He had just returned from a journalists' conference in Kathmandu, Nepal. Shafeeq was released after police interrogated him. According to human rights groups, the arrest was part of a government crackdown on dissidents prior to the Dec. 2 parliamentary elections. He was previously sentenced to 11 years in prison in December 1991 for allegedly plotting to detonate a petrol bomb in a public park, but he was released in May 1993.

Myanmar

The Burmese media—directly controlled by the government's Ministry of Information and Culture—remains one of the most repressed in Asia. Laws in effect in 1994 prohibited any expression considered harmful to national security and "socialist social order." In October, dissident writer Daw San San Nwe and journalist U Sein Hla Oo were sentenced to 10 years and seven years in prison, respectively, on charges of disseminating anti-government reports and contacting pro-democracy groups. Both journalists belonged to the opposition party National League for Democracy (NLD).

The country's transition to democracy has been stalled by the ruling State Law and Order Restoration Council (SLORC), which seized power in 1988 following a violent crackdown on a pro-democracy uprising. Opposition political leader and Nobel Peace Prize winner Daw Aung San Suu Kyi has been under house arrest since 1989, without charge or trial. In the 1990 national elections, her political party—the NLD—won a landslide victory that was later annulled by the Burmese military. A new constitution that was being drafted by SLORC in 1994 includes provisions that ensure the military's continued grip on power—among them, representation of the armed forces in the legislature.

August 5
Daw San San Nwe, IMPRISONED
U Sein Hla Oo, IMPRISONED
Dissident writer Daw San San Nwe and journalist U Sein Hla Oo were arrested on charges of spreading information damaging to the state and contacting anti-government groups. Daw San San Nwe and U Sein Hla Oo were sentenced on Oct. 6 to 10 years and seven years in prison, respectively. Three other dissidents, including a former UNICEF worker, were sentenced to between 7 and 15 years in prison on similar charges. Officials said all five had "fabricated and sent anti-government reports to some diplomats in foreign embassies, foreign radio stations and visiting foreign journalists." Daw San San Nwe allegedly met two French reporters visiting Burma in April 1993 and appeared in a video they produced to spread "false" propaganda about the government. Authorities said they seized confidential Energy Ministry data, as well as documents and compact discs containing anti-government materials from one of the dissidents. Both U Sein Hla Oo and Daw San San Nwe were previously imprisoned for their involvement in the National League for Democracy, Burma's main pro-democracy party. As of December 1994, all five were being held at the Insein Prison in Rangoon.

Pakistan

Sectarian and factional violence in the southern city of Karachi claimed hundreds of lives over the course of 1994. The situation was aggravated considerably by the withdrawal in November of federal troops—stationed in the city for over two years—and the attendant transfer of authority to an ill-prepared police force. Two journalists were among those killed in the withdrawal's immediate aftermath. The first was Mohammed Salahuddin, editor of the conservative weekly *Takbeer* and a prominent critic of the locally dominant Muhajir Quami Movement (MQM), a party supported exclusively by Muslim migrants from India and their descendants. The subsequent slaying of Mohammed Samdani Warsi, business manager of the pro-MQM daily *Parcham,* was seen by some as a retaliatory move against Salahuddin's assassination.

Pakistan's blasphemy laws were invoked against five journalists belonging to the minority Ahmadi community—followers of a sect that the government regards as un-Islamic and which it bars from proselytizing. Facing mandatory capital punishment if convicted, the journalists are charged with having "misrepresented" themselves as Muslims, offended the majority group's sensibilities and propagated Ahmadi beliefs in their articles.

February 7
Noor Muhammad Saifi, *Al Fazal,*
  LEGAL ACTION
Agha Saifullah, *Al Fazal,* LEGAL ACTION
Qazi Munir Ahmed, *Al Fazal,* LEGAL ACTION
Mirza Muhammad Din Naz, *Ansarullah,*
  LEGAL ACTION
Mohammad Ibrahim, *Ansarullah,*
  LEGAL ACTION
Five journalists from the minority Ahmadi community were arrested and charged with blasphemy for preaching the Ahmadi faith, "passing" themselves off as Muslims, and for having "injured the religious feelings of Muslims." Three journalists from the daily *Al Fazal*—editor Saifi, publisher Ahmed and printer Saifullah—as well as two editors from the monthly *Ansarullah,* Naz and Ibrahim, face mandatory capital punishment if convicted of blasphemy under the Pakistani Penal Code. On March 7, all five were released on bail after being held in Chiniot, Punjab province. The complaints against the journalists were related to several July 1993 issues of *Al Fazal* and a June 1993

issue of *Ansarullah.* Pakistani law now makes it an offense for Ahmadi community members to practice or spread their faith. By the year's end, the cases were pending in court and no trial date had been set.

December 4
Mohammed Salahuddin, *Takbeer,* KILLED
Salahuddin, editor of Urdu-language weekly *Takbeer,* was fatally shot by two unidentified gunmen on a motorcycle. The assailants ambushed him outside *Takbeer*'s offices in Karachi as he was stepping into his car. Generally supportive of the policies of the religiously and politically conservative Jamaat-i-Islami party, Salahuddin frequently wrote editorials criticizing the governing Pakistan People's Party. But he reserved his strongest criticism for the Muhajir Quami Movement (MQM), a Karachi-based party supported by many Muslim migrants from India. MQM members were suspected of having attacked and burned Salahuddin's home in 1991. And in 1992, unidentified assailants had set *Takbeer*'s offices on fire. CPJ condemned the murder and called for an investigation.

December 6
Mohammad Samdani Warsi, *Parcham,* KILLED
Samdani, business manager of the Urdu-language daily *Parcham,* was shot and killed by unidentified gunmen in the newspaper's office in Karachi. The assailants entered the office looking for the paper's editor, but turned on Samdani after being unable to find their original target. *Parcham* editorially supports the Muhajir Quami Movement (MQM), a Karachi-based political party of Muslim migrants from India. CPJ condemned Samdani's murder and called for a nonpartisan investigation.

Singapore

Former Prime Minister Lee Kuan Yew's belief that press freedom must take a back seat to economic growth and national unity remained the guiding policy under his successor, Goh Chok Tong, in 1994. The city-state's major newspapers were mainly pro-establishment and adhered to the government line on domestic issues. Foreign publications were frequently subject to strict limits on their circulation, especially those that published critical reporting on domestic politics. And many foreign journalists were only allowed to work in the country for a limited time. In May, for example, the immigration department summarily rejected *Asiaweek* correspondent Alejandro Reyes' request to renew his employment pass.

Reporters charged with transgressing Singapore's press policies faced prosecution twice during the year. In March, two *Business Times* editors were found guilty of violating the Official Secrets Act, for publishing an unofficial estimate of Singapore's second-quarter economic growth rate. They were fined a total of US$4,800 and released. Christopher Lingle, formerly a professor at the National University of Singapore, was charged in November and found guilty on Jan. 17, 1995, of contempt of court for an opinion piece he wrote for the *International Herald Tribune* that ambiguously referred to "intolerant regimes" in Asia and their "compliant" judiciaries. He was fined US$6,900. Other defendants in the case included the *Tribune*'s publisher and the Singapore-based editor of its Asia edition. The two were fined US$1,725 and US$3,450, respectively.

In a bold move to improve the human rights situation and loosen the government's hold on freedom of expression, the opposition Singapore Democratic Party (SDP) called for the establishment of a human rights commission in July. The SDP also sought the abolition of the Internal Security Act, which allows for detention without trial.

March 31
Patrick Daniel, *Business Times,* LEGAL ACTION
Kenneth James, *Business Times,* LEGAL ACTION
Daniels and James, editors at *Business Times,* were found guilty of violating Singapore's Official Secrets Act and fined a total of approximately US$4,800 for publishing unofficial economic data. The two had been charged in December 1992 with endangering state security by obtaining and publishing a classified estimate of Singapore's second-quarter growth rate in the June 29, 1992, edition of *Business Times.* Their joint trial with alleged collaborators Tharman Shanmugaratnam, Singapore's monetary authority director, and two economists, began Oct. 21, 1993. The prosecution claimed one of the economists saw the secret estimate in a Monetary Authority report that Shanmugaratnam had brought to a meeting with the economist on June 19, 1992. The economist was accused of passing the information to James. Shanmugaratnam was charged with handling confidential information in a way that endangered its secrecy.

May 31
Alejandro Reyes, *Asiaweek,* CENSORED
Singapore's immigration department rejected a request to renew the employment pass of Reyes, *Asiaweek*'s Singapore correspondent. The employment pass is renewable annually and is required for journalists to work in Singapore. Immigration officials gave no reason for their decision. Foreign journalists are reportedly allowed to work in the city-state only for a limited time period so as to mimimize their involvement in domestic politics. Reyes, whose pass had been renewed once in 1993, had worked for two years in Singapore. Among the articles he had written was one about Singaporean political exile Francis Seow, who was detained in 1988 for allegedly collaborating with U.S. diplomats to foster opposition to the Singaporean government.

November 18
Christopher Lingle, LEGAL ACTION,
  HARASSED
Richard McClean, *International Herald Tribune*
  (Paris), LEGAL ACTION
Michael Richardson, *International Herald Tribune*
  (Singapore), LEGAL ACTION
International Herald Tribune Pte Ltd. (Singapore),
  LEGAL ACTION
Singapore Press Holdings, LEGAL ACTION
Singapore's attorney general charged Lingle,
former senior fellow in European studies at the
National University of Singapore, with con-
tempt of court over an opinion piece he wrote
for the *International Herald Tribune* that criticized unnamed "intolerant regimes" in Asia and
their "compliant" judiciaries. The Oct. 7 article
was criticized by the government for questioning the independence of Singapore's court system. Also named in the suit were McClean,
publisher and chief executive of the *Tribune* in
Paris; Richardson, Asia editor for the *Tribune;*
International Herald Tribune Pte Ltd., the
paper's Singapore distributor, and Singapore
Press Holdings Ltd., which prints the paper's
local edition. In mid-October, Lingle was questioned by police and investigated for possible
criminal defamation. He fled to the United
States on Oct. 20. Following an in absentia
trial, Lingle was found guilty on Jan. 17, 1995,
and fined US$6,900. Richardson and McLean
were fined US$3,400 and US$1,725 respectively. The distributor and printer were ordered to
pay US$1,035 each.

Sri Lanka

**Press freedom emerged as a major issue in
Sri Lanka's 1994 parliamentary and presidential election campaigns. This development was due in a large part to the efforts
of the local Free Media Movement, a journalists' group that has taken the lead in raising
public awareness of press freedom violations. For five years under President Ranas-**
**inghe Premadasa and his successor, Dingiri
Banda Wijetunge, the ruling United National
Party (UNP) had maintained a dismal record
of censorship and violent attacks on journalists. In both of the year's back-to-back elections, the UNP was soundly defeated.
Unfortunately, the change in leadership did
not hail a clean break with past abuses.**

　　**The Peoples Alliance (PA), led by Chan-
drika Kumaratunga—a daughter of two former heads of state—campaigned on a
platform that included the privatization of
the government-owned Lake House publishing group. It therefore came as a disappoint-
ment to many when the newly elected PA
government censored news stories in state-
owned media about the separatist Liberation
Tigers of Tamil Eelam (LTTE), who were
allegedly implicated in the assassination of
UNP presidential candidate Gamini Dissanayake and with whom the PA advocated
negotiations. Equally alarming was the PA
government's rewriting of news stories in
Lake House publications on two occasions
during the presidential campaign.**

January 10
Daya Lankapura, *Divaina,* HARASSED
Edmund Ranasinghe, *Divaina* and *Island,*
  HARASSED
Niresh Eliyathamby, *Island,* HARASSED
Sharmindra Ferdinando, *Island,* HARASSED
Sri Lankan police visited the offices of the
dailies *Divaina* and *Island* to question several
journalists who reported on the discovery of
mass graves containing the remains of hundreds
of murder victims in Suriyakande. The victims
were reported to have been killed in a 1989
crackdown on left-wing activists by government
death squads. According to press reports, officials from the Criminal Investigation Department recorded statements from Lankapura and
Ranasinghe of the Singhalese-language *Divaina,*
as well as from Eliyathamby and Ferdinando of
the English-language *Island.* Investigators asked
them who their sources for the stories were, and

whether they had reported the stories with the intention of discrediting the government.

February 21
Free Media Movement, ATTACKED
Yukthiya, ATTACKED
Police tear-gassed a group of journalists who had assembled at Koralawella for a procession in remembrance of journalist Richard de Zoysa, whose 1990 slaying was widely attributed to the government of the late President Ranasinghe Premadasa, and human rights activist Rajani Thiranagama, who was reportedly killed in 1989 by the separatist Liberation Tigers of Tamil Eelam (LTTE). Later in the day, police armed with batons attacked several of the journalists involved in the procession as they entered the Vihara Mahadevi Park Town Hall for a public meeting about press freedom. In a Jan. 24 letter, Colombo police had refused the organizers—Sri Lanka's Free Media Movement and the Singhalese-language tabloid *Yukthiya*—permission to hold the procession. The Free Media Movement is seeking to reopen the official inquiry into de Zoysa's killing.

April 6
Chandana Keerthi Bandara, *Haraya,*
   LEGAL ACTION, HARASSED
Police arrested Bandara, features editor of *Haraya* and assistant secretary of Sri Lanka's Free Media Movement, on his way home to Avissawalle. He was held for 24 hours, and was reportedly beaten and assaulted. Bandara subsequently filed charges of unlawful arrest and assault against two Avissawalle police officers; the charges were dropped after he received an apology from the officer-in-charge.

May
Ravaya, THREATENED
Housing, Construction and Urban Development Minister B. Sirisena Cooray demanded US$2 million in compensation from the weekly *Ravaya* for allegedly damaging his reputation and political career. Cooray threatened to bring

legal action against the paper if compensation was not paid. On May 1, *Ravaya* had published an article linking Cooray and Sri Lankan Army Chief of Staff Maj. Gen. Lakshman Algama to a planned military coup. Both officials denied the charge. Cooray, however, was forced to resign May 1 as general secretary of the United National Party (UNP).

May 1
R.M.A. Ajit Seneviratne, *Aththa,*
   LEGAL ACTION, HARASSED
Seneviratne, a photographer for the Singhalese-language weekly *Aththa,* was arrested while covering a protest outside the president's house in Colombo. He was detained at the police station for 24 hours, without notification of his family or employer, and questioned by the National Intelligence Bureau. He was released on bail on May 2, with the stipulation that he report to the police on the last Sunday of each month until his case was settled. Attorney General Tilak Marapana said in June that the department would investigate the incident.

October 24
Sena Vidanagamage, *Agence France-Presse,*
   ATTACKED
AFP photographer Vidanagamage was assaulted by a group of unidentified men while on assignment at Colombo's General Hospital, where the body of slain opposition presidential candidate Gamini Dissanayake had been taken earlier in the day. Vidanagamage sustained injuries to his chest, arm and leg, and his cellular phone was taken from him during the attack.

October 25
Sudath Malaweera, *Island,* ATTACKED
About a dozen unidentified men assaulted *Island* photographer Malaweera as he attempted to take pictures at a Colombo funeral parlor, where the body of slain presidential candidate Gamini Dissanayake had been brought for embalming. Malaweera's camera was damaged in the attack.

October-November
All media, CENSORED
The government of President Chandrika Kumaratunga imposed restrictions and censorship on news coverage of the November presidential election campaign. The state-owned Sri Lanka Broadcasting Corporation and the Independent Television Network were prohibited from broadcasting reports implicating the separatist Liberation Tigers of Tamil (LTTE) in the assassination of UNP presidential candidate Gamini Dissanayaka. Printing of the Oct. 28 issue of *Dinamina* and the Nov. 4 issue of the *Ceylon Daily News* was interrupted until several articles had been rewritten to support the political campaign of the People's Alliance. Both papers belong to the government-owned Lake House publishing group.

Taiwan

While Taiwan's print media today present a broad array of political viewpoints, the country's broadcast media have remained largely in the hands of the ruling Kuomintang (KMT), or Nationalist Party. Under pressure from the political opposition, the KMT relented somewhat in 1993 and began issuing licenses to nongovernment radio stations. However, capitalization requirements for new stations were prohibitively high for many would-be applicants. The result was a boom in pirate radio, pioneered by Voice of Taiwan in November 1993, and followed over the succeeding months by roughly 40 other unlicensed stations.

The new, unregulated stations quickly drew a vast working-class audience in 1994, with their caustic criticism of the KMT, live call-in talk shows, and Taiwanese and Hakka-language broadcasts (a stark contrast to the Mandarin spoken on most official stations). Taxi drivers, in particular, emerged as a conspicuous and often volatile segment of their audience. Unfortunately, authorities responded to demonstrations by taxi drivers and others by accusing the stations of incitement, and cracking down on them with massive police raids. In addition, formal charges were pressed against Voice of Taiwan owner Hsu Rong-chi. Although the Information Office said in August that it would issue licenses to low-power stations with dramatically reduced capitalization requirements, only about a quarter of the 174 applicants were granted licenses at year's end.

Journalists working for KMT or state-owned media were once again excluded from the United Nations, which contended that they were ineligible for accreditation as the official news agencies of a government that had been expelled from the General Assembly. In a move that suggested that U.N. accreditation officials were responding to stepped-up political pressure from the People's Republic of China, two Taiwanese journalists who had been accredited at the United Nations since 1990 and 1992, respectively, were abruptly denied renewal of their press passes in March.

February 1
Ming Young, *China Television System (CTS),* CENSORED
Chiou Yueh, *Taiwan Television Enterprise (TTV),* CENSORED
The United Nations refused to renew Young and Chiou's press passes, on the grounds that the journalists' news organizations are partly owned by the Taiwanese government. The government of Taiwan is not recognized by the General Assembly, and U.N. officials said Taiwanese state-owned media are ineligible for accreditation under terms of a 1972 U.N. Legal Counsel opinion. Until February, however, the U.N. Department of Public Information (UNDPI) had regularly renewed Young and Chiou's press passes. Young and Chiou were first accredited by the UNDPI in February 1990 and October 1992, respectively. Chiou had also been a member of the U.N. Correspondents Association since October 1993. CPJ

protested the revocation of their press credentials in a July 29 letter to U.N. Secretary General Boutros Boutros Ghali. In an Aug. 17 letter
to CPJ, the UNDPI reiterated the 1972 opinion and denied CPJ's assertion that it was acting
under pressure from the delegation of the People's Republic of China. Two other Taiwanese
journalists, David Wang of the Central News
Agency (CNA) and Lisa Shen of the China
Television Company (CTV), had lost their
U.N. press passes on the same grounds in 1993.

April 21
Voice of Taiwan,
   CENSORED, LEGAL ACTION, ATTACKED
Hsu Rong-chi, *Voice of Taiwan,*
   CENSORED, LEGAL ACTION, ATTACKED
Police raided the Voice of Taiwan, an unlicensed
radio station, and confiscated its broadcasting
equipment. Taipei district prosecutor Chang
Chen-hsing charged the station with endangering
public security by allegedly inciting an April 11
demonstration by taxi drivers in central Taipei.
The drivers had clashed with riot police when
they attempted to prevent the demolition of the
two-story headquarters of the Nationalist Party,
one of the few Japanese colonial-era buildings left
in Taipei. Hsu Rong-chi, the owner and popular
talk-show host of Voice of Taiwan, resumed
broadcasting on April 24 with hidden backup
equipment. Hsu was arrested on July 22 for
allegedly inciting the protest, which was illegal
under Taiwanese law, and released the same day.

July 30
14 radio stations, CENSORED, ATTACKED
More than 6,000 police raided 14 unlicensed
radio stations and seized their broadcasting
equipment in a nationwide government crackdown on illegal broadcasting. Dozens of people
clashed with police outside the Voice of Taiwan
radio station in Taipei as they shut it down. Several operators of the stations are members of
the opposition Democratic Progressive Party.
Most of the stations subsequently resumed
transmitting.

August 30
Voice of Taiwan, CENSORED, ATTACKED
Voice of the People, CENSORED, ATTACKED
Police raided Voice of Taiwan and Voice of the
People, two popular unlicensed radio stations in
Taipei, and confiscated their transmitting
equipment. The Government Information
Office said the stations were broadcasting illegally, had incited public disorder and had provoked anti-government sentiments with
criticism of the ruling Nationalist Party. Hsu
Rong-chi, Voice of Taiwan owner and talk-show
host, resumed broadcasting within three hours
using backup equipment. Voice of the People
subsequently resumed broadcasting as well.

September 13
Hsu Rong-chi, *Voice of Taiwan,* LEGAL ACTION
Hsu, owner and host of underground radio station Voice of Taiwan, was arrested for ignoring
orders to appear in court, and detained for 46
days on several charges, including inciting
demonstrations in Taiwan. Taiwan's laws governing demonstrations make it illegal to have
any large public gathering without prior government approval. On Oct. 1, Hsu was sentenced to eight months in prison for mobilizing
thousands of taxi drivers to blockade the
Finance Ministry in February to protest high
insurance premiums. On Oct. 29, in a separate
case, Hsu was given the choice of five months in
prison or a US$5,200 fine for allegedly inciting
a protest by taxi drivers in April against the
demolition of a historic site, but he was released
the same day on bail. Hsu has appealed both
cases.

October 12
Voice of Taiwan, ATTACKED
Nearly 10 unidentified assailants raided the
Voice of Taiwan, a popular underground radio
station in Taipei. Three people were hurt in the
raid, and office and broadcasting equipment
were damaged. Voice of Taiwan resumed broadcasting two days later.

Asia

141

Thailand

Since returning to multiparty rule in 1992, Thailand has seen a gradual relaxation of government control over the media. In 1994, Prime Minister Chuan Leekpai continued efforts to form a legal and institutional framework to promote democracy in a society shaped by political patronage, money and corruption. The media, especially the print media, were largely unrestricted, and the majority of weekly and daily newspapers were privately owned. Although journalists continued to practice self-censorship with regard to the royal family and Buddhist clergy, they were often harshly critical of government officials—but not without reprisal. *Thai Rath*, the nation's largest Thai-language daily, was hit with a grenade in early December by a group of unidentified men. No one was injured in the explosion. Local sources linked the attack to the newspaper's aggressive coverage of recent domestic political scandals and corruption among the Thai military.

Lively, independent broadcast media were just emerging amidst the many television and radio stations still owned by the state or military. The powerful Thai army continued to selectively restrict freedom of the press, and in May, the Territorial Defense Department suspended the army-owned FM-96 news radio station for three days for broadcasting commentary considered to be critical of the military on its "News Talk" show. FM-96 is leased to NPG Broadcasting Network, an affiliate of The Nation Publishing Group, and the daily newspaper *Nation* provides news programs for the station.

Foreign journalists were also restricted during the year. The Foreign Ministry threatened to ban the sales of the Japanese daily *Asahi Shimbun* and bar its journalists from reporting in the country for a story published on July 5 that alleged Thai army involvement

in Cambodia's failed July 3 coup attempt. The army demanded a retraction and an apology.

May 15
FM-96, CENSORED
The Thai Territorial Defense Department temporarily suspended the radio station FM-96 because the May 14 broadcast of its "News Talk" program included comments by a guest that were allegedly "biased" against the military. Although owned by the army, FM-96 is leased to NPG Broadcasting Network, an affiliate of The Nation Publishing Group. The *Nation*, a respected English-language daily, provides news stories to the station. FM-96 resumed broadcasting on May 18.

July 6
Asahi Shimbun, THREATENED
The Foreign Ministry threatened to ban the sale of the Japanese daily *Asahi Shimbun* and bar its journalists from working in Thailand because of a story alleging Thai army involvement in Cambodia's failed July 3 coup. *Asahi Shimbun* reported on July 5 that 14 Thais who were arrested in Cambodia in connection with the coup attempt may have been members of Thai special forces that were planning to assassinate Cambodia's two co-prime ministers. The paper quoted an unidentified source as saying that Thai special forces were in charge of up to 300 troops, including armored vehicles, who tried to enter Phnom Penh during the coup bid. The Army demanded an apology and a retraction. On July 14, the paper's management expressed "deep regret" to Foreign Minister Prasong Sunsiri for hurting Bangkok's reputation. However, *Asahi Shimbun* refused to run a retraction.

December 5
Thai Rath, ATTACKED
A group of unidentified men fired a rocket-propelled grenade at the Bangkok headquarters of *Thai Rath*, the nation's largest Thai-language daily. No one was injured in the early morning

attack. The explosion shattered several windows, and damaged an office wall and two cars parked outside. Local media sources intimated that the attack was instigated by the newspaper's recent reports on political scandals and a corruption case involving a prominent Thai army general. CPJ condemned the attack and called for a thorough investigation.

Asia

Central Europe and the Republics of the Former Soviet Union

RUSSIA

ESTONIA
LATVIA
LITHUANIA
BELARUS

CZECH REPUBLIC

HUNGARY

POLAND

ROMANIA

KAZAKHSTAN

SLOVAKIA

SLOVENIA

UKRAINE

AZERBAIJAN

KYRGYZSTAN

BOSNIA-HERZEGOVINA

CROATIA

MOLDOVIA

GEORGIA

UZBEKISTAN

ARMENIA

YUGOSLAVIA

BULGARIA

ALBANIA

MACEDONIA

TURKMENISTAN

TAJIKISTAN

OVERVIEW
OF # Central Europe and the Republics of the Former Soviet Union

by Leonid Zagalsky

Leonid Zagalsky, *a native of Russia, is the program coordinator for Central Europe and the republics of the former Soviet Union. Formerly a journalist with the respected Moscow-based weekly* Literaturnaya Gazeta, *Zagalsky was the recipient of a John S. Knight fellowship for professional journalists at Stanford University. He has written widely on science and political and economic affairs for publications in the former Soviet Union and the United States. Zagalsky is also a contributing editor for* The Bulletin of the Atomic Scientists.

    Yalman Onaran, *a CPJ research associate, wrote the sections on Albania, Bosnia-Herzegovina, Croatia and Yugoslavia.* **Dimitry Danilyuk** *and* **Sorin Matei,** *both research assistants at CPJ, contributed extensively to this report.*

The research carried out by CPJ's program on Central Europe and the republics of the former Soviet Union was made possible in part by a grant from The John D. and Catherine T. MacArthur Foundation.

S INCE THE END OF THE COLD WAR, press freedom has taken root in Central Europe and the former Soviet Union. The newly independent governments that make up this vast and diverse region profess to support the transition to democracy, and the independence of the press has been encoded into law. Yet many of these regimes continue to repress the media or control them outright. In 1994, several governments cited national security to justify crackdowns on independent reporting, and journalism became still more hazardous as armed conflicts and ethnic strife intensified throughout the region.

In Russia, the press displayed increasing courage and independence in its coverage of crime, civil conflicts and public institutions, including the military. In response, many journalists came under official censure, and even direct physical attack. No case better exemplifies the risks facing Russian journalists today than the murder of Dmitry Kholodov, an investigative reporter for Moscow's most popular newspaper, *Moskovski Komsomolets,* who was killed when he opened a booby-trapped briefcase he had collected from a source. Kholodov had been writing extensively on corruption in the Russian military. His murder was especially chilling because it was so clearly linked to his activities as a reporter.

The crisis in Chechnya, which began in December, presented another set of problems. During the first three weeks of fighting two journalists were killed, and officials in Moscow bitterly criticized reports aired by Russian television that were critical of the government's actions in the conflict. The Russian military ordered journalists out of the war zone, jammed their satellite transmissions, exposed their film, and, occasionally, took potshots at reporters' cars. The press responded to these attacks with some of the best independent reporting Russia has ever seen.

Central Asia is the region of the former Socialist bloc least covered by international media. It is also the most repressive. Turkmenistan and Uzbekistan set the tone for the area with strict party-line controls on all print and news broadcasting services. The most severe restrictions on press freedom are found in Tajikistan, which continues to be torn by civil war and remains one of the most dangerous countries in the world for journalists. Since May 1992, at least 27 reporters and editors have been killed there in what appear to have been assassinations directly related to their profession. There is strong evidence of official complicity in many of these murders. In addition, a ruthless campaign against independent media by the government of President Emomali Rakhmonov led to the closure of all magazines and newspapers considered sympathetic to the opposition, and to the suppression of all dissident viewpoints on radio and television. Four journalists from Tajikistan's state television spent 20 months in a Dushanbe prison awaiting trial on charges of treason before being released. Most independent and pro-opposition journalists were either killed, intimidated into silence or forced into exile.

The governments of Armenia and Azerbaijan also adopted authoritarian measures to deal with independent journalists. Both official censorship and intimidation were used to silence dissent in the media, and the conflict between the two republics over the disputed enclave of Nagorno-Karabakh served as a convenient pretext for cracking down on the press.

The war in Bosnia claimed the lives of six journalists in 1994, and the death of a seventh is under investigation. In all, at least 45 reporters have been killed on the job in Bosnia and its neighboring republics since 1991, making the war in the former Yugoslavia the most dangerous conflict for war correspondents since Vietnam.

The press in the nations of the former Soviet satellites of Central Europe faced severe economic and political problems, though in these countries journalists were less likely to face direct physical attacks. Governments continued to monopolize the airwaves, but independent newspapers and magazines proliferated. Still, independent news outlets were subject to economic coercion by government overseers, and legal constraints were widespread, including stiff penalties and lax standards of proof for libel and defamation.

Central Europe

Albania

Albania shed its totalitarian past with democratic elections in 1991. Since then democratic institutions, including an independent press, have formed in this society, which only a few years ago was one of the most isolated in the world.

Although Albania got off to a rocky start on its road to full-fledged democracy, the situation for journalists improved a great deal in 1994. Following a pardon of several journalists convicted of press law violations by Albanian President Sali Berisha on World Press Freedom Day (May 3), attacks against journalists as well as their arrests and trials almost came to a halt. A repressive press law that was passed in 1993 and had been used against journalists and news organizations was no longer actively enforced.

The ethnic Greek minority in the south of the country was the focus of tensions between Albania and Greece. In August 1994, there were several instances of the police mistreating Greek journalists who were covering the trial of ethnic Albanian-Greeks. These incidents seem to have been directed at Greek nationals, though, rather than journalists specifically.

The government employed subtler economic means of pressuring the opposition press but with little success. The press in Albania not only survived an increase in taxes, which was targeted at newspapers, but has continued to flourish with each passing day. Private broadcasting is still not permitted, however, and radio and TV remain in the government's hands.

January 7
Apollon Bace, *Deutsche Welle*
   and *Dita Informacion*, ATTACKED
Somebody attempted to stab Bace, a correspondent for the German radio station Deutsche

Welle and a reporter for the Tirana biweekly *Dita Informacion*. The police have not identified any suspects.

January 17
Fatmir Zanaj, *Zeri i Popullit*, LEGAL ACTION
Zanaj, a journalist for *Zeri i Popullit*, was tried and given a suspended sentence of three months in jail and a year on probation for publishing an article that criticized reform in the army.

January 31
Aleksander Frangaj, *Koha Jone*, LEGAL ACTION
Martin Leka, *Koha Jone*,
   IMPRISONED, LEGAL ACTION
Frangaj, the editor in chief of *Koha Jone*, and Leka, a reporter, were arrested in connection with an article published in the newspaper. The article, referring to a government document leaked to *Koha Jone*, talked about disarming off-duty military officers. Leka was charged with collaboration and conspiracy with the government official who leaked the document. Frangaj was charged with not keeping his newspaper free of punishable violations. On Feb. 25, Leka was convicted and sentenced to 18 months in prison. Frangaj was acquitted and released. On March 21, the appeals court upheld Leka's conviction and reversed Frangaj's acquittal, sentencing him to five months in prison. Because Frangaj was out of the country when this decision came through, he was not arrested immediately. On May 3, a day after CPJ wrote a second appeal to Albanian President Sali Berisha appealing for the release of Leka and the overturning of the two journalists' convictions, Berisha pardoned Leka and Frangaj. The case against them was dropped.

March 3
Gjergj Zefi, *Aleanca*, ATTACKED
Zefi, a deputy editor in chief at *Aleanca*, the newspaper of the opposition Democratic Alliance Party, was hit on the head by unidentified persons. After the beating Zefi was hospitalized. Two weeks earlier, Zefi was sued for

libel by the government because of a story he wrote accusing the government of being a mafia gang.

March 10
Teodor Keko, *Aleanca*, ATTACKED, HARASSED
Keko, the editor in chief of the opposition newspaper *Aleanca*, was beaten by unknown persons outside his home. Many Albanian journalists told CPJ that he was beaten because he published many articles in his newspaper that were critical of the government. Keko was also harassed constantly by government prosecutors, who demanded that he appear in court once a week to testify about a journalist who anonymously wrote an article about the murder of a Democratic Alliance politician in *Aleanca*. Keko refused to name the journalist each time, but authorities continued to summon him for a few months. CPJ expressed its concern for the beating and harassment of Keko in a letter to the Albanian government.

April
Shyqyri Meka, *Zeri i Popullit*,
HARASSED, LEGAL ACTION
Meka, the deputy editor in chief of the Socialist Party's daily *Zeri i Popullit*, was fined $1,000 for publishing a letter to the editor that criticized the government. The conviction was based on an article of the press law passed in 1993 that holds editors responsible for publishing articles that violate the law. On May 3, a day after CPJ protested this conviction, the Albanian president revoked the fine and pardoned Meka.

He was also detained for seven hours on April 3 at the police department and fined for allegedly resisting arrest. Meka claims, however, the police did not show a warrant for his arrest.

April 7
Ilirian Zhupa, *Popullit Po*, LEGAL ACTION
Zhupa, the managing editor of the opposition newspaper *Popullit Po*, was sentenced to two months in prison on charges of publishing an article that defamed the head of the secret

police. His sentence was suspended on condition that he would not repeat the offense within a year. On May 3, a day after CPJ protested the conviction, Albanian President Sali Berisha overturned the conviction and pardoned Zhupa.

May
Opposition and independent press, HARASSED
A government decision in May to make newspapers pay a 15 percent "advertisement tax" on top of all the other taxes they had been paying has made it financially difficult for the independent press to survive. A new tariff of 30 percent on newsprint has increased the price of paper tremendously. In July, editors of the seven major dailies, including the government paper *Rilindja Demokratike*, appealed to the Albanian president to eliminate some of the taxes paid by newspapers; he agreed to do so during a press conference a few days later, but no such cuts were put into effect in 1994. Protesting what they called "unfair" taxes aimed at destroying the independent and opposition press, nine Albanian newspapers suspended publication for four days in August.

July 27
Koha Jone, HARASSED
The police sealed the Tirana offices of *Koha Jone*, the largest independent newspaper in Albania, on the grounds that it owed the state-owned printing facilities long overdue payments. The staff managed to publish the paper the next day by working out of a colleague's house, using only one computer. When the publishers proved to the court that the payments were made but had been delayed in the banking system, the seal was removed and staff moved back into their offices the day after the police had shut them down. In an editorial about the incident, the newspaper claimed that the financial charges and temporary closure of *Koha Jone* were another attempt by the government to silence the press.

149

August 23 to September 10
Takis Diamandis, *ET-1 (Greek state television)*
and Greek daily Eleftherotypia, EXPELLED
Thekla Kittou, *Cypriot journalist,* EXPELLED
Kostas Markellos, *Sky Channel (Greece),*
EXPELLED
Agni Vravoritou, *Star Channel (Greece),*
EXPELLED

During the much-publicized trial of five ethnic
Greek-Albanians accused of treason, many
Greek journalists were harassed and detained
briefly along with lawyers, politicians and others from Greece who were observing the trial.
On Aug. 23, Kittou, a Cypriot journalist, was
arrested and deported the next day for "not
having any press credentials and not being able
to explain why she was there," according to
state-owned Albanian Television. On Sept. 6,
Vravoritou of Greece's Star Channel was
detained along with his three technicians. They
were deported the next day. Similarly, on Sept.
7, Markellos was arrested with his technician
and deported a day later. Diamandis, a well-
known journalist in Greece who was the Tirana
correspondent for Greek state television as well
as for a major daily newspaper, was arrested on
Sept. 10 and expelled the following day. In
addition, he was banned from entering Albania
for five years.

In all the cases, the Albanian authorities
claimed that the journalists were not at the trial
as journalists but as Greek nationalists trying to
slander Albania's court system. In some of the
detention cases, the Greek journalists were
arrested as they were leaving the Greek
embassy and accused of being spies. They were
usually released when their press credentials
were confirmed.

The harassment of Greek journalists was
part of the mistreatment by Albanian authorities
of all Greek nationals observing the trial, and
the increased tensions between the two countries during this time also fueled the crackdown.

Armenia

Armenia's independence from the Soviet
Union in September 1991 gave rise to an
independent media, the first in the republic's
history. But with economic problems and six
years of bitter fighting with neighboring Azerbaijan, the Armenian government became
more despotic in the way it dealt with the
independent press in 1994, and instances of
violence against journalists by authorities
increased.

On Oct. 28, the representatives of 20
news organizations signed a joint statement
that condemned violence against journalists,
and demanded that the president and law-
enforcement agencies take decisive measures to protect the lives and guarantee the
safety of journalists. At the same time a
meeting of journalists in Yerevan, the Armenian capital, discussed setting up their own
independent trade union. They also proposed
a much more radical endeavor: pressing for
legislation that would allow journalists to
bear arms.

August
Golos Armenii, HARASSED, LEGAL ACTION
Golos Armenii, an independent Russian-language
daily newspaper published in Yerevan, was
under pressure to close down by the Armenian
government, which controls all newsprint and
printing facilities. Authorities first tried to shut
the publication down by raising its rates for
newsprint, but when this failed, the government
sued the newspaper later in the month. The
charges were dismissed as groundless, but *Golos
Armenii* continued to suffer financial problems
and had to stop publishing for one month. It
resumed publishing at the end of January 1995.

October-November
AZG, ATTACKED
Akop Avetikyan, *AZG,* ATTACKED
Two arson attempts were made against the editorial office of the republic's popular newspaper *AZG* on Oct. 19 and 25. Akop Avetikyan, the chief editor, was also severely beaten by unidentified assailants on Nov. 3. There were no investigations into any of these cases, but sources in Armenia told CPJ that these actions were taken in an effort to pressure the newspaper, which is not affiliated with any group, to align with a political party.

October 20
Aram Abramyan,
Armenian Television, ATTACKED
Abramyan, a correspondent for Armenian Television and the former press secretary to the Armenian president, was beaten up late at night by unidentified persons at the entrance to his house.

November 21
Armen Bagdasarian, *AZG,* ATTACKED
Bagdasarian, a reporter with the Liberal-Democratic newspaper *AZG,* was beaten not far from his office by persons who represented themselves as police officers. He was hospitalized after the attack. The attackers seized the reporter's tape recorder and tapes of a speech made by Armenia's president at a session of the Supreme Council.

December 29
Yerkir, LEGAL ACTION, CENSORED
Azatamard, LEGAL ACTION, CENSORED
Arakast, LEGAL ACTION, CENSORED
Munetik, LEGAL ACTION, CENSORED
Marzashkharh, LEGAL ACTION, CENSORED
Andratarts, LEGAL ACTION, CENSORED
Nork, LEGAL ACTION, CENSORED
Mikayel Varandian Publishing House,
LEGAL ACTION, CENSORED
Haylour News Agency,
LEGAL ACTION, CENSORED

Horizon Television Agency,
LEGAL ACTION, CENSORED
Armenian Documentation Center,
LEGAL ACTION, CENSORED
The government of Armenia closed down eleven news organizations because they were allegedly financed by illegal sources of an extremist faction of the Armenian Revolutionary Federation (ARF), a leading political opposition group. The alleged secret faction of the ARF is called the Dro. The activities of ARF, also known as Dashnaks, had been "temporarily suspended" one day earlier following a televised decree by Armenian President Levon Ter-Petrossian, in which he accused the Dro of criminal activities, including political assasination and drug trafficking. Only four of the organizations ordered closed— *Yerkir, Azatamard, Marzashkharh* and the Haylour News Agency—were directly affiliated with the ARF. The other seven were independent organizations, some of whose staff were ARF members.

Azerbaijan

The six-year undeclared war with neighboring Armenia over the disputed enclave of Nagorno-Karabakh went terribly wrong for Azerbaijan in 1994. The instability created dozens of armed gangs and interest groups with regional power bases, all of whom presented a serious challenge to Azerbaijan's president, Haydar Aliyev. His response was to impose an even more intense crackdown on opposition groups and the media than had been in effect in previous years.

In October, Aliyev declared a state of emergency after a two-day standoff with police troops. He claimed that the police and armed supporters were attempting a coup backed by former Prime Minister Suret Huseinov. During the state of emergency, which was still in effect by year's end, Aliyev had carte blanche to shut down political par-

Central Europe

ties, impose censorship and dismiss officials. He managed to remain in power and to restore order, but only by crushing all opposition, reappointing his supporters and reactivating the department that censored the media in Soviet days. Since that time, the country's 600 newspapers have been scrutinized and often forced to publish with blank space in place of stories critical of Aliyev's regime. And the government decreed that independent publications must pay for information provided by the state news agency, which they are required to carry.

February 11
Dick Gordon, *Canadian Broadcasting Corporation (CBC),* EXPELLED
Douglas Alteen, *CBC,* EXPELLED
Mike Trickey, *Southam,* EXPELLED
CBC radio reporter Gordon; his producer, Alteen; and Trickey, a reporter for the Canadian Southam newspaper chain, were arrested and expelled from Azerbaijan after being told by authorities that their accreditation documents were "no longer valid." The journalists had been asking questions about the conditions in refugee camps, where settlers were complaining that the Azerbaijan government was not providing them with sufficient assistance. CPJ condemned the expulsion in a letter to Azerbaijan authorities.

March
Thomas Goltz, *Free-lancer,* HARASSED
Goltz, a free-lance writer who published several articles in the *New York Times,* was arrested at the end of the month in Baku while covering a demonstration by opposition movements. He was released in a few hours. No charges were pressed.

April 18
Azadlig, ATTACKED, HARASSED
The editorial office of *Azadlig,* the largest opposition newspaper in Azerbaijan, was attacked by several uniformed police. Without having pre-

sented any warrants for arrest or detention, they held 15 people in the newspaper's offices for the entire day. Among those detained were Ganimat Zahidov, a former editor of *Azadlig,* staff writers Hikmet Zeynalov, Rafig Mammadly, Gorkhmaz Ibrahimov and Kanan Salimov, as well as members of the Popular Front who were inside the building at the time.

November 4
Seyfullah Mustafayev, *Azerbaijan News Service (ANS),* HARASSED
Mustafayev, president of the Azerbaijan News Service, which runs the only independent radio and TV news stations in Baku, was beaten in the office of Babek Huseyinov, head of State Radio and Television. Mustafayev claims that Huseyinov's bodyguards assaulted him. The next day ANS radio and TV stations were prevented from broadcasting by city officials in Baku. They were allowed to resume airing programs on Nov. 7 after several appeals by ANS to government officials. Mustafayev told CPJ he believes that his beating and the suspension of his stations's broadcasting rights were part of a campaign to force ANS radio and television off the air.

Belarus

Presidential elections in July 1994 promised to break the Communists' grip on power that had remained firm in Belarus despite the collapse of the Soviet Union in 1991. The winning candidate, Alexander Lukashenko, promised during his campaign that, if elected, he would liquidate the state's monopoly of the media, ban political censorship, end political persecution of journalists, and permit the independent distribution of information irrespective of the will of officials.

But Lukashenko did not make good on his promises. In December, he reimposed political censorship, and as a result major newspapers began running white space in place of censored stories. The president also refused to release a report on government corruption to the media, and he fired editors of the largest newspapers in the republic.

March
Alexander Chulanov, *Belarus National Television,*
KILLED
Chulanov, a sports correspondent for Belarus National Television, was found dead in his Minsk apartment in March. He was killed by a blow to the head with a heavy object. The motive for his killing remains unknown. CPJ wrote to the president of Belarus asking for a thorough investigation.

December 23, 1994
Sovetskaya Belarus, CENSORED
Respublika, CENSORED
Zvezda, CENSORED
Narodnaya Gazeta, CENSORED
In accordance with a presidential order, the newspapers ran white space in place of stories on a report about corruption in the presidential administration, which was written by a member of the Belorussian Parliament. The exception was *Narodnaya Gazeta,* which did not publish at all that day.

December 25, 1994
Igor Osinski, *Sovetskaya Belarus,* HARASSED
Osinski, the chief editor of *Sovetskaya Belarus,* was dismissed by order of Belarus President Alexander Lukashenko because he protested Lukashenko's order to censor stories about a report on corruption in the presidential administration.

Bosnia-Herzegovina

All the problems encountered by journalists and news organizations in Bosnia in 1994 were directly related to the war that has raged

in the country since 1992. Security remained the prime issue. Often caught in the crossfire, injured or killed by land mines or targeted by different warring factions for their coverage, journalists, both local and foreign, were—and continue to be—at high risk. Six journalists were killed in 1994 in Bosnia, and the death of a seventh is under investigation. This brings to at least 45 the total number of journalists killed during the first three years of the conflict in the republics of the former Yugoslavia.

Local news organizations were constantly limited by the material scarcities and other difficulties caused by the war. Newspapers had to struggle to find enough newsprint to publish regularly. TV and radio stations did not have a sufficient supply of blank tapes, forcing them to reuse old ones and thereby delete valuable archive material. Phone lines did not work, and travel proved extremely dangerous, which made the gathering of information a daunting task, even for the locals.

January 28
Dario D'Angelo, *RAI-TV,* KILLED
Marco Luchetta, *RAI-TV,* KILLED
Alessandro Otta, *RAI-TV,* KILLED
The three Italian journalists working for RAI were killed by mortar fire from the Bosnian Croats as they were entering Mostar in their car. They were going to film a documentary about children orphaned by war in Mostar. Croatian Foreign Minister Mate Granic expressed his "deep concern and regret" over the deaths of the journalists in a letter to the Italian government, but he refrained from openly condemning the Bosnian-Croat (HVO) forces responsible for the shelling. CPJ issued a press release calling for all sides in the conflict as well as the United Nations to offer greater protection to journalists.

March
Frane Jedzicic, *Slobodna Dalmacija,*
IMPRISONED
Jedzicic, a correspondent for the Croatian daily

153

Slobodna Dalmacija, based in Split, was arrested by Bosnian-Serb authorities in Bugojna. He was still in prison at the end of 1994.

March 1
George Eykyn, *BBC*, HARASSED

Despite having received all the necessary permission from the Serbian authorities, BBC correspondent Eykyn was detained after he had finished shooting in Gorazde. His tapes were seized, and he was detained for five hours. When he was allowed to leave, his tapes were not returned to him. Eykyn protested strongly to the military officials who knew him and had given him permission to do what he was doing. He was especially disturbed because he had shot footage of the Bosnian-Muslim side and the unedited footage would give the Serbs access to some classified enemy information. Eykyn argued that the confiscation of his tapes made it appear that he was a spy for the Serbs and compromised his role as an objective journalist covering both sides of the conflict.

April 14
All American journalists, EXPELLED
Srdjan Ilic, *Associated Press (AP)*, EXPELLED
Mike Montgomery, *Daily Telegraph*, EXPELLED
Misha Slavic, *AP*, EXPELLED

Following NATO air strikes on its positions in Bosnia, the self-declared Bosnian-Serb government ordered the expulsion of all American journalists and local journalists working for U.S. media organizations from the Serbian-held territory of Bosnia. The journalists to whom the order applied who were there at the time were two AP correspondents, both Yugoslav nationals, and Mike Montgomery, an American working for Britain's *Daily Telegraph*. CPJ wrote to the Bosnian-Serb authorities in Pale criticizing the ban. By June, Serbian authorities had started to ease their restrictions. Although no formal announcement about the lifting of the ban was ever made, American journalists and others working for U.S. media organizations can now get permission from the Serbs to enter Serbian-controlled Bosnia.

May 1
Brian Brinton, *Free-lancer*, KILLED
Francis Tomasic, *Free-lancer*, KILLED
William Vollman, *Spin magazine*, WOUNDED

Brinton, Tomasic and Vollman were driving to Mostar when their car hit a land mine, according to U.N. accounts. Brinton, a free-lancer on assignment from the Seattle-based *Magnolia News*, and Tomasic, a translator for Vollman of *Spin* magazine, died at the site of the incident. Vollman was injured slightly and was rescued by Bosnian Muslim soldiers who arrived at the scene shortly after the explosion. The road was known to have mines, but it is not clear if the three men knew that.

August 30
Mohammed Hussein Navab, *Keyhan*, KILLED

A correspondent for the Tehran daily *Keyhan*, Navab was killed in Mostar by unidentified gunmen. He disappeared on Aug. 28, and his body was discovered on Sept. 5. A coroner determined that he died on Aug. 30. A fact-finding mission sent to Mostar by the Iranian government concluded that Navab was abducted and killed by Croat militiamen. Iran vigorously protested the incident to the Croatian ambassador in Tehran. CPJ issued a press release calling on the Bosnian government, local Croat leaders, Mostar's European administration and the U.N. Protection Force to investigate the murder.

September
Risto Djogo, *Bosnian-Serb Television*, KILLED

Djogo, the editor in chief of Bosnian-Serb Television in Pale, was last seen on Sept. 10 at a hotel near the border between Muslim-led Bosnia and Serbian-controlled Bosnia. His body was found in a lake, and he is assumed to have been murdered. Djogo was a staunch nationalist who regularly ridiculed the Bosnian Muslims on his TV news show. Just before his death, he had started to voice opposition to Serbia's President Slobodan Milosevic for cutting ties with the Bosnian-Serb government. Serbian authorities announced later that an autopsy revealed no signs of violence on Djogo and that it appeared he died by drowning. Local journalists told CPJ that his death is too suspicious to write off as an accident.

October 5
Boro Maric, *Vecernje Novosti,* IMPRISONED
Maric, the Banja Luka correspondent of the pro-government Belgrade daily *Vecernje Novosti,* was detained by the Bosnian-Serbs in Pale. He was subsequently released in November.

Croatia

Like the governments in many former Communist countries, the Croatian government has used mostly economic means to pressure the opposition press. Though independent media are gaining strength in the country and laws have been passed that favor a free press, the printing houses are still owned by the state, as is the system of distribution. This gives the government a powerful economic weapon to fight news organizations that criticize the state. But not all independent media have bowed to the pressure, and in 1994, many continued to be critical in their coverage despite the economic consequences.

Other problems faced by journalists in Croatia during the year were directly related to the war in neighboring Bosnia. For instance, journalists were often detained by ethnic Serbs who lived in the Krajina district of Croatia and who controlled some of the territory. They were also subject to harassment and attacks by Croat nationalists who would act out of sympathy for ethnic Croats in Bosnia. The war's effect on the region economically also made it very difficult for news organizations to survive.

April 1994
Tatjana Tagirov, *Arkzin,* ATTACKED
Tagirov, a journalist with the anti-war magazine *Arkzin,* was stopped by the police as she

returned from visiting a friend at night. When the two officers recognized her name after checking her ID, they started beating her, first with their hands, then with their guns. When she pleaded to go to the police station, the officers radioed for support and the officers arriving on the scene joined in the beating. Tagirov was finally taken to the station and questioned about her writing in the magazine. She was released after three hours. A few days later the deputy police commissioner of Zagreb called and apologized, saying it was only a few officers who were unruly and that they would be punished. Tagirov saw the same officers' names in the newspapers when some human rights activists were beaten a few months later. She told CPJ that she believes she was beaten because of her anti-war writing and that while the government does not systematically support them, it tolerates attacks on anti-war activists.

July 1
Feral Tribune, HARASSED
Arguing that the *Feral Tribune* had become a "pornographic" publication, the Ministry of Education and Culture increased the tax rate of the newspaper to 50 percent. One of the few independent publications in Croatia, the *Feral Tribune* is a satirical political weekly with one of the highest circulations of any newspaper in the country. The tax rate increase was seen as a punishment by the government, which was not happy with the regular criticism meted out by the newspaper.

December 4
Lucia Annunziata, *Corriere della Sera,*
    IMPRISONED, HARASSED
Federico Bugno, *Expresso,*
    IMPRISONED, HARASSED
Guido Picchio, *Olimpia Agency,*
    IMPRISONED, HARASSED
The three Italian journalists were arrested by the Serbian militia in the Croat region of Krajina. They were held for 34 hours in Turanj, Croatia. They were released on the night of

Central Europe

Dec. 5, but their car, their money and their documents were stolen.

December 5
Luc Delahaye, *Magnum,*
   IMPRISONED, HARASSED
Ron Jacques, *Saba Press Photo,*
   IMPRISONED, HARASSED
Jacques, an American photographer, and Delahaye, a French photographer, were both on assignment for *Newsweek* when they were arrested by the Serbian militia division in Vojnic, in the Croat region of Krajina. They were released unharmed on Dec. 7, but their car, their personal documents and most of their equipment that had been confiscated were not returned.

Georgia

Since April 1991, Georgia has been torn by a civil war that has left thousands dead and hundreds of thousands homeless and near starvation. In 1994, internal conflicts intensified and, as a result, independent media came under constant government pressure. CPJ was able to confirm two violent attacks against journalists that were directly tied to their professional responsibilities, as well as the bombings of two major news organizations in the nation's capital of Tbilisi.

March 23
Zazou Chenguelia, *Ibervizia Television,*
   ATTACKED
Chenguelia, director of Ibervizia Television, had to be hospitalized after being beaten by several armed men who stormed the station's offices. The attack followed a number of threats made to the staff of Ibervizia for airing a report critical of the former defense minister. No investigation was conducted, and no suspects were questioned.

March 26
Ibervizia Television, ATTACKED
The Tbilisi offices of the independent television station Ibervizia were bombed three days after the station director, Zazou Chenguelia, was beaten in the Ibervizia's offices. The blast caused structural damage to the building, and destroyed the building's roof, antennas and broadcast equipment. It is believed the bombing was in retaliation for a report the station aired that was critical of the former defense minister, but no one has claimed responsibility for the attack, and no investigation of the case was conducted.

April 8
Svobodnaya Gruzia, ATTACKED
A bomb exploded at the editorial office of *Svobodnaya Gruzia* newspaper at approximately 1 p.m. No one was injured in the blast. According to an official account, someone threw a grenade into the office of the newspaper, and it landed on a couch. No investigation of the case was conducted.

July 27
Giorgi Ratishvili, *Ostankino Television,*
   ATTACKED
Ratishvili, a correspondent for the Russian state radio and television company, Ostankino, was stopped in his car by police in Tbilisi. After checking Ratishvili's accreditation as a representative of the Russian media, the police began searching his car. When he asked them not to throw his belongings around, the officers beat him until he was unconcious. Ratishvili suffered a concussion and eye damage in the attack. By order of the Georgian minister of internal affairs, Shota Kviraia, two policemen were fired for the beating, and severe reprimands were issued to the chief of Tbilisi's Saburtalo district police department and the commander of a special subunit of the main directorate of the Tbilisi police. The minister announced that he will "personally ensure the safety of every journal-

ist," and measures will be taken to avoid similar incidents in future.

Hungary

Before losing the national elections in May 1994, the Hungarian Democratic Forum (MDF) had been coming down hard on the broadcast media in the first few months of the year. In March, 129 journalists were dismissed from Hungarian Radio, allegedly for budgetary reasons. But journalists told CPJ that the dismissals were an attempt to silence criticism of the government before the elections. Previously, MDF leaders had expressed annoyance with Hungarian Radio because it had not given the prime minister, Peter Boros, exclusive air time before the municipal elections.

The coalition government of Socialists and Liberal-Democrats that ousted MDF proved to be no less heavy-handed when it came to silencing media criticism. Made up of former Communists and former anti-Communist dissidents, the coalition fired the directors of Hungarian Radio and Television, and appointed Adam Horvath to head up state television. One of Horvath's first decisions was to cancel the popular and controversial "Hirado" news program, which had been critical of the Socialist Party before the elections, and to fire the show's executive producer, Istvan Stefka.

The heavy hand of the government in state-run television was particularly hard felt because of the fact that there are still no independent broadcast TV stations in Hungary. A bill that would have allowed for privatization of television was shelved on Oct. 17, 1994, because members of the ruling coalition could not agree upon its terms.

Cable television fared somewhat better, in part because of the absence of a media law to govern it. In 1994, Hungary, by some reports, had nearly one million households subscribing to cable service, a major portion of which was provided by Kábelkom/HBO, a joint venture with Time Warner and United Communications International.

As in previous years, the print media enjoyed success and influence throughout 1994. Boosted by foreign investment, new private publications and some former state dailies thrived in the new commercial environment. But the process of press privatization, begun by the MDF government, was sometimes hampered by political discord.

March 4
Hungarian Radio, LEGAL ACTION
The head of Hungarian Radio, Laszlo Csucs, announced that he was firing 129 journalists for budgetary reasons. But Hungarian journalists told CPJ the dismissals were intended to silence government criticism before the national elections in May. Prior to the dismissals, the Hungarian government had expressed annoyance with the live coverage of a Budapest taxi strike and the fact that the prime minister, Peter Boros, was not given exclusive air time before the municipal elections. On March 22, CPJ wrote a letter to Boros denouncing the dismissals.

July 21
"Hirado," CENSORED
Istvan Stefka, *"Hirado,"* CENSORED
Adam Horvath, who had recently been appointed head of Hungarian Television [MTV] by the newly elected Socialist-Liberal coalition government, cancelled the controversial news program "Hirado" ("Newsreel") and fired its executive producer, Istvan Stefka. "Hirado" had been critical of the Socialist party before the election. In a letter to the Hungarian government, CPJ was critical of Horvath's decisions.

Romania

Passage of amendments to Romania's Penal Code in 1994 stiffened the penalties for libel. As a result, a prison sentence of up to eight years may be handed down for a journalist convicted of slandering the head of state.

In December, 17 Romanian publications protested the decision by the country's only newsprint supplier to stop production for a few months. In spite of a temporary cancellation of import taxes for newsprint, the factory supplied paper only erratically, and some newspapers complained that they were being discriminated against politically.

The picture was somewhat brighter for the broadcast media. By August 1994, the Romanian National Broadcasting Council, had awarded 63 licenses to local broadcast television stations in 35 large and medium-size cities of the country. Bucharest, the capital, has five such stations in operation. And by year's end, there was a total of more than 90 radio and television stations operating throughout the country, not including cable networks.

Still, the viability of the new stations was jeopardized by the Communication Ministry's restrictive regulations on the power of the radio and television transmitters. The government severely reduced the power of local TV transmitters, thereby limiting their reach. In addition, commercial code regulations limited the amount of money a company could spend on radio and television advertising, which deprived broadcasters of a critical source of revenue.

Despite its willingness to license privately owned local TV stations, the National Broadcasting Council would not award a license to a private nationwide broadcaster. In the spring, parliament passed a special law that regulates radio and television and designates national television frequencies as state assets, thereby prohibiting their privatization.

February 14
Nicolae Andrei, *Conflict*, IMPRISONED
Andrei, a journalist working with the small local weekly *Conflict* in Craiova, about 120 miles west of Bucharest, was arrested for "insulting the

head of state" in a satirical piece he wrote that combined elements of a well-known fairy tale—whose main character is a pig—with the biography of Romania's president, Ion Iliescu. Andrei was released on bail on Feb. 21, and his case was still pending in the local court at the end of the year. If convicted, he faces up to eight years in jail. This was the first time since 1989 that a Romanian journalist was arrested for a press offense. He was prosecuted under a provision in Article 238 of the Penal Code that had been amended recently to increase the prison terms for slandering the head of state.

October 1
Gigi Nicolau, *Free-lancer,* ATTACKED
Nicolau, a free-lance reporter and photojournalist for the satirical weekly *Academia Catavencu* and for the weekly magazine *Tinerama*, was assaulted by Miron Cozma, the leader of one of the largest coal miners' unions in Romania. The incident occurred during a rock concert sponsored by the trade union. It started when Cozma noticed that Nicolau was photographing him. Cozma began to punch him repeatedly, and afterward, one of Cozma's bodyguards took the journalist's camera and never returned it. According to eyewitnesses, police were present during the assault but did not intervene. The Romanian Journalists Association distributed a letter of protest, and on Oct. 6, Nicolau sued Cozma for physical assault. By year's end, the case was still pending.

Russia

One major achievement of *glasnost* and *perestroika,* the breakdown of the Soviet Empire, and President Boris Yeltsin's hectic reign has been the lifting of official censorship in Russia. But a new type of censorship has emerged, one that is enforced by the media's continuing dependence on state support, the intimidation of journalists and even contract killings.

The murder of Dmitry Kholodov, an investigative reporter for Moscow's most popular newspaper, *Moskovski Komsomolets,* marked a new era in the history of Soviet/Russian journalism. Before his death, Kholodov, 27, had been writing extensively on corruption in the Russian military. He was killed in October 1994 when a booby-trapped briefcase he had collected from a source at Moscow's Kazanski railroad station exploded in the offices of his newspaper. His murder especially frightened colleagues because it was so clearly linked to his activities as a reporter.

In 1993, eight journalists were killed in Russia–all but one died during the confrontation between Yeltsin and supporters of ousted parliamentarians. In 1994, however, the attacks against journalists, though fewer, became far more personal. At least two were murdered because of their work, and CPJ is still investigating the motives for two other homicides. No arrests have been made in any of these cases.

Russians still believe in the written word. And the Russian press is one of the few progressive institutions operating in the country, playing a crucial role in the building of democracy and free enterprise. Thus, in the long run, this ruthless campaign against journalists could be even more dangerous than the smuggling of nuclear weapons or the spread of rabid anti-Semitism.

But violence was not the only threat to press freedom in Russia in 1994. Much of the print media still depended on state support and ran the risk of losing critical funding if a government official disagreed with something he had read in a publication. And even though many media organizations became joint-stock companies in 1992, they still had to go to the state for printing, paper and distribution services. The costs charged for these government monopolies soared way above world prices, and proved to be the best means for the state to keep the media on a short leash.

In addition to being pursued by the government, many news outlets were also subject to influence from criminal syndicates as well as commercial and political groups from which they received funding. Many entrepreneurial publishers, for instance, with close ties to political organizations, often encouraged their papers to sponsor certain politicians at voting time. Similarly, firms that offered lavish funding to newspapers tended to want a say in the paper's content. To ward off such interference, some newspapers kept a majority of their shares in the hands of their editorial staff.

While Russia has worked to eliminate government involvement in the print media in the last three years of transition, there was little movement to divorce television from state control during the year. Independent channels emerged, but mostly on a local or regional basis. And two nationwide television broadcast outlets—Channel 1 (Ostankino) and Channel 2 (RTR)—remained in the government's hands.

Still, one independent national station, Independent TV (NTV), which siphoned talent and advertising from the state channels, managed to provide some competition for government broadcasting. NTV proved to be a reliable news source in 1994, especially at year's end with its coverage of the Chechen conflict. Whereas the state channels mostly repeated government misinformation, NTV, like the independent newspapers, made an effort to report events as they really happened.

During the early stages of the conflict, Russian troops attempted to force journalists out, particularly television media, by jamming satellite transmissions, stealing journalists' cameras and shooting at their cars. But the government's efforts to censor the war proved unsuccessful, and the Russian public experienced its first television war, a result of which has been the overwhelming public disapproval of Yeltsin's policy toward the breakaway republic.

Central Europe

January 27
Vil Mirzayanov, *Institute of Organic Chemistry,*
IMPRISONED
Mirzayanov, a scientist who contributed to the weekly *Moscow News,* was arrested for refusing to appear in court because the proceedings were to be kept secret. He was sent to Matrosskaya Tishina, a maximum security prison, where he faced a seven-year sentence if convicted. CPJ wrote to President Boris Yeltsin and General Prosecutor Alexei Kazannik in protest of Mirzayanov's arrest. On Feb. 22, he was released. On March 11, the Office of the Prosecutor General announced that all charges against the defendant had been dropped due to lack of evidence. On May 17, Mirzayanov filed a 40-million ruble (US$10,000) lawsuit against the counterintelligence service, the Office of Prosecutor General and the Institute of Organic Chemistry from which he was fired. Mirzayanov's legal problems began after he wrote an article entitled "A Poisoned Policy," which was published in the Sept. 20, 1992, issue of *Moscow News.* The article alleged that Russia was continuing to develop chemical weapons in violation of international agreements. On Oct. 22, 1992, Mirzayanov was arrested, imprisoned and charged with disclosing state secrets, thereby becoming the first political prisoner in the post-Soviet era. But the charges did not stand up in court, and the case was dropped. In March 1993, however, Prime Minister Victor Chernomyrdin signed a resolution making it a crime to reveal past or present state secrets and, as a result, Mirzayanov was once again detained.

February 1
Sergei Dubov, *Vsyo Dlya Vas, Novoye Vremya,*
International and *Moscow Business Week,*
KILLED
Dubov, publisher of several newspapers and magazines (*Vsyo Dlya Vas, Novoye Vremya, International* and *Moscow Business Week)* was shot dead in front of his house. He was killed by a single bullet, shot by an assailant standing in a telephone booth. The Russian media reported that Dubov's killing was related to his activities

as a newspaper publisher, although CPJ was not able to confirm this. Russian authorities said that they were conducting an investigation of the case, but they have not made public any information about it.

February 4
Alexei Kostin, *Yeshcho,* IMPRISONED
Kostin, founder and publisher of the Latvian-based newspaper *Yeshcho,* was arrested for the second time for allegedly continuing to publish and distribute his publication, which according to the government is pornographic. However, *Yeshcho* has never been ordered to cease publication. Kostin's arrest followed a debate on what constitutes pornography, and he has been in jail awaiting trial since February 1994. His imprisonment violates the Russian Processing Code, which sets a maximum term of imprisonment prior to trial at nine months. Kostin was first arrested on Oct. 6, 1993, in the wake of the standoff at the Russian White House, when Russian President Boris Yeltsin temporarily banned a dozen newspapers, including *Yeshcho.* He was held in custody until Oct. 28, 1993, when he was formally charged with production and distribution of pornography and possession with intent to distribute under Article 228 of the Criminal Code. Two hearings were held in Kostin's case, one in late summer and another in November of 1994. Both times, the judges denied the motion by defense to release Kostin pending trial.

April 26
Andrei Aizderdzis, *Who's Who,* KILLED
Aizderdzis, publisher of the weekly newspaper *Who's Who* and a member of the Russian State Duma (the lower house of parliament), was killed by a shotgun blast to the throat as he returned to his home in the Moscow suburb of Khimki. Although the killer has not been apprehended, Russian lawmakers believe the slaying stems from the publication in Aizderdzis' newspaper of the names of 266 organized crime figures. In a letter to President Boris Yeltsin and Moscow General Prosecutor

Yuri Ilyushenko, CPJ urged the Russian government to thoroughly investigate the murder. The investigation is still in progress. CPJ attempted find new information on this case using its sources in Moscow, but no new information was available by the end of 1994.

May 12
Zufar Gareyev, *Writer*, IMPRISONED
Gareyev, a well-known Moscow fiction writer, was arrested for allegedly selling copies of the banned newspaper *Yeshcho* to an undercover policeman. He and his wife were charged with distributing pornography under Article 228 of the Criminal Code and with distributing items subject to seizure under Article 185. Gareyev was released after 30 hours in custody, and the charges were dropped. The writer is one of the principle supporters of Alexei Kostin, founder and publisher of the banned newspaper, who has been in prison since February 1994. With the help of other Moscow writers, Gareyev organized a letter-writing and media campaign to pressure Russian officials to drop the charges against Kostin.

June 12
Yuri Soltis, *Interfax*, KILLED
Soltis, a crime reporter for the independent news agency Interfax, was found dead at a train station in the Stroitel district on the outskirts of Moscow. Apparently, he was killed while on his way home. The day before, a train conductor saw Soltis being followed by an unidentified man as he stepped off the train. He was so badly beaten that it took police until June 15 to identify him. Soltis' colleagues in Moscow told CPJ that they believe the reporter's murder is linked to his investigation of Russia's criminal underworld.

September 24
Bella Kurkova, *St. Petersburg Television*,
   ATTACKED
Kurkova, director St. Petersburg Television's Channel 5, was assaulted near her home by two men dressed in black. She was seriously injured and spent nearly two months in the hospital. Two weeks later, her news director, Viatcheslav Netchaev, was attacked under similar circumstances. CPJ was told by local journalists that Kurkova and her news director were attacked because she initiated major layoffs from St. Petersburg Television as part of an effort to restructure the station and take extremist points of view off the air. Some of the people were dismissed for their alleged anti-Semitic and ultra-nationalist views. CPJ wrote to President Boris Yeltsin, protesting these and other attacks against journalists in Russia.

October 9
Viatcheslav Netchaev, *St. Petersburg Television*,
   ATTACKED
Netchaev, news director for St. Petersburg Television's Channel 5, was brutally beaten with an iron bar by two men dressed in black. He was hospitalized with head injuries and a broken arm. As a result of the attack, his vision is permanently impaired. The assault occurred two weeks after a similar attack on his supervisor, Bella Kurkova. The attack may have been in retaliation for the major layoffs at St. Petersburg Television. In a letter to President Boris Yeltsin, CPJ protested the attacks on Netchaev and Kurkova.

October 17
Dmitry Kholodov, *Moskovski Komsomolets*, KILLED
Kholodov, an investigative reporter for the Moscow-based newspaper *Moskovski Komsomolets*, was killed in a bomb blast at the offices of the newspaper. Kholodov, who had been investigating Mafia connections with the military, was killed when he opened a briefcase that he had been told contained secret documents exposing military corruption. Defense Minister Pavel Grachev described the murder of the journalist as "the result of a big and dirty political game and a struggle between the Mafia and Russia's leaders." Nevertheless, the outraged public accused Grachev of involvement in the

killing and demanded his resignation. Kholodov's murder touched a nerve among thousands of Russians who saw it as an example of the high level of crime and corruption in the government. CPJ wrote a letter to President Boris Yeltsin, expressing deep concern about the deteriorating state of press freedom in the Russian Federation. Yeltsin is unlikely to force Grachev to resign because Grachev is his ally and an influential figure in the Russian military. The prosecutor's office, which has been criticized for its handling of the case, announced three arrests in connection with the killing, but refused to name the suspects. This heightened the Russian media's scepticism about whether those responsible had in fact been brought to justice. On Nov. 1, Yeltsin dismissed the First Deputy Defense Minister Col. Gen. Matvei Burlakov after continuing allegations that the colonel general was involved in corruption and Kholodov's murder.

November 24
Murad Esenov, *Radio Liberty,*
   LEGAL ACTION, IMPRISONED
Khalmurad Soyunov, *Radio Liberty,*
   LEGAL ACTION, IMPRISONED
Esenov and Soyunov, dissident journalists from Turkmenistan living in Moscow and working for Radio Liberty, were detained in Moscow by the Russian Federal Counterintelligence Service at the request of the Turkmen Prosecutor's Office, which accused them of plotting to assassinate Turkmen President Saparmurat Niyazov. The Turkmen authorities urged Russia to extradite the two men to stand trial in Turkmenistan, where they would face a possible death sentence or prison sentences of up to 15 years if convicted. The dissidents were held in detention at Lefortovo Prison in Moscow for nearly a month before being released on Dec. 22. Charges against them, however, have not been dropped. In fact, they may face additional charges from the Russian authorities. After being released, Esenov went to live with his family in Moscow,

and Soyunov was admitted to a Moscow hospital on Dec. 25 for treatment of an aggravated ulcer, a condition that resulted from his incarceration. Both were granted refugee status in Sweden, but must wait for their documents to be processed before they are allowed to leave Russia.

December 22
Cynthia Elbaum, *Free-lancer,* KILLED
Elbaum, a 28-year-old American free-lance photographer, was killed during a Russian air raid in Grozny, the capital of the breakaway republic of Chechnya. CPJ sent a letter to President Boris Yeltsin, expressing concern over the treatment of journalists covering the conflict and urging him to respect the right of journalists to cover events there without government interference.

December 31
Vladimir Zhitarenko, *Krasnaya Zvezda,* KILLED
Zhitarenko, a war correspondent for the Russian Armed Forces daily, *Krasnaya Zvezda,* was hit by two bullets as he stepped out of an armored personnel carrier on a front line near the Chechen capital of Grozny. He died of his wounds on New Year's Day. Zhitarenko, 54, who held the army rank of colonel, covered the war in Afghanistan as well as numerous conflicts in the former Soviet Union during his 30-year career. CPJ wrote a letter to President Boris Yeltsin, expressing concern over the treatment of journalists covering the conflict in Chechnya and urging him to recognize the right of reporters to cover events there without government interference.

Slovakia

Independent Slovak journalists had to deal with increasing pressure from the government over the course of 1994. The prevalence of state-owned media raised the stakes in this confrontation, and offered, at

times, a shade of legitimacy to government intervention.

On Sept. 30, 1994, the Movement for Democratic Slovakia (HSDZ), won parliamentary elections but was unable to form a government for another three months because it had not garnered an absolute majority. On Nov. 4, however, HSDZ forced parliament to dismiss all but one of the 18 members of the state radio and television supervising councils on political grounds.

HSDZ then fired several journalists working for state broadcasting. Svatozar Kosicki, head of one of the Slovak Television news departments, was replaced the week after the broadcasting councils were disbanded. The official reason given for Kosicki's dismissal was that he "did not work enough with the young staff." But local observers believe that his dismissal stemmed from the content of the news program "Aktuality," which had not supported parliament's decision to fire members of the broadcasting councils.

Vladimir Stefka, the head of Slovak National Radio since the overthrow of Communism in 1990, was also fired at the same time as Kosicki, and replaced by Jan Tuzinsky, a prominent figure in the Movement for Democratic Slovakia, the party dominating parliament. Among Tuzinsky's first actions in his new job was promising to shorten the most popular news program on Slovak Radio, "Radiozurnal," from one hour to 20 minutes. Tuzinsky had said, upon his nomination, that there was too much news and commentary on Slovak Radio and that the public would be better served with music and cultural programs.

State-subsidized periodicals that carried articles criticizing the prime minister and the government suffered financial retribution. The Ministry of Culture removed subsidies from a number of cultural periodicals on the grounds that their readership was too small.

Besides dismissals or direct financial pressures, the government accumulated a towering position over the media through indirect economic means. Danubiaprint, the printing plant used by all newspapers in the country, continued as a government monopoly after its privatization process was halted in 1992 by Vladimir Meciar's government.

March 16
Stefan Hrib, *Radio Free Europe (RFE),* ATTACKED
Milan Zitny, *RFE,* ATTACKED
Ljuba Lesna, *RFE,* ATTACKED
Hrib, RFE's Bratislava editor, and Zitny and Lesna, journalists with the Czech bureau of RFE, were attacked by a crowd of demonstrators who were gathered in front of the presidential palace in Bratislava in support of the ousted Prime Minister Vladimir Meciar. No one was seriously injured, and Hrib was the only one who required medical care after the attack, suffering bruises on his neck, head, chest and back. Bratislava police said that they arrested one of the attackers.

November 4
Slovak Radio and Television, LEGAL ACTION
The Slovak National Council dismissed all but one of the 18 members of the state radio and television supervising councils and appointed new members. Among those dismissed were two journalists: Svatozar Kosicki, head of the Slovak Television news department, and Vladimir Stefka, head of Slovak Radio. CPJ wrote a letter to Slovak President Michal Kovak and to speaker of the National Council, Ivan Gasparovic, protesting the decision to replace the members of the councils. On Dec. 8, CPJ received a reply from Kovac stating that he agreed that the council's dismissals were very disturbing developments that threatened to undermine the independent role of public broadcasting. But he also wrote that he is not constitutionally entitled to revoke the Slovak National Council's decision. CPJ also received a letter from Gasparovic, in which he expressed his disagreement with CPJ's position.

Central Europe

Tajikistan

In 1994, CPJ conducted an investigation into the killings of journalists and the status of press freedom in Tajikistan. As a result of its investigation, CPJ was able to confirm and document for the first time the killing of 27 reporters and editors in Tajikistan since May 1992 (see Special Report: Tajikistan, p. 165). Four of them were killed in 1994. Those who were murdered appear to have been deliberately assassinated for reasons directly related to their profession, and there is strong evidence of official complicity in many of the journalists' deaths.

CPJ was particularly critical of the government's plans to hold national elections in November, considering the complete lack of independent media coverage. Despite numerous protests by opposition groups and human rights organizations, the elections went on as scheduled. Emomali Rakhmonov, chairman of the Tajik Supreme Soviet, won the presidential election. Rakhmonov had been one of the chief field commanders of the People's Front, the paramilitary organization thought to be responsible for most of the journalists' murders.

May 16
Olim Abdulov, *Tajikistan State Television*, KILLED
Abdulov, a staff member of Tajikistan State Television, was shot and killed by unknown persons near Dushanbe.

May 18
Khushvakht Haydarsho, *Jumhuriyat*, KILLED
Haydarsho, secretary of the editorial board of the Tajik-language government newspaper *Jumhuriyat*, was shot dead near his home in Dushanbe. He had recently published articles on the "criminal and political Mafia" in Tajikistan, and the possibility that they were involved in his murder has not been ruled out.

August 9
Maksud Husseinov, *Sadoi Mardum*,
IMPRISONED
Husseinov, a leading journalist for the parliamentary newspaper *Sadoi Mardum*, was arrested in Dushanbe after state security agents searched his home and discovered copies of the opposition newspaper *Charogi Ruzh*, which is published in Moscow and circulates clandestinely inside Tajikistan. In a letter to Tajik authorities, CPJ condemned his arrest and called for his release. On Aug. 14, Husseinov was set free.

August 11
Mukhammadrakhim Saydar, *Sadoi Mardum*,
IMPRISONED
Like his colleague Maksud Husseinov, Saydar, a journalist for the parliamentary newspaper *Sadoi Mardum*, was arrested in the capital, Dushanbe, after state security agents searched his home and discovered copies of the opposition newspaper *Charogi Ruzh*, which is published in Moscow and circulates clandestinely inside Tajikistan. CPJ called for Saydar's release in a letter of protest to Tajik authorities. He was released on Aug. 16.

August 18
Davlatali Rakhmonaliev, *Tajikistan State Television*,
KILLED
Rakhmonaliev, director of programming at the national television station, was fatally shot in front of his home in Dushanbe. He was reported to have close ties to the pro-Communist government, even after it was driven from Dushanbe by rebels in a 1992 civil war. CPJ wrote to the government of Tajikistan, urging it to conduct a thorough investigation of Rakhmonaliev's murder.

November 17
Khamidjon Khakimov, *Khaksuz*, KILLED
Khakimov, editor of the Uzbek-language newspaper *Khaksuz*, was shot in the head in Dushanbe and died overnight. He was a promi-
—*continued on p. 184*

A Retreat to Tyranny: Tajikistan's Unreported War Against Press Freedom

OVER THE PAST THREE YEARS, Tajikistan has been the scene of one of the most brutal yet least noticed campaigns against press freedom in the world. All independent publications and broadcast outlets have been banned or forced out of business. Most Tajik journalists are now in hiding at home or in exile abroad.

Since May 1992, at least 27 reporters and editors in Tajikistan have been murdered. A CPJ investigation revealed that most of these deaths appear to have been deliberate political assassinations carried out by paramilitary forces loyal to the current regime. Tajik authorities in Dushanbe confirmed to a CPJ fact-finding team that there have been no official investigations into these murders. The government, led by President Emomali Rakhmonov, is unapologetic about the crackdown on independent media, which is in turn part of a broader suppression of civil liberties by former Communists whose power is ultimately dependent on the 25,000 Russian troops stationed in the country. Armed opposition groups also appear to have been responsible for attacks on journalists, including the recent murders of several pro-government broadcasters.

IN OCTOBER 1994, CPJ released a special report that documented these deaths for the first time and traced the systematic suppression of press freedom in Tajikistan over the past three years. The CPJ staff and board felt strongly that the situation in Tajikistan merited close attention not just because of the scale and viciousness of the attacks against the press there, but because of its implications for all of Central Asia and, by extension, the other republics of the former Soviet Union.

This special report is an adaptation of a longer report published by CPJ in October 1994. The original report was written by **Leonid Zagalsky,** *CPJ's program coordinator for Central Europe and the republics of the former Soviet Union, and* **William A. Orme, Jr.,** *CPJ's executive director.*

Based on months of research and scores of interviews with local and foreign journalists, government officials, diplomats, Tajik exile sources and human rights investigators, the report brought international attention to the complicity of the present Tajik leadership in many of these murders. It also highlighted the complete absence of independent local media coverage during the period leading up to the Nov. 6 presidential elections.

The report's findings have been cited by the Helsinki Commission, U.S. Congressional committees and other governmental bodies reviewing policies toward and within Central Asia. Yet Tajikistan still seems to be viewed as a tragic, but strategically insignificant, nation condemned by history and geography to remain a protectorate of Moscow. Like much of the rest of Central Asia, it is backsliding into a particularly venal combination of Soviet-style authoritarianism and post-Cold War gangsterism. But because of its poverty and isolation, and the oppressive character of its general neighborhood—Tajikistan borders China, Afghanistan and Uzbekistan, and is closest culturally to Iran—the country has felt little pressure to honor its proclaimed democratic ideals.

The Russian Federation, which provides crucial military and economic support to the Rakhmonov regime, is bound by bilateral treaty obligations to push for progress on human rights issues in Tajikistan. Russia is seeking United Nations recognition of its military forces there as sanctioned "peacemakers," but has failed to control or even protest the systematic assaults by its client government on journalists and other independent voices. With Russian policymakers asserting their right to maintain a strategic presence elsewhere in the "near abroad," the precedent of Tajikistan is especially important. As part of CPJ's campaign to protect journalists in Tajikistan, we have asked President Boris Yeltsin to push for the restoration of press freedom and other civil liberties as a condition of continuing Russian support.

IN DISCUSSIONS IN DUSHANBE, Tajikistan's capital, government spokesmen told CPJ that the prosecutor general's office had been unable to investigate the deaths of journalists, due to a lack of resources and personnel. Yet the prosecutor general's office did find the time to assemble an exhaustive dossier on four former state television journalists who had been jailed for 22 months awaiting trial on charges of treason, a crime punishable by death. The journalists' real crime had been their participation in the accurate television reporting of the civil disorders that culminated in the previous government's overthrow. While in prison, the journalists were denied opportunities to discuss their case with representatives from CPJ and other international organizations that had requested such meetings. (The television journalists were later released as part of a prisoner exchange with armed opposition groups that was brokered by the United Nations.)

Since 1992, hundreds of journalists from Tajikistan have fled to Russia, Afghanistan, Iran and Pakistan. Most of the journalists who were killed or who had to leave the country worked for Tajik-language publications associated with political factions, ethnic groups and Islamic religious forces represented in the coalition government, which was in power for less than a year. In November 1992, that coalition was overthrown by former Communists backed by a paramilitary organization known as the People's Front. Accounts corroborated by journalists, opposition sources, diplomats, foreign experts and other credible sources indicate that the People's Front murdered scores of independent community leaders, including journalists, in its fight for power. Among the first "field commanders" of the People's Front were Emomali Rakhmonov, the country's current president, and his powerful internal security minister, Yakub Salimov.

A Compelling Crisis

In sheer numbers, the killings of journalists in Tajikistan rival the worst levels documented by the Committee to Protect Journalists in Central America and Argentina in the late 1970s and early 1980s. As in Latin America, the paramilitary death squads responsible for these killings appear to enjoy immunity from prosecution, and are in some cases direct extensions of state internal security forces.

In recent years, only Algeria and the former Yugoslavia have seen comparable numbers of journalists killed because of their profession. But in Algeria, these murders were the work of anti-government insurgents, while the journalists killed in Yugoslavia were caught in crossfire or shot by snipers from rebel militias. In Tajikistan, by contrast, most of the murders of journalists appear to have been carried out by paramilitary operatives who have since become an integral part of the state internal security apparatus.

Over the course of 1993, CPJ had received credible reports of the

Regionalism and Power in Tajikistan

FOR MOST OF THE TAJIK POPULATION, regional identity clearly supersedes national identity, and many of the atrocities during the civil war have been committed by the people of one region against those from another. Kinship-based patronage dominates Tajikistan's political and economic system, and this tends to reinforce the regional divisions in society.

Tajikistan's four major regions, which differ in terms of economic development, culture and religion, include:
a) The province of Gorno-Badakhshan in the Pamir Mountains, which is the poorest and least-populated of Tajikistan's provinces. Its residents consider themselves Pamiris;
b) The province of Garm (also called the Karategin zone), which is located northeast of Dushanbe. It is an agricultural area whose inhabitants, mainly peasants, are reputed to be the most religious in Tajikistan;
c) The province of Leninabad (renamed Khojand), an industrial center and the most economically developed region in Tajikistan. This is the home territory of the "Leninabadi clan," which was in power from the 1930s until the breakup of the U.S.S.R. Almost all state bureaucrats and Communist Party officials were selected from this region;
d) The former provinces of Kulyab and Kurgan-Tyube provinces, south of Dushanbe, which were joined together into the Khatlon province. The current government of Tajikistan is dominated by people of Kulyab origin called the "Kulyabi clan." Under Stalin's policy of forced migration, when migrants had to create *kolkhozes* (collective farms) on so-called "new lands," Garmis and Pamiris were forced to settle in irrigation colonies in Kurgan-Tyube, which has seen some of the harshest fighting of the civil war.

Tajikistan's civil war has pitted the people of Leninabad and Khatlon—the regions that benefited the most from years of Soviet domination—against the people of Garm and Pamir, the regions that were most neglected under Communism.

murders of 15 journalists in Tajikistan—more than in any other country in the world. But only four of those cases could be confirmed at the time. Limited, contradictory accounts of these incidents appeared in the Russian press, and Western correspondents in the region had done only limited reporting in the country. The government of Tajikistan did not respond to CPJ's multiple requests for information about the murders, and their diplomatic representatives in New York and Moscow refused requests for meetings. CPJ could not contact independent sources in Tajikistan by fax or phone for fear of jeopardizing their safety. It was essential to research and document these killings with as much detail as possible. And it was equally important to dramatize to authorities in Tajikistan the grave concern with which such murders were viewed by journalists around the world. Leonid Zagalsky, CPJ's program coordinator for the former Soviet Union and Central Europe, began to research the cases extensively in early 1994. His investigation included extensive field interviews during a two-week visit to Russia and Central Asia in June 1994. He was accompanied on the mission to Tajikistan by William A. Orme Jr., CPJ's executive director. Before traveling to Tajikistan, Orme and Zagalsky interviewed journalists and opposition leaders in exile in Moscow, as well as local and foreign journalists and human rights researchers. En route, in Kazakhstan and Uzbekistan, they also spoke to local and Russian journalists who have closely followed the Tajik wars.

In Dushanbe, they met with local journalists, foreign diplomats, representatives of nongovernmental organizations and other sources. They were received formally by several high-ranking Tajik officials, including the minister of press and information and key policy-makers at the prosecutor general's office. They also held a press conference convened by the chairman of the Tajik branch of the Confederation of Journalist Unions.

The minister of press and information, Bobokhon Makhmadov, denied any knowledge of journalists being murdered. When presented with CPJ's preliminary information, he blamed bandits and opposition forces. CPJ's request for a meeting with Prosecutor General M. S. Salikhov was turned down. Orme and Zagalsky met privately with officials in the prosecutor general's office, who confirmed that there had been no official investigation into the killing of journalists, nor was there likely to be one.

In a press conference hosted by the Confederation of Journalist

The Origins of Tajikistan's Civil War

AFTER THE BREAKUP of the Soviet Union and the collapse of the Communist Party in August 1991, Tajikistan's acting president, Khadriddin Aslonov, banned the Communist Party in his republic and passed an order to seize its property. Several days later former Communist Party leaders forced Aslonov to resign, replacing him with the former first secretary of the Communist Party of Tajikistan, Rakhmon Nabiev. The political opposition demanded that Nabiev's government resign. To resolve the political crisis, Nabiev resigned and declared presidential elections. On Nov. 25, 1991, Nabiev was elected president of Tajikistan. These elections were held under the state of emergency in Tajikistan and cannot be considered free and fair.

In March 1992, anti-government demonstrations were held in the capital, prompted by the dismissal of the Pamiri minister of the interior. The Pamiri movement was joined by supporters of the Democratic Party of Tajikistan (DPT) and the Islamic Renaissance Party (IRP). Violent clashes ensued, and in May 1992 Nabiev formed a government of national reconciliation that included some members of the opposition. This sparked a violent campaign in Khatlon by forces spearheaded by the People's Front, which objected to the government's concessions to the opposition.

Violence in Khatlon spilled into the capital in August and September 1992, when anti-government demonstrators forced Nabiev to resign. The opposition installed the chairman of the Supreme Soviet, Akbarsho Iskandarov, as head of state.

The Supreme Soviet then abolished the office of president, appointing Emomali Rakhmonov chairman of the Supreme Soviet. It also appointed a government of national reconciliation, which mostly consisted of the People's Front field commanders during the civil war and political leaders from Leninabad province.

With the capital besieged by the People's Front and other pro-Communist militias, Iskandarov and the coalition government resigned in November 1992. Rakhmonov's government has held power since then, with Rakhmonov elected president in November 1994, in elections without opposition participation.

Unions, Orme and Zagalsky discussed their concerns and preliminary findings. Journalists from the official Khovar News Agency, three government newspapers, several Russian publications and Radio Liberty attended. Those from Tajikistan's press remained silent.

Later, Orme and Zagalsky were interviewed at length on the nightly state television newscast. They expressed CPJ's concerns about the murder of journalists and about the situation of the four imprisoned journalists charged with treason. To their surprise, and, as they later learned, to the surprise of state management, the interview ran intact.

After returning to New York with new sources and information, Zagalsky was able to piece together the list of 27 journalists killed in Tajikistan since 1992. Many other cases, however, are still under investigation.

The Media in Tajikistan: Under State Control

Tajikistan has no tradition of press freedom. Under the former Soviet Union, Tajikistan had only state-owned newspapers and magazines and a few hours of broadcasting on state television and radio, all of which were controlled by the Communist Party. In the latter days of Gorbachev and *perestroika*, a few independent periodicals were founded, and broadcast media began reporting the news more freely. In a newly independent Tajikistan from November 1991 to November 1992—under governments that at times included democratic reformers, Islamic fundamentalists, Tajik nationalists, and regional clans that had been shut out of power under Communist rule—several new periodicals in Dushanbe and in the provinces began publishing a wider range of political, cultural and religious views. Though during that time the succession of governments—that of First Communist Party Secretary Rakhmon Nabiev until May 1992, then a coalition government from May to September, and lastly a short-lived democratic-Islamic government from September to November—often expressed displeasure with dissenting voices, the Tajik media experienced the most freedom they had ever known.

This brief period of relative openness came to a brutal end, however, with the civil war that began in December 1992, when journalists became primary targets of forces linked to the country's ex-Communist rulers. Aside from the 22 local journalists who are

Confirmed: 27 Journalists Murdered in Tajikistan (1992-1994)

SPECIAL REPORT: Tajikistan

THE GREATEST number of journalists killed in Tajikistan since 1992 were murdered during the first full year of the country's civil war, which began in December 1992. Most of the deaths are believed to have been deliberate assassinations carried out by the People's Front, a paramilitary group loyal to the country's current regime, which has stamped out all remnants of an independent media. The Front is also known for targeting various regional and ethnic groups in the country, and indeed, in many cases, those killed appear to have been marked as much for their regional identity as for their profession.

The list below chronicles the deaths of journalists that CPJ was able to confirm, a task that took no less than a year to complete. Several more cases, however, are still under investigation and could not be confirmed by the time this report went to press.

The death toll for journalists in Tajikistan from 1992 to 1994—one of the highest CPJ has ever documented in any one country—is but one indication of the organized terror and systematic suppression of civil liberties being carried out in the republic. It serves as an alarm for the international community to take immediate action on behalf not only of the Tajik people but on behalf of the entire region of Central Asia, which is vulnerable to the Soviet-style authoritarianism and post-Cold War gangsterism dominating Tajikistan today.

1994

Olim Abdulov, *Tajikistan State Television*
May 16, 1994
Near Dushanbe
Abdulov, a correspondent for Tajikistan State Television, was murdered on May 16, 1994, by unknown persons near Dushanbe.

▶

believed to have been killed during 1992 and 1993, scores of reporters and editors fled the country, and most of the new publications closed. Financial pressures—including the loss of state subsidies, the rising cost of imported ink and newsprint, and the overall deterioration of the economy—also contributed to the collapse of independent newspapers.

But the biggest single factor stamping out press freedom was organized repression. Perhaps nothing reflects the recent events in Tajikistan better than the fate of *Navidi Vakhsh*, a pro-Islamic, Tajik-language newspaper published three times a week in the Khatlon region, 100 miles south of Dushanbe. Four of its staff journalists were murdered in 1993 between June and September. One by one, the journalists disappeared under suspicious circumstances; their bodies were later discovered in remote locations outside the capital city. Reports received independently from local journalists, foreign diplomatic sources and exiled leaders all indicate that the People's Front, a paramilitary group loyal to the current regime, was responsible for most, if not all, of these killings. The newspaper has since ceased publication.

Today, the national press in Dushanbe consists of a few state-owned newspapers, with one exception. The most important state newspaper is the Russian-language *Narodnaya Gazeta*, published by Tajikistan's Supreme Soviet. Other branches of government publish the Tajik-language *Jumhuriyat* and the Uzbek-language *Khalqi Ovozi*. The Council of Ministers runs the Russian-language *Golos Tajikistana* and its Tajik- and Uzbek-language sister publications, *Tojikiston* and *Tojikiston Ovozi*. None run independently reported news. Their pages feature government orders and decrees or official reports from government-organized conferences and meetings.

The sole private publication, the Russian-language *Biznes i Politika*, can hardly be considered a newspaper. It publishes mostly advertising and sparse statistical information about the economy. *Biznes i Politika*'s editor is the foreign minister's brother and its owner is a local businessman who obtained a valuable cotton trading license from the current government.

Outside the capital, a small number of provincial tabloids run entertainment features and reprint decrees and official statements, but these have no independent news reports either.

On Feb. 21, 1994, Emomali Rakhmonov, then chairman of the

Khushvakht Haydarsho, *Jumhuriyat*
May 18, 1994
Dushanbe

Haydarsho, secretary of the editorial board of the Tajik newspaper *Jumhuriyat*, was shot dead on May 18, 1994, near his home in Dushanbe. Local journalists believe his murder is connected to a series of articles he published on "the criminal and political Mafia" in Tajikistan.

Davlatali Rakhmonaliev, *Tajikistan State Television*
Aug. 18, 1994
Dushanbe

Rakhmonaliev, director of programming at Tajikistan State Television, was fatally shot in front of his home in Dushanbe on Aug. 18, 1994. He was reported to have close ties to the pro-Communist government. Rakhmonaliev was known for his loyalty after the government was driven from Dushanbe by rebels in 1992. He sought temporary refuge in the southern city of Kulyab.

Khamidjon Khakimov, *Khaksuz*
Nov. 17, 1994
Dushanbe

Khakimov, editor at the Uzbek-language newspaper *Khaksuz*, was shot in the head in Dushanbe on Nov. 17, 1994, and died overnight. Khakimov was a prominent member of the Uzbek minority in Tajikistan.

1993

Saidmurod Yerov, *Farkhang*
January or February 1993
Dushanbe

Yerov, executive director of the Tajik-language *Farkhang* magazine, was abducted by People's Front members in January 1993. Yerov's body was found in a mass grave in Dushanbe on Feb. 2, 1993, local journalists told CPJ.

Yerov was a Pamiri, from the Gorno-Badakhshan province, located south of Dushanbe. Gorno-Badakshan is located in the Pamir Mountains and is the poorest and least populated of the Tajik provinces. People from this region have been frequent targets of the People's Front.

Saidjonol Fakhriddinov, *Navidi Vakhsh*
June 1993
Dushanbe

Fakhriddinov was killed in June 1993; his body was found on the streets of Dushanbe. He was a reporter for *Navidi Vakhsh*, a pro-Islamic, Tajik-language newspaper published three times a week in the province of Khatlon, 100 miles

▶

Supreme Soviet, passed "temporary" Order Number 220, which banned all independent broadcasting. The country's few local independent television stations were forced to close, pending new television regulations to be drafted by the Council of Ministers. Journalists say they fear the new law will grant the government permanent control over all electronic media.

The only opposition newspaper, *Charoghi Ruz*, was once published in Dushanbe but is now edited and printed by exiled journalists in Moscow. It publishes articles both in Russian and Tajik and circulates clandestinely among intellectuals and journalists in Dushanbe. Meeting in Moscow with CPJ representatives, *Charoghi Ruz*'s editor in chief, Dododzhon Atovuloyev, spoke nostalgically of the days when his newspaper was published at home and was popular among city residents.

Charoghi Ruz publishes bitter criticism of the current government of Tajikistan and the ongoing negotiations for a cease-fire on the Tajik-Afghan border. The newspaper maintains contact with members of the opposition in Iran and Afghanistan—almost every issue has interviews with Tajikistan's exiled Islamic religious leaders. At one point, two journalists were arrested by Tajikistan's security forces for possessing a copy of *Charoghi Ruz*. They were later released, though Human Rights Watch/Helsinki received reports that they were beaten while in custody. Western diplomats who complained about their detention noted that *Charoghi Ruz* has never been listed as a banned publication under Tajikistan's press laws.

TELEVISION JOURNALISTS IN JAIL

Government officials told CPJ that a lack of resources prevented them from properly investigating the murders of local journalists. But this did not stop them from compiling extensively detailed accusations of treason against four former journalists from Tajikistan State Television. Mirrahim Mirbobo, Ahmedshoh Komilov, Miriddin Kosimov and Khurshed Nazarov were held in a Dushanbe prison from January 1993 until November 1994. They had been charged with treason and stealing state property—charges that carry the death penalty.

During their visit, CPJ representatives were not allowed to meet with the imprisoned journalists, who had then been awaiting trial for more than 18 months. The First Deputy of the General Prose-

south of Dushanbe. The People's Front is believed by local journalists to have been responsible for his killing and for the murder of three other journalists from the staff of *Navidi Vakhsh* between June 1993 and September 1993.

Fakhriddinov was of Garmi descent, as were two other of his murdered colleagues from the paper. People from the Garm region, a poor and heavily Islamic district of central Tajikistan, have been frequent targets of the People's Front.

Sharofuddin Kosimov, *Navidi Vakhsh*
June or July 1993
Place of death unknown

Kosimov, a reporter for *Navidi Vakhsh* of Garmi descent, was abducted in June or July 1993 by members of the People's Front, according to local journalists. His body was discovered in July and subsequently identified by family members.

Tokhirjon Azimov, *Maktabi Sovieti*
June or July 1993
Place of death unknown

Azimov was a reporter at the state-owned, Tajik-language magazine *Maktabi Sovieti*. He disappeared in June or July 1993. Tajik opposition sources in Russia and the United States say he was killed by one of several small paramilitary groups loosely affiliated with the People's Front.

Sharif Ahrorov, *local newspaper in Kuibishev district of Khatlon province*
June or July 1993
Place of death unknown

Ahrorov, editor of a local newspaper in Kuibishev district of Khatlon province, disappeared in June or July 1993. He was a Garmi. Tajik opposition sources in Russia say he was killed by one of several small paramilitary groups loosely affiliated with the People's Front.

Garmis are a minority in the province of Khatlon, which is dominated by people of Kulyab origin. The so-called "Kulyabi clan," which includes Tajikistan President Emomali Rakhmonov, is heavily represented in the current Tajik government.

Olimjon Yorasonov, *regional newspaper in Vakhsh, Khatlon province*
June or July 1993
Vakhsh, Khatlon province

Yorasonov, a reporter for a regional newspaper in Vakhsh, Khatlon province, was killed in June or July 1993. Local journalists and Tajik opposition sources in Moscow say he was murdered by members of the People's Front.

▶

cutor of Tajikistan told Orme and Zagalsky that the criminal investigation against the four men was over, though they had yet to be
brought to trial because they had not signed a requisite statement
indicating that they had reviewed the state's evidence against them.

After CPJ's visit, the government began negotiating an exchange
of political prisoners with members of opposition groups, who had
submitted a list of 52 people. The four television journalists were on
that list.

In late November 1994, the four men were finally released.
They were permitted to leave the country, and they went to
Afghanistan to receive medical treatment, which CPJ was able to
confirm through sources in Tajikistan, Moscow and Kabul. The
journalists told CPJ's sources that they had been severely tortured
and beaten while in jail.

Russian Complicity

The deliberate killings of journalists could not have been carried out
without Russian complicity. The People's Front, thought to be
behind the murders, was organized with help from Uzbekistan and
Russia. And the Rakhmonov government, which has incorporated
many elements of the People's Front into the state security apparatus, is sustained in power primarily by Russian economic and military support, including the presence of 25,000 Russian troops.

THE PEOPLE'S FRONT

The People's Front was organized in 1992 in the province of Kulyab
by Sangak Safarov, a notorious criminal who spent 23 years in
prison for murder and robbery. The Front targeted Islamic religious
groups, democratic reformers and regional clans who were strong
supporters of the coalition government in power at the time. Journalists were also singled out for attack.

Two of the Front's first "field commanders" were Rakhmonov,
now Tajikistan's president, and Salimov, the current internal security
minister.

In the spring of 1992, just before the coalition government came
to power, then President Nabiev handed out thousands of weapons
to pro-Communist demonstrators in Dushanbe. The guns were
made available to him by the Russian 201st Motorized Division,
according to press accounts at the time. Among the demonstrators

Zikrullo Valiev, *Khalqi Ovozi*
Summer 1993
Place of death unknown

Valiev, a reporter for the state-owned Uzbek-language *Khalqi Ovozi*, was killed in the summer of 1993. Sources in Tajikistan believe that he was killed by an armed band that claims loyalty to the current Tajik government. Valiev was a member of Tajikistan's large Uzbek minority. The motives for his murder are unclear.

Pirimkul Sattori, *Navidi Vakhsh*
July-September 1993
Kurgan-Tyube

Sattori, a reporter for *Navidi Vakhsh*, was killed in Kurgan-Tyube between July and September 1993 by members of the People's Front. Tajik journalists say he was killed for a speech in which he criticized the "Kulyabi clan."

Emma Podobed, *Narodnaya Gazeta*
Missing since September 1993
Place of death unknown

Podobed, a reporter with *Narodnaya Gazeta* in Dushanbe, disappeared in September 1993. The circumstances of his disappearance are unknown.

Tabarali Saidaliev, *Ba Pesh*
Oct. 21, 1993
Place of death unknown

Saidaliev, an editor of the Tajik-language *Ba Pesh*, was killed on Oct. 21, 1993. Witnesses say he was abducted from the paper's office by men dressed like government security officials. Several days later his body was found in a cotton field.

Kishvaroy Sharifova, *Navidi Vakhsh*
Fall of 1993
Place of death unknown

Sharifova, a reporter for *Navidi Vakhsh*, disappeared in the fall of 1993. The circumstances of her disappearance are unknown. Other staff journalists at *Navidi Vakhsh* are believed to have been killed by members of the People's Front. Sharifova was a Garmi.

1992

Olim Zarobekov, *Tajik National Radio*
May 1992
Dushanbe

Zarobekov, a radio journalist, was killed in Dushanbe in May 1992, by mem-

▶

was Safarov, who soon organized the People's Front and recruited many former criminals into its ranks.

In a few months, Safarov expanded his forces and began mass killings of people from Garm, a poor and heavily Islamic district in central Tajikistan, and Pamir, the poorest and least-populated region of the country.

Safarov's forces had tanks, armored personnel carriers and helicopters, along with specialists to service the equipment. Its soldiers were armed with Kalashnikovs. Safarov also received support from neighboring Uzbekistan, whose president, Islam Karimov, was a high-ranking Communist Party official. The Front's officers were trained in Uzbekistan, and the Uzbek army also assisted the People's Front in carrying out its military operations.

On Dec. 9, 1992, following a previously failed attempt, the People's Front captured Dushanbe and moved into Garm, burning villages, destroying mosques and murdering people in its way. The People's Front is reported to be responsible for carrying out attacks on civilians on the basis of the victims' ethnic or regional identity.

Safarov was killed in a shoot-out with his deputy, Fayzali Saidov, in March 1993. And many members of the People's Front are now believed to have been integrated into the official state security apparatus under Internal Security Minister Salimov. Other Front members, who did not receive official positions, have formed their own armed criminal groups.

THE MOSCOW-DUSHANBE "FRIENDSHIP TREATY"
Tajikistan declared its independence from the U.S.S.R. on Sept. 9, 1991, and in March 1992, the former Soviet republic became a member of the United Nations. But Moscow has been reluctant to relinquish its interests in Tajikistan and continues to maintain the Central Asian states as protectorates of Russia.

In July 1993, Moscow and Dushanbe signed the Tajik-Russian Treaty on Cooperation, also known as the "Friendship Treaty," in order to further entrench Russian troops in Tajikistan. The Friendship Treaty provides for wide military, economic, legal and cultural cooperation between Russia and Tajikistan. It also requires the government of Tajikistan to respect human rights and contains a little-known clause calling for the establishment of a bilateral commission on human rights, but nothing has been reported on the activities of

bers of the then newly organized, pro-Communist paramilitary group that later became the People's Front, members of the Tajik opposition in exile told CPJ. Zarobekov, a Pamiri, was among the first Tajik journalists killed in the civil war.

Shirindzhon Amirdzhonov, *Tajik National Radio*
May 1992
Dushanbe
    Amirdzhonov, a Pamiri radio journalist, was killed in Dushanbe in May 1992. Sources in the Tajik opposition in exile say he was murdered by members of the People's Front.

Murodullo Sheraliev, *Sadoi Mardum*
May 1992
Dushanbe
    Sheraliev, the editor in chief of the Tajik-language newspaper of the Supreme Soviet, *Sadoi Mardum,* and member of parliament, was killed by unknown assailants in May 1992 in the building of the Tajikistan Supreme Soviet in Dushanbe. His regional background was Leninabadi.
    Leninabad province, which was renamed Khojand, is the most economically developed in Tajikistan and is an industrial center. This is the home territory for the "Leninabadi clan" which was in power since the 1930s. Almost all state bureaucrats and the Communist party officials were selected from this region.

Tura Kobilov, *Bairaki Dusti*
June 1992
Bokhtar district of Khatlon province
    Kobilov, a reporter for the *Bairaki Dusti* newspaper in Bokhtar district of Khatlon province, was killed in June 1992. Kobilov, a Kulyabi, was taken as a hostage and then killed by his captors. According to local sources, he was killed for his writing after the opposition was removed from the district, where he had chosen to remain.

Arkadi Ruderman, *Channel 1 (Ostankino)*
September 1992
Place of death unknown
    Ruderman, a journalist from Minsk (Belarus) who was working for Russia's state-run television station Channel 1, was killed while on assignment in September 1992. The circumstances of his death are not known.

Zuhurruddin Suyari, *Tojikiston*
September 1992
Place of death unknown
    Suyari, correspondent for the Tajik-language government magazine *Tojikiston,* was killed in September 1992. His body was found in March 1993. Local

▶

this commission, which may or may not have been put into operation.

The Rakhmonov government favors Russian involvement because of the threat of Islamic opposition groups, which are supported by Muslim fundamentalists in Afghanistan, Iran and Pakistan. The vacuum created after the departure of the Communists and the disintegration of the Soviet Union must be filled by someone—and if not by Russia and other Central Asian countries, then Tajikistan may be destined to exist in a perpetual state of anarchy, much like Afghanistan. Already a sizable stream of weapons is flowing into the country from Afghanistan, where many Tajik opposition forces are based, along with the message of Islamic fundamentalists, which has considerable appeal among some of the people. And the mujahideen seem eager to penetrate the Tajik frontier themselves, weapons in hand.

To date, negotiations have failed to quell the conflict. Tajik opposition forces and the Rakhmonov government had agreed to a cease-fire at their meeting in Tehran in October, but clashes continued unabated across the Afghan border. Their most recent round of U.N.-backed negotiations took place in January 1995 in Moscow, but nothing was resolved.

Russian soldiers patrol the Tajik-Afghan border, and the 25,000 Russian troops in Tajikistan represent the largest armed Russian force anywhere outside the borders of the Russian Federation. According to the Friendship Treaty, they are to remain until the country is able to defend its own borders.

Economically, Russian support is vital for the Tajik government, and Tajikistan is the only country of the former Soviet Union that still uses the Russian ruble as its currency. Russia provides as much as 70 percent of Tajikistan's economic aid and military assistance, and Western diplomats estimate that Russia provides up to 50 percent of the country's state budget. Rakhmonov has said that if it were not for Russia and Boris Yeltsin personally, and Uzbekistan and Islam Karimov personally, Tajikistan would already have ceased to exist.

SEEKING THE WORLD'S COMPLICITY
In the fall of 1994, the Russian Foreign Ministry sought explicit U.N. sanction for its forces in Tajikistan. In his October 1994 address to the U.N. General Assembly, Yeltsin stated that "Russia's priority interests lie in the newly independent nations of the former

Tajik journalists and Tajik journalists in exile say he was murdered by members of the People's Front because he was from Garm.

Makhsum Olimi, *affiliation unknown*
October 1992
Place of death unknown

Olimi, a poet and journalist from the Aini district, was killed in October 1992. The circumstances of his death are not known.

Tavakkal Faizulloev, *Subhi Yovon*
Nov. 17, 1992
Place of death unknown

Faizulloev, a correspondent for *Subhi Yovon*, a Yovon district newspaper in Khatlon, was killed on Nov. 17, 1992, in retaliation for his anti-Islamic articles. His regional background was Kulyabi.

Mukhtor Bugdiev, *Khovar Information Agency*
December 1992
Dushanbe

Bugdiev, a photojournalist with Khovar, the official state news agency, was killed in December 1992 in Dushanbe by members of the People's Front, according to local Tajik journalists. He was a Pamiri.

Jamshed Davliyatmamatov, *Khovar Information Agency*
December 1992
Dushanbe

Davliyatmamatov, a correspondent for Khovar and a Pamiri, was killed in Dushanbe in December 1992. Local journalists say that he was murdered by members of the People's Front.

Filolisho Khilvatshoev, *Payomi Dushanbe*
December 1992
Place of death unknown

Khilvatshoev, a correspondent of *Payomi Dushanbe*, was killed in December 1992. Local Tajik journalists say he was killed by members of the People's Front. He was a Pamiri.

Khushvaht Muborakshoev, *Tajikistan State Television*
December 1992
Place of death unknown

Muborakshoev, a television journalist and a Pamiri, was killed in December 1992. Local Tajik journalists say he was killed by members of the People's Front. ∎

Soviet Union, and Moscow believes it has the prime responsibility for ensuring peace and stability among those neighboring states."

One month later, the heads of state from the Commonwealth of Independent States (CIS) decided to extend the mandate of CIS peacekeeping troops in Tajikistan until June 1995. In December, the United Nations sent 40 military observers to the country, thereby formally establishing its first peacekeeping operation in more than a year. A resolution, adopted unanimously by the U.N. Security Council, however, puts a time limit on the venture that is known as the U.N. Mission of Observers in Tajikistan (UNMOT). The observers are to help implement a temporary cease-fire agreement, investigate violations and maintain contact with Russian peacekeeping forces in the country. But the mission, which is subject to renewal, could be pulled out at any time if the brokered cease-fire fails to take hold.

Conclusion

If Tajikistan is an example of how Russia will carry out its self-assigned responsibilities elsewhere in the near abroad, then the international community should be very concerned.

When the Russian foreign ministry sought explicit U.N. sanction for its forces as "peacemakers," Russia took upon itself the responsibility of developing Tajikistan into a democratic state. But given its tremendous leverage with the Rakhmonov government and its failure to insist on adherence to the human rights clause of the Friendship Treaty, it is clear that Russia is not doing enough to push the Tajikistan government in the direction of respecting freedom of the press, pluralism and human rights.

The totalitarianism of the Rakhmonov government, its brazen repression of opposition forces and independent media, and its contempt for international opinion should not be tolerated. The Yeltsin government has not addressed the human rights and press freedom issues raised by the government, nor has he been adequately pressured to do so by the United States and Europe. Indeed, given their acceptance of Russia's far-from-neutral military intervention, they, too, bear some responsibility for the continuing tragedy in Tajikistan.

—continued from p. 164

nent member of Tajikistan's Uzbek minority. CPJ wrote to the government of Tajikistan, requesting a full investigation into the murder.

Ukraine

Despite the continued presence of Communists at the highest levels of government, a number of independent publications and broadcast stations have emerged in Ukraine in recent years. But while the Ukrainian press enjoyed a relatively high degree of freedom in 1994, the same cannot be said for those journalists in the country who were working for Russian media.

President Leonid Kravchuk, the former first Secretary of the Ukrainian Communist Party who was in power until June 1994, began a campaign against the Russian media, accusing them of "rabid and dishonest" reporting on the dispute between Ukraine and the rebel region of Crimea. As a result, Ukraine's Foreign Ministry announced it withdrew the credentials of three reporters, all of whom were Ukrainian citizens working for Commonwealth of Independent States Television in the Black Sea port of Odessa, and in the eastern cities of Donetsk and Kharkov. A ministry spokesman said their accreditation had been withdrawn because they had produced "provocative" stories on the former Soviet republic. At one point in the spring, only one journalist who worked for a Russian media organization in Ukraine had proper accreditation.

May 23

Yuri Selivanov, *Commonwealth of Independent States Television (CIS-TV),* LEGAL ACTION
Vitaly Pidchenok, *CIS-TV,* LEGAL ACTION
Gennady Kondaurov, *CIS-TV,* LEGAL ACTION
Ukraine's Foreign Ministry spokesman announced that it had withdrawn the credentials of three CIS-TV reporters who worked

out of bureaus in the Black Sea port city of Odessa and in the eastern cities of Donetsk and Kharkov. They were among 20 journalists who had applied for renewal, and they were the only Ukrainian citizens in the group. The reporters were singled out for allegedly having produced "provocative" stories on the former Soviet republic. Ukrainian President Leonid Kravchuk accused the Russian media of "rabid and dishonest" reporting on the dispute between Ukraine and its rebel Crimea region, and the government of Ukraine accused the Russian media of being partial toward ethnic Russians in the region. Russian journalists protested the decision, and it was reversed.

Uzbekistan

Uzbekistan, the most populous Central Asian state, remains one of the last bastions of Communism among the republics of the former Soviet Union, with an almost total absence of independent media. Since coming to power in December 1991, President Islam Karimov has banned all opposition parties and imposed strict measures of media censorship.

In 1994, Karimov continued this crackdown on dissident newspapers and journalists, both local and foreign. Moreover, he rejected Western criticism of his regime's human rights record, citing the need for strong executive powers to guard against conflicts spilling over from neighboring Afghanistan and Tajikistan. As a regional power broker, Uzbekistan has been actively involved in these conflicts. In one instance, the Karimov regime supplied and trained the People's Front, a paramilitary group thought to be responsible for the killing of many journalists in Tajikistan.

Karimov also clamped down on free expression in the university. In November, the journalism department at Tashkent State University was shut down after two students

asked questions at a workshop about the censorship of the media and the absence of a democratic press in Uzbekistan. Both students were expelled, and police searched their residences for books and pamphlets produced by opposition leaders. The publications that were found were burned. University Professor Azat Sherakhutdinov, a prominent writer who had tried in vain to persuade Karimov to defend the students, was forced to resign.

March
Salavat Umurazakov, *Erk*, IMPRISONED
Umurazakov, a journalist for the banned opposition newspaper *Erk*, was arrested, tried and convicted for possession of the publication. According to authorities, having copies of *Erk* violated the conditions of a suspended sentence that he had received following a trial on charges that he organized an attempted coup d'etat, carried out other anti-government activity, and insulted the honor and dignity of President Islam Karimov. As a result, he was sentenced to serve the remaining 33 months of his original three-year sentence in a labor colony. On Nov. 3, however, Karimov issued a decree ordering Umurazakov's release from prison along with four other members of the Uzbek opposition movement, Birlik, to which Umurazakov belongs.

March 3
Mamadali Makhmudov, *Writer and Journalist,*
    IMPRISONED
Makhmudov, a leading writer and chairman of the Cultural Foundation of Uzbekistan, was arrested at his home and charged with possession of a firearm. There have been concerns that the charges against him were fabricated as part of the crackdown on *Erk*, the newspaper of the Uzbek opposition party of which the writer is a known member. The paper, which Makhmudov contributed to, was banned by the government in November 1993. By December 1994, Makhmudov was still in prison.

April 20
Abdunabi Adiyev, *Erk*, IMPRISONED
Adiyev, a journalist for the banned opposition newspaper *Erk*, was arrested for possession of the banned publication and was briefly detained.

October 11
Steve Le Vine, *Newsweek*, EXPELLED
Le Vine, Central Asia correspondent for *Newsweek* magazine, was denied press accreditation renewal by the Foreign Ministry's Press Department. Consequently, Le Vine was expelled from Uzbekistan. In a letter to President Islam Karimov, CPJ called on him to reactivate Le Vine's press credentials and to ensure that foreign journalists are allowed to work unhindered in Uzbekistan.

Yugoslavia

Government harassment and intimidation of foreign correspondents in Belgrade, capital of the Yugoslav federation that today consists of Serbia and Montenegro, increased dramatically in 1994. Upset with the reporting and portrayal of Serbs as "the guilty party," the government in Belgrade took away accreditation from many journalists and expelled them. And Western reporters trying to get into Yugoslavia had a very difficult time obtaining visas.

The biggest problems for the local media were the financial penalties, bureaucratic appointments and state takeovers imposed by the government on its opponents in the press. For instance, some news organizations were forced to nationalize because of minor technicalities having to do with the way they were privatized during the transition from communism to a market economy. International economic sanctions against the Milosevic regime were felt most acutely by an unintended target: the independent maga-

zines and radio outlets that criticize the government and hence have no official economic support.

April 12-21

Helene Despic-Popovic, *Agence France Press (AFP)*, LEGAL ACTION, EXPELLED

Rosi Gavrilovic, *AFP*, LEGAL ACTION

Florence Hartman, *Le Monde*, LEGAL ACTION, EXPELLED

Mina Ivanovic, *Cable News Network (CNN)*, LEGAL ACTION

Eli Jurukova, *Demokratia*, LEGAL ACTION, EXPELLED

Jonathan Landay, *Christian Science Monitor*, LEGAL ACTION, EXPELLED

Arnold van Linden, *Sky Television*, LEGAL ACTION, EXPELLED

Nikola Miletic, *AFP*, LEGAL ACTION

Musa Sever, *CNN*, LEGAL ACTION

Viktorija Stegic, *AFP*, LEGAL ACTION

Mirjana Tomic, *El Pais*, LEGAL ACTION

Oliver Vujovic, *Die Presse*, LEGAL ACTION

Joco Znidarsic, *CNN*, LEGAL ACTION

Immediately after the first NATO strikes on Bosnian-Serbs in April, the Serb-dominated Yugoslavian government began a campaign of revoking press credentials of Western journalists based in Belgrade and local journalists working for Western news organizations. Particularly hard hit were correspondents for French and American news organizations. On April 12, the press credentials of all CNN and AFP correspondents were revoked. Likewise, on April 15, Jonathan Landay of the *Christian Science Monitor*, Eli Jurukova of the Sofia-based *Demokratia* and Arnold van Linden of British Sky Television lost their credentials. In the following days, so, too, did Mirjana Tomic of Spain's *El Pais*, Florence Hartman of France's *Le Monde* and Oliver Vujovic of Austria's *Die Presse*. The government cited "anti-Yugoslavian" attitudes and "unfair coverage" as the reasons for its decision. The correspondents who lost their credentials called it "retaliation" for the NATO air strikes. With their press credentials revoked,

foreign correspondents based in Belgrade were forced to leave the country when their visas expired because they could not get them renewed. The Yugoslav nationals who were affected switched jobs to regain accreditation. CPJ sent a protest letter to the Belgrade government twice, after each of the two phases of the revoking campaign.

April 29

Carol Williams, *Los Angeles Times*, LEGAL ACTION

Williams, the Balkans correspondent for the *Los Angeles Times*, learned on April 29 that her credentials as a correspondent were no longer recognized by the Yugoslav government. Williams told CPJ that she has applied for a visa to Yugoslavia more than once since then, but she has not received word on the status of her applications. Other foreign journalists also report that their efforts in recent months to visit Belgrade have been in vain.

July 1994

Studio-B TV, CENSORED

Studio-B TV, the only independent TV station in Yugoslavia, was denied permission to broadcast outside of Belgrade. Although the station's application for a permit to broadcast outside the city was approved by the Ministry of Communications, the Federal Broadcasting Authority refused to honor the decision and told the ministry so. In July, the ministry decided to revoke its original decision. The maneuver was widely seen as a political decision to prevent the station, which is highly critical of the government, from reaching more people.

September

Aleksander Tijanic, *Politika TV*, CENSORED

Tijanic, editor in chief of the semi-independent TV station Politika TV, was forced to resign, and he was replaced by the minister of information. Politika TV, although state-owned, had managed to stay independent and to criticize the government. Commentators said the move to replace Tijanic with the information minister was intended to end that freedom and to silence Politika TV. Tijanic later won a victory in the lower court, which decided that he should be reinstated as the editor in chief. By then, however, he had already started to work for a new independent TV station and did not return to Politika TV.

October 6

Dick Verkijk, *Free-lancer*, EXPELLED

Verkijk, a correspondent for a number of Dutch broadcasters, including Radio Holland, was based in Belgrade when his credentials were withdrawn by the Yugoslav government. His visa was not renewed, and he was asked to leave the country by Oct. 6, which he did. He was also banned from entering Yugoslavia for the next five years. The reason given for his expulsion—carrying out "anti-Serbian activities"—is the same that was used during the April incidents in which foreign correspondents lost their credentials. In a letter to the authorities, CPJ denounced their continued harassment of foreign correspondents in Belgrade and called on them to renew Verkijk's credentials.

November 8

Borba, LEGAL ACTION

Arguing that the independent daily *Borba* (Struggle) was not privatized properly in 1992, the government asked the District Court of Belgrade to annul the privatization and nationalize the newspaper. The court did just that on Nov. 8. *Borba* is highly criticial of the government, and its editors believe that the state is trying to silence it by owning it. As the decision was being appealed, another court decision on Dec. 19 annulled *Borba*'s 1992 privatization. On Dec. 26, the government appointed a state official as the editor in chief of the paper, but *Borba*'s staff rejected the takeover as too premature and refused to cooperate with the new appointee. A "pirate" version of the newspaper began to be published along with the government version. In early January of 1995, the staff moved to another site and started publishing *Nasha Borba* (Our Struggle). The Appeals Court had not yet ruled on the status of *Borba* as this book went to press.

The Middle East and North Africa

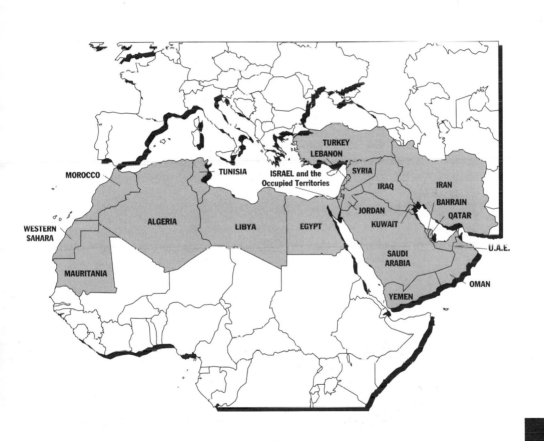

OVERVIEW
OF # The Middle East and North Africa

by Avner Gidron

CIVIL WARS and low-intensity conflicts in the Middle East and North Africa imperiled recent gains for the media and, in some cases, made journalists' work all but impossible in 1994.

Nowhere was this more evident than in Algeria, where 19 journalists were murdered—more than in any other country in 1994. Religious extremists fighting the military regime are believed to be responsible for most of these murders. But before the Islamic militants began their ruthless extermination campaign against journalists in May 1993, it was the Algerian government that was the primary violator of media rights. And though organizations such as the Armed Islamic Group now pose the existential threat to the profession of journalism, the government continues to impose restrictions on the embattled media, essentially banning independent coverage of the country's most pressing issues. Algerian authorities have given journalists the unenviable choice of reprinting official bulletins on security matters (thereby incurring the wrath of the fundamentalists) or printing nothing at all.

Turkey held 74 journalists in prison at the end of 1994—the largest number ever documented by CPJ anywhere. The war between Kurdish separatists and government security forces is the main reason for the systematic oppression. The government treats not only pro-Kurdish writing, but any independent reporting that contradicts the goverment's account of the conflict, as "separatist propaganda." As a result, newspapers and magazines are routinely confiscated by the authorities; edi-

Avner Gidron *is CPJ's director of research and program coordinator for the Middle East and North Africa. Fluent in Arabic and Hebrew, Gidron has lived and studied in Egypt, Jordan and Israel. He is a contributing editor to* World Press Review, *and holds an M.A. in Middle East studies and international economics from the Paul H. Nitze School of Advanced International Studies at Johns Hopkins University.*

   Marlé Hammond, *a research consultant at CPJ, contributed extensively to this report, and* **Yalman Onaran,** *a CPJ research associate, wrote the section on Turkey.*

tors and reporters are regularly harassed, detained, sentenced to prison terms and fined; and news organizations are often ordered shut down.

In September, for the first time in over two years, armed Islamic opponents of the Egyptian government killed a journalist. The radical Islamic Group (al-Gamaa al-Islamiya) claimed responsibility. No group, however, took credit for the assassination attempt on writer and columnist Naguib Mahfouz in October. But most violations of press freedom in Egypt during the year were committed by the government. Citing the ongoing struggle with the Islamists, the government extended the state of emergency, which has been in effect since 1981, for three more years. And it used its emergency powers to jail opposition reporters and editors without due process.

The government of Tunisia, having used the threat of fundamentalism to silence critical reporting in the domestic press for the last several years, turned its attention to the foreign media in 1994. It banned foreign publications that criticized its human rights policies, and censored foreign correspondents who reported on the presidential candidacy of a former leader of a human rights organization.

Attacks on reporters working in the Israeli Occupied Territories were common in 1994, despite implementation of the Israel-PLO agreement. The introduction, in May, of partial Palestinian self-rule in Gaza did reduce violations of journalists' rights. But the Palestinian National Authority (PNA), faced with an increasingly popular Islamic opposition and pressure from Israel to crack down on terrorism, quickly resorted to banning newspapers, arresting journalists and even shooting reporters covering confrontations.

Yemen's two-and-a-half-month civil war, which began in May, put three years of unprecedented press freedom to the test. Independent newspapers emerged weakened and more vulnerable to the government's use of economic pressure and legal harassment. And many papers in the port city of Aden, capital of the defeated secessionist southern rebels, were permanently shut down.

CPJ was unable to confirm any attacks on the press in Syria, Saudi Arabia, Libya or Iran in 1994. While this may appear to be good news, the truth is there are almost no independent journalists left in these countries to get into trouble. None of the governments, with the exception of Iran, allow any critical reporting in their media, and all of them, except Saudi Arabia, can be found in the list of countries currently holding journalists in prison (see page 241). That some have kept journalists in jail for more than 20 years is testament to the fact that they are among the world's most implacable opponents of free expression.

Algeria

Ever since the army intervened to halt the electoral process and prevent the fundamentalist Islamic Salvation Front (FIS) from winning parliamentary elections in 1991, Algeria has been embroiled in a brutal civil war. The government estimates that 11,000 people have been killed, but Western intelligence suggests the number is closer to 30,000.

Nineteen journalists were murdered in Algeria in 1994, the highest number documented by CPJ for the year. They were each targeted because of their profession, as were many of their other colleagues who, unlike them, have been lucky enough to escape assassination attempts. Nearly all the murders appear to be the work of opponents of the regime, especially the radical Armed Islamic Group (GIA). In some cases, such as the murder of Saïd Mekbel, editor in chief of the French-language daily *Le Matin,* the GIA has claimed responsibility. But most assassinations go unclaimed.

Journalists are not the only professionals under attack. Intellectuals, doctors, schoolteachers and foreigners have all been killed. But members of the media are disproportionately represented on the militants' death lists. The first journalist killed in 1995, a reporter for the independent daily *Liberté* who was shot dead on Jan. 6, knew that he was marked for death. His name, Zineddine Aliou Salah, was written on the walls of mosques in his hometown of Blida. Algerian journalists have told CPJ that this is a common phenomenon.

The role of the Islamic Salvation Front (FIS) in the killings is less clear. Throughout 1994, CPJ repeatedly urged FIS leaders to recognize the status of journalists as noncombatants. In a communiqué sent to CPJ in response to our condemnation of the February murder of French free-lancer

Olivier Quemener, the head of the Parliamentary Delegation of the FIS, Anwar Haddam, stated that the FIS "is opposed to and condemns the attacks against individuals who express themselves through exercising their right to freedom of thought and expression (writers, politicians, journalists and scholars). . . . The Parliamentary Delegation of FIS calls on everyone to renounce the violence against Algerian civilians or military and foreigners who are not directing or taking part in security operations involving the use of force." But FIS leaders have not unanimously backed this position. Nor has Haddam himself stuck with it consistently. In August, the publisher of the magazine *Horoscope* was kidnapped by the armed wing of the FIS. He was released after a CPJ appeal to the FIS leadership, but upon being set free he was given a warning to deliver to journalists: Repent or face the consequences.

Algerian journalists repeatedly told CPJ that the Algerian government is not doing all that it can to protect the press. And not only are they not receiving adequate protection, but journalists are actually imperiled by government restrictions that make objective reporting impossible. Militant Islamists have always been suspicious of Algerian journalists, particularly those working for state news outlets or independent papers that espouse an anti-fundamentalist line. The media are seen by opponents of the regime as puppets of the security forces, a perception the government reinforces by monopolizing the distribution of information. In June, the Interior Ministry established a "communications office" the sole purpose of which is to release official communiqués, fed to the press through the government news agency (APS). The ministry also sent a secret directive to all members of the national media forbidding independent coverage of security matters. Such prohibitions have left independent and opposition papers with little more than Hobbesian choices: censor news stories and face the wrath of militant Islamists or expose their publications to lengthy suspensions; reprint APS stories or ignore "security" matters altogether.

In the last two months of 1994, the government showed that newspapers that flaunt its draconian restrictions will be punished. It suspended six papers for periods ranging from two weeks to six months, and seized copies of the most widely read Arab-language daily. Officials offered either vague explanations for the bans or none at all.

February 1

Olivier Quemener, *Free-lancer*, KILLED
Scott Allan White, *Free-lancer*, ATTACKED
French free-lance television journalist Quemener and his colleague White, an Australian free-lance journalist, were shot while on assignment. Quemener was killed, and White suffered a bullet wound to the head and was hospitalized in serious condition. The two cameramen were attacked in the Casbah section of Algiers while shooting video footage that they had hoped to sell to ABC News. The Algerian state news service, APS, referred to them as victims "of a terrorist attack," a term the government uses to describe attacks by Muslim extremists. In a press release, CPJ condemned the shootings and called on the Islamic Salvation Front (FIS) to unequivocally renounce all attacks on journalists in Algeria.

February 14

Abdelaziz Smati, *Algerian Television*, ATTACKED
Smati, a television producer who also produced musical broadcasts for a French-language radio station, was shot repeatedly in the chest and stomach outside his home in Cheraga, a suburb of Algiers. A man reached for a gun tucked inside a notebook and opened fire on him.

Some reports indicate the presence of a second gunman. Smati, who now lives in exile in France, is paralyzed in his legs as a result of his injuries. No one has claimed responsibility for the attack, but it is believed that he was targeted by Islamic militants. CPJ wrote a letter urging the Algerian government to investigate the case, bring those responsible to justice and take urgent action to protect journalists and news organizations from such attacks in the future.

February 28

Abdelkader Hireche, *Algerian Television*, KILLED
Hireche, a journalist with Algerian Television (ENTV), was shot and killed in an eastern suburb of Algiers by three men bearing automatic weapons. Two men who were accompanying Hireche were wounded—one seriously. Later there were unconfirmed reports that security forces had "eliminated" the suspects in the case in an armed clash. In addition to condemning the murder of Hireche and three other journalists, CPJ again called on the Algerian government to make every possible effort to protect journalists and bring to justice those responsible for attacks against them.

March 1

Miloud Zaatar, *Alger Républicain*, ATTACKED
Zaatar, the correspondent in Tiaret (a city southwest of Algiers) for the French-language daily *Alger Républicain*, was hit by five bullets outside his home at night. He was hospitalized and recovered from his wounds. As with the assassination attempt against Abdelaziz Smati, CPJ denounced the attack in a letter to Algerian authorities.

March 1

Mohamed Hassaine, *Alger Républicain*, KILLED
Hassaine, correspondent for the daily *Alger Républicain*, was taken from his home in Larbatache in the Blida region. According to the paper's director, his decapitated body was later found.

Middle East

193

March 5
Hassan Benaouda, *Algerian Television,* KILLED
Benaouda, a journalist with Algerian Television
(ENTV), was shot in the head by a group of
armed assailants in the Casbah section of
Algiers. He died of his wounds one week later.
Security Services later reported that their forces
stormed the suspects' hideout, killed two mem-
bers of the alleged gang and took three others
into custody. CPJ denounced the murder of
Benaouda and other journalists assassinated in
Algeria and demanded that the Algerian gov-
ernment do more to protect journalists.

March 8
Abed Charef, *La Nation,* ATTACKED
Charef, a journalist with the French-language
weekly *La Nation,* survived two attempts on his
life in one day. In the morning, one of his neighbors, who somewhat resembled Charef, was
gunned down in front of his home. Later in the
day gunmen sprayed Charef's car with bullets in
front of his children's day care facility. He was
not in the car, and his driver, who was there to
pick up Charef's children, escaped injury. It is
believed that Charef was targeted by Islamic
militants. In a protest letter about this attack and
others, CPJ urged the Algerian government to
protect journalists and to bring to justice those
responsible for attacks against them.

March 8
Saïd Mekbel, *Le Matin,* ATTACKED
Mekbel, director of the independent French-lan-
guage daily *Le Matin,* escaped injury when his car
was sprayed with bullets by unknown gunmen.
The attack reportedly occurred near his home
while he was on his way to work. In December,
Mekbel was not so fortunate. He was assassinated
while eating in a restaurant in downtown Algiers.
[See Dec. 3 entry.]

March 12
Cherif Rizki, *El Khabar,*
 ATTACKED, THREATENED
Rizki, a journalist with the independent Arabic-

language daily *El Khabar,* was visiting his parents in his hometown of Sidi Naamane in the
district of Tizi Ouzou about 100 kilometers east
of Algiers, when he eluded a group of armed
men who came calling on him. The men
reportedly entered the quarter after the breaking of the Ramadan fast and started asking
questions about him. Cherif was alerted to this
by one of the neighbors and took refuge in
another house. Three armed men then showed
up at his house, roughed up his parents and
vandalized his car.

March 19
Yahia Djamel Benzaghou, *Prime Minister's press
 department,* KILLED
Benzaghou, director of Prime Minister Redha
Malek's press department and formerly a
reporter for the National Liberation Front
(FLN) daily, *El Moudjahid,* and the state news
agency, Algerian Press Service (APS), was
gunned down in Bab El Oued, Algiers, where he
lived. It is believed that he was targeted for
assassination by Islamic militants. CPJ condemned the murder and wrote to the Algerian
government demanding that it make every effort
to protect journalists.

March 20
Madjid Yacef, *L'Hebdo Libéré,* KILLED
Rachid Benhaddou, *L'Hebdo Libéré,* KILLED
Men armed with automatic weapons and disguised as policemen raided the Algiers offices of
the independent French-language weekly
L'Hebdo Libéré and opened fire on those inside
the composing room, killing photojournalist
Madjid Yacef and driver Rachid Benhaddou.
Three other employees were seriously wounded. The attack fell on a Monday, the day the
paper goes to press. Normally, the magazine's
director is present on Mondays, but that morning he was attending the funeral of slain journalist Djamel Benzaghou. The "center-left"
weekly is anti-fundamentalist. In a letter to
Algerian authorities concerning this case and
several others, CPJ urged that the government

take urgent action to ensure the safety of journalists and news organizations.

April 13
L'Indépendant, CENSORED

L'Indépendant received a facsmile from the Ministry of Communication, ordering a six-month suspension of the French-language daily for publishing articles "undermining public order, safety and the higher interests of the state." The order did not cite any specific articles or offer any further explanation. CPJ wrote a letter of protest to the Algerian government about the suspension, which was lifted two weeks later after an appeal by L'Indépendant's director, Chafik Abdi. Though the paper resumed publication on April 26, it shut down again in the summer for financial reasons.

April 13
Mohamed Meceffeuk, Détective, KILLED

Meceffeuk, a journalist with the weekly magazine Détective and a contributor to the independent El Watan, was shot and killed about 35 kilometers outside the town of Chlef.

May 26
Tayeb Belghiche, El Watan, HARASSED
Khaled Messaoudi, El Watan, HARASSED

El Watan's editor in chief, Belghiche, and Messaoudi, a journalist with the paper, were summoned for questioning in connection with an article that appeared on May 25 in the independent French-language daily. The disputed article was about administrative changes within the office of the president. In a meeting on May 26, two high officials from the Ministry of Communication told Belghiche and Messaoudi, who wrote the offending article, that they had revealed a sensitive state secret. He warned that this matter would be pursued in court and that, unless Messaoudi revealed his source, the government may consider permanently closing El Watan. CPJ sent a letter to the minister of communication, asking that the government stop the judicial harassment of El Watan and allow it to publish without further government interference.

June 6-7
Hichem Guenifi, Algerian Radio, KILLED

Guenifi, a 21-year-old trainee technician with the Berber-language Seconde Radio, a division of the state-run Algerian Radio, was shot and wounded on the night of June 6 or the morning of June 7 in Bachdjarah, a suburb of Algiers. He later died of his wounds. It is believed that he was targeted by Islamic militants. CPJ expressed dismay about Guenifi's death and the rash of murders of other journalists, and urged the government to take stronger action to protect the press and its practitioners.

June 7
Ferhat Cherkit, El Moudjahid, KILLED

Cherkit, adjunct editor in chief of the National Liberation Front (FLN) daily El Moudjahid, was shot and killed in downtown Algiers, not far from the paper's headquarters. It is believed that he was targeted for assassination by armed Islamic militants, from whom he had been receiving threats. CPJ condemned the murders of Cherkit and other journalists in a letter to the Algerian government and urged that investigations into the matters be launched and that their results be made public.

June 28
Veronique Tavot, France 2, ATTACKED
Philippe Fremont, France 2, ATTACKED

Tavot and Fremont, members of a France 2 television crew, were injured by a bomb blast while covering a demonstration in Algiers. The demonstration was led by Saïd Sadi, secretary-general of the Rally for Culture and Democracy, and the protestors were demanding that the government release a report about the death of Algerian President Mohamed Boudiaf. They were also protesting against religious extremists, and it is believed that the bomb was planted by Islamic militants.

July 10

Yasmina Drici, *Le Soir d'Algérie,* KILLED

On the evening of July 10, a group of men in police uniforms stopped Drici, a proofreader with the French-language daily *Le Soir d'Algérie,* and a friend as they were driving near her home in the Algiers suburb of Rouiba. Drici objected when the men removed her friend from the car. The men then searched Drici's pocketbook and discovered her press card. Her friend was released. Police found Drici's body with her throat slit the next day. To date no group has claimed responsibility for her death. Drici's colleagues at the paper are convinced that she was murdered by Muslim extremists. CPJ issued a press release condemning the killing and wrote to the Algerian government demanding that it conduct a public investigation into the case.

July 21

Mohamed Lamine Legoui, *Algerian Press Service (APS),* KILLED

Unidentified gunmen shot and killed Legoui outside his home in Bou-Saada, in the M'Sila region. There were no witnesses to the murder, and no group has claimed responsibility. Legoui was the M'Sila correspondent for APS. CPJ issued a press release condemning the murder and called for a thorough investigation into the matter in a letter to Algerian authorities.

July 27

Ali Ben Si Ali, *Free-lancer,* IMPRISONED

Ben Si Ali, a journalist who had been living in Egypt for three years and had been detained there by State Security Investigations since July 8, was deported from Egypt and returned to his native Algeria. Ben Si Ali's family went to meet him at the airport but did not find him because upon arrival he was taken to a prison in Algiers. CPJ protested Ben Si Ali's arrest to the Algerian government, and he was subsequently released. While in Egypt, Ben Si Ali contributed articles to opposition newspapers, including *Al-Shaab.* He also served as a contact between several Western news organizations and Islamist groups.

August 4

Le Patriote, CENSORED

For reasons that are unclear, *Le Patriote,* a French-language weekly based in Oran, was banned by the Ministry of Justice on the day its first issue was published. CPJ wrote to the Algerian government to inquire about the ban.

August 14

Brahim Taouchichet, *Horoscope,* ATTACKED

Taouchichet, director and founder of the monthly astrological magazine *Horoscope,* was kidnapped by men dressed in police uniforms in Algiers, near the *Maison de la Presse* where many independent publications are based. When he refused to go with them, the men forced Taouchichet at gunpoint into a car, eyewitnesses told Algerian news organizations. Two hours later, newspapers and press agencies received a communiqué from the Islamic Salvation Army, the armed wing of the Islamic Salvation Front (FIS), claiming responsibility for the kidnapping. The message, signed by Hocine Abdellatif, said that Taouchichet would be put on trial, presumably for blasphemy, since astrology is formally forbidden in Islam. CPJ wrote to the exiled spokesman for the FIS, demanding Taouchichet's immediate release. His captors let him go two days later along with a "final warning" to journalists to mend their secular ways.

August 16

Khaled Bougherbal, *Algerian Television,* KILLED

Bougherbal, an administrator with Algerian Television (ENTV), was knifed to death in Bouchaoui.

September 25

Mouloud Barroudi, *National Agency of Filmed News (ANAF),* KILLED

The body of Barroudi, a cameraman with the National Agency of Filmed News (ANAF), was found near his home, west of Algiers. He was killed with a knife. In a letter, CPJ urged the government of Algeria to step up efforts to protect journalists.

—continued on p. 199

The Torment of a Targeted Journalist

by Saïd Mekbel

SPECIAL REPORT: Algeria

I MUST BEGIN by addressing a few words to the terrorists. First, they don't make my work any easier. No, not at all. And it is already complicated enough without them. Each day that God creates, I wrack my brains to write my daily column, to find an entertaining subject and give it that light and witty cast that my readers expect from me, as if all I have to do is pull it out of a drawer. In short, I live a daily torture so painful that I wonder how the terrorists are able to ignore it. Have they no humorists in their ranks who can empathize with a colleague?

Consider this, for example: on two occasions several shots were fired at me. At this rate, they'll succeed in killing me, don't you think? And this is something that I must drive home with the terrorists—tell them that their little game is fatal. Perhaps they are unaware that the bullets in their pistols can actually hurt and kill. If only that were all I had to tell them. Do you suppose that they know that they're causing problems between me and my wife, my lover and faithful companion of 20 years? Why? Simply because I have not managed to convince my better half that if, on certain nights, I fail to return to my conjugal abode, it is simply out of prudence. The last time, in order to cast away any doubts about my fidelity, I explained that I had spent the night with a friend from the paper. The look that she shot me! I'm sure she was wondering about me.

Another thing: sometimes I have to do acrobatics to elude the eyes of the moles who study my habits on the terrorists' behalf. When, for example, I cover my tracks by walking backwards toward my house to make it look like I've gone out. Or when I do the opposite to make it look like I've come home. I don't know whether or

Saïd Mekbel *was the director of the independent French-language daily* Le Matin. *He was assassinated on Dec. 3, 1994. The radical Armed Islamic Group (GIA), which is believed to be responsible for the majority of the 33 murders of journalists in Algeria since May 1993, claimed responsibility for his killing. Two previous attempts had been made on Mekbel's life, and before his death he published this column in* Le Matin. *It was reprinted on the cover of the Dec. 15, 1994, edition of the Moroccan newspaper* Libération. *The article was translated from French by Marlé Hammond.*

not this ruse has successfully thrown off the enemy, but at least my bizarre behavior has attracted the attention of the neighbors who have recommended to my wife that she get me examined by a psychiatrist. I must admit that often when I'm engaged in these acrobatics I get disoriented—forgetting for the moment if I'm going home and just pretending that I am leaving, or vice versa.

And these long detours I must make to avoid being tailed, even though the paper's only a 15-minute drive from my house. In essence, I squander the time I could be spending with my family. Maybe I should leave the car behind and go on foot—but that could conceivably be dangerous, couldn't it? And there is one thing I want the terrorists to know most of all. On the advice of friends concerned about my safety, I've altered my physical appearance by changing a few details. I shaved my mustache, cut my hair very short, and replaced my glasses with contact lenses. If you could only see the effect, I have become simply unrecognizable. To the point where I can pass between two columns of terrorists.

In the street, no one notices me any more. No more fond gestures or nice words. Nothing. I really feel as if I've vanished, as if I'm dead. Sometimes this feeling is so intense and overpowering that I open the paper to see if my assassination has been announced.

—continued from p. 196

September 25
Smail Sbaghdi,
Algerian Press Service (APS), KILLED
Sbaghdi, a reporter with the official Algerian Press Service (APS), was killed in Algiers when gunmen opened fire on the taxi in which he was a passenger. In a press release, CPJ condemned Sbaghdi's murder and included a listing of the 20 journalists killed in Algeria since May 1993.

September 28
Nadir Boulegroune,
El Moudjahid-Hebdo, IMPRISONED
Boulegroune, director of the National Liberation Front's weekly *El Moudjahid-Hebdo*, was arrested after answering a summons to appear before the Sidi M'Hamed court in Algiers. He was held for less than a week. The reasons for his arrest are unclear.

October 12
Lahcene Bensaadallah, *El Irshad*, KILLED
Bensaadallah, director of *El Irshad*, a publication affiliated with the moderate Islamist party Hamas, was shot and killed outside his home in Badr, a neighborhood in Algiers.

October 16
Tayeb Bouterfif, *Algerian Radio*, KILLED
Bouterfif, who worked for the government's Berber-language radio station, was fatally shot outside his home, south of Algiers. No one claimed responsibility for his murder, but it is likely that Bouterfif was targeted by religious extremists. CPJ issued a press release condemning the murder and included a list of the 23 journalists killed in Algeria since May 1993.

October 20
Farah Ziane, *Révolution Africaine*, KILLED
Ziane, editor of the French-language weekly *Révolution Africaine*, was shot and killed outside his home in Blida, south of Algiers. *Révolution Africaine* is published by the National Liberation Front (FLN), the party that ruled Algeria

from independence in 1962 until the army coup in January 1992. No one has claimed responsibility for his murder. In a press release, CPJ called on all parties to the Algerian conflict to recognize the role of journalists as noncombatants and to unequivocally condemn their murders.

October 27
Mohamed Salah Benachour, *Algerian Press Service (APS)*, KILLED
Benachour, a reporter for the official Algerian Press Service (APS), was shot and killed in Boufarik, south of Algiers, as he was returning from work. No one has claimed responsibility for his murder, but it is believed to be the work of armed Islamic militants. In a press release, CPJ called on all parties to the Algerian conflict to recognize the role of journalists as noncombatants and to unequivocally condemn their murders.

October 29
Kaddour Bouselham, *Horizons*, IMPRISONED
Bouselham, a correspondent with the government-controlled daily *Horizons*, was kidnapped in Hacine, in the Mascara district west of Algiers. Bouselham, who was living in a tent since an earthquake destroyed his home in August, was abducted by a group of about 50 armed men. CPJ wrote to the Algerian government urging the authorities to do their utmost to locate Bouselham. His whereabouts are unknown, and no one has claimed responsibility for the kidnapping.

November 7
El Ouma, CENSORED
Al-Wajh al-Akhar, CENSORED
The Interior Ministry imposed one-month suspensions on *El Ouma* and *Al-Wajh al-Akhar* for allegedly publishing "subversive information apologizing for crime." CPJ protested the suspensions to the Algerian government.

Middle East

November 12
Le Libre, CENSORED

Hichem Aboud, *Le Libre,* LEGAL ACTION

The Interior Ministry suspended the Setif-based weekly *Le Libre* for an indefinite period. Hichem Aboud, the paper's editor in chief, was taken in for questioning by the police. The paper is accused of disseminating information "harmful to public order and the higher interests of the state." Aboud has since been placed under the jurisdiction of the courts—he must appear before a tribunal once a week, and he is barred from leaving the country. CPJ wrote a letter to the Algerian government urging it rescind the order of suspension of *Le Libre.*

November 16
El Khabar, CENSORED

El Hiwar, CENSORED

El Watan, CENSORED

In one day, Algerian authorities prevented the distribution of one paper and suspended two others. In one instance, security forces seized 25,000 copies of the country's most widely read newspaper, the Arabic-language daily *El Khabar,* in a dawn raid on the paper's three printers in Algiers, Oran and Constantine. They then stopped the print run of that day's edition. No reason was given for the action. Authorities also suspended *El Hiwar,* an organ of the National Liberation Front (FLN), for six months, which is the maximum length of suspension permitted under Algerian law. Again, the reason for the suspension is unclear. In the third instance, the Interior Ministry suspended the independent French-language daily *El Watan* for 15 days. No official explanation was offered, but press accounts suggest the measure may have stemmed from *El Watan's* criticism of the Justice Ministry's handling of a prison riot that resulted in several fatalities. CPJ sent a letter to the Algerian government urging that it rescind the orders of suspension for the newspapers.

November 30
Ahmed Issaad, *Algerian Television,* KILLED

Nasseredine Lekhal, *El Massa,* KILLED

Issaad, a reporter for Algerian Television, and Lekhal, a reporter for the state-owned Arabic-language daily *El Massa,* were killed in Boufarik, about 30 km south of Algiers. They were among five residents of Boufarik whom gunmen killed in a raid on the neighborhood. The journalists were forced out of their homes, then shot and beheaded, according to Algerian Television. In a press release, CPJ condemned the murders and called on all parties to the conflict to recognize the status of journalists as non-combatants.

December 3
Saïd Mekbel, *Le Matin,* KILLED

Mekbel, director of the independent French-language daily *Le Matin,* was shot in the head by unknown assailants as he ate in a restaurant in downtown Algiers near his paper's offices. He went into a coma and died of his wounds the next morning at Ain-Naadja Hospital. Mekbel had been the target of previous assassination attempts, one of which occurred on March 8. In the last piece he wrote for his satirical column, "Mesmar J'ha," Mekbel likened the life of the Algerian journalist to that of "the thief who scales the walls to go home at night, the father who warns his son not to tell anyone what he does for a living." The Armed Islamic Group claimed responsibility for his murder.

December 19
L'Opinion, CENSORED

The Interior Ministry suspended the independent French-language daily *L'Opinion* for 40 days. Government spokesman Ahmad Attaf accused the paper of "manipulation" for featuring what *L'Opinion* described as a draft election law for the presidential elections scheduled for the end of 1995. The previous two editions had not been published because the government-run press house refused to print them.

Egypt

As the battle between government forces and armed religious extremists continued in 1994, the Egyptian government became increasingly sensitive to criticism. That, combined with an atmosphere of intolerance generated both by the religious opposition and the conservative religious establishment, exacted a high toll on press freedom.

In mid-April, members of the Egyptian Journalists' Syndicate banded together to protest the treatment of their colleagues. They objected in particular to the prosecution of journalists in military courts, the unlawful manner in which reporters and editors were being summoned in for questioning, and the way in which coverage of certain topics, such as corruption, incurs the wrath of the authorities.

In the fall, the government resorted to legislative measures to tame the opposition press through draconian amendments to the Political Parties Law. In Egypt, newspapers are licensed by political parties, and the government argued that certain newspapers were not adhering to their parties' lines, and that, in effect, unaffiliated individuals were buying licenses from political parties in order to air unlicensed views. The legislation, which was enacted in late October through a decree announced by President Husni Mubarak, and which is currently under review by parliamentary committees, prohibits a newspaper from publishing articles that do not reflect its party's platform. This restriction is aimed at publications like *Al-Shaab,* the mouthpiece of the formerly leftist Labor Party, and *Al-Ahrar,* organ of the Liberal Party, both of which have pro-Islamist bents.

The October stabbing of Naguib Mahfouz on the sixth anniversary of the day he received the Nobel prize for literature was a chilling reminder of the danger posed by religious extremism to freedom of expression in Egypt. The 83-year-old Mahfouz is an outspoken critic of religious extremism and is himself criticized in many corners, both for his alleged blasphemy and for his acceptance of the Egyptian peace treaty with Israel. In the wake of the attack, the government allowed Mahfouz's novel *Children of Gebelawi* to be published by newspapers in serial form. The book, whose central characters are modeled on Moses, Jesus and Muhammad, was banned in 1959 by the country's official religious institution, Al-Azhar. It should be noted, however, that the novel was serialized once before, when the ban was initially imposed. Though some have tried to make the case that the most recent serialization of Mahfouz's work indicates an ease in censorship, it cannot be seen as such given the fact that books that offend Egypt's conservative clerical establishment, especially those written about Islam, are regularly banned.

The year closed on a sour note. On Dec. 24, Adel Hussein, the secretary-general of the Labor Party and former editor in chief of *Al-Shaab,* was arrested and kept in solitary confinement on charges of possessing leaflets of the Islamic Group (al-Gamaa al-Islamiya). The Defense Ministry also accused him of revealing military secrets in an article he wrote for *Al-Shaab.*

January-June
Middle East Times, CENSORED
The censors banned three issues of the Egyptian edition of *Middle East Times*, an Athens-based English-language weekly, and seriously delayed the release of six others. Among the offending topics were domestic violence, Islamic militants and security at a telecommunications conference.

February 8

Ibrahim Shukri, *Al-Shaab*, LEGAL ACTION

Magdi Hussein, *Al-Shaab*, LEGAL ACTION

Mahmoud Bakri, *Al-Shaab*, LEGAL ACTION

Emad Mahjoub, *Al-Shaab*, LEGAL ACTION

Shukri, chairman of the moderate pro-Islamist Labor Party and, as such, chairman of the party's daily organ *Al-Shaab*, Hussein, *Al-Shaab's* editor in chief, and Bakri and Mahjoub, editors with the paper, were summoned before the Second Degree Criminal Court in Cairo by Public Prosecutor Ragaa al-Arabi to answer charges of slander. Three figures—Prime Minister Atef Sidqi, Cairo Gov. Omar Abdel Akher, and the head of the Presidential Office, Zakariya Azmi—had filed complaints of libel against them for articles published on Jan. 11, 14 and 21. In April, the cases were postponed, and in August, Sidqi and Abdel Akher dropped their charges. Azmi did not, however, and his lawsuit awaits trial.

March 3

Khaled Dawoud, *Associated Press (AP)*, ATTACKED

Norbert Schiller, *AP*, HARASSED

Dawoud, an AP reporter, was beaten by a police officer, and Schiller, an AP photographer, had his film confiscated while covering a student demonstration in Cairo against the Hebron mosque massacre in the West Bank. Police were firing tear gas canisters and warning shots to disperse the crowd. An officer was angered when Dawoud pointed out an instance of police brutality to Schiller. He ordered Dawoud's arrest and beat him. Dawoud identified himself as a reporter. The officer responded, "So what?" and continued beating him on the arms and back with a baton. The beating stopped when a police captain intervened.

April 7

Mohamed Zaki, *Al-Wafd*, HARASSED

Zaki, a reporter for *Al-Wafd*, the daily organ of the conservative secularist party of the same name, was arrested by State Security police in an early morning raid on his mother's apartment.

He was reportedly detained at Lazoughli prison and interrogated for several hours before being released. There were reports that he had been beaten. Zaki, who covers the Interior Ministry for the paper, had written an article about a certain group of armed extremists. The authorities claimed that Zaki had violated a ban on coverage that could interfere with the security forces' efforts to locate members of the group. The paper denied that it violated the ban.

April 30

Abdessattar Abu Hussein, *Al-Shaab*, IMPRISONED

Abu Hussein, military editor of *Al-Shaab*, was convicted of revealing military secrets in an article published in his paper, which is the organ of the pro-Islamist Labor Party. A military court originally sentenced him to one year in prison and fined him 500 Egyptian pounds (US$150). Abu Hussein was first detained and interrogated on April 3, two days after the article appeared. He was released on bail three days later. The disputed article was about joint Egyptian-U.S. military maneuvers called Bright Star. Abu Hussein reported that several European NATO members would join the maneuvers in 1995. According to his lawyers, this information had already appeared in other Egyptian papers in 1993. And *Al-Shaab* claims that the real reason for the prosecution was a series of articles by Abu Hussein that accused certain government officials of receiving commissions from U.S. companies. Abu Hussein remained free while filing petitions for clemency with the court—military court verdicts cannot be appealed—and was imprisoned in the beginning of May. On July 9, his sentence was commuted from one year to three months, and he was released in early August.

May 28

Ibrahim Saad, *Middle East News Agency*, IMPRISONED

Saad, a journalist with the the official Middle East News Agency (MENA) press service, was arrested at his home in Cairo on charges that he

202

was implicated in a case involving an extremist group. An article in the July 11 issue of the semiofficial daily *Al-Ahram* reported that Saad was released and cleared of all charges.

July 8
Ali Ben Si Ali, *Free-lancer,*
IMPRISONED, EXPELLED
Ben Si Ali, an Algerian journalist who had been living in Egypt for three years, was arrested by State Security Investigations (SSI). His whereabouts were unknown to his family and colleagues until July 26, when Egyptian authorities informed the Algerian Embassy that they were going to deport Ben Si Ali the next day. On July 27, he was put on a plane to Algiers, where he was arrested immediately. CPJ sent a letter to the Algerian government condemning the action. The journalist was later released. While in Egypt, Ben Si Ali contributed articles to opposition newspapers, including *Al-Shaab*. He also served as a contact between several Western news organizations and Islamist groups.

September 1
Hamed Yassin, *Al-Ard: Sawt al-Fellah,*
IMPRISONED
Yassin, editor of *Al-Ard: Sawt al-Fellah*, a small, Tanta-based magazine advocating peasants' rights, was detained by members of State Security Investigations (SSI) as he was collecting the latest issue from the printer. All copies of the magazine were confiscated. Apparently the authorities were angered by an article written by Nabil al-Hilali, a prominent attorney, criticizing the government-sponsored "conference of national dialogue" between the ruling and opposition parties. The prosecutor in the case ordered that Yassin be held at the Tanta prison for 15 days, but as of Sept. 23 he was still in detention.

September 11
Nevine Hamdan, *Free-lancer,*
LEGAL ACTION, HARASSED
Hamdan, a free-lance television producer and professor at the American University in Cairo,

was detained by police overnight and questioned about a story that aired on CNN the previous week. Hamdan had arranged for a CNN film crew to videotape the circumcision of a 10-year-old girl. Members of the girl's family, the man who performed the circumcision and another man who helped him were reportedly detained as well. Hamdan was released the next day. The airing of the story coincided with the International Conference on Population and Development in Cairo. Hamdan's case is still under investigation, and she could face charges of "damaging Egypt's image."

September 17
Labib Ibrahim, *Egyptian Television,* KILLED
Ibrahim, a cameraman for Egyptian Television on assignment for UNICEF, was killed when gunmen attacked a convoy of UNICEF employees and Egyptian police as they were driving from Luxor to Qena in southern Egypt. Four policemen were also killed in the attack. The next day Al-Gamaa al-Islamiya (the Islamic Group) sent a statement to news bureaus claiming responsibility for the attack. CPJ urged the Egyptian government to thoroughly investigate the attack and disclose its findings.

September 18
Mustafa Bakri, *Al-Ahrar,*
IMPRISONED, LEGAL ACTION
Bakri, editor in chief of *Al-Ahrar*, organ of the pro-Islamic Liberal Party, was summoned for questioning by State Security Investigations (SSI). During his detention, he was interrogated in the presence of representatives of the Egyptian Press Syndicate and the Egyptian Organization for Human Rights. CPJ protested Bakri's arrest. He was released on Sept. 19, but faces several charges including "publishing material attacking the government with the aim of inciting the public" and "accepting money from foreign states for undermining Egypt's national interest." In the weeks before Bakri's arrest, *Al-Ahrar* had published articles critical of the gov-

Middle East

ernment's hosting of the International Conference on Population and Development.

October 2
Imad Abd al-Aziz, *Al-Ahrar,* HARASSED
Iyhab Abd al-Sattar, *Al-Ahrar,* HARASSED
Issam Kamel, *Al-Ahrar,* HARASSED
Khaled Husni, *Al-Ahrar,* HARASSED
Al-Ahrar, ATTACKED
Abd al-Aziz, Abd al-Sattar, Kamel and Husni, all journalists with the pro-Islamic Liberal Party organ *Al-Ahrar,* were arrested as police forces were evicting the party and its paper from their headquarters. The journalists were charged with rioting and resisting eviction. They were held until late the next day, when prosecutors released them on bail. The landlord had been trying to evict the Liberal Party and its paper for nine years, and *Al-Ahrar* was in the process of appealing a ruling in the landlord's favor. On the day of the eviction, an appeals court upheld that ruling. The staffers of *Al-Ahrar,* however, were given no time to remove their property from the premises. Riot police cordonned off the building early in the morning before the decision was announced. Those who were outside the building were not allowed in, and those who were inside were forcibly removed. Property was damaged.

October 14
Naguib Mahfouz, ATTACKED
Mahfouz, a world-renowned author who regularly contributed columns to the semiofficial daily *Al-Ahram,* was stabbed in the neck by an unidentified assailant while sitting in a car in front of his home at about five in the afternoon in the Cairo neighborhood of Agouza. The attack fell on the sixth anniversary of the day Mahfouz was awarded the Nobel Prize for literature. The 83-year-old Mahfouz was taken to a nearby police hospital where he received surgery and recovered from his wounds. He was released from the hospital in early December. CPJ wrote to Egyptian President Hosni Mubarak urging the government to investigate the attack thoroughly. The Egyptian ambassador in Washington sent a reply on Oct. 24 assuring that "the Egyptian government spares no effort in protecting its citizens...and bringing terrorists who perpetrate such despicable acts to justice."

In January 1995, the trial of 16 Islamist militants accused of the stabbing came to a close. A military court sentenced two of the defendants to death, 11 to lengthy prison sentences and acquitted the others.

Mahfouz has long been an outspoken critic of religious extremism and was rumored to have been on several hit lists. One of his novels, *Children of Gebelawi* (1959), is considered by some to be blasphemous for its allegorical depictions of the prophets Moses, Jesus and Muhammad. The book was banned by Al-Azhar, Egypt's official religious institution.

December 24
Adel Hussein, *Al-Shaab,* IMPRISONED
Hussein, secretary-general of the opposition Labor Party and former editor in chief of the party's newspaper, *Al-Shaab,* was detained by State Security authorities for questioning on charges of possessing leaflets of the outlawed Islamic Group. The next day, State Security Prosecutors ordered Hussein detained for 15 days pending investigation of these charges. The Defense Ministry was simultaneously pressing charges against him for an article he wrote, published on Dec. 23 in *Al-Shaab,* about U.S. military presence in the Sinai Peninsula. He is accused of jeopardizing the "higher interest" of the state and of revealing military secrets. During at least part of his detention, he was held in isolation in a small, unlit cell at the Tora Istiqbal prison. At first he was not given adequate clothing or blankets, and he had no access to his heart medication. Hussein had previously suffered two heart attacks and has a blood clot in his brain.

On Jan. 5, 1995, his 15-day detention order was renewed. Many of Hussein's colleagues with the Egyptian Journalists' Syndicate staged a sit-in at the syndicate's headquarters in protest of his detention and his treatment by prison officials. A number of them went on a hunger strike, calling for either his release or his transfer to the hospital. They ended their hunger strike about a week later, when Adel Hussein requested that they do so for the sake of their health. Reports in the international press in mid-January revealed that Hussein had been transferred from his unventilated cell to a room with windows, and that he was being allowed to leave the room and walk around. He was released on Jan. 18. In a Dec. 27 letter to the Egyptian government, CPJ denounced the arrest and expressed concern for Hussein's health.

Iraq

Journalists writing for the Iraqi press have always known that independent reporting can be deadly. But the disappearance of Subhy Haddad, a reporter for Japan's *Asahi Shimbun* who wrote an article about Iraqi military maneuvers, served as a reminder that Iraqis working for foreign news organizations must also beware. On Jan. 27, 1994, Haddad was summoned to the offices of Iraqi intelligence, and later that day agents searched his home and confiscated documents. He has not been seen or heard from since.

Iraqi President Saddam Hussein's son, Uday, is perhaps the only journalist in Iraq who can speak his mind without fear of retribution. His paper, *Babil,* sometimes challenges the powers that be, offering some semblance of debate. But Uday can hardly be considered a friend to the press. As head of the Iraqi Journalists' Union, all Iraqi journalists are subject to his whims. In April, the international Arabic daily *Al-Sharq al-Awsat* reported that the younger Hussein had dismissed five journalists from the union, effectively preventing them from practicing their profession.

The continued sanctions on Iraq, which have weakened the country's economy as a whole, also had a direct impact on the press in 1994. Due to a shortage of newsprint over the past few years, Iraqi publications have had to reduce their size and circulation.

The situation of the newly independent press in the U.N. protected Kurdish region of Northern Iraq deteriorated in 1994 due to fighting between the armed wings of the two main parties in Iraqi Kurdistan. International coverage of the area is slight, partly because the situation is dangerous for foreign reporters. In April, Lissy Schmidt, a freelance journalist of German nationality, was shot and killed when gunmen opened fire on her car. She was reportedly the only foreign journalist in Iraqi Kurdistan at the time.

January 27
Subhy Haddad, *Asahi Shimbun,* IMPRISONED
Haddad, Baghdad correspondent for the Japanese daily *Asahi Shimbun,* received a telephone call from Iraqi intelligence early in the morning, summoning him to their offices for questioning. A couple of hours later agents searched his house and confiscated some of his documents. He had recently written a piece about military exercises northeast of Baghdad. Haddad has been missing since he was summoned for questioning.

March 13
Two Swedish journalists, ATTACKED
Two free-lance Swedish journalists whose names have not been released were targeted for attack by an unknown party when a TNT bomb blew up their unattended car in the Kurdish-controlled area of northern Iraq. They were slightly injured in the attack.

April 3
Lissy Schmidt, *Free-lancer,* KILLED
Schmidt, a free-lance journalist who filed with Agence France-Presse (AFP) and the German newspapers *Frankfurter Rundschau* and *Der Tagesspiegel,* was shot and killed when gunmen opened fire on her and a companion, Aziz Qadir,

Middle East

as they were driving outside the city of Sulaymaniyah in the Kurdish-controlled area of northern Iraq. Qadir also died in the attack. Schmidt, a German national, was reportedly the only foreign journalist based in Iraqi Kurdistan at the time. There was a report in mid-April that Kurdish authorities had arrested two men who had confessed to the killings. The men said that the Iraqi authorities in Kirkuk were holding their families hostage as a means of forcing them into carrying out attacks against foreigners. Others speculated that Turkish intelligence was behind the attack. Schmidt had clashed with the Turkish authorities in the past and, in fact, had moved to Iraqi Kurdistan in 1991 after having been expelled from Turkish territory. A week before her death she reported on an influx of Kurdish refugees from Turkey and their stories of repression. She had also written about inter-Kurdish fighting, and attacks on Kurds by Iraq and Iran.

August 22
Al-Jumhuriyyah, ATTACKED
A car bomb exploded near the offices of the government-owned *Al-Jumhuriyyah* newspaper. The offices were only slightly damaged, but, according to the Iraqi News Agency, the explosion killed a child and wounded 13 residents of the adjacent buildings. No group has claimed responsibility for the attack.

October 10
Elisa Gambino, *CNN*, ATTACKED
Jassim Mohammed, *Associated Press*, ATTACKED
Jack Redden, *Reuters*, ATTACKED
Journalists with Fuji television
    and Agence France-Presse, ATTACKED
Others, ATTACKED
A busload of 30 passengers, including 25 journalists and Ministry of Information officials, were robbed and assaulted by a gang armed with AK-47s about half an hour north of Basra, where they were headed to observe military deployment along the border with Kuwait. The bus was ambushed after dark. The gunmen ordered the passengers off the bus and lined

them up, threatening to kill them. Some of the victims received blows to the head. Most of the men were forced to strip down do their underwear. The gunmen robbed the passengers of all their cash, equipment (including television cameras) and personal effects. Before leaving, the gunmen shot the tires of the bus. Reuters reported that Iraqi police later arrested a group of suspects in the case and found some of the stolen items.

Israel and the Occupied Territories

The fact that Israel is officially at peace with two of its Arab neighbors, Jordan and Egypt, and is working out a modus vivendi with the Palestinians has yet to yield significant improvements for the Palestinian press in the West Bank, which continues to operate under military occupation.

For the first half of 1994, Israel was still in full control of all of the West Bank and Gaza, and its army continued to harass, beat, detain and shoot Palestinian reporters, especially those carrying video cameras. In the tense aftermath of February's Hebron massacre, there was an alarming increase in incidents of Israeli soldiers shooting journalists. Most shooting victims were either foreigners or Palestinians working for Western news organizations. The only case in which a soldier was eventually disciplined for shooting a reporter came after the March shooting in Gaza of John Gaps III, a U.S. photographer working for the Associated Press. Gaps was wounded by a plastic bullet fired by a sharpshooter, long after a confrontation between the army and demonstrators had been dispersed. CPJ and Israel's Foreign Press Asso-

ciation demanded an investigation of the incident. But the army's investigation concluded only that the soldier did not follow proper procedure for using plastic bullets. He was given a warning.

Even after the Palestinian National Authority (PNA) took control in Gaza, Israel continued to make the job of Gazan journalists difficult. Because all Palestinians are subject to permanent travel restrictions, and no exceptions are made for journalists except those few accredited with the Israeli Government Press Office, the Israeli army barred dozens of reporters in Gaza from traveling to Jerusalem, the center of the Palestinian press, where their employers—both Palestinian and international news outlets—are based.

On the positive side, Palestinians told CPJ that censorship has eased. But in August, the Israeli army closed a Palestinian weekly, *Al-Bayan,* for allegedly having ties with the Islamic Resistance Movement (Hamas). The closure followed rumors that the PNA was about to ban distribution of the weekly in areas under its control.

As for broadcast media, Israel began to implement a law permitting private ownership of radio stations in 1994. This followed on the heels of the establishment of the country's first privately owned television station. The law permits only regional radio stations to be licensed, and, according to a section of the law that divides the country into 11 zones, there are 17 such stations eligible. Initial reports indicate that the Second Channel Board, which is the licensing body, will not allow any exclusively Arabic-language stations to apply for a license despite the fact that at least 18 percent of Israel's population is Arab.

January 10
Robert Friedman, *Free-lancer,* ATTACKED
Friedman, a free-lance reporter on assignment for *New Yorker* magazine, was assaulted by a group of men in the West Bank settlement of Kfar Tapuach. Friedman, escorted by Jerusalem Post reporter Mitch Pilcer, travelled to Kfar Tapuach to interview members of the militant right-wing Kahane Chai (Kahane Lives) organization. After interviewing David Cohen, a member of the town council, for 90 minutes, Friedman was set upon by at least five armed settlers. After fighting off the attackers, Friedman and Pilcer drove to the nearby settlement of Ariel to file a complaint at the police station. Mr. Friedman reports that the police were reluctant to take their statements and refused to show them mug shots so that they could identify their assailants. Later that day, the mayor of Kfar Tapuach, David Axelrod, issued a news release claiming responsibility for the attack on behalf of Kahane Chai. CPJ wrote a letter of protest to the Israeli government condemning the attack.

Friedman is the author of *The False Prophet*, an unflattering biography of Rabbi Meir Kahane. Kahane's supporters accuse Friedman of inciting the 1990 murder of the militant founder of the Jewish Defense League and the anti-Arab Kach Party. Friedman has received death threats from Kahane loyalists for the past six years.

January 28
Atta Wessat, *Zoom* 77, ATTACKED
Wessat, a journalist with the Israeli news agency *Zoom* 77, was attacked by Israeli troops while taking pictures of confrontations between demonstrators and soldiers in the West Bank town of Ramallah. Apparently, he had unwittingly photographed members of an undercover army unit. It is reportedly forbidden to take photographs of these officers, who are disguised as Palestinian civilians. Wessat was beaten by uniformed soldiers after he refused to hand over his film, and at one point he received a blow to the head from the butt of an assault rifle. He was then hospitalized. According to the prime minister's media advisor, Oded Ben-Ami, who addressed the incident in a letter to the Canadian Center of Inter-

Middle East

national PEN, a border guard had asked Wessat to move "so as not to obstruct the view of the soldiers." Ben-Ami added, "The photographer himself admits that he was hit inadvertently by the butt of the soldier's gun." The wound to Wessat's head required 12 stitches.

March 1
Suher Ismael, *Free-lancer*, ATTACKED
Soldiers raided Ismael's home in the Dheisheh refugee camp, near Bethlehem. Ismael, a camerawoman accredited with the Israeli Government Press Office, was working on the documentary "Peace Chronicles," an Israeli-Palestinian-Dutch-British coproduction. She filmed the soldiers as they ransacked her house and tried to forcibly remove the camera from her. Ismael asked to see an order declaring the camp a closed military zone, but the soldiers never showed her one. They failed in their attempts to seize her camera, but they physically assaulted two of her relatives and left the house in a state of disarray. CPJ wrote a letter of protest about the incident and received a response from the Office of the Prime Minister, stating that the letter had been forwarded to the Ministry of Justice. CPJ, however, never received any communication from that office.

March 7
John Gaps III, *Associated Press (AP)*, ATTACKED
Gaps, an AP photographer, was shot above the knee with a plastic bullet by an Israeli army sniper in the Jabalya refugee camp in Gaza. He was then hospitalized at Al-Ahli Hospital in Gaza City. It appears that Gaps, who was photographing the sniper at a distance of about 100 yards, was deliberately targeted. In a response to a CPJ letter, the prime minister's media advisor, Oded Ben-Ami, wrote that "the officer in question maintains he fired in the direction of individuals involved in a disturbance in order to disperse them" and that the matter was under investigation. A Palestinian reporter who was with Gaps at the time of the incident said that the shooting occurred about an hour and a half after a demonstration had ended;

a few young men were still present near a burning tire, but they were not throwing stones. Though CPJ was never officially informed of the results of the military's investigation of the incident, the U.S. Embassy in Tel Aviv sent a copy of a letter it received on Oct. 18 from the Ministry of Foreign Affairs. The investigation concluded that the soldier who fired at Gaps "acted in accordance with the law." But because he did not strictly follow the procedure for using plastic bullets, the soldier was "tried before the Officer Commanding Southern Command on Sept. 18, 1994. He was found guilty and given a warning."

March 8
Awad Awad, *Agence France-Presse (AFP)*,
   ATTACKED
Eyal Warshavsky, *Associated Press (AP)*,
   ATTACKED
Awad, a photgrapher with the French news agency AFP, was shot in the calf with a plastic bullet from a distance of less than a yard while covering a demonstration commemorating International Women's Day in East Jerusalem. As policemen and mounted guards were breaking up the protest with clubs and tear gas, Awad was warned by one officer that if he continued to take photographs he would be shot. He was hospitalized for his injuries. Warshavsky, an AP photographer, was trampled by a police horse during the same incident. His wrist was broken, he received an injury to the head, and his camera and lens were smashed. Warshavsky did not file a complaint.

March 24
Majdi al-Arabid, *Worldwide Television News*,
   IMPRISONED
Hamza Zaqout, *ABC News*, IMPRISONED
Al-Arabid and Zaqout, both cameramen, were detained for filming in a closed military zone in Gaza. They were held for two days and released.
—continued on p. 214

Strange Bedfellows:

Israeli Editors Tacitly Support Government Censorship

by Avner Gidron

DURING ISRAEL'S 1982 INVASION of Lebanon, no newspaper reported that Prime Minister Menachem Begin was suffering from severe depression, which may have impaired his decision-making abilities and cost Israeli soldiers their lives. Yet Israel's top editors knew about Begin's condition. Moshe Negbi, legal affairs columnist for the Hebrew-language daily *Maariv*, explained that editors obtain such information off the record in regular meetings with government officials. The briefings are part of a system of self-censorship and arbitration known as the editors' agreement, entered into by editors to circumvent Israel's harsh press laws.

The Israeli government wields tremendous power over newspapers under the 1933 Press Ordinance and the 1945 Defense Regulations, laws inherited from British rule of the region and incorporated into Israel's legal system after independence. Under these regulations, publications must obtain licenses and submit all material to prior review by a military intelligence censor—and can be closed down by the Ministry of the Interior without a court hearing. The laws also allow prolonged detention of journalists.

Since independence, a committee of editors of mainstream Hebrew-language dailies and state broadcast news programs has met regularly with the defense ministry for briefings about security issues and military operations. Participating news organizations don't need to submit all their material to censorship—only articles on a list of topics drawn up by the censor. The government agrees not to punish participating news organizations for broaching sensitive issues, and the news organizations agree to settle any disputes with the army censor in arbitration instead of taking their grievances to court.

Last year Negbi led the way in drafting a bill to change the cozy relationship between the government and the mainstream press by reducing censorship. The bill, introduced in 1993 by a coalition of

Avner Gidron, *CPJ's director of research,*
traveled to Israel, the West Bank and Gaza in June 1994.

left-wing, centrist and right-wing politicians, is now before the Knesset, Israel's parliament. The bill would limit censorship strictly to military and security issues. It would require prompt court hearings for newspapers that dispute censorship decisions. It would also require the censor to be a civil servant rather than a military intelligence officer. And finally, it would require continued censorship only when a state of emergency is in effect. Thus, theoretically, the Negbi bill could end censorship in the foreseeable future if the state of emergency is lifted.

Predictably, the government opposes the proposal. What is surprising is the strong opposition from Israel's media barons.

Dina Goren, a communications professor at Bar Ilan University who helped draft the legislation, believes the opposition of the editors' committee stems from a fear that members will lose their privileged status.

"The agreement gives its members clout, entrée to high places and off-the-record information," she explained. "If there were real press freedom, the committee would become superfluous."

But Israeli editors say the bill would not increase press freedom and would actually hinder their work.

Yoel Estheron, deputy editor of *Haaretz*, Israel's most respected daily, conceded that the editors' agreement, from which his paper recently withdrew, "is far from ideal. But Israel is an imperfect democracy." He believes that editors are opposed to the bill because it would be a bad law. "Any good press law would not allow journalists to go to prison," he said. "At least the laws we have now aren't really Israeli laws. They're from the [British] Mandate."

Estheron said the editors' committee described by Negbi and Goren is a thing of the past. "We no longer collaborate with the government. Nor do we receive privileged information," he said. "A new generation is running the papers, one that grew up watching American television. We no longer consider ourselves a branch of the government." He also maintained that any newspapers that wanted to join the committee, including Israeli-Arab papers, would be welcomed.

Negbi insists that Israeli editors have not really changed. "Part of the problem is that the leaders of Israel's media don't understand the real function and contribution of a free press," he said. Recently, he noted, it has come to light that Gen. Amnon Shahak, the army's deputy chief of staff and the leading candidate to become chief of staff, has leukemia. "For three years, senior journalists have known that he has suffered from leukemia, but didn't write about it," Negbi said. "This is the man who was heading autonomy negotiations with the Palestinians."

Under the current laws, the editors' agreement facilitates the work of the mainstream press. But it has excluded Israel's Arabic-language papers, as well as Hebrew-language weeklies. Nonmembers face the full powers of the censor and risk sanctions, including closure, if they violate censorship regulations.

In 1992, the Ministry of the Interior closed *Al-Siyasa*, an Arabic-language weekly based in Haifa, because of "information about the involvement of hostile elements in its publication." The paper's publisher, who denies the charge, was never given a satisfactory explanation for the shutdown. In 1984, the newly founded Hebrew-language daily *Hadashot* (which had not yet been invited to join the editors' committee), was closed for three days by the army after publishing photos of Palestinian hijackers killed by the security services after they had been captured. The General Security Services (GSS), Israel's domestic intelligence agency, had claimed that all the hijackers were killed when rescuers stormed the bus. The *Hadashot* story eventually led to the resignation of the chief of the GSS.

The editors' agreement has limited legal challenges to censorship, stunting Israeli jurisprudence on press freedom. Several media experts argue that it has fundamentally distorted the relationship between the press and the government.

On a few occasions, newspapers have challenged the censor in Israel's High Court of Justice (a three-member panel drawn from the Supreme Court, which hears challenges to administrative orders). In two key cases, the winning petitioners were newspapers who were not parties to the editors' agreement. The 1953 Kol Ha'am decision, which overturned the suspension of a Hebrew-language Communist daily, set the standard for deciding when speech may be suppressed. For an item to be suppressed, its publication must have "a near certainty" of endangering public peace.

In 1988, the Tel Aviv weekly *Ha'ir* successfully challenged deletions by the chief censor in an article criticizing the performance of the head of the Mossad, Israel's intelligence agency, whose identity remains a state secret. The High Court's ruled unanimously that a "near certainty" of "severe and substantial damage to public order" must be shown to justify prior restraints on the press. Many more positive rulings, however, might have been won if the most influential news organizations, with the greatest resources, had not agreed to settle disputes with the censors outside the legal system.

The Negbi bill would apply the same legal standards to all media. Its sponsors claim that it would make it easier for journalists to work, especially those with publications that are not members of the editors' agreement.

But Yoram Perry, editor in chief of *Davar*, a daily published by the confederation of labor unions (the Histadrut), thinks passing the Negbi bill would be disastrous. "It would hurt all journalists," he predicted. "The whole atmosphere is changing with the peace process. The political culture, professional ethics... The government no longer uses the [British] Mandate laws to curb the press. A new Israeli law would constitute a tremendous setback for the process of normalizing the Israeli press."

Pnina Lahav, a professor at Boston University's School of Law and a leading expert on Israel's press law, is disappointed with the Negbi bill, which she fears would "solidify practices that are inherently dangerous to the press." But she is also critical of Israel's editors. "To say that the laws inherited from the British Mandate, which have been used by Israel for nearly 50 years, are not 'Israeli' laws is absurd." Press freedom has improved, along with other civil and political liberties, but Lahav believes that Israeli editors should not be too comfortable. "As long as the current laws are on the books, they can be used against the press," she warned.

Recent polls show little support for the press among Israelis. A 1993 survey conducted by Israel's Institute of Applied Social Research found that two-thirds or more of Israelis, both Jews and Arabs, would fail to protect many basic media rights "all the time." The progress toward peace in the last year is not likely to improve the press's image—terrorist outrages, such as the Oct. 20, 1994, bus bombing in Tel Aviv, perpetuate a siege mentality and can be used by the government to justify press restrictions.

Israeli editors' complacency could have consequences beyond Israel. Yasser Arafat, chairman of the Palestinian National Authority, has already demonstrated his disregard for press freedom by suspending *Al-Nahar*, one of only two Palestinian dailies, for six weeks in 1994 because of its favorable coverage of Jordan's King Hussein.

The ban was lifted only after the editor pledged to adhere to the national line. In October 1994, Palestinian police arrested four Palestinian journalists from Reuters' Gaza bureau for having obtained videotapes of a kidnapped Israeli soldier and his Hamas captors. The journalists were released four days later—after the soldier was killed during a botched Israeli rescue attempt.

Israel could set a good example by liberalizing its own restrictive press laws. The initiative must come from journalists themselves, according to Lahav. "Editors are justified in finding fault with the Neghi bill," she said. "But they must propose a more liberal press law that would have the full support of the journalistic community."

—continued from p. 208

March 29
Mohamed Attallah Hassan, *Reuters Television,*
ATTACKED
Hassan, a cameraman with Reuters Television, was shot in the forehead with a rubber bullet while recording a confrontation in the West Bank.

April 25
Adnan Abu Hasna, *Qatar Radio* and *Abrar,*
IMPRISONED
Abu Hasna, a part-time correspondent for Qatar Radio and Abrar, a press office connected to Jerusalem's *Al-Quds* newspaper, was arrested by members of the General Security Service (GSS) and the army at his home in Gaza City. He was given three and a half months' administrative detention. As is usually the case with administrative detainees, the reason for his detention was not made public. CPJ wrote to the Israeli government requesting information on Abu Hasna's whereabouts and on his legal status. He was released in August.

May 11
Hervé Deguine, *Reporters Sans Frontières,*
ATTACKED
Deguine, director of international relations for the French press freedom advocacy group Reporters Sans Frontières (Reporters Without Borders) who was in Israel and the Occupied Territories in an official capacity, was hit in the jaw by a rubber bullet during a confrontation in Jericho between Israeli soldiers and Palestinians. He was shot while conversing with Palestinian shopkeepers who were not engaged in the confrontation. Deguine believes he was deliberately targeted by an Israeli soldier. CPJ urged the Israeli government to conduct a full investigation of the case and to make its findings public.

August
Al-Bayan, CENSORED
Al-Bayan, an East Jerusalem-based weekly, was shut down by the Interior Ministry for allegedly having ties to the Islamic Resistance Movement (Hamas). The paper was not charged with violating any laws. Just prior to the closure, rumors were circulating that the Palestinian National Authority was going to ban *Al-Bayan*'s distribution in the self-rule area as it had done on July 28 with Al-Nahar and Akhbar al-Balad.

August 20
Khaled Zaghari,
Reuters and the *Jerusalem Post,* ATTACKED
Zaghari, a photographer with Reuters and the *Jerusalem Post,* was shot in the left shoulder while covering a confrontation between an Israeli army unit and Palestinian protestors in the West Bank town of Ramallah. Undercover soldiers among the crowd opened fire. Zaghari was shot while trying to take cover.

September
Nasser Shiyukhi, *Associated Press (AP),*
ATTACKED, HARASSED
Shiyukhi, a Hebron-based stringer for AP, was attacked twice by soldiers at Israeli military checkpoints. On Sept. 12, he was beaten for having attempted to take a picture of a U.N. vehicle that soldiers had stopped. He was treated for his injuries at the Alya Hospital in Hebron, and later that day he filed a complaint with the authorities. On Sept. 17, soldiers beat him and detained him for several hours because, according to the army, his identity card had expired. Shiyukhi denies that allegation. It is unclear whether or not the reporter filed another complaint after the second beating or whether the two incidents were related. Shiyukhi is not pressing the case, according to his employers.

October 12
Munis Abu Shilbayeh, *Reuters,* IMPRISONED
Abu Shilbayeh, a cameraman with Reuters TV in Jerusalem, was detained overnight by Israeli police. His family reported that the police officers came to the house to arrest him and spent two hours going through his footage, which

they confiscated. It is believed that he was taken in for questioning about videotapes that Reuters had obtained of kidnapped Israeli soldier Nachson Waxman and his abductors. That same night, four Reuters journalists in Gaza were detained by Palestinian police.

Areas under the Palestinian National Authority

When the Israeli army handed over power in Gaza and Jericho to the Palestinian National Authority (PNA) in May 1994, expectations were high that people's lives would improve dramatically. But the effects of 27 years of occupation and economic devastation have proven difficult to overcome, especially by a governing body that lacks crucial elements of sovereignty and is hampered by inadequate funds.

One inexpensive way to improve the situation would be to allow free expression. Unfortunately, PNA Chairman Yasser Arafat demonstrated little regard for freedom of the press in 1994. At the end of July, *Al-Nahar* newspaper, one of only two Palestinian dailies, was suspended due to its positive coverage of Jordan's King Hussein. The paper was allowed to resume publishing after six weeks, but only after pledging allegiance to the Palestine Liberation Organization. At least one smaller paper, *Akhbar al-Balad,* was suspended at the same time, but it never returned to newsstands.

Several Palestinian journalists working in Gaza were jailed for up to 10 days by Palestinian police, but none reported being physically abused in custody, an improvement over the treatment they used to receive under Israeli authority.

No formal charges were ever brought against any reporter during the year, though some journalists who criticized the banning of *Al-Nahar* were subjected to harassment and censorship.

Even though the PNA leadership did not support free expression, Palestinian journalists stood up for their right to report independently. When their own institutions (such as their union, the Arab Journalists Association) failed to take action, individual members of the press mobilized on behalf of detained and silenced colleagues, using petitions, sit-ins and demonstrations to pressure the PNA into rectifying its repressive measures. At the end of the year, journalists in Gaza held a 24-hour strike to protest their poor access to PNA officials and the travel restrictions imposed on them by Israel. Only a handful of journalists in Gaza are accredited with Israel's Government Press Office and only they can get permits to travel to Jerusalem and the West Bank.

In other positive developments, authorities refrained from practicing prior censorship, and by year's end three private weekly newspapers were publishing in Gaza—one independent paper, another sympathetic to Islamic Jihad and the third sympathetic to the Islamic Resistance Movement (Hamas).

In terms of broadcast media, no private radio or television stations were established—to do so requires Israeli permission and generous financial backing. But the official Palestinian Broadcasting Company (PBC) began transmitting the Jericho-based radio station Voice of Palestine in the summer. To date, however, its programs have not exhibited editorial independence. PBC also experimented with television programming but did not broadcast regularly.

Middle East

215

June 22
Sakher Abu al-Oun,
Agence France-Presse (AFP), ATTACKED
Abu al-Oun, a correspondent for AFP, was struck with a rifle butt by a security officer in Gaza City. Al-Oun was waiting outside a heavily guarded building to interview Palestine Liberation Organization representative and negotiator Nabil Shaath. Al-Oun was hospitalized for his injuries, and he later registered a complaint with the police.

July 28
Al-Nahar, CENSORED
Akhbar al-Balad, CENSORED
The Palestinian National Authority banned the distribution of the East Jerusalem-based daily *Al-Nahar* in the self-rule areas of Gaza and Jericho as policemen confiscated issues of the papers at the Israel-Gaza border. It seems that the pro-Jordanian daily was banned for its insufficient coverage of the Palestinian National Authority. In a letter to Palestinian National Authority Chairman Yasser Arafat, CPJ urged him to recognize international standards of free expression and Article 66 of the Palestine Draft Constitution, which guarantees freedom of the press. In August, *Al-Nahar* applied for a distribution permit, and it resumed publication on Sept. 5, after pledging loyalty to the authorities and cutting back drastically on its coverage of Jordan. Issues of the pro-Jordanian weekly *Akhbar al-Balad* were also confiscated on July 28, as a ban on its distribution had been ordered as well.

September 6
Muhammad al-Ejla, *Free-lancer,* IMPRISONED
Palestinian police arrested al-Ejla, a reporter whose articles have appeared in the East Jerusalem-based daily newspaper *Al-Nahar,* as part of a roundup of supporters of Islamic Jihad, a group opposed to the peace agreement between Israel and the Palestine Liberation Organization (PLO). CPJ issued a press release and wrote to PLO Chairman Yasser Arafat to protest the arrest. Al-Ejla, a resident of Gaza

City and a journalism student at the Islamic University in Gaza, was held in Gaza Central Prison and released two days later.

October 12
Sawah Abu Seif, *Reuters,* IMPRISONED
Ahmad Jadallah, *Reuters,* IMPRISONED
Shams Oudeh, *Reuters,* IMPRISONED
Taher Shriteh, *Reuters,* IMPRISONED
Shriteh, a stringer; Jadallah, a photographer; Oudeh, a cameraman; and Abu Seif, a soundman—all working for Reuters—were detained by Palestinian police on the night of Oct. 12 for questioning about videotapes they had obtained that featured kidnapped Israeli soldier Nachson Waxman and his Hamas abductors. They were released the next morning, then taken in again that afternoon, at which time they were held at Gaza Central Prison. CPJ issued a press release and sent a letter of protest condemning the arrests to the Palestinian National Authority. By Oct. 17, all four had been released.

October 26
Taher Shriteh, *Reuters* and *CBS News,*
IMPRISONED
Amer Shriteh, *Reuters* and *CBS News,*
IMPRISONED
Taher Shriteh, a stringer for Reuters and CBS News, was arrested by Palestinian police officers. Later that evening police arrested his brother, Amer, who works as Taher's assistant. They were held at police headquarters in Gaza City and were denied access to lawyers and family members. According to local sources, their arrest stemmed from having received a statement, by fax, that was signed by the Islamic Resistance Movement (Hamas) and entitled "An Open Letter to Bill Clinton." CPJ wrote to Palestine Liberation Organization Chairman Yasser Arafat to protest the arrests, and received a reply on Nov. 1 from Marwan Kanafani, an advisor to Arafat, explaining that CPJ's letter had been brought to Arafat's attention and that he asked Kanafani to look into the case. Kanafani added that Shriteh was not arrested,

but was being held only for questioning. Shriteh and his brother were released on Nov. 4.

November 18

Shamseddin Oudeh, *Reuters,* ATTACKED
Adel Hanna, *Associated Press (AP),* ATTACKED
Ahmad Jadallah, *Reuters,* ATTACKED
Alexandra Vakaian, *Contact,* ATTACKED
Heidi Levine, *Free-lancer,* ATTACKED
During a day of deadly confrontations between Palestinian police and demonstrators, three reporters were shot. Oudeh, a cameraman with Reuters TV, was shot in the shoulder by police and hospitalized in Israel. Hanna, an AP photographer, and Jadallah, a photographer with Reuters, were also shot and wounded by police. Eyewitness accounts suggest that both police and demonstrators attempted to stop photographers from covering the confrontations. A Palestinian policeman threatened to shoot Vakaian, a photographer with the Contact photo agency, if she did not leave the scene. And Levine, a free-lancer on assignment for AP, was roughed up by demonstrators. CPJ wrote to the Palestinian National Authority denouncing the police's treatment of the press at the confrontations.

November 28

Al-Nahar, HARASSED
Al-Quds, HARASSED
Jerusalem Post, HARASSED
For five days in a row beginning on Nov. 28, the authorities in the self-rule areas of Gaza and Jericho held up the distribution of three Jerusalem-based dailies, the Arabic-language *Al-Quds* and *Al-Nahar* and the English-language *Jerusalem Post,* for six hours each day. The papers, which are normally distributed at dawn, were not reaching the newsstands until the afternoon, and the delay caused a marked decrease in sales and readership. The Palestinian National Authority denied that they were holding up the papers and attributed the delays to traffic and weather conditions. Many reports, however, suggest that the authorities were angry with the papers for publishing what offi-

cials considered to be an inflated head count of the number of people who participated in a demonstration in Gaza the previous Saturday.

Jordan

While the print media in Jordan enjoy a fair amount of freedom, the government continues to invoke certain clauses of the Press and Publications Law (enacted in May 1993) to rein in journalists who go too far. For example, the article prohibiting the defamation of the armed forces or the security forces and the article prohibiting the publication of a trial transcript without the court's permission were both used to prosecute journalists in 1994.

In the fall, journalists and observers alike were stunned when prosecutors charged the editor of a tabloid with criminal libel and jailed him overnight after he published an erroneous report that the head of the medical association had paralyzed a patient because of a botched operation.

The negotiations for and signing of the treaty that formally ended the state of war that had existed between Jordan and Israel since 1948, put the Jordanian government's tolerance of press freedom to the test. In attempts to stifle criticism of the treaty, authorities detained Nidal Mansour, the editor in chief of the weekly *Al-Bilad,* twice in August—the first time for having reported on the activities of parties hostile to the normalization of relations with Israel, and the second time for having published the statements of such parties. The following month other editors whose publications spoke out against the peace process were summoned for questioning by prosecutors about their papers' editorial policies.

May 16

George Hawatmeh, *Jordan Times,*
  LEGAL ACTION
Sana Atiyeh, *Jordan Times,* LEGAL ACTION
Hawatmeh, editor in chief of the English-

language daily *Jordan Times*, and Atiyeh, formerly a reporter with the paper and currently the Amman correspondent for United Press International (UPI), were convicted of violating articles 40 and 42 of the Press and Publications Law and fined 300 Jordanian dinars (US$450) each for an article that appeared in the paper in October 1993 about the trial of 10 men accused of conspiring to assassinate King Hussein. They were charged with publishing a trial transcript without the court's permission and of harming the image of the army or of security forces. The two are appealing the decision.

September
Fahd al-Rimawi, *Al-Majd*, LEGAL ACTION
Prosecutors summoned al-Rimawi for questioning about two articles and charged him with two counts of violating the Press and Publications Law. Al-Rimawi, editor in chief of the pan-Arabic weekly *Al-Majd* and formerly a columnist with the daily *Al-Ray*, is outspoken in his criticism of the peace process with Israel and had already faced three charges filed against him in the preceding three months.

September
Hilmi al-Asmar, *Al-Sabeel*, HARASSED
Al-Asmar, editor in chief of the weekly organ of the Islamic Action Front *Al-Sabeel*, was summoned for questioning by prosecutors about his paper's editorial policies. The paper opposes the normalization of relations with Israel.

September 17
Nidal Mansour, *Al-Bilad*,
    IMPRISONED, LEGAL ACTION
Mansour, editor in chief of the weekly *Al-Bilad*, was summoned for questioning by military intelligence and then detained for three days after refusing to reveal the source of a story published in his paper on Aug. 10. The article reported that a number of Jordanians returning from U.N. peacekeeping duty in Croatia were HIV-positive. Mansour was charged with "harming the image of the armed forces" in vio-

lation of the Press and Publications Law. Prime Minister Abd al-Salam al-Majali ordered Mansour's release on Sept. 20 after a group of journalists waged a protest outside the ministry. Mansour had also been detained twice in August. On Aug. 2, a prosecutor with the civil courts ordered his detention for reporting on the activities of parties hostile to the normalization of relations with Israel. And later in the month he was detained for four hours for publishing the statements of parties hostile to the normalization of relations with Israel. In both cases he was promptly released on bail.

November 17
Shihan, ATTACKED
One or more unidentified individuals attempted to set a pair of time bombs outside the offices of the weekly newspaper *Shihan*. According to one of the paper's security guards, at about four in the morning he heard some strange voices and movement outside. He exited the building to investigate the situation. He was hit on the head with a stone, briefly lost his balance, and then took out his pistol and fired shots. He noticed three people fleeing the scene. Police arrived and discovered two bottles of benzine, wires, batteries and a fuse. The bombs were disabled. The motive for the attack is unclear.

November 27
Abd al-Rahman Abushi, *Al-Rasif*, IMPRISONED
Abushi, editor in chief of the tabloid *Al-Rasif*, was arrested, charged with criminal libel, and imprisoned overnight after a journalist with Al-Rasif erroneously reported in one of his articles that an operation performed by Ishaq Maraqa, head of the Jordanian Medical Association, had led to the paralysis of the patient. As editor in chief, Abushi was held accountable. He was released on bail on Nov. 28.

Lebanon

The durability of Lebanon's independent broadcast media was tried in 1994. In late March, the Middle East's only privately owned and fully independent radio and television stations were slapped with a ban on all news broadcasts and political programming. The government claimed that the media were stirring up sectarian strife. The decision, which was backed by Prime Minister Rafiq Hariri, coincided with a crackdown on members of the Lebanese Forces who were implicated in a number of violent attacks, including the Feb. 27 bombing of Sayyidat al-Najat Church that killed 11 people. The group, which was one of the most powerful Christian militias during the civil war, runs the Lebanese Broadcasting Corporation (LBC), the most popular television network in the country.

The ban on television and radio marked the first time since the civil war that the state had a monopoly on news broadcasts. Though it was lifted temporarily in July, the ban was in effect throughout the government's investigation into the incidents allegedly involving the Lebanese Forces, which was one of the most important political cases since the end of the war. A temporary ban was also imposed on detailed press accounts of ongoing investigations, a move clearly aimed at curtailing newspaper coverage of the prosecution of the leaders of the Lebanese Forces.

Still, there were some promising developments for the media in 1994. Passage of the Audio-Visual Media Law on Oct. 19 permanently legalized news broadcasts on private radio and television stations. The law is the only one of its kind in the region. But there are some troubling restrictions. Under the law, broadcasters may not slander heads of state or religious leaders. They are also not allowed to air anything that would foster sectarian strife, or "promote relations with the Zionist enemy." Those found guilty of serving the interests of a foreign power, endangering the political system or provoking confessional discord may be sentenced to prison. Whether these restrictions are interpreted stringently or leniently remains to be seen.

March 23
Private TV and Radio Stations, CENSORED
Following a series of bombing incidents, the government banned all news broadcasts and political programming from airing on the country's privately owned television and radio stations. The authorities argued that these news outlets, which were allied with former militias and political parties, were fostering sectarian strife. The decision, which was backed by Prime Minister Rafiq Hariri, came after many officials of the Lebanese Forces were implicated in the Feb. 27 bombing attack of a Maronite church. The Lebanese Forces operate the Lebanese Broadcasting Corporation (LBC), the most popular television station in the country. The ban was lifted on July 29, when President Elias Hrawi signed a draft of a media bill.

April 26
All newspapers, LEGAL ACTION
The Minister of Justice ordered the Public Prosecutor, Munif Oweidat, to press charges against all newspapers reporting on an investigation into a series of bombings, arguing that it was a violation of the press law to publish accounts of such ongoing investigations.

July 5
Al-Wasat, CENSORED
Security forces seized nearly 10,000 copies of the July 4 issue of the London-based weekly magazine *Al-Wasat* after a ban on its entry and distribution in Lebanon was imposed by Gen. Nabil Khairallah, director of General Security and head of the Bureau for Censorship and the Media. The issue contained an interview with

Middle East

Ghassan Touma, security chief of the Lebanese Forces, in which he discussed the charges brought by the government implicating members of his organization in the bombing of the Sayyidat al-Najah Church on Feb. 27, and the 1990 assassination of rival Christian leader Dani Chamoun and his family.

November 3
Al-Sharq, LEGAL ACTION
Public Prosecutor Munif Oweidat brought charges against the pro-Syrian daily *Al-Sharq* for publishing a cartoon depicting the Maronite patriarch hanging women's underwear on a laundry line in Paris. The patriarch, Cardinal Nasrallah Boutros Sfeir, who had only recently been made a cardinal by Pope John Paul II, was in France to confer with officials about the concerns of the Maronite community. The specific charges are unclear, but Lebanon's press law prohibits slander against religious leaders. At a press conference held on the same day, Parliament's vice chairman, Eli al-Farzali, argued that when the media, through words or images, mock a religious or spiritual figure, they are not merely expressing a certain stance but are wounding the dignity of this figure and, in effect, insulting a segment of Lebanese society.

Mauritania

Article 11 of the 1991 ordinance regulating the Mauritanian press gives the interior minister the power to ban the circulation, distribution or sale of newspapers and other written material, periodical or otherwise, if they are of foreign inspiration or origin, or if they are likely to harm Islamic principles or the authority of the state, jeopardize the common good, or compromise public order and security. In May 1994, the then newly appointed Interior Minister Mohamed Lamine Salem Ould Dah began to invoke this article repeatedly, often to silence reports about human rights violations

committed against black Mauritanians by the Arab- and Berber-dominated government.

One independent weekly paper that publishes editions in both French and Arabic, Le Calame, had a particularly difficult year. It was seized three times in May, suspended for the entire month of June and raided by vigilantes in November. One of its banned issues contained reports from two human rights organizations about the government's forced exile of black citizens to Senegal.

On Sept. 1, papers affiliated with the National Association of the Independent Press (ANPI), including Le Calame, went on strike in protest of the series of seizures and suspensions. They demanded, among other things, the modification of the press ordinance, but their demands were ignored by the government. Despite this fact, they ended their strike in October.

May
Le Calame, CENSORED
Three issues of the Nouakchott-based opposition weekly *Le Calame* were seized by the authorities at the printers. The first, the May 18 Arabic edition, published excerpts of a report by two human rights organizations, the Fédération Internationale des Droits de L'Homme (International Federation of Human Rights) and Agir Ensemble (Work Together). The report covered the plight of Mauritanian exiles in Senegal and the human rights abuses by government officials, particularly the new interior minister, Mohamed Lamine Salem Ould Dah, during the 1990-91 crackdown that forced many black Mauritanians to flee the country. The other confiscated issues—the May 23 French edition and the May 27 Arabic edition—also covered Ould Dah's involvement in human rights abuses. CPJ condemned the seizures in a letter to Mauritanian authorities.

May 23
Al-Bayane, CENSORED
The May 23 issue of the independent weekly *Al-Bayane* was seized for criticizing the govern-

ment's censorship of *Le Calame*. The seizure was carried out under the orders of Interior Minister Mohamed Lamine Salem Ould Dah, who is in charge of the national press, according to the publisher of *Le Calame* and the Association Nationale de la Presse Indépendante (National Association of Independent Press). CPJ sent a letter of protest condemning the seizure.

June
Le Calame, CENSORED
Although no formal charges were filed against the opposition weekly *Le Calame*, a May 31 decree issued by Interior Minister Mohamed Lamine Salem Ould Dah suspended publication of the newspaper, which has both Arabic and French editions, for the entire month of June. According to *Le Calame*'s publisher, Habib Ould Mahfoud, and the press association, the government says it suspended the newspaper because it published an allegedly offensive news item about Spain's King Juan Carlos during his recent visit to Mauritania. However, Mahfoud maintains that the suspension decree was issued in retaliation for the newspaper's critical reporting of the government's human rights record, especially that of the interior minister. CPJ denounced the suspension in a press release and in a letter to Mauritanian authorities.

July 25
L'Éveil Hebdo, CENSORED
For reasons that are unclear, authorities seized the July 25 edition of the weekly *L'Éveil Hebdo* by order of the Bureau of Political Affairs and Public Freedoms, which is a division of the Interior Ministry. An editor with the paper reportedly attributed the seizure to one or possibly two articles. The first, "I accuse France," was an opinion piece critical of Operation Turquoise, the French military operation in Rwanda. The second was a report on the coup d'état in Gambia.

August
Mohamed Fall Ould Oumere,
  Le Calame, HARASSED
Mr. Mousa, *Le Calame*, HARASSED
Oumere, editor in chief of the Nouakchott-based opposition weekly *Le Calame*, and Mousa, one of the paper's senior editors, were forced to decide between their journalistic pursuits and their day jobs. The two men, like many journalists in Mauritania, earn their living as high school teachers. In August, the Department of Education, apparently under orders from the President's Office, transferred Oumere to Maqta al-Hijar, a city 400 kilometers east of Nouakchott, and Mousa to Nowathebo, a city that borders the Western Sahara. Oumere stated to the London-based daily *Al-Hayat* that the neither he nor Mousa have any intention of leaving Nouakchott or *Le Calame* and that they will appeal the decision in the courts. He also said that his transfer is nonsensical, since he teaches history and geography in French and the high school in Maqta al-Hijar has no French department.

August 30
Al-Bayane, CENSORED
Le Calame, CENSORED
The government stopped the Arabic edition of the biweekly *Al-Bayane* at the presses. This was followed on Sept. 1 by the seizure of the French-language edition of *Le Calame*. These actions prompted a strike by the National Association of the Independent Press (ANPI) in protest of the numerous violations of press freedoms.

November 5
Le Calame, ATTACKED
Néné Diakité, *Le Calame,* ATTACKED
Seventeen men raided *Le Calame's* headquarters in Nouakchott and destroyed furniture, computers, fax machines and other equipment. Néné Diakité, a female editor at the paper, was badly beaten and hospitalized. The assailants, described as members of the Ideyboussat tribe,

Middle East

221

were reportedly angered by an article in *Al-Qalam*, the Arabic-language edition of *Le Calame*, which alleged that the first wife of tribal leader and Member of Parliament Mohamed Mahmoud Ould al-Ghazwani had attempted to kill him after he had remarried. Two of the assailants, who were restrained by employees of the paper, were later taken into custody by police. CPJ wrote to the Mauritanian government asking for a thorough investigation of the attack and received a response from the Interior Ministry on Dec. 27, announcing that the perpetrators had been apprehended and brought before an examining magistrate.

Tunisia

In early February 1994, the former director of the Tunisian Human Rights League, Dr. Moncef Marzouki, announced his candidacy for the March 20 presidential elections, challenging the incumbent, Zine El Abidine Ben Ali, who has ruled the country since 1987. The government responded, in part, by cracking down on the press. Since criticism in the domestic press has, for the most part, already been silenced, the primary targets of repression were reporters for foreign news outlets.

On Feb. 17, the correspondent for the Kuwaiti News Agency (KUNA) was temporarily ordered to stop working after KUNA had relayed a statement by Rachid Ghannouchi, exiled leader of the outlawed Tunisian Islamist movement Al-Nahda, in which he declared his support for Marzouki's candidacy. On the same day, BBC correspondent Alfred Hermida was expelled from Tunisia, reportedly because of his coverage of the government's suppression of Marzouki's press conference, at which he planned to announce his candidacy. A Tunisian journalist who published an interview with Marzouki in the French daily *La Croix* was dismissed from the Tunis-Afrique-Presse (TAP) agency on charges that he was working for foreign

media without TAP authorization. Other journalists were prevented from entering the country to cover the elections.

Marzouki's candidacy was blocked on technical grounds. And on March 23, after he was interviewed by the Spanish newspaper *Diario 16,* he was arrested for "propagating false news" that would "disturb the public order." Although he is not a journalist, he was charged under the Press Code. Marzouki was released on bail in July.

Immediately prior to and in the weeks that followed the elections—in which President Ben Ali was re-elected with more than 99 percent of the vote—the government imposed bans of indefinite duration on a number of foreign publications, such as the French dailies *Le Monde* and *Libèration,* on March 18 and April 2 respectively, and the London-based, Saudi-owned Arabic weekly *Al-Majalla* in mid-July.

February 17
Alfred Hermida, *BBC*, EXPELLED
Hermida, the North Africa correspondent for the BBC, was expelled by the authorities after they had revoked his press accreditation. According to a BBC report, the Tunisian government issued a statement that Hermida had devoted too much coverage to "defamatory and baseless rumours spread from abroad by…fugitive terrorists belonging to the fundamentalist sphere." Apparently the authorities were annoyed by his coverage of the arrest of Moncef Marzouki, former director of the Tunisian Human Rights League. On Feb. 5, Marzouki announced his candidacy for president in the elections that were to be held on March 20. Five days later, shortly before he was to hold a press conference, Marzouki was arrested.

February 17
Kuwaiti News Agency (KUNA), CENSORED
The Tunis correspondent of KUNA was ordered to stop working, and the phone lines at the KUNA bureau were disconnected after the

agency broadcast a statement by the leader of the outlawed Tunisian Islamic movement al-Nahda. In that statement, Rachid Ghannouchi, declared his support for presidential candidate Moncef Marzouki, former director of the Tunisian Human Rights League. Marzouki announced his candidacy on Feb. 5 and was arrested by the authorities five days later. On Sunday, Feb. 20, KUNA officials reported that the Tunis Bureau had been authorized to reopen and that its phone lines had been restored.

March 18
Le Monde, CENSORED

The French daily Le Monde was banned for an indefinite period. Michel Deure, a correspondent who was reporting from the country at the time, was informed of the ban by the Tunisian Foreign Communications Agency (ATCE) just two days before the presidential and legislative elections were held on March 20. A statement issued by the Foreign Ministry a few days later affirmed Tunisia's commitment to freedom of the press, but added that the country "cannot accept that, in the name of this freedom, certain media commit extremes and violate the ethics of their profession." The statement referred to Le Monde as being persistently "hostile and disparaging in its attitude toward a country known for its tolerance." As of Dec. 31, 1994, there was no indication that the ban had been lifted.

March 28
Kamel Labidi, La Croix, HARASSED

Labidi, Tunisia correspondent for the French daily La Croix, was dismissed from the Tunis-Afrique-Presse (TAP) agency and thus stripped of the privileges accorded to foreign press correspondents, such as a press card granting him access to national and international conferences held in Tunisia. The dismissal came shortly after he had published an interview with Moncef Marzouki, former head of the Tunisian Human Rights League, who was arrested first in February after announcing his candidacy in

the presidential elections and then again on March 24. The agency claimed that Labidi had violated one of its statutes by working for the foreign media without TAP authorization. Appeals made to the Information Ministry by La Croix and United Press International on behalf of Labidi requesting that his accreditation be reinstated have been rejected.

April 2
Libération, CENSORED

A government paper published a piece entitled "The Dignity of Tunisia and the Honor of Her People Before All," which announced that the daily French newspaper Libération was banned due to its "openly hostile attitude." The next day the decision was confirmed by the Tunisian Foreign Communications Agency (ATCE). Libération's March 23 edition had already been banned in Tunisia. The issue featured an article written by a Tunisian intellectual about the absence of democracy in his country.

April 6
Science et Nature, CENSORED

The monthly French environmental magazine Science et Nature was banned indefinitely. Its March edition contained an article about human rights violations in Tunisia.

July 15
Al-Majalla, CENSORED

The Saudi-owned, London-based weekly magazine Al-Majalla announced that the government had indefinitely banned it on the grounds that it "promotes extremist religious and political thinking." The authorities were reportedly upset by the regular contributions of Fahmi Howeidi, a prominent Egyptian writer and Islamist.

Middle East

Turkey

As the undeclared civil war in Turkey's Kurdish-populated Southeast escalated in 1994, the obstacles facing journalists increased. They were often subject to fines, arrest, imprisonment, beatings, torture and kidnapping. And their news organizations were equally at risk. Newspapers and periodicals had issues confiscated and many were temporarily shut down. Police raids at news bureaus were commonplace and many offices were bombed. But perhaps one of the most telling facts about the state of press freedom in Turkey in 1994 is that by year's end 74 journalists—the highest number of any country in the world—were in prison.

The justification for many of the arrests and much of the harassment was the Anti-Terror Law, which prohibits "separatist propaganda." According to that law, writing anything but the government's account of what happened or should happen in the Southeast is considered propaganda for the insurgent Kurdistan Workers' Party (PKK). And since no line is drawn between commentary and news reports in the application of this law, straightforward reporting about a battle between the PKK and the government is considered "separatist propaganda" if it did not conform to the government line. Equally treasonous under this law were reports that criticized the military. Attempts in 1994 to limit the definition of "separatist propaganda" failed.

Basing their decisions on the Anti-Terror Law, Turkish courts arrested hundreds of journalists throughout the year, and most were held in detention for several weeks without any charges pressed against them. Many remained in prison for a few months after being charged and formally arrested, and still others were kept in prison during their trials while others were set free.

Though the mainstream media were not spared punishment if they covered the Kur-dish conflict in ways the government did not like—a fact that resulted in a great deal of self-censorship—it was the small, left-wing and pro-Kurdish publications that suffered most heavily from government harassment. The daily newspapers *Özgür Gündem* and *Özgür Ülke,* are cases in point. In a systematic campaign of censorship by the government, both papers suffered bombings, the temporary detention or long-term imprisonment of many on staff and several court-ordered shut downs, not to mention the confiscation of the majority of issues published.

CPJ sent several letters to the Turkish government denouncing the closure decisions imposed on *Özgür Gündem,* as well as police raids on news bureaus of various periodicals, confiscations of newspapers and magazines, beatings of journalists, and the trials against them. On several occasions, CPJ urged the authorities to release journalists under arrest. Other CPJ appeals were addressed to members of the Turkish parliament requesting changes in the Anti-Terror Law and the recent broadcasting law. CPJ also wrote the PKK for the immediate release of two Turkish journalists it had detained.

Despite these obstacles, Turkish journalists continued to be as independent, critical and colorful as ever, and perhaps more so. Left-wing and pro-Kurdish publications faced with too many sentences disbanded and restarted under new names. Fresh faces joined the ranks and took up where their colleagues left off before being jailed. And because most of the harassment was carried out under the guise of legal action, the slow court system allowed time for the news organizations to find ways to publish despite the restrictions. But as a result of the pressures and polarization in the Turkish society because of the conflict in the Southeast, mainstream media either tended to stay away from the taboo subjects or offered coverage of them that sounded the government line more and more. Objectivity was also compromised in the left-wing, right-wing and pro-Kurdish publications, which were forced toward the extremes.

January 13
Sabah, ATTACKED
A grenade was thrown into the Cağaloğlu office of the mainstream daily *Sabah.* The bomb bounced off a window pane and exploded on the sidewalk below. No one was injured. Nobody claimed responsibility for the attack, and no clear motive has been identified.

January 27
Kutlu Esendemir, *TGRT Television,* IMPRISONED
Levent Öztürk, *TGRT Television,* IMPRISONED
The two Turkish television journalists were kidnapped by the Kurdistan Workers' Party (PKK) for disobeying the PKK ban on journalists in southeastern Turkey. The PKK had banned Turkish journalists from reporting from the region in October 1993. Most news bureaus shut themselves down following the ban, which was imposed with what amounted to a virtual death threat. Öztürk and Esendemir were shooting a documentary near Diyarbakir when they were abducted by the PKK. CPJ appealed to the PKK for their release, at first to no avail. But the two were set free on April 26, a week after CPJ issued its second appeal for their release and called various Kurdish organizations to inquire about their situation. Esendemir wrote a letter thanking CPJ for the efforts made on his behalf.

January 27
Özgür Gündem, ATTACKED
The Ankara bureau of the pro-Kurdish daily *Özgür Gündem* was rocked by the explosion of a bomb. Windows were shattered, but no one was hurt. No group or individual claimed responsibility for the attack.

February
Gerçek, ATTACKED
Police raided the Adana bureau of the left-wing periodical *Gerçek* and confiscated photos, documents and publications. The periodical's Diyarbakir bureau had been raided two days earlier.

February 3
Ayşe Önal, *Nokta,* ATTACKED
Figen Turna, *Nokta,* ATTACKED
Önal, editor in chief of the mainstream weekly *Nokta,* and Turna, a reporter accompanying her, were shot at by a news source. The attacker, Uğur Çakici, had invited the two journalists to interview her at the hospital where she was being treated. She fired a shot at them but missed. Çakici is the daughter of Dundar Kiliç, a famous Mafia figure about whom *Nokta* had published a news article on Jan. 30. Her anger about that article is believed to be the reason for the shooting.

February 7
Nevzat Yilmaz, *Aydinlik,* ATTACKED
Yilmaz, a photographer with the leftist newspaper *Aydinlik* was beaten by the police while he was covering a funeral procession at Kocatepe Cemetery in Istanbul. Yilmaz told CPJ that he was beaten not only during the procession but on the way to the police station in Umraniye and again once there. "At the police station, they started beating me just because I was working for *Aydinlik,*" Yilmaz said. "They told me to 'go work for another newspaper. Take pictures of naked women instead of political rallies,' they said." Yilmaz was beaten so badly that he passed out at the station and spent the rest of the night at the hospital. Pictures of his body taken the day after the beating showed clear signs of abuse. CPJ demanded an investigation from the Turkish government.

February 11
Erhan Akyildiz, *HBB-TV,* LEGAL ACTION
Ali Tevfik Berber, *HBB-TV,* LEGAL ACTION
HBB-TV producers Akyildiz and Berber were each convicted and sentenced to two months in prison by a military court for their report about conscientious objectors, which aired in Decem-

ber 1993. The two journalists had been arrested and kept in detention for a week before their trial was launched. On April 7, CPJ appealed to the Turkish government for the charges against the two men to be dropped. On June 23, the Military Court of Appeals reversed the lower court's decision and sent it back for retrial. The lower court acquitted them on Dec. 6.

February 17
Adnan Akfirat, *2000'e Doğru,* LEGAL ACTION
An appeals court upheld the 1993 conviction and sentencing of Akfirat, an editor of the now defunct leftist weekly *2000'e Doğru.* The conviction stemmed from an article titled "PKK Camps in Turkey," which appeared in the magazine in May 1991. Based on the Anti-Terror Law, he was sentenced to one year in prison and US$3,000 in fines. But because of his poor health, Akfirat's jail sentence was put off until his recovery.

March 4
Hincal Uluç, *Sabah,* ATTACKED
Uluç, a columnist of the mainstream daily *Sabah,* was shot at a gas station near his home. He was taken to a nearby hospital, where he was treated for wounds. Two men, believed to be bodyguards of the Mafia figure Alaaddin Çakici, were arrested after the incident and charged with the crime. Uluç had written columns defending Ayşe Önal, editor of the weekly *Nokta,* who was shot at by Çakici's wife in February. The attack on Uluç was considered to be in retaliation for his defense of Önal.

March 12
Nazim Babaoğlu, *Özgür Gündem,* KILLED
Babaoğlu, Urfa correspondent for the pro-Kurdish daily *Özgür Gündem,* disappeared in Siverek, a small town near Urfa. He had traveled there to follow up on a news tip from a colleague, Murat Yoğunlu, who later denied phoning him. Yoğunlu disappeared the day after Babaoğlu, but reappeared briefly in May. At that time *Özgür Gündem* interviewed him, but he continued to deny he had anything to do

with the kidnapping. Babaoğlu has been missing since March 12 and is presumed dead. Soon after his disappearance, CPJ appealed to the Turkish government to locate Babaoğlu.

March 16
Tacettin Vural, *Flash TV,* ATTACKED
Özbey Özay, *Flash TV,* ATTACKED
Serdar Cebe, *Kanal D television,* ATTACKED
Hasan Polat, *Günaydin,* ATTACKED
Ertuğrul Onursal, *Türkiye,* ATTACKED
Journalists covering the election campaign of Prime Minister Tansu Çiller were beaten by the police at Antalya airport. Anti-terror police teams were called in to disperse the journalists when they complained about the lack of space on helicopters to carry journalists accompanying the prime minister. Several journalists received blows on their backs from the police. In a letter to the Turkish government, CPJ condemned the beating and demanded that there be an investigation into the matter.

March 19
Michael Enger, *Spiegel TV,* HARASSED
Corinna Gutstadt, *Spiegel TV,* HARASSED
Hans Peter Wymar, *Spiegel TV,* HARASSED
Enger, Gutstadt and Wymar were hassled by police officers who confiscated their film and damaged some of their equipment. Later that day, they were told to leave the town of Tatvan immediately. Four days later, on March 23, in the village of Dolunay, near Lice, they were forced into their cars by village guards, escorted out of the village, blindfolded and taken to another village's gendarmerie station for an 11-hour interrogation. Their film was confiscated again. The three journalists were investigating reports about abuses by the Turkish security forces in the region. CPJ denounced the way the journalists were treated in a letter to the Turkish government.

March 22
Hürriyet, ATTACKED
The Cağaloğlu office of the mainstream daily *Hürriyet* was attacked by a gunman who was

angry about an article about a murder published in the newspaper on March 20. The gunman fired several shots at the building, shattering windows. No one was hurt.

March 25
Özgür Gelecek, CENSORED
The left-wing periodical *Özgür Gelecek* was forced to shut down for 15 days after the Supreme Court ratified a lower court's decision. The magazine was shut down for "separatist propaganda," which is considered criminal under the Anti-Terror Law.

April
Mazhar Günbat, *Welat*, LEGAL ACTION
Günbat, the former editor in chief of the now defunct Kurdish-language weekly *Welat*, was sentenced to two years in prison on charges of "separatist propaganda," and the magazine was ordered to shut down for a month. Günbat claims that the trial was unfair because he was not allowed to testify in Kurdish and thus could not defend himself properly. The articles in question, which were written in Kurdish, were not translated to Turkish correctly, and he was not allowed to request new translations. *Welat* ceased publication in May 1994. Günbat is now the editor of *Welate Me*, the successor to *Welat*, and his case is being appealed.

April 14
Özgür Gündem, CENSORED
The first in a series of court decisions to temporarily shut down the pro-Kurdish daily *Özgür Gündem* was ratified by the highest appeals court. The 15-day ban on the publication resulted from an interview with Abdullah Öcalan, the leader of the outlawed Kurdistan Workers' Party (PKK), which was published in two parts in the paper in April 1993. Expecting that the appeals court would soon ratify similar decisions that together would have resulted in an eight-month shutdown of the paper, *Özgür Gündem* chose to cease publication indefinitely. Afterwards, however, the paper's staff started publishing a new daily, *Özgür Ülke*, on April 28. It was similar in editorial tone and coverage. A week before the appeals court approved the initial 15-day shutdown of *Özgür Gündem*, CPJ had criticized the Turkish government for the courts' numerous closure decisions.

April 14
Metin Uca, *Kanal D Television*, ATTACKED
Uca, a reporter for the mainstream TV station Kanal D, was reporting on the student demonstrations in Ankara when he was beaten by police officers. Uca's cameraman was recording scenes of a badly beaten student when the police tried to block his view and prevent him from shooting. Uca told the police he and his colleague had the right to record the event based on the principle of freedom of the press and that the cameraman was only doing his job. The officers attacked Uca and beat him severely right there, in the middle of the street. Uca could not work for four days because of his injuries. He told CPJ in December that in the spring of 1994 the police regularly intervened in the work of reporters and treated them roughly, but that things have improved since then.

April 20
All broadcast media, LEGAL ACTION
A new law governing the establishment and operation of radio and television stations was passed by the Turkish Parliament and signed into law by the president on April 20. The new law imposed many restrictions on freedom of the press and gave extraordinary powers to the government. Article 4 of this law listed 20 "principles of broadcasting," which in effect were guidelines defining what could be broadcast and what could not. Some of the principles were so vaguely worded that they could be used to censor anything. The law also created a radio and television supervision council, for which the majority of seats are reserved for the governing party. The council has broad powers to control broadcasting activity in the country, and the prime minister is given the authority to ban the broadcasting of any station

Middle East

without having to obtain a court decision. Political parties, newspapers, labor and trade unions, and foundations and local governments are banned from operating radio or TV stations. CPJ lobbied the Turkish Parliament to overturn the law or send it to Constitutional Court for examination to see if it violates the Turkish Constitution. But there was not enough support garnered in the parliament for either action.

May 13
Azadi, LEGAL ACTION, CENSORED
Sedat Karataş, *Azadi*, LEGAL ACTION
Ikramettin Oğuz, *Azadi*, LEGAL ACTION
The pro-Kurdish weekly magazine *Azadi* was ordered shut down for 15 days when the Supreme Court upheld a verdict of the lower courts. The decision for closure was based on the Anti-Terror Law, which makes it a crime to spread "separatist propaganda." The article in question had appeared in the weekly in March 1992. The high court also approved an 18-month prison sentence and $10,000 fine for Karataş, the former editor, and a $12,000 fine for Oğuz, who owned the newspaper. After the 15-day closure was ordered, Oğuz decided to shut down *Azadi* permanently because he expected more closure decisions to be ratified by the courts. The staff of *Azadi* and the defunct monthly *Deng* started publishing a weekly magazine under the name *Denge Azadi* on May 21.

A month before *Azadi* shut down, CPJ wrote a letter to the Turkish government criticizing the courts' decisions in the case, and expressing concern about the pressure brought to bear on the press in Turkey.

June 14
Nokta, CENSORED
The 25th edition of the mainstream political weekly magazine *Nokta* was confiscated by the authorities for spreading "separatist propaganda." A staunch defender of secularism, *Nokta* was accused of disseminating propaganda on behalf of the ultra-religious Islamic Avengers' Front of the Great East (IBDA-C). The State Security

Court found the investigative article about IBDA-C to be in violation of the 28th Article of the Turkish Constitution, which guarantees freedom of expression and freedom of the press.

June 28
Servet Engin, *Zaman*, LEGAL ACTION
Engin, editor in chief of the biggest-selling right-wing newspaper, *Zaman*, was sentenced to seven months in prison in two trials that were concluded in the penal court of Istanbul. The sentence, however, was reprieved. Engin resigned from his post in July after a pile of convictions and ongoing trials against him mounted for articles he published in *Zaman*. He later went to work in the paper's newsroom. Engin told CPJ that he was involved in almost 30 trials, mostly on charges of insulting the Turkish president, the prime minister or other government ministers. He received jail sentences in many of these cases, but they were converted to fines, and some of the cases were still in progress by year's end.

July 6
Beklenen Vakit, ATTACKED
A time bomb was found in the main office of the radical Islamic daily *Beklenen Vakit*. The bomb was defused by the police bomb squad before it went off. Nobody claimed responsibility for the attack.

August 1
Bülent Çiftçi, *Özgür Ülke*, IMPRISONED
Çiftçi, the Van correspondent of the pro-Kurdish daily *Özgür Ülke*, was taken into custody by the police. On Aug. 26, he was charged with assisting the outlawed Kurdistan Workers' Party (PKK). According to his colleagues at *Özgür Ülke*, Çiftçi had obtained a government memo, signed by a former interior minister, that allegedly ordered the nation's police force to do "everything in its power" to prevent *Özgür Ülke* and the pro-Kurdish Democratic Party from functioning. Çiftçi had called the Istanbul office telling them about this memo and that he was on his way to
—continued on p. 232

Fanaticism's Flames

by Aziz Nesin

O N JULY 2, 1993, fundamentalists thugs surrounded the hotel where I was staying in Sivas, a city near Ankara. "We want the rule of Islamic law," they chanted. And "Sivas will become Aziz Nesin's graveyard." They wanted my head.

Why? Because my books and newspaper columns have always warned of the danger of religious fundamentalism. Fundamentalists were further angered because I tried to publish Salman Rushdie's *The Satanic Verses* in Turkish. Excerpts from the novel had just run in the newspapers where I was a front-page columnist. I was attending a conference in Sivas along with other Turkish intellectuals who believe in secularism. To religious fanatics, it all meant blasphemy.

A few hours later, the hotel was in flames. The mob had spilled gasoline and set the building on fire. A friend and I were trapped in our upstairs room. When we opened the door, we saw fire racing up the stairs. The smoke made it impossible to breathe. I thought I was going to die within minutes.

Then a fire truck arrived and, to our relief, a ladder was soon raised to our window. I started climbing down the ladder and saw a fireman clambering up to meet me. When he reached me, however, he started beating me. He realized that he was saving the man who was supposed to be killed. Down below, a city councilman from the fundamentalist Welfare Party was shouting, "He is the real infidel! He is the one who should be killed! Hit him! Kill him!" Luckily, I tumbled down the ladder and was carted away to the hospital unconscious.

While I survived this incident, 37 other Turkish writers and intellectuals did not. They were burned to death by religious fanatics who are demanding an Islamic state and will not tolerate people who think otherwise.

Religious fanaticism and fundamentalism are the main threat to the world's future. Fundamentalism is not unique to Islam, but a

Aziz Nesin, *who was given CPJ's 1994 International Press Freedom Award, is a Turkish journalist and author of 107 books, including* Istanbul Boy, Part III. *This article, which was translated by Yalman Onaran, CPJ's research associate, first appeared in* New York Newsday.

danger in all religions. Recently we learned of the mass suicide committed by followers of a fundamentalist Christian sect in Switzerland. Less than a year ago we watched on TV as Hindus destroyed a mosque in India. Moreover, fundamentalist ideology, and its recent rise is an indicator of increasing fundamentalism in the Western world. Regardless of where and how it manifests itself, fanaticism is an enemy of peace and freedom.

Ayatollah Khomeini's *fatwa* (religious decree) condemning Rushdie to death for *The Satanic Verses* was a serious blow to human rights and freedom of thought. Publication of the book is banned in my country by government decree. If a book can still be banned in the 1990s, the nation that does so is not civilized or modern. One of the foremost conditions for civil society is freedom of expression. That's why I've tried to defy this decree.

Many people in my country have threatened to kill me and anyone else who seeks to publish *The Satanic Verses*. The Sivas incident was one of several attempts to carry out this threat. I have not been able to publish the book because translators and publishers are scared. But I believe that, not only in Turkey but around the world, a writer is responsible for what he has not written as well as for what he has written. He is responsible for everything he doesn't write because of fear.

Copies of the newspaper in which excerpts from *The Satanic Verses* appeared were confiscated by Turkish prosecutors, and a trial is proceeding against the newspaper, which is named, ironically, *Aydinlik* (The Light of Day). Fundamentalists also attacked the publishing house where the paper is printed while the excerpts were running. A Turkish Muslim cleric living in Germany has issued a fatwa, demanding my death. But I will not be scared away. I am determined to prove that, even under the threat of death, we intellectuals will not shy away from our responsibilities.

People often ask me, "Will Turkey become another Iran or Algeria?" Turkey will never become another Iran, Algeria, Saudi Arabia or Libya. Religious fundamentalism is one thing these countries share, but they all have unique conditions. Turkey might become undemocratic, but it will always be Turkey. If Turkey becomes an Islamic state one day, its style of Islamic government will mirror our country's own social conditions. Will this happen? Realistically, I think such a possibility is greater today than it ever has been since Turkey became a secular republic in 1923.

In a section of Istanbul called Ümraniye is a big dumping ground for most of the city's garbage. Slums have been built around this disposal site, and entire neighborhoods eke out a livelihood by scavenging the garbage. One day last year, the Umraniye dump exploded, claiming 33 lives. The whole country was shocked, but there was no reason to be surprised. The explosion could have been predicted long in advance because it is common knowledge that organic reactions occur within garbage, and the gases that result from these reactions can accumulate underneath and explode under pressure. City officials knew this but didn't do anything about it.

Religious fundamentalism in my country is like that garbage dump. And the incident in Sivas was like that explosion. Fundamentalism's strength results from the accumulation of "social garbage" over many years. This social garbage is the compromises past and present Turkish governments have made with fundamentalism. Since the death in 1938 of Kemal Atatürk, modern Turkey's founder, every government has promoted religion, currying favor with the fundamentalists in hopes of winning uneducated rural voters.

Today Turkey is no longer a secular country in practice, although its constitution states that it is. The nation's slip from secularity is acknowledged and accepted by most Turks. Despite this awareness, the advance of fundamentalism has not slowed down.

How can we stop the rise of fundamentalism? This is a question that not only Turkish intellectuals, but all intellectuals around the world, need to ask themselves before it is too late.

Recently the Bengali writer Taslima Nasrin was forced out of Bangladesh into asylum in Sweden because of fundamentalists' threats to her life. In Egypt, the Nobel Prize-winning novelist Naguib Mahfouz was stabbed in the throat by an Islamic fanatic. Two weeks later, the Iranian writer Ali Akbar Saidi Sirjani died after eight months in an Iranian prison. But fundamentalism recognizes no borders. Salman Rushdie is not Iranian; his book is not written in Persian; it was never published in Iran. Still, Iran's fundamentalist regime sentenced a British citizen to death.

The *fatwa* on my head is just another example of the fundamentalism that is threatening freedom around the globe.

It's time for the world community to wake up and counter this rising threat before it's too late.

continued from p.228

deliver the document personally. He was arrested before he could board the bus to Istanbul, his editors say. As of Dec. 31, Çiftçi was still in prison, awaiting the conclusion of his trial. CPJ has demanded that the Turkish government release Çiftçi and drop all charges against him.

August 6
Faruk Deniz, *Özgür Ülke*, IMPRISONED
Adil Harmanci, *Özgür Ülke*, IMPRISONED
Correspondents Deniz and Harmanci were taken into custody by the local police during a raid of the Van bureau of *Özgür Ülke* five days after the bureau chief, Bülent Çiftçi, was detained. CPJ appealed to the government for the two men's release on Aug. 18. Harmanci and Deniz were freed on Aug. 31, after a 25-day detention.

August 10
Berivan Kutlay, *Özgür Ülke*, IMPRISONED
Safyettin Tepe, *Özgür Ülke*, IMPRISONED
Mustafa Aladağ, *Özgür Ülke*, IMPRISONED
Nevzat Bulut, *Özgür Ülke*, IMPRISONED
The four correspondents of the newspaper's Ağri bureau in eastern Turkey were taken into custody by the police. Three days later, on Aug. 13, Kutlay and Tepe were released, while Aladağ and Bulut were arrested. The two are charged with being members of the outlawed Kurdistan Workers' Party (PKK). Their news reports about Turkish security operations in the region are being used against them in the trial as evidence of their PKK membership. The two released journalists claimed that they were tortured while in detention, and a Turkish journalist who saw Tepe on Aug. 15 told CPJ that his feet were so swollen from beating that he could not wear shoes. Five days after Bulut and Aladağ were arrested, CPJ wrote the Turkish government demanding their release.

August 13
Hüsnü Akgül, *Özgür Ülke*, IMPRISONED
Şükrü Kaplan, *Özgür Ülke*, IMPRISONED
Emine Iğdi, *Özgür Ülke*, IMPRISONED
Hüsniye Tekin, *Özgür Ülke*, IMPRISONED
The Mardin bureau of *Özgür Ülke* was raided by the police, who took all four correspondents present into custody. On Sept. 5, after being detained for 24 days, they were taken before a judge and arrested. Subsequently, Akgül and Kaplan were released, while Iğdi and Tekin remained in prison. They are charged with being members of and aiding the outlawed Kurdistan Workers' Party (PKK). CPJ wrote the "supergovernor" of the Southeast, demanding an explanation for the four journalists' detention. The supergovernor's office replied by stating the charges brought against them. CPJ then appealed to the government in Ankara for their release.

September 4
Abdullah Kiraci,
Taraf, IMPRISONED, LEGAL ACTION
Kiraci, editor in chief of the radical Islamic weekly *Taraf*, was arrested and put on trial under the Anti-Terror Law for articles published in the periodical. He was released on Nov. 18, but his trial continued.

September 5
Toktamiş Ateş, *Cumhuriyet*, ATTACKED
Ateş, a well-known columnist, was spared assassination when the bomb planted near his desk during a book signing failed to explode. The extremist group Islamic Avengers' Front of the Great East (IBDA-C) claimed responsibility for the attempt on Ateş' life. A few days after the attack, the Istanbul police announced that the bomb was not strong enough to cause any harm. Following that announcement, *Cumhuriyet* claimed that the first ballistics report from the police, which had come the day after the attempt, had asserted that the bomb was powerful and would have killed many people. *Cumhuriyet* claimed that police were trying

to reduce publicity around the bombing attempt in an effort to protect IBDA-C.

September 6
Aydinlik, CENSORED

The Sept. 3 issue of the left-wing weekly *Aydinlik* was confiscated by the local penal court for not obeying the closure order handed down when it was a daily newspaper. That initial closure was ordered because the newspaper reprinted an *Özgür Ülke* article about the pro-Kurdish political party that had been shut down by the Supreme Court in the beginning of 1994. The daily *Aydinlik* ceased publication on Feb. 20, and the weekly started immediately after that. Since the company that owns the weekly and its editorial staff are not the same as the defunct daily's, the closure decision should not have applied to them, editors of the weekly argued, but to no avail. The decision to close *Aydinlik* for five days was handed down on June 5 by the Istanbul State Security Court.

September 8
Erol Akgün, *Devrimci Çözüm*, KILLED

Akgün, editor in chief of the left-wing weekly *Devrimci Çözüm*, was killed by unidentified assailants as he left his home in Gebze, near Istanbul. His colleagues at the paper believe he was killed by a rival left-wing faction because of his role as the weekly's editor. One of the assailants' aims was to silence *Devrimci Çözüm*, according to Akgün's colleagues. The magazine continues to publish under the direction of a new editor.

September 11
Cumhuriyet, CENSORED

The Sept. 11 issue of *Cumhuriyet* was confiscated by the Istanbul State Security Court for "terrorist propaganda" because it published interviews with leaders of the ultrareligious organization IBDA-C, which had claimed responsibility for the Sept. 5 assassination attempt on *Cumhuriyet* columnist Toktamiş Ateş.

September 12
Emeğin Bayraği, CENSORED

The publication of the left-wing weekly *Emeğin Bayraği* was suspended indefinitely by the courts on the grounds that both the editor in chief and owner of the publication were in prison. *Emeğin Bayraği* continued to publish as a special insert to another left-wing weekly for three weeks after the closure decision. The publication was disbanded on Oct. 8, and its staff joined forces with another left-wing periodical to publish *Atilim* magazine.

September 29
Berin Nadl, *Cumhuriyet*, LEGAL ACTION
Aydin Engin, *Cumhuriyet*, LEGAL ACTION

Nadi, the owner of the mainstream daily *Cumhuriyet*, was fined 296 million Turkish liras (US$8,500) for a news report about the the Kurdistan Workers' Party (PKK) that was published in the newspaper on Aug. 30. Engin, the paper's editor in chief, was fined 148 million liras (US$4,200) in the same trial. The trial was launched in 1993 and had ended with acquittal, but the appeals court had sent the case back for a retrial, demanding conviction.

October 17
Mücadele, CENSORED, LEGAL ACTION

The Turkish Supreme Court upheld a one-month closure verdict for the left-wing weekly *Mücadele*. At the end of this period, the court upheld three more successive closure verdicts, thus effectively shutting down the magazine. *Mücadele* disbanded during this series of closures.

October 27
Oral Çalişlar, *Cumhuriyet*,
CENSORED, LEGAL ACTION

Cumhuriyet reporter Çalişlar was sentenced to two years in prison and 250 million Turkish liras (US$7,100) for writing a book about the Kurdish problem. The book is a collection of news reports, interviews and investigative research originally published in the daily *Cumhuriyet*. The book was confiscated by the authories, who deemed it "separatist propaganda," but the articles featured in the book, which included interviews with the leader of the outlawed Kurdistan Workers' Party (PKK), did not result in any charges when they originally ran in the newspaper in 1993.

November 23
Mehmet Ali Birand, *Show TV,* LEGAL ACTION
Deniz Arman, *Show TV,* LEGAL ACTION
Halil Abonoz, *Show TV,* LEGAL ACTION
Birand, the producer of the news show "32nd Day" on Show TV; Arman, Show TV's editor in chief; and Abonoz, a cameraman; were each sentenced to five months in prison for a report they aired about the increase in mandatory military service. Birand's show is the most watched news hour in Turkey. The three men were convicted of "discouraging people from serving in the military." Their conviction is being appealed.

November 24
Havva Suiçmez, *Devrimci Gençlik,* IMPRISONED
Mehmet Akdemir, *Işçi Hareketi,* IMPRISONED
Mir Ali Demir, *Halkin Gücü,* IMPRISONED
Devrimci Gençlik, HARASSED
Işçi Hareketi, HARASSED
Halkin Gücü, HARASSED
Mücadele, HARASSED
The central offices of four left-wing magazines, *Devrimci Gençlik, Işçi Hareketi, Halkin Gücü* and *Mücadele* were raided by the police on Nov. 24. Thirty-one journalists were detained, of which nine were released two days later. CPJ wrote the Ankara State Security Court prosecutor and police chief on Dec. 2, requesting information about the raids and the fate of those journalists in detention, as well as expressing concern about their treatment. The remaining 22 journalists were taken before a judge on Dec. 6. Demir, Suiçmez and Akdemir were charged with "terrorist propaganda" and arrested as the others were released. By year's end, the three were in prison, awaiting trial.

December 3
Özgür Ülke, ATTACKED
Ersin Yildiz, *Özgür Ülke,* KILLED
The *Özgür Ülke* headquarters in Istanbul, the paper's Ankara bureau and local Istanbul bureau were bombed on the same day. In the bomb attack on the main office, Ersin Yildiz, a receptionist, lost his life. Also, 21 staff members, including reporters, editors and other personnel, were injured. The editors of the newspaper claimed that the attacks were instigated by the government, a charge vehemently denied by the officials. The three buildings were not usable after the attack, but the pro-Kurdish newspaper did not interrupt its publishing. Working out of different newspapers' offices as temporary guests, the staff managed to put out the paper daily. In a Dec. 5 letter, CPJ criticized the Turkish government for its inability to protect journalists from such highly organized attacks.

December 9
Hüseyin Esen, *Atilim,* ATTACKED
Sultan Seçik, *Atilim,* ATTACKED
Atilim, CENSORED
Two reporters for the left-wing weekly *Atilim* were detained by police while covering a funeral procession of a left-wing leader. The two reported being beaten and tortured while in custody. Photographs of Esen received by CPJ showed clear marks of severe beating on his body. *Atilim* started publishing in October, but all 10 issues of the weekly published between October and December were confiscated by authorities.

December 28
Milliyet, ATTACKED
Meydan, ATTACKED
Kanal D, ATTACKED
The Doğan Media Center, which houses the mainstream dailies *Milliyet* and *Meydan* as well as the television station Kanal D, came under attack by unidentified gunmen. The attackers fired a round of shots at the building and fled in a stolen car. No one was hurt during the inci-

234

dent. Someone called *Milliyet* and claimed responsibility for the attack on behalf of the militant Islamist organization IBDA-C.

December 28
Ocak Işik Yutçu, *Özgür Gündem,*

IMPRISONED, LEGAL ACTION

Yutçu, the first editor in chief of the defunct *Özgür Gündem,* was sentenced to 25 years in prison for articles published in the pro-Kurdish daily in 1991. He was arrested and sent to jail when the appeals court upheld the sentencing. Now serving time, Yutçu may be given additional prison sentences when the appeals court reviews a series of other lower-court decisions against him.

December 28
Ismail Beşikçı, *Özgür Gündem,*

IMPRISONED, LEGAL ACTION

Beşikçi, a prominent Kurdish writer, was sentenced to two more years in prison for his 1993 columns in the defunct pro-Kurdish daily *Özgür Gündem.* By the end of 1994, the prison sentences imposed on him for his books and newspaper articles came to a total of 67 years and one month.

December 31
Gerçek, ATTACKED, HARASSED,
LEGAL ACTION, CENSORED

The left-wing weekly was a regular target for harassment by the Turkish government for its reporting and editorial stance. In verdicts upheld by the appeals court in 1994, editors of the magazine were fined a total of $12,000 and sentenced to six months in prison. For verdicts reached during the year but not upheld yet, the fines totaled $10,000 and the prison sentences came to one year and 10 months. A one-month closure of the magazine was also handed down by the courts, but is being appealed. There are 37 other trials in progress. The magazine's Adana bureau was raided twice by police, and its reporters taken into custody many times. Nearly 15 issues were confiscated throughout the

year, and shipments of the magazine to various cities in Turkey were intercepted by police at the post office.

1994
Sosyalist Alternatif,

HARASSED, LEGAL ACTION, CENSORED
Fahrettin Dülçek, *Sosyalist Alternatif,*

HARASSED, LEGAL ACTION

Nearly all issues of the left-wing weekly *Sosyalist Alternatif* were confiscated by the authorities in 1994. The offices of the paper were raided by the police on Jan. 12. Editor in chief Fahrettin Dülçek was detained during this raid and held until Aug. 19. He is on trial for aiding an outlawed leftist organization. Two former editors of *Alternatif* have been convicted by courts for articles published in the periodical. Taken together, their sentences total eight years in prison and $30,000 in fines so far, but that may change, since many trials against them are still in progress.

1994
Azadi, ATTACKED, HARASSED,
LEGAL ACTION, CENSORED
Deng, ATTACKED, HARASSED,
LEGAL ACTION, CENSORED
Denge Azadi, ATTACKED, HARASSED,
LEGAL ACTION, CENSORED

Following months of legal harassment by the Turkish government, two pro-Kurdish publications, *Azadi* and *Deng,* disbanded in May and the staff joined forces to publish *Denge Azadi.*

Though there are nearly 50 trials still in progress against the defunct *Azadi,* its former editors have been sentenced to a total of 11 years in prison and $80,000 in fines thus far for various articles published in the magazine. On May 13, 1994, the first of three closure orders—this one for 15 days—was handed down by the courts. The owners of *Azadi* decided to disband after this decision, expecting more closures. A second one, for a month, came in November, and a third one, again for one month, came in December.

Middle East

The editor of the defunct *Deng*, Hikmet Çetin, is in prison while being tried for articles published in the magazine.

Denge Azadi has had its share of pressure, too. Twenty-eight out of the 34 issues published between May and December were confiscated by authorities, and its Adana bureau was raided by police five times between November and December.

1994
Mücadele, LEGAL ACTION, ATTACKED, HARASSED, CENSORED
One of the major left-wing weeklies, *Mücadele*, has been a prime target of government harassment and prosecution. Police raided the newspaper's Antakya bureau six times, its Adana bureau five times and its other bureaus at least once each, bringing to 22 the total number of raids on *Mücadele* offices in 1994. The weekly's correspondents were taken into custody many times throughout the year, and by December, 21 staff members were in prison, on trial or convicted for articles published in the magazine. As for the editor in chief, he has received prison sentences totaling 10 years and 5 months to date.

1994
Taraf, ATTACKED, HARASSED, LEGAL ACTION, CENSORED
In 1994, *Taraf* was the token right-wing publication targeted by the government. Begun as a monthly, *Taraf*'s first five issues in 1994 were confiscated by the authorities, and the magazine was ordered by the courts to shut down for a month in May. The magazine became a weekly in June, and all 30 issues published between June 10 and Dec. 31 were also confiscated. The editors say they cannot keep track of all the court cases against them, but they estimate the number to be roughly 100. They also said that the police raided the magazine's offices regularly to confiscate documents and detain staffers. By the end of 1994, two editors and four reporters were in jail awaiting trial.

1994
Devrimci Gençlik, ATTACKED, HARASSED, LEGAL ACTION, CENSORED
The left-wing monthly magazine *Devrimci Gençlik* was under constant pressure from the government throughout 1994. In November, the appeals court upheld a lower-court decision to shut down the periodical for one month because of articles published in 1993. The closure was put into effect at the end of December. There are 12 other trials against the magazine still in progress. One of its reporters has been in prison since April 1993, on trial for membership in an illegal organization. Out of 15 editions published in 1994, including special issues, 12 were confiscated by authorities. In addition, the magazine's bureaus were raided by the police several times, and staff were detained for a few days in each instance.

1994
Özgür Ülke, CENSORED, LEGAL ACTION
The daily newspaper *Özgür Ülke* had to endure a systematic campaign of censorship by the Turkish government. The paper began publishing in April 1994. By December, all but five of its 234 issues had been confiscated by the authorities. A total of 329 trials were launched against the newspaper in 1994, mostly in the State Security courts, but none of them had finished by year's end.

Yemen

The civil war that shook Yemen from May to July in 1994 nearly repartitioned the country and eroded the foundations of the country's relatively free press. Few independent publications emerged unscathed or unaligned, and all suffered financial devastation. Papers that criticized the victorious ruling coalition of the Islah Party and the General People's Congress (GPC) were branded secessionists. These publications included, but were not limited to, organs of the Yemeni Socialist

Party (YSP), the party that ruled Southern Yemen before unification and shared power with the Northern-based GPC before the outbreak of the civil war.

In mid-July, the government demonstrated its uneasiness with free expression in the wake of the civil war. Seven journalists were among those arrested and detained at a Political Security prison in Sanaa for having participated in a conference on the postwar future of Yemen, which was organized by the *Yemen Times*, an independent English-language weekly. At the time of the arrests, the phone lines of the *Yemen Times* were disconnected, and service was not restored until late August.

Throughout 1994, government officials used a three-pronged approach to stifle criticism in the press. First, they deployed Political Security forces to detain journalists, like the seven mentioned above, or to occupy YSP premises in Sanaa, where the YSP organ, *Al-Thawri,* is published. Secondly, they sued numerous newspapers for slander, which cost the publications a great deal in time and money. And lastly, they placed technical obstacles in their paths. A host of Aden-based independent papers were unable to publish because the government's 14th of October press house refused to print them. The press claimed that its equipment was in disrepair even though it continued to publish official and semiofficial papers.

The print media, which for the past four years have flourished under one of the region's most liberal press laws, have managed to resist government repression, however. In early October, the Ministry of Information tried to impose a draconian law requiring newspapers to submit copies of their editions before sending them to press. Journalists protested the decision, and it was revoked in less than a week. In December, charges filed by the Interior Ministry against *Al-Shoura*, organ of the Tagammu party, were dropped when the judge, who happens to be the chairman of the Yemeni

Organization for Human Rights, threw the case out for lack of evidence.

May 9

Abdulaziz al-Saqqaf, *Yemen Times,* HARASSED Al-Saqqaf, publisher and editor in chief of the independent English-language weekly *Yemen Times*, was summoned to a meeting with President Ali Abdullah Saleh after his paper published information that contradicted the official government account of a battle between loyalist troops and secessionist southern forces. Following the meeting, al-Saqqaf temporarily suspended publication of the *Yemen Times*.

July 17

Abdulaziz al-Saqqaf, *Yemen Times,* IMPRISONED
Ahmad al-Sufi, *Press Association,* IMPRISONED
Abdallah Saad, *Al-Shoura,* IMPRISONED
Izzedin Said, *Al-Gumhurriyyah,* IMPRISONED
Nu'man Qaid Saif, *Al-Tagammu,* IMPRISONED
Muhammad al-Mikhlafi, *Al-Thawri,*
  IMPRISONED
Abd al-Rahman Saif Ismail, *student,*
  IMPRISONED
Political Security officers arrested Al-Saqqaf, editor of the independent English-language weekly *Yemen Times;* al-Sufi, a member of the Press Association's central committee; Saad, editor in chief of the weekly *Al-Shoura;* Said, a journalist with the government-owned, Taiz-based daily *Al-Gumhurriyyah;* Saif, a journalist with *Al-Tagammu* newspaper, the weekly organ of the opposition Unionist Rally Party; al-Mikhlafi, a contributor to the weekly *Al-Thawri* newspaper, which is published by the central committee of the Yemeni Socialist Party; and Ismail, a journalism student. On July 14, the seven men had participated in a seminar in Sanaa on the postwar future of Yemen, which was organized by the *Yemen Times.* They were held at a Political Security prison. Al-Sufi reported that he was chained with leg irons, and that he and al-Saqqaf were beaten while in custody. They were neither interrogated nor officially charged before they were released on July

18. The other five men were released a few days later. It should be noted that on the day of the arrests the phone lines of the *Yemen Times* were cut, and the paper's phone service was not restored until late August.

October 1
The print media, CENSORED
The Ministry of Information announced that all newspaper editions must obtain prior authorization from the ministry before going to the printers. Journalists protested the decision, and it was reversed within a week.

October 13
Abdullah Saad, *Al-Shoura,* LEGAL ACTION
Al-Shoura, LEGAL ACTION
Abdullah Saad, editor in chief of the weekly organ of the Union of Popular Forces *Al-Shoura,* was summoned to appear in penal court to answer to charges filed against his paper in a lawsuit by the Ministry of Information. The ministry charged that an article published on Sept. 18 slandered the president and fostered sectarian strife. Saad himself was charged with "impropriety." Judge Hamoud al-Hitar, who is also the chairman of the Yemeni Organization for Human Rights, presided over the series of hearings and threw out the case in December.

October 16
Abdullah al-Wazeer, *Al-Balagh,* IMPRISONED,
     CENSORED, LEGAL ACTION
Al-Balagh, CENSORED, LEGAL ACTION
Al-Wazeer, editor in chief of *Al-Balagh,* an organ of the Islamic Action Movement, was detained by Political Security forces in Sanaa for three days, then released on his own recognizance. He and his paper are charged with slandering the president. *Al-Balagh* had recently published a poem called "Tell the Generals," which was addressed directly to the president and reportedly included scathing criticism of his government. The pressure applied by the authorities on *Al-Balagh*'s editor effectively shut the paper down. In addition, al-Wazeer's car

was impounded. The paper was able to resume publication in mid-November.

Mid-October
Al-Wahdawi, LEGAL ACTION
Al-Wahdawi, the Aden-based mouthpiece of an Arab nationalist opposition party, was effectively shut down after the Ministry of Information filed a lawsuit against it. The paper is charged on three counts: slander against the president, disclosure of military secrets and insulting senior government officials. One of the offending articles reportedly refered to these officials as "dinosaurs who would not die." The first hearing in the case was held on Nov. 12.

Mid-November
Mohammed al-Mugahid,
     Al-Gumhurriyyah, HARASSED
Al-Mugahid, editor in chief of the Taiz-based, government-owned daily *Al-Gumhurriyyah,* was suspended from his position after Col. Mohammed al-Iryani, the governor of Taiz, ordered his replacement. According to the English-language *Yemen Times,* the governor claimed that he took this action because *Al-Gumhurriyyah* Press refused to publish the newspaper *Taiz,* an organ of the People's General Congress. Others, however, believe al-Iryani was reacting to corruption allegations. Al-Mugahid had written editorials accusing the colonel of using public assets to build a private fortune and calling on him to disclose financial records.

December 11, 1994
Al-Thawri, CENSORED, HARASSED
The offices of *Al-Thawri,* a weekly newspaper published by the central committee of the Yemeni Socialist Party (YSP), were raided at about 10 a.m., when Political Security forces took over the party's headquarters in Sanaa, claiming that the landlord had turned the building over to the authorities. Political Security occupied the building, and party employees, including journalists, were evicted.

Late December

Abu Bakr al-Saqqaf, *Al-Ayyam,* HARASSED

Al-Saqqaf, a philosophy professor at the Uni versity of Sanaa and a columnist with local and regional papers, including the independent Ara- bic weekly *Al-Ayyam,* was dismissed from his chair by the university's vice-president as the government had instructed him to do. Al- Saqqaf, a prominent leftist writer, had recently published a series of articles in *Al-Ayyam* enti- tled "The Invasion of the South and Domestic Imperialism," in which he criticized the actions of the government in southern Yemen.

Journalists in Jail
A Record 173 Cases of Reporters Imprisoned Around the World

A T THE END OF 1994, at least 173 journalists in 23 countries were in prison for their reporting. The only crime committed by these journalists was to have published or broadcast something their governments disliked.

This is the largest number ever documented by the Committee to Protect Journalists. A year ago, CPJ had documented 126 cases of imprisoned journalists in 28 countries.

In the Middle East and North Africa, 109 journalists are in prison, 74 of them in Turkey alone. There are 41 imprisoned journalists in Asia. Twelve are in prison in the Americas, and seven in Africa. Two journalists are in prison in Central Europe and the former Soviet Union. The list does not include the many journalists who were jailed briefly in 1994 and later released.

In Turkey, a crackdown on independent and opposition reporting on the Kurdish insurgency in the Southeast has landed scores of journalists in prison on charges of disseminating "separatist propaganda." China, with 21 imprisoned journalists, continued to hand down harsh prison sentences in 1994. Xi Yang, a correspondent for the Hong Kong daily *Ming Pao*, was sentenced to 12 years in prison for reporting on interest rate changes. And dissident journalist Gao Yu was sentenced to six years in prison for leaking state secrets. Kuwait holds 18 journalists in prison, all of whom were accused of collaboration for having worked for a newspaper published during the Iraqi occupation.

Ten journalists are in prison in Peru after trials that fell far below international standards of due process. Half of them are serving prison terms of 20 or more years. Six of the nine reporters in Syrian prisons have been there more than nine years. Nine journalists are jailed in Vietnam; all but one were convicted for their work on the pro-democracy newsletter *Freedom Forum*.

International pressure can help free these journalists. We ask you to take the time to write to at least one of the leaders listed below, respectfully urging them to release these prisoners immediately.

Imprisoned Journalists

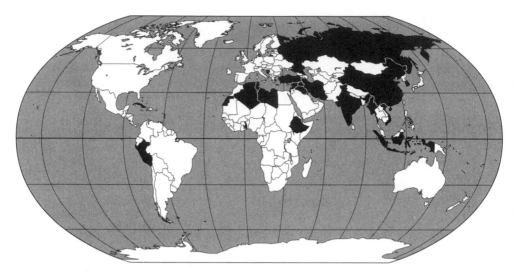

Countries Holding Journalists in Prison

Algeria (1)

Kaddour Bouselham, *Horizons*
Kidnapped: October 29, 1994

Bouselham, a correspondent with the government-controlled daily *Horizons*, was kidnapped in Hacine, in the Mascara district in Western Algeria on Oct. 29, 1994. Bouselham, who had been living in a tent since an earthquake destroyed his home in August, was abducted by a group of about 50 armed men. CPJ wrote to the Algerian government urging the authorities to do their utmost to locate Bouselham. His whereabouts are unknown, and no one has claimed responsibility for the kidnapping.

APPEALS TO:
His Excellency Liamine Zeroual
President of the High Council of State
The Presidential Palace
El Mouradia
Algiers, Algeria   Fax: 213-2-590-407

Bosnia-Herzegovina (1)

Frane Jedzicic, *Slobodna Dalmacija*
Imprisoned: March 1994

Jedzicic, a Split-based correspondent for the Croatian daily *Slobodna Dalmacija*, was arrested in March 1994 by the Bosnian Serb authorities in Bugojna.

Imprisoned Journalists

APPEALS TO:
Radovan Karadzic, President
Republika Srpska
Pale, Bosnia-Herzegovina   Fax: 387-71-783-324

China (21)

Liu De, *Jianna Literature
and Arts Journal*
Sentenced: February 1987

Liu, a member of the editorial board of the literary magazine *Jianna Literature and Arts Journal* in Sichuan Province, was sentenced to seven years' imprisonment in February 1987 for "vilifying the Socialist system." Liu had also been active during the 1979-81 Democracy Wall period. His release, which was expected in February 1994, has not been confirmed.

Fan Jianping, *Beijing Ribao*
Imprisoned: 1989

Fan, an editor at *Beijing Ribao* (Beijing Daily), was arrested sometime after June 4, 1989.

Ji Kunxing, *Pioneers*
Imprisoned: September 1989

Ji was tried in Kunming in September 1989 on charges of fomenting a counterrevolutionary plot. He and three others had published an underground magazine called *Pioneers*, circulated anti-government leaflets, and put up anti-government posters.

Jin Naiyi, *Beijing Ribao*
Imprisoned: 1989

Jin, with *Beijing Ribao* (Beijing Daily), was arrested sometime after June 4, 1989.

Li Jian, *Wenyi Bao*
Imprisoned: July 1989

Li, a journalist with *Wenyi Bao* (Literature and Arts News), was arrested in July 1989.

Ren Wanding,
   China Human Rights League
Imprisoned: June 9, 1989

Ren, a former Democracy Wall journalist who founded the underground publication *China Human Rights League*, actively supported the 1989 student democracy movement in speeches and articles calling for freedom of expression. He was arrested June 9, 1989, and sentenced on Jan. 26, 1991, to seven years in prison and three years' subsequent deprivation of political rights. Ren, who previously spent four years in prison, has reportedly been denied proper treatment for his cataracts and is said to be in danger of losing his eyesight. His chronic sinusitis, chest infections, acute gastritis, and severe internal and external hemorrhoids have also gone untreated.

Shang Jingzhong, *Pioneers*
Tried: September 1989

Shang was tried in Kunming in September 1989 on charges of fomenting a counterrevolutionary plot. He and three others had published an underground magazine called *Pioneers*, circulated anti-government leaflets, and put up anti-government posters.

Imprisoned Journalists

Shi Qing, *Pioneers*
Tried: September 1989

Shi was tried in Kunming in September 1989 on charges of fomenting a counterrevolutionary plot. He and three others had published an underground magazine called *Pioneers,* circulated anti-government leaflets, and put up anti-government posters.

Yang Hong, *Zhongguo Qingnian Bao*
Imprisoned: June 13, 1989

Yang, a reporter for *Zhongguo Qingnian Bao* (China Youth News), was arrested on June 13, 1989, in Kunming. He was charged with circulating "rumor-mongering leaflets" and protesting against corruption.

Yu Anmin, *Pioneers*
Tried: September 1989

Yu was tried in Kunming in September 1989 on charges of fomenting a counterrevolutionary plot. He and three others had published an underground magazine called *Pioneers,* circulated anti-government leaflets and put up anti-government posters.

Yu Zhongmin, *Fazhi Yuekan*
Imprisoned: 1989

Yu, a journalist with *Fazhi Yuekan* (Law Monthly) in Shanghai, was arrested sometime after June 4, 1989. He was later described in an article in *Wenhui Daily* as an "agitator" of the Shanghai student demonstrations.

Chen Yanbin, *Tielu*
Imprisoned: Late 1990

Chen, a former Qinghua University student, was arrested in late 1990 and sentenced to 15 years in prison with four years' subsequent deprivation of political rights. Together with Zhang Yafei, he had produced an unofficial magazine called *Tielu* (Iron Currents). The government termed it reactionary and charged Chen with making counterrevolutionary propaganda and incitement. Several hundred mimeographed copies of the journal were distributed.

Zhang Yafei, *Tielu*
Imprisoned: September 1990

Zhang, a former student at Beifang Communications University, edited an unofficial magazine called *Tielu* (Iron Currents), about the 1989 crackdown at Tiananmen Square. He was arrested in September 1990, charged with making counterrevolutionary propaganda and incitement, and in March 1991 was sentenced to 11 years in prison and two years' subsequent deprivation of political rights.

Liao Jia'an, *Da Jia*
Imprisoned: June 8, 1992

Liao, a People's University graduate student and co-editor with Wang Shengli of the unofficial student journal *Da Jia* (Everyone), received a three-year prison sentence from the Beijing People's Intermediate Court in August 1993. Liao was arrested on June 8, 1992, and is said to have been formally charged with counterrevolution on December 1992. He was initially held at the Banbuqiao Detention Center in Beijing, where a hepatitis infection he contracted was left untreated.

Wang Jun,
People's Daily Overseas Edition
Imprisoned: May 1992

Wang, a *People's Daily Overseas Edition* reporter, was handed a two-year prison sentence in May 1993, a year after his arrest for allegedly giving state secrets to the international media. Active in the press protests of 1989, Wang had been put on disciplinary probation. His release, which was expected in May 1994, has not been confirmed.

Wu Shishen, *Xinhua News Agency*
Imprisoned: October or November 1992

Wu, a Xinhua News Agency reporter, received a life sentence in August 1993 for allegedly providing a "state-classified" advance copy of President Jiang Zemin's 14th Party Congress address to a Hong Kong journalist. Wu had been arrested in October or November of 1992.

Fu Shenqi
Imprisoned: June 26, 1993

Fu, a former Democracy Wall activist who had just been released from a two-year detention for his involvement in publishing an underground human rights journal, was again detained on June 26, 1993, and sentenced without trial to three years in "education through labor" camps for inciting trouble and speaking to foreign journalists.

Gao Yu
Imprisoned: October 2, 1993

Gao, a free-lance journalist, was tried without counsel and sentenced to six years in prison on Nov. 10, 1994, for "leaking state secrets" about China's structural reforms in articles for the pro-Beijing Hong Kong magazine *Mirror Monthly*. She was detained on Oct. 2, 1993, two days before she was to depart for the United States to start a one-year research fellowship at Columbia University's Graduate School of Journalism. Gao was previously jailed for 14 months following the June 1989 Tiananmen Square demonstrations and released in August 1990, after showing symptoms of a heart condition.

Ma Tao,
China Health Education News
Sentenced: August 1993

Ma, editor of *China Health Education News*, received a six-year prison term in August 1993 for allegedly assisting Xinhua News Agency reporter Wu Shishen in providing President Jiang Zemin's "state-classified" 14th Party Congress address to a Hong Kong journalist. According to the Associated Press, Ma is believed to be Wu's wife.

Xi Yang, *Ming Pao*
Imprisoned: September 27, 1993

Xi, Beijing correspondent for the Hong Kong daily *Ming Pao*, was arrested on Sept. 27, 1993, and sentenced to twelve years in prison on March 28, 1994, for "stealing and espionage of state secrets." The "secrets" in question included unpublished savings and loans interest rate changes for the People's Bank of China, as well as information on the Bank's international gold transaction plans, provided to Xi in both cases by Bank official Tian Ye.

Imprisoned Journalists

Wei Jingsheng
Imprisoned: April 1, 1994

Wei, a prominent dissident journalist, was arrested on April 1, 1994, and charged with violating his parole terms by attempting to enter the capital; Wei's parole had expired the previous day. Wei had been released on parole on Sept. 14, 1993, after serving 14 and a half years of a 15-year prison sentence for articles he had written in the pro-democracy journal *Tansuo.* He had been briefly detained in March 1994 for alleged parole violations. Earlier in the year Wei had received several official warnings for granting interviews to foreign journalists, contributing an opinion piece to the *New York Times,* and signing a contract to write his prison memoirs. Wei is being held incommunicado at an unknown location.

APPEALS TO:
His Excellency Tao Siju
Minister of Public Security
Gong'anbu
14 Dongchang'anlu
Beijing 100741
People's Republic of China   Fax: 86-1-5241596

Cuba (2)

Yndamiro Restano
Imprisoned: December 20, 1991

Restano, a former radio journalist and founding member of the Cuban Association of Independent Journalists (APIC), has been serving a 10-year prison term in Cuba since 1992 for organizing The Harmony Movement (MAR), a popular, nonviolent political movement. He was arrested on Dec. 20, 1991, and tried and convicted of rebellion in May 1992. In November 1994, Restano received CPJ's International Press Freedom Award. He is being held in the Combinado del Este prison in Havana.

Alexis Castaneda Perez,
Vanguardia and Huella
Imprisoned: May 15, 1994

Castaneda Perez, a journalist, art critic and essayist with *Vanguardia* and *Huella,* was sentenced on May 15, 1994, to five years in prison for "enemy propaganda."

APPEALS TO:
President Fidel Castro Ruz
c/o Permanent Mission of Cuba in the United Nations
315 Lexington Avenue
New York, NY 10016
United States   Fax: (212) 779-1697

Ethiopia (6)

Tefera Asmare, *Ethiopis*
Imprisoned: November 1993

Tefera, editor in chief of *Ethiopis*, was arrested in November 1993 and sentenced in late March 1994 to two years in prison for "inciting people against the government" and spreading "false rumors." The charges stemmed from an article about ethnic conflict in the Gondar region and an editorial entitled "The President Pretends Everything is O.K." In late June, Tefera was given an additional 18-month suspended sentence for having published an editorial entitled "Fascism in Tigray" and an article about conflict in western Ethiopia. An appeal to the Supreme Court was pending at the end of 1994.

Daniel Kifle, *Fendisha*
Imprisoned: January 15, 1994

Daniel, editor of *Fendisha*, was arrested by police on Jan. 15, 1994, and sentenced to 18 months in prison on June 1. His conviction stemmed from articles that alleged corruption on the part of Prime Minister Tamirat Layne and reports claiming that Eritrean troops were deployed in Ethiopia.

Ezedin Mohammed, *Ye Fikir Chawata*
Imprisoned: January 1994

Ezedin, editor of *Ye Fikir Chawata* (Love Games), was arrested in January 1994 and subsequently sentenced to one year in prison on charges of offending public morals. He is scheduled to be released in February 1995.

Habtamu Belete, *Ruhama*
Imprisoned: July 1994

Habtamu, a reporter for *Ruhama*, and Girma Endrias, his colleague, were each sentenced in July 1994 to six months in prison for contempt of court. Girma was reportedly released at the end of the year, but Habtamu remained in prison.

Nayk Kassaye, *Beza*,
Disappeared: May 9, 1994
Yohannes Abebe, *Beza*,
Imprisoned: October 1994

Nayk, editor in chief of *Beza*, and Yohannes, the paper's deputy editor, were arrested by police on Jan. 22, 1994, for reasons that are unclear. The two were released on bail in March. Then, on May 9, Nayk disappeared on his way to the Central High Court. It is believed that the State Security Services are holding him in their custody. Yohannes was rearrested in October and fined 10,000 birr on Dec. 12.

APPEALS TO:
Minister Mahteme Solomon
Ministry of Justice
PO Box 1370
Addis Ababa, Ethiopia   Fax: 251-1-550722

Imprisoned Journalists

India (1)

Gurdip Singh, *Aaj di Awaz*
Imprisoned: January 11, 1994

Singh, managing editor of the Punjabi daily *Aaj di Awaz*, was detained by state police officers on Jan. 11, 1994. Ten days later, Singh was charged with violating the Terrorist and Disruptive Activities Act (TADA). The charge was based on allegedly incriminating statements made by Kashmiri separatist Nisar Ahmed, who has been in police custody for two years.

APPEALS TO:
His Excellency Narasimha Rao
Office of the Prime Minister
South Block, Gate No. 6
New Delhi 110011   India   Fax: 91-11-3016857

Indonesia (1)

Adnan Beuransyah,
Serambi Indonesia
Imprisoned: August 16, 1990

Beuransyah, a journalist with the newspaper *Serambi Indonesia*, was arrested on Aug. 16, 1990. He was tried in March 1991 in Banda Aceh on charges of subversion and sentenced to eight years in prison.

APPEALS TO:
His Excellency Suharto
Office of the President
Istana Merdeka
Jakarta, Indonesia   Fax: 62-21-778182

Iran (2)

Salman Heidari, *Salam*
Imprisoned: June 1992

Heidari, a reporter for the Tehran daily *Salam*, was arrested in late June 1992 and accused of espionage. Some view Heidari's arrest as an attempt by President Rafsanjani to intimidate the hard-line opposition. It is unclear whether he has been formally charged and tried.

Manouchehr Karimzadeh, *cartoonist*
Imprisoned: April 11, 1992

Karimzadeh, a cartoonist, was arrested on April 11, 1992, after a piece of his appeared in the science magazine *Farad*. It depicted a soccer player with an amputated arm and wearing a turban, and the image was interpreted by the authorities to be a caricature of the late Ayatollah Khomeini. An Islamic revolutionary court originally sentenced him to one year in prison, but he was retried in 1993 by order of the Supreme Court and sentenced to 10 years imprisonment.

APPEALS TO:
His Excellency Ali Akbar Hashemi Rafsanjani
The Presidency

Palestine Avenue, Azerbaijan Intersection
Tehran, Islamic Republic of Iran
Telex: 214231 MITI IR or 213113 PRIM IR

Iraq (2)

Aziz al-Syed Jasim, *Al-Ghad*
Imprisoned: April 18, 1991

Jasim, editor of *Al-Ghad* magazine and former editor of the official daily, *Al-Thawra*, was taken into custody at a secret police station in Baghdad on April 18, 1991, and has not been heard from since. Government officials deny that he is under arrest. During a previous term of imprisonment that began in 1989, he was forced to write a number of books in support of Iraqi President Saddam Hussein.

Subhy Haddad, *Asahi Shimbun*
Imprisoned: January 27, 1994

Haddad, Baghdad correspondent for the Japanese daily *Asahi Shimbun*, received a telephone call from Iraqi intelligence early in the morning on Jan. 27, 1994, summoning him to their offices for questioning. A couple of hours later agents searched his house and confiscated some of his documents. Haddad had recently written a piece about military exercises northeast of Baghdad. Haddad, like Aziz al-Syed Jasim, has not been seen nor heard from since.

APPEALS TO:
President Saddam Hussein
c/o Iraqi Mission to the United Nations
14 East 79th Street
New York, NY 10021 United States

Israel and the Occupied Territories (1)

Mousa Qous, *Al-Fajr*
Imprisoned: October 21, 1991

Qous, a reporter with the English-language edition of *Al-Fajr* weekly, was arrested on Oct. 21, 1991. On Nov. 19, 1991, he was sentenced by the Lod Military Court to four years in prison for membership in the Popular Front for the Liberation of Palestine and for instructing others to write graffiti. His appeal of the sentence was rejected on Dec. 26, 1991.

APPEALS TO:
Prime Minister Yitzhak Rabin
Rappin Street
Jerusalem, Israel   Fax: 972 2 664 838

Imprisoned Journalists

Kuwait (18)

**Fawwaz Muhammad
al-Awadi Bessisso
Ibtisam Berto Sulaiman al-Dakhil
Usamah Suhail Abdallah Hussein
Abd al-Rahman Muhammad
Asad al-Husseini
Ahmad Abd Mustafa**
Sentenced to life in prison:
June 1991

The five journalists were given life sentences for working with the Iraqi occupation newspaper *Al-Nida*. They were taken into custody after Kuwait's liberation and charged with collaboration. The trials, which began on May 19, 1991, in martial-law courts, failed to comply with international standards. The defendants were reportedly tortured during their interrogations. Their defense —that they were coerced to work for the Iraqi newspaper—was not rebutted by prosecutors. On June 16, 1991, the journalists were sentenced to death. Ten days later all martial-law death sentences were commuted to life terms, following international protests.

**Wafa Wasfi Ahmad
Belqiss Hafez Fadhel
Zekarayat Mahmoud Harb
Walid Hassan Muhammad Karaka
Rahim Muhammad Najem
Ghazi Mahmoud al-Sayyed**
Sentenced to 10 years in prison:
June 1991

A martial law tribunal in June 1991 sentenced the three men and three women to 10 years in prison with hard labor for their "supporting role...in helping to publish the [Iraqi occupation] paper [*Al-Nida*]." The defendants reportedly were tortured during interrogation. The prosecution did not offer direct evidence to rebut the coercion defense of the accused. Four other staffers were also sentenced to 10 years in prison for allegedly working at the paper, though it appears that they did not work as journalists: Riyadh Fouad Shaker Ali; Ahmad Muhammad Hannoun; Zuhra Muhammad Adel Abd al-Khaleq; and Lefta Abdallah Menahi.

**Daoud Suleiman al-Qarneh
Hassan al-Khalili
Muhammad Zahran
Nawwaf Izzedin al-Khatib**
Sentenced to 10 years in prison:
June 20, 1992

On June 20, 1992, Kuwait's State Security Court sentenced four Palestinian journalists convicted of having worked for *Al-Nida*, organ of the Iraqi occupation, to 10 years in prison. They are: al-Qarneh, formerly deputy chief editor at the Kuwait News Agency (KUNA); al-Khalili, formerly an editor at KUNA; Zahran, accused of translating for *Al-Nida*; and al-Khatib. The court fined them KD 2000 each and ordered that they be expelled from the country upon termination of their sentences.

Bassam Fouad Abiad
Sentenced to 15 years in prison:
July 28, 1992
**Mufid Mustafa Abd al-Rahim
Ghazi Alam al-Dine**
Sentenced to 10 years in prison:
July 28, 1992

On July 28, 1992, the State Security Court convicted Abiad, Abd al-Rahim and Alam al-Dine of working for *Al-Nida*, news organ of the Iraqi occupation. Abiad, a Lebanese citizen, was sentenced to 15 years in prison. Abd al-Rahim, a Palestinian, was sentenced to 10 years in prison. And Alam al-Dine, a Jordanian citizen and former editor at KUNA, was sentenced to 10 years in prison, although he had only worked a total of 12 hours for *Al-Nida*. The court also fined each of the three men KD 2000 and ordered that they be expelled from the country upon termination of their sentences.

APPEALS TO:
His Highness Shaikh Sa'ad al-'Abdallah al-Sabah,
Crown Prince and Prime Minister
Al-Diwan al-Amiri
Al-Safat
Kuwait City, Kuwait   Fax: 965 243 0121

Libya (1)

Abdallah Ali al-Sanussi al-Darrat
Imprisoned: 1974 or 1975

Al-Darrat, a journalist and writer from Benghazi, was arrested in 1974 or 1975 and has been held in the interim without trial.

APPEALS TO:
Revolutionary Leader
Col. Muammar al-Qadhafi
c/o Libyan Mission to the United Nations
309-315 East 48th Street
New York, NY 10017 United States

Maldives (1)

Mohamed Saeed Moosa Wajdee
Imprisoned: October 19, 1994

Free-lance journalist Wajdee was arrested in connection with an article he wrote for the daily *Haveeru* alleging that government officials regularly bought votes and used "strong arm tactics" to influence voters during presidential and general elections. Wajdee had been detained several times in 1990 for articles published in *Hukuru*, a weekly newspaper he edited that was banned the same year.

APPEALS TO:
President Maymoon Abdul Gayoom
The President's Office
Marine Drive (North)
Male, Maldives   Fax: 960-325-525

Myanmar (Burma) (7)

U Win Tin
Imprisoned: July 4, 1989

U Win Tin, former editor of two daily newspapers and vice-chair of Burma's Writers Association, was active in establishing independent publications during the 1988 student democracy movement. He also worked closely with imprisoned National League for Democracy (NLD) leader Daw Aung San Suu Kyi. He was arrested on July 4, 1989, and sentenced to three years' hard labor. His sentence was subsequently extended. U Win Tin is reported to be gravely ill, and was seen wearing a neck brace by U.S. Congressman Bill Richardson during a February 1994 prison visit.

Imprisoned Journalists

U Myo Myint Nyein,
What's Happening
Imprisoned: September 1990

U Myo Myint Nyein, who was arrested in September 1990 for contributing to *What's Happening*, was sentenced to seven years in prison under the 1950 Emergency Provisions Act.

U Nay Min, *BBC*
Imprisoned: 1988

U Nay Min, a lawyer and BBC correspondent, was arrested in 1988 and sentenced in October 1989 to 14 years of hard labor.

U Sein Hlaing, *What's Happening*
Imprisoned: September 1990

U Sein Hlaing, publisher of *What's Happening*, a satirical news magazine, was arrested in September 1990 and sentenced to seven years in prison under the 1950 Emergency Provisions Act.

U Maung Maung Lay Ngwe
Imprisoned: September 1990

U Maung Maung Lay Ngwe was arrested in September 1990, and charged with writing and distributing publications which "make people lose respect for the government." The publications were titled *Pe-Tin-Tan* and *U Wisara Hnint U Ottama Ko-Sarr-Pyu.*

Daw San San Nwe
U Sein Hla Oo
Imprisoned: August 5, 1994

Dissident writer Daw San San Nwe and journalist U Sein Hla Oo were arrested on charges of spreading information damaging to the state and contacting anti-government groups. Daw San San Nwe and U Sein Hla Oo were sentenced on Oct. 6, 1994, to 10 years and seven years in prison, respectively. Officials said they had "fabricated and sent anti-government reports to some diplomats in foreign embassies, foreign radio stations and visiting foreign journalists." Both U Sein Hla Oo and Daw San San Nwe were previously imprisoned for their involvement with the National League for Democracy (NLD), Burma's main pro-democracy party. As of December 1994, they were being held at the Insein Prison in Rangoon.

APPEALS TO:
His Excellency General Than Shwe
Prime Minister and Minister of Defense
Chairman of the State Law and Order Restoration
    Council
Ministry of Defense
Signal Pagoda Road
Yangon, Myanmar   Telex 21316

Peru (10)

Javier Tuanama Valera, *Hechos*
Imprisoned: October 16, 1990.

Tuanama, editor in chief of the magazine *Hechos*, was sentenced on Nov. 7, 1994, to 10 years in prison for alleged links with the terrorist group Revolutionary Movement Tupac Amaru (MRTA). Although he was found not guilty of charges of terrorism on two previous trials he remains in prison at the Picsi penitentiary. He was first arrested on Oct. 16, 1990.

Pedro Valdez Bernales, *El Diario*
Imprisoned: November 19, 1992

Valdez, a layout artist for *El Diario*, a daily that became the mouthpiece for the terrorist group Shining Path, was first arrested on Nov. 19, 1992, and sentenced to 20 years in prison on Aug. 19, 1993, on charges of belonging to the Shining Path. Valdez's defense lawyer said his client worked for the newspaper before it became linked to the terrorist group.

Eduardo Sihue Cano, *Cambio*
Imprisoned. June 12, 1992

Sihue, a layout artist for the left-wing weekly *Cambio*, was detained on June 12, 1992. He was sentenced to six years in prison for allegedly "apologizing for terrorism," a crime under the anti-terrorism legislation instituted in Peru in 1992. He is being held in the Miguel Castro Castro prison in Lima.

Hermes Rivera Guerrero,
Radio Oriental
Imprisoned: May 8, 1992

Rivera, a reporter for Radio Oriental, was sentenced to 20 years in prison in February 1994 for alleged terrorist activity. He was arrested on May 8, 1992. Rivera is currently being held in the Picsi prison near Chiclayo.

Jose Antonio Alvarez Pachas,
Cambio
Imprisoned: June 11, 1992

Alvarez, a journalist with the left-wing weekly *Cambio*, was detained on June 11, 1992, and sentenced on May 24, 1993, to six years in prison under the anti-terror legislation. He is currently being held in the Miguel Castro Castro prison in Lima.

Alfonso Castiglione Mendoza,
Radio Amistad FM Stereo
Imprisoned: April 29, 1993

Castiglione, journalist and owner of Radio Amistad FM Stereo, was detained on April 29, 1993, on charges of alleged collaboration with terrorists. He was sentenced to 20 years in prison on Aug. 19, 1994.

Emilio Carrasco Moreno,
Radio Sensación
Imprisoned: December 2, 1993

Carrasco, owner of Radio Sensación, was arrested on December 2, 1993. A lower court found Carrasco innocent of charges of terrorism. But under anti-terrorism legislation, his case was referred to a higher court, where the anonymous judge sentenced him on May 12, 1994, to 30 years in prison. Carrasco is being held in the Picsi prison near Chiclayo.

Antero Gargurevich Oliva
Imprisoned: March 6, 1993

Gargurevich, a journalist and university professor, was arrested and put in jail on March 6, 1993, for allegedly being a member of a terrorist group. Under the anti-terror legislation, he was sentenced on April 14, 1994, to 12 years in prison.

Pedro Carranza Ugaz,
Radio Oriental de Jaén
Imprisoned: November 29, 1993

Carranza, a journalist with Radio Oriental de Jaén, was detained on Nov. 29, 1993, and sentenced on Nov. 7, 1994, to 20 years in prison on charges of being a member of the terrorist group Revolutionary Movement Tupac Amaru (MRTA).

Imprisoned Journalists

David Cajahuamán Picoy
Imprisoned: March 1994

Cajahuamán, a journalist and public employee in Huanuco, was arrested in March 1994 on charges of terrorism. He is currently imprisoned at a Trujillo penal center.

APPEALS TO:
Su Excelencia Alberto Fujimori
Presidente de la República del Peru
Palacio de Gobierno
Lima, Peru   Fax: 5114-326-535

Russia (1)

Alexei Kostin, *Yeshcho*
Imprisoned: February 4, 1994

Kostin, the founder and publisher of the Latvian-based newspaper *Yeshcho*, was arrested on Feb. 4, 1994. He was first detained on Oct. 6, 1993, and held until Oct. 28, 1993, when he was charged with publishing and distributing pornography. His second arrest came about because he continued to publish and distribute *Yescho*, even though it was never ordered to cease publication. While Kostin awaits trial in jail, in violation of the Russian Processing Code, which sets a maximum term of imprisonment prior to trial at nine months, *Yeshcho* continues to publish. At each of two hearings in the case, one held in late summer and another in November 1994, the presiding judges denied motions by the defense to release Kostin pending trial.

APPEALS TO:
His Excellency Boris Yeltsin
President of the Russian Federation
Moscow, Russia   Fax: 70-95-206-5137

South Korea (1)

Choi Chin-sop, *Mal*
Imprisoned: September 14, 1994

According to Amnesty International, Choi, a journalist with the monthly current affairs magazine *Mal*, was arrested on Sept. 14, 1992, as part of a crackdown on an alleged North Korean "spy ring." Choi was sentenced to three years in prison on Feb. 3, 1993, for belonging to an alleged "anti-state" organization—the pro-reunification 1995 Committee—and disseminating material in support of North Korea. Several of Choi's articles on human rights issues in South Korea were introduced as evidence against him at his trial.

APPEALS TO:
His Excellency Kim Young-Sam
Office of the President
Chong Wa Dae (The Blue House)
1 Sejong-no, Chongno-ku
Seoul, Republic of Korea   Fax: 82-2-770-0253

Syria (9)

Rida Haddad, *Tishrin*
Imprisoned: October 1980

Haddad, an editorial writer for the daily *Tishrin*, was arrested in October 1980 and accused of membership in the Communist Party Political Bureau. He was sentenced to 15 years in prison with hard labor, and the court deprived him of his civil rights.

Ahmad Swaidan,
Kifah al Umal al-Ishtiraki
Imprisoned: January 1982

Swaidan, a reporter for *Kifah al-Umal al-Ishtiraki*, was arrested in January 1982 on suspicion of membership in the Ba'ath Party's February 23 movement. His trial began in the summer of 1993. The sentence given in the case was such that he should have been set free by now, but his release has not been confirmed.

Izzat al-Mahmoud
Imprisoned: 1982

Al-Mahmoud, a Syrian journalist working in Beirut, was handed over to the Syrian government by Lebanese authorities in 1982.

Faisal Allush
Imprisoned: 1985

Allush, a journalist and political writer held since 1985, was sentenced in June 1993 to 15 years imprisonment for membership in the banned Party for Communist Action (PCA).

Anwar Bader,
Syrian Radio and Television
Imprisoned: December 1986

Bader, a reporter for Syrian radio and television, was arrested in December 1986 by the Military Interrogation Branch. He was accused of membership in the Party for Communist Action (PCA). In March 1994, he was convicted and sentenced to 12 years in prison.

Samir al-Hassan, *Fatah al-Intifada*
Imprisoned: April 1986

Al-Hassan, Palestinian editor of *Fatah al-Intifada*, was arrested in April 1986 because of his membership in the Party for Communist Action. In June 1994, he was convicted and sentenced to 15 years in prison.

Jadi Nawfal
Imprisoned: December 18, 1991

Nawfal, a free-lance journalist, was arrested on December 18, 1991 and sentenced the following March to five years in prison for belonging to Committees for the Defense of Democratic Freedoms and Human Rights in Syria (CDF).

Nizar Nayouf
Imprisoned: January 1992

Nayouf, a free-lance journalist who contributed to *Al-Huriyya* and *Al-Thaqafa al-Ma'arifa*, was arrested in January 1992 in Damascus with several human rights activists from the Committees for the Defense of Democratic Freedoms and Human Rights in Syria (CDF). In March 1992, he was sentenced by the State Security Court to 10 years in prison for "disseminating false information and receiving money from abroad." He was severely tortured during his interrogation.

Imprisoned Journalists

Salama George Kila
Imprisoned: March 1992

Kila, a Palestinian writer and journalist, was arrested in March 1992 by the Political Security division in Damascus. His trial began in the summer of 1993. The court ruled that he was guilty of a misdemeanor rather than a felony. Since the maximum sentence for a misdemeanor is three years, he should be released in March 1995.

APPEALS TO:
His Excellency Hafez al-Assad
President of the Syrian Arab Republic
Presidential Palace
Damascus, Syria   Telex: 419160 munjed sy

Togo (1)

Martin Dossou Gbenouga,
Tribune des Démocrates
Imprisoned: April 26, 1994

Gbenouga, editor and publisher of the independent biweekly *Tribune des Démocrates,* was arrested on April 26, 1994, following the publication of an article in the April 22 edition that quoted the French Minister of Cooperation reproaching President Eyadema for the delay in appointing a new prime minister. The issue also carried an editorial by Gbenouga that criticized the president's military rule, corruption, falsification of facts and exploitation of ethnic politics. On May 6, he was sentenced to five years in prison and five million CFA for slandering President Eyadema. Gbenouga was held in the Civil Prison in Lome until May 18, when he was transferred to a remote prison in Mango. On Jan. 12, 1995, an appeals court reduced his sentence to one year and his fine to one million CFA.

His Excellency General Gnassingbe Eyadema
President of the Republic of Togo
Presidential Palace
Avenue de la Marina
Lome, Togo   Fax: 228-21-20-40; 21-08-50

Tunisia (2)

Hamadi Jebali, *Al-Fajr*
Imprisoned: January 1991

Jebali, editor of *Al-Fajr,* the weekly newspaper of the banned Islamist Al-Nahda party, was sentenced to 16 years in prison by the military court in Bouchoucha on Aug. 28, 1992. He was tried along with 170 others accused of membership in Al-Nahda. Jebali was convicted of "aggression with the intention of changing the nature of the state" and "membership in an illegal organization." During his testimony Jebali denied the charges against him and displayed evidence that he had been tortured while in custody. In January 1991, Jebali had been sentenced to one year in prison after *Al-Fajr* published an article calling for the abolition of military courts in Tunisia. International human rights groups monitoring the mass trial concluded that it fell far below international standards of justice.

Abdellah Zouari, *Al-Fajr*
Imprisoned: February 1991

Zouari, a contributor to *Al-Fajr*, was sentenced to 11 years in prison by the military court in Bouchoucha on Aug. 28, 1992. He was tried along with 170 others accused of membership in the banned Islamist Al-Nahda party. He had been in detention since February 1991 when he was charged with "association with an unrecognized organization." International human rights groups monitoring the trial concluded that it fell far short of international standards of justice.

> APPEALS TO:
> M. Zine El Abidine Ben Ali
> President of the Republic
> Presidential Palace
> Tunis, Tunisia   Fax: 216-1-744721

Turkey (74)

IMPRISONED BEFORE 1994 **(19)**

Naile Tuncer, *Devrimci Proletarya*
Imprisoned: May 1992

Tuncer, former responsible editor of left-wing *Devrimci Proletarya* magazine, was arrested in May 1992. She was sentenced to two years in prison for articles published in the periodical. The sentence was upheld by the appeals court in May 1994.

Ünsal Zor, *Taraf*
Imprisoned: November 26, 1992

Zor, a reporter for the right-wing weekly *Taraf*, was arrested on Nov. 26, 1992.

Serhat Aktuğ, *Devrimci Gençlik*
Imprisoned: April 18, 1993

Aktuğ, a reporter for the left-wing monthly *Devrimci Gençlik*, was taken into custody on April 18, 1993, from the magazine's Fatih office in Istanbul. He was charged with membership in an illegal organization and arrested. His trial continues at the Istanbul State Security Court.

Tuncay Atmaca, *Emek*
Imprisoned: August 1993

Atmaca, former responsible editor of the left-wing monthly *Emek*, was arrested and put in jail in August 1993 when his conviction was upheld by the appeals court. He was sentenced to two and a half years in prison for articles published in the magazine.

Ismail Beşikçi
Imprisoned: November 12, 1993

Beşikçi, a prominent writer and journalist, was arrested on Nov. 12, 1993, and sentenced to one year in prison for an article he had written in the now-defunct *Yeni Ülke* daily. Since then, he has been convicted in other cases on charges stemming both from articles he published in the now defunct *Özgür Gündem* and from books he has written on the Kurdish question. By the end of 1994, the prison sentences he had received totaled 67 years. More cases against him are pending.

Bektaş Cansever, *Devrimci Çözüm*
Imprisoned: January 7, 1993

Cansever, a reporter for the left-wing *Devrimci Çözüm* magazine, was taken into custody on Jan. 7, 1993, during a police raid on the magazine's headquarters in Istanbul. He was subsequently arrested. His trial has not been concluded.

Hikmet Çetin, *Deng* and *Azadi*
Imprisoned: December 29, 1993

Çetin, owner of the now defunct *Deng* and *Azadi* magazines, was arrested on Dec. 29, 1993, and sent to prison when the 20-month prison sentence against him for "separatist propaganda" was upheld by the appeals court.

Sakine Fidan, *Mücadele*
Imprisoned: July 20, 1993.

Fidan, Diyarbakir correspondent of the left-wing weekly *Mücadele*, was arrested on July 20, 1993.

Ismail Güneş, *Özgür Gündem*
Imprisoned: December 11, 1993

Güneş, a correspondent for the pro-Kurdish daily *Özgür Gündem*, was taken into custody on Dec. 11, 1993, during a police raid on the Ağri bureau of the newspaper. He was subsequently charged with being a member of the outlawed Kurdistan Workers' Party (PKK) and arrested. His trial continues in Erzincan.

Mustafa Kaplan, *Beklenen Vakit*
Imprisoned: September 28, 1993

Kaplan, a writer at the right-wing daily *Beklenen Vakit*, was arrested on Sept. 28, 1993. He was convicted of insulting Kemal Atatürk, the founder of modern Turkey, and of insulting the Turkish president. He was originally sentenced to five years in prison, but is expected to spend a little longer than a year because he was covered in a recent amnesty.

Salih Özçelik, *Azadi*
Imprisoned: September 26, 1993

Özçelik, a contributor to *Azadi* was charged with "separatist propaganda" on Sept. 26, 1993, for an article he wrote for the now defunct pro-Kurdish weekly. He was sentenced to two years in prison on Aug. 20, 1994, and is serving his sentence in Hatay prison.

Ibrahim Özen, *Devrimci Çözüm*
Imprisoned: January 7, 1993

Özen, a reporter for *Devrimci Çözüm*, was taken into custody on Jan. 7, 1993, during a police raid on the magazine's headquarters in Istanbul. He was subsequently arrested. His trial has not been concluded.

Hasan Özgün, *Özgür Gündem*
Imprisoned: December 9, 1993

Özgün, Diyarbakir correspondent for *Özgür Gündem*, was taken into custody during a police raid on the paper's bureau in Diyarbakir on Dec. 9, 1993. He was subsequently charged with aiding the outlawed Kurdish insurgent organization PKK and arrested. His trial continues in Diyarbakir State Security Court.

Fethiye Pekşen, *Devrimci Çözüm*
Imprisoned: January 7, 1993

Pekşen, a reporter for *Devrimci Çözüm*, was taken into custody on Jan. 7, 1993, during a police raid on the magazine's headquarters in Istanbul. She was subsequently arrested. Her trial has not been concluded.

Zena Sezen, *Azadi*
Imprisoned: October 18, 1993

Sezen, editor in chief of *Azadi*, was arrested on Oct. 18, 1993 and charged with "separatist propaganda" under the Anti-Terror Law for various articles published in the weekly. There are three trials against her in progress. One has resulted in a two-year sentence, but is being appealed.

Hüseyin Solak, *Mücadele*
Imprisoned: September 1993

Solak, Gaziantep bureau chief of *Mücadele* magazine, was arrested in September 1993.

Kemal Topalak, *Devrimci Çözüm*
Imprisoned: January 7, 1993

Topalak, a reporter for *Devrimci Çözüm*, was taken into custody on Jan. 7, 1993, during a police raid on the magazine's headquarters in Istanbul. He was subsequently arrested. His trial has not been concluded.

Cemal Uç, *Mücadele*
Imprisoned: December 24, 1993

Uç, *Mücadele*'s Tunceli correspondent, was arrested on Dec. 24, 1993.

Sinan Yavuz, *Yoksul Halkin Gücü*
Imprisoned: 1993

Yavuz, former responsible editor of the left-wing weekly *Yoksul Halkin Gücü*, was arrested in 1993 for articles published in the magazine.

IMPRISONED IN 1994 **(55)**
Mehmet Akdemir, *İşçi Hareketi*
Imprisoned: November 24, 1994

Akdemir, a reporter for the left-wing magazine *İşçi Hareketi*, was taken into custody on Nov. 24, 1994, during a police raid on the magazine's main offices in Istanbul. He was subsequently arrested.

Mustafa Aladağ, *Özgür Ülke*
Imprisoned: August 10, 1994

Aladağ, one of *Özgür Ülke*'s Ağri correspondents, was taken into custody on Aug. 10, 1994, during a police raid on the paper's Ağri bureau. He was subsequently charged with being a member of the PKK. Articles he wrote about the security forces and their operations and human rights violations in the Southeast are cited as evidence of his PKK membership. The trial continues.

Metin Alhas, *Mücadele*
Imprisoned: October 23, 1994

Alhas, one of the Antakya correspondents for the weekly *Mücadele*, was detained during a police raid on the magazine's Antakya bureau on Oct. 23, 1994. He was subsequently formally arrested.

Mehmet Sait Alpaslan, *Newroz*
Imprisoned: October 1994

Alpaslan, a writer at the pro-Kurdish *Newroz* magazine, was arrested in October 1994.

Imprisoned Journalists

Gürsel Avci, *Taraf*
Imprisoned: January 1, 1994

Avci, a reporter for *Taraf*, was arrested on Jan. 1, 1994.

Fatih Aydin, *Taraf*
Imprisoned: January 25, 1994

Aydin, a reporter for *Taraf*, was arrested on Jan. 25, 1994.

Hayrettin Ayhan, *Gerçek*
Imprisoned: December 2, 1994

Ayhan, a reporter for the left-wing weekly *Gerçek*, was taken into custody on Dec. 2, 1994, while he was covering a demonstration in Istanbul. He was arrested 15 days later and charged with belonging to an illegal organization and participating in an unauthorized rally.

Aysel Bölücek, *Mücadele*
Imprisoned: October 11, 1994

Bölücek, one of *Mücadele*'s Ankara correspondents, was picked up by the police at her home on Oct. 11, 1994, and detained. She was later arrested.

Sabri Bölek, *Özgür Gündem*
Imprisoned: January 3, 1994

Bölek, a correspondent for *Özgür Gündem*, was arrested on Jan. 3, 1994. He was charged with belonging to the PKK. Articles he wrote about the security forces and their operations and human rights violations in the Southeast are cited as evidence of his PKK membership. The trial continues.

Ali Asker Bal, *Alinteri*
Imprisoned: October 17, 1994

Bal, a reporter for left-wing magazine *Alinteri*, was arrested on Oct. 17, 1994.

Mehmet Balamir, *Özgür Ülke*
Imprisoned: September 6, 1994

Balamir, a correspondent for *Özgür Ülke*, was detained following a police raid on the daily's Diyarbakir bureau on Sept. 6, 1994. He was later arrested and charged with violating the Anti-Terror Law.

Nevzat Bulut, *Özgür Ülke*
Imprisoned: August 10, 1994

Bulut, a correspondent for *Özgür Ülke*, was taken into custody during a police raid on the newspaper's Ağri bureau on Aug. 10, 1994. He was subsequently charged with being a member of the outlawed Kurdish insurgent organization PKK and arrested. Articles he wrote about the security forces and their operations and human rights violations in the Southeast are cited as evidence in his trial, which is in progress.

Ali Sinan Çağlar, *Mücadele*
Imprisoned: August 6, 1994

Çağlar, *Mücadele*'s Ankara correspondent, was arrested on Aug. 6, 1994, and charged with membership in an illegal organization. On Jan. 23, 1995, he was sentenced to 12 and a half years in prison. His articles in *Mücadele* and his status as a staff correspondent were used as evidence that he belonged to an outlawed left-wing organization.

Şaban Çavdar, *Taraf*
Imprisoned: January 25, 1994

Çavdar, a reporter for *Taraf*, was arrested on Jan. 25, 1994.

Sadık Çelik, *Mücadele*
Imprisoned: March 16, 1994

Çelik, *Mucadele*'s Zonguldak bureau chief, was taken into custody on March 16, 1994, and subsequently arrested.

Bülent Çiftçi, *Özgür Ülke*
Imprisoned: August 1, 1994

Çiftçi, Van correspondent for *Özgür Ülke*, was detained on Aug. 1, 1994, at the bus terminal. He was heading for the newspaper's headquarters in Istanbul. *Özgür Ülke* claims that Çiftçi was delivering documents signed by the former interior minister ordering the security forces to curtail the newspaper's activities. He was subsequently arrested and charged with aiding the PKK. His trial continues.

Cemal Dağ, *Özgür Gündem*
Imprisoned: January 10, 1994

Dağ, one of the Diyarbakir correspondents for *Özgür Gündem*, was arrested on Jan. 10, 1994, on charges that he was a member of the PKK and was aiding the outlawed organization. His trial continues.

Kadir Dara, *Mücadele*
Imprisoned: November 5, 1994

Dara, one of *Mücadele*'s Mersin correspondents, was detained by the police on his way to an assignment on Nov. 5, 1994, and was later arrested.

Mir Ali Demir, *Yoksul Halkın Gücü*
Imprisoned: November 24, 1994

Demir, a reporter for the left-wing weekly *Yoksul Halkın Gucu*, was taken into custody on Nov. 24, 1994, during a police raid on the magazine's main offices in Istanbul. He was arrested on Dec. 6, 1994.

Gürsel Eroğlu, *Özgür Gelecek*
Imprisoned: February 2, 1994

Eroğlu, a correspondent for left-wing *Özgür Gelecek* magazine, was taken into custody on Feb. 2, 1994, during a police raid on the magazine's Tokat bureau. He was subsequently arrested.

Recep Gedik, *Mücadele*
Imprisoned: October 29, 1994

Gedik, one of *Mücadele*'s Mersin correspondents, was detained by the police on his way to an assignment on Oct. 29, 1994, and was later arrested.

Serdar Gelir, *Mücadele*
Imprisoned: April 16, 1994

Gelir, one of *Mücadele*'s Ankara correspondents, was detained on April 16, 1994, and arrested 10 days later.

Nuran Gezici, *Yoksul Halkın Gücü*
Imprisoned: April 1994

Gezici, a reporter for *Yoksul Halkın Gücü*, was arrested in April 1994.

Özgür Güdemoğlu, *Mücadele*
Imprisoned: May 20, 1994

Güdemoğlu, *Mücadele*'s Konya bureau chief, was taken into custody on May 20, 1994, and arrested a few days later.

Teoman Gül, *Newroz*
Imprisoned: November 1994

Gül, a reporter for *Newroz* magazine, was arrested in November 1994.

Imprisoned Journalists

Asli Güneş, *Hedef*
Imprisoned: June 7, 1994

Güneş, who served as the responsible editor of the left-wing weekly *Hedef* in 1992 and 1993, was arrested and sent to prison on June 7, 1994, to serve a one-year sentence for articles published in the weekly. Because she cannot afford to pay the fines imposed upon her in the same case, the fines were converted to prison time and she is expected to remain in prison until 1997.

Ramazan Güngör, *Taraf*
Imprisoned: June 10, 1994

Güngör, a reporter with *Taraf,* was arrested on June 10, 1994.

Hanim Harman, *Mücadele*
Imprisoned: January 24, 1994

Harman, one of *Mücadele's* Malatya correspondents, was taken into custody on Jan. 24, 1994, and arrested 15 days later.

Veysi Harman, *Özgür Ülke*
Imprisoned: November 9, 1994

Harman, responsible editor of *Özgür Ülke,* was arrested on Nov. 9, 1994, for various articles published in the newspaper. He is charged with disseminating "separatist propaganda" and "insulting the state." His trial continues.

Ahmet Ibili, *Mücadele*
Imprisoned: October 30, 1994

Ibili, Mersin bureau chief of the weekly *Mücadele,* was detained by the police on his way to an assignment on Oct. 30, 1994, and was later arrested.

Emine Iğdi, *Özgür Ülke*
Imprisoned: August 13, 1994

Iğdi, one of *Özgür Ülke's* Mardin correspondents, was detained on Aug. 13, 1994, during a raid on the paper's Mardin bureau. She was later charged with aiding the PKK and arrested. Her trial continues.

Özkan Kiliç, *Alternatif*
Imprisoned: 1994

Kiliç, editor in chief of the now defunct left-wing monthly *Alternatif,* was sentenced in 1994 to four years in prison for articles published in the magazine in 1993. He is in Bursa prison serving his sentence.

Zehra Kurtay, *Mücadele*
Imprisoned: May 1, 1994

Kurtay, a correspondent in *Mücadele's* Bursa bureau, was taken into custody on May 1, 1994, and subsequently arrested.

Sevim Lekesif, *Newroz*
Imprisoned: November 1994

Lekesif, a reporter at *Newroz* magazine, was arrested in November 1994.

Botan Önen, *Özgür Gündem*
Imprisoned: February 1, 1994

Önen, one of *Özgür Gündem's* Diyarbakir correspondents, was arrested on Feb. 1, 1994, on charges that he was a member of the PKK and was aiding the outlawed organization. His trial continues.

Kadriye Özcanli, *Özgür Ülke*
Imprisoned: September 6, 1994

Özcanli, one of *Özgür Ülke's* Diyarbakir correspondents, was detained following a police raid on the paper's Diyarbakir bureau on Sept. 6, 1994. She was later charged with membership in the PKK and arrested. Her trial continues.

Haydar Özdemir,
Yoksul Halkin Gücü
Imprisoned: October 1994

Özdemir, a reporter for *Yoksul Halkin Gücü* magazine, was arrested in October 1994.

Nezahat Özen, *Özgür Ülke*
Imprisoned: September 20, 1994

Özen, a correspondent for *Özgür Ülke*, was detained during a police raid on the paper's Diyarbakir bureau on Sept. 20, 1994. She was subsequently arrested and charged with aiding the PKK.

Veysel Şahin, *Mücadele*
Imprisoned: January 12, 1994

Şahin, Mücadele's Bursa bureau chief, was arrested on Jan. 12, 1994.

Murat Saraç, *Özgür Ülke*
Imprisoned: December 14, 1994

Saraç, responsible editor of *Özgür Ülke*, was arrested on Dec. 14, 1994, on charges that articles published in the daily violated the Anti-Terror Law.

Gülcan Sarioğlu, *Mücadele*
Imprisoned: October 23, 1994

Sarioğlu, one of the Antakya correspondents for the weekly *Mücadele*, was detained during a police raid on the magazine's Antakya bureau on Oct. 23, 1994. She was subsequently arrested.

Emine Serhat, *Özgür Gündem*
Imprisoned: February 3, 1994

Serhat, one of *Özgür Gündem*'s Iğdir correspondents, was detained on Feb. 3, 1994, during a raid on a village near Iğdir where she was doing a story for her newspaper. A week later she was charged with PKK membership and arrested. The trial continues.

Yusuf Şit, *Özgür Ülke*
Imprisoned: October 11, 1994

Şit, a former responsible editor of *Özgür Ülke*, was arrested on Oct. 11, 1994, in connection with 27 articles published in the newspaper in September and October, all of which allegedly violated the Anti-Terror Law prohibiting "separatist propaganda."

Hayrettin Soykan, *Ak-Zuhur*
Imprisoned: January 13, 1994

Soykan, owner and responsible editor of the now defunct right-wing *Ak-Zuhur* magazine, was sentenced to 20 months in prison and US$8,000 in fines for publishing "propaganda on behalf of an illegal organization." He was arrested and sent to jail on Jan. 13, 1994, when the appeals court upheld his conviction. His fines were converted to three years in prison because he could not pay them.

Havva Suiçmez, *Devrimci Gençlik*
Imprisoned: November 24, 1994

Suiçmez, a reporter for *Devrimci Gençlik*, was detained on Nov. 24, 1994, during a police raid on the main offices of the magazine in Istanbul. She was arrested on Dec. 6 and charged with membership in an illegal organization. By the end of 1994, her trial had not yet started.

Imprisoned Journalists

Leyla Taşdar, *Yoksul Halkın Gücü*
Imprisoned: October 1994

Taşdar, a reporter for *Yoksul Halkın Gücü*, was arrested in October 1994.

Hüsniye Tekin, *Özgür Ülke*
Imprisoned: August 13, 1994

Tekin, a correspondent for *Özgür Ülke*, was detained during a raid on the Mardin bureau of the newspaper on Aug. 13, 1994. She was subsequently charged with aiding and belonging to the PKK. Her trial continues.

Meral Tikiz, *Özgür Gündem*
Imprisoned: January 21, 1994

Tikiz, one of *Özgür Gündem*'s Iğdir correspondents, was taken into custody on Jan. 21, 1994. She was formally arrested a week later and charged with membership in the PKK. Articles she has written about the security force operations and human rights violations in the Southeast are cited as evidence in her ongoing trial.

Mehmet Toruş, *Hedef*
Imprisoned: December 12, 1994

Toruş, who served as the responsible editor for *Hedef* between 1989 and 1991, was arrested on Dec. 12, 1994, and put in jail to serve an 18-month sentence because of articles published in the weekly.

Fatma Hülya Tungan, *Mücadele*
Imprisoned: February 21, 1994

Tungan, Samsun bureau chief of *Mücadele* magazine, was taken into custody on Feb. 21, 1994, and arrested four days later. On Nov. 30, she was sentenced to 12 and a half years in prison.

Mehmet Emin Unay, *Özgür Ülke*
Imprisoned: May 16, 1994

Unay, Izmir correspondent for *Özgür Ülke*, was taken into custody on May 16, 1994, in Izmir. His trial is underway.

Ali Yolcu, *Mücadele*
Imprisoned: December 12, 1994

Yolcu, Antakya bureau chief of weekly *Mücadele*, was arrested on Dec. 12, 1994.

Halim Yurtoğlu, *Mücadele*
Imprisoned: April 1994

Yurtoğlu, one of the correspondents for *Mücadele* in Kırşehir, was detained in April 1994 and arrested in May.

Işık Ocak Yutçu, *Özgür Gündem*
Imprisoned: December 28, 1994

Yurtçu, a prominent writer and journalist who served as *Özgür Gündem*'s responsible editor in 1991 and 1992, was arrested and sent to prison on Dec. 28, 1994, when the appeals court upheld a 25-year sentence against him. He was charged under the Anti-Terror Law and convicted of "separatist propaganda" for various articles published in the daily while he was the editor. He faces charges in other, similar cases.

Ali Osman Zor, *Taraf*
Imprisoned: January 25, 1994

Zor, former responsible editor of the right-wing *Taraf* weekly, was arrested on Jan. 25, 1994, for articles that were published in the magazine.

APPEALS TO:
Tansu Çiller
Prime Minister
Basbakanlik
06573 Ankara, Turkey   Fax: 90 312 418 04 76

Vietnam (9)

Doan Viet Hoat
Imprisoned: November 17, 1990

Hoat, editor and publisher of the pro-democracy newsletter *Freedom Forum*, was sentenced to 20 years of hard labor in late March 1993 for his involvement with the publication. He is currently serving out his sentence, lowered to 15 years on appeal, in Thanh Cam Prison. Located in northern Vietnam, near the Laotian border, Thanh Cam is normally reserved for serious criminal offenders. Hoat suffers from kidney stones, a condition that developed during his previous 12-year incarceration by the Hanoi regime.

Pham Duc Kham
Imprisoned: Late 1990

Kham was sentenced to 16 years in prison in late March 1993 for his involvement with *Freedom Forum*. His sentence was reduced on appeal to 12 years. Kham is presently interred at Xuan Phuoc labor camp with Doan Viet Hoat and Le Duc Vuong.

Nguyen Van Thuan (Chau Son)
Imprisoned: Late 1990

Thuan was sentenced to 12 years in prison in late March 1993 for his involvement with *Freedom Forum*. His sentence was reduced on appeal to eight years. Thuan suffered a stroke on Feb. 25, 1994, that left him partially paralyzed. Authorities ordered him to return to Ham Tan prison camp within 30 days of his hospitalization.

Le Duc Vuong
Imprisoned: Late 1990

Vuong was reportedly sentenced in late March 1993 to seven years in prison for his involvement with *Freedom Forum*. Vuong is presently interred at Xuan Phuoc labor camp with Pham Duc Kham.

Nguyen Dan Que
Sentenced: November 1991

Que, sentenced to 20 years in prison in November 1991 on charges of compiling and distributing subversive literature, had distributed political handbills and sent documents abroad. Que, who suffers from hypertension and a bleeding gastric ulcer, is imprisoned at the Xuyen Moc labor camp in Dong Nai province.

Nguyen Xuan Dong
Sentenced: March 1993

Dong was reportedly sentenced in late March 1993 to four years in prison for his involvement with *Freedom Forum*.

Imprisoned Journalists

265

Nguyen Thieu Hung
Sentenced: March 1993

Hung was reportedly sentenced in late March 1993 to four years in prison for his involvement with *Freedom Forum.*

Hoang Cao Nha
Sentenced: March 1993

Nha was reportedly sentenced in late March 1993 to eight months in prison for his involvement with *Freedom Forum.* His release, which was expected by the end of 1993, has not been confirmed.

Pham Thai Thuy
Sentenced: March 1993

Thuy was reportedly sentenced in late March 1993 to four years in prison for his involvement with *Freedom Forum.*

APPEALS TO:
His Excellency Do Muoi
General Secretary of the Central Committee
Communist Party of Vietnam
1 Hoang Van Thu
Hanoi, Socialist Republic of Vietnam
Fax: 84-42-59205

Western Sahara (1)

Bahi Mohamed Ould Deif
Imprisoned: 1986

Bahi Mohamed, a Moroccan journalist, disappeared in 1986 while reporting from Tindouf, in western Algeria. An Algerian newspaper reported, after his disappearance, that he had been arrested by the Polisario, for plotting the assassination of Mohamed Abdelaziz, general secretary of the Polisario. Abdelaziz's claim that Bahi Mohamed is at liberty and free to return to Morocco have not been confirmed. In 1993, the Moroccan National Press Syndicate wrote to CPJ that he is still being held against his will and has not been tried.

APPEALS TO:
Mohamed Abdelaziz
Secretary General of the Polisario Front
B.P. 10
El Mouradia
Algiers, Algeria

The Death Toll

72 Confirmed Cases of Journalists Killed in the Line of Duty in 1994

P OLITICAL ASSASSINATION was once again the leading cause of job-related death for journalists around the world last year. The following list documents the deaths of 72 journalists who were killed in 1994 as a direct consequence of their profession—the largest number ever recorded in CPJ's annual press freedom surveys. Evidence in 58 of these cases strongly suggests that the journalists were deliberately targeted by killers whose intent was to suppress independent or critical reporting. In most instances these crimes were carried out with apparent impunity. As of February 1995, no one in any of the 18 countries where these murders took place had been arrested.

Another 14 journalists were killed in 1994 while on assignment in battle zones—five in Bosnia, three in Somalia, two in Chechnya, two in South African townships, one in Angola, and one in Rwanda. In Bosnia and Somalia, some of the victims may have been deliberately targeted because of their profession, but that is difficult if not impossible to prove.

Algeria suffered the highest death toll in 1994. Fundamentalist rebels murdered 19 Algerian journalists, the largest number of journalists deliberately killed in one country since the assassination campaigns of Argentina's "Dirty War" in the 1970s. All but one of the victims were Algerian nationals; most were reporters for French-language newspapers, magazines and wire services. The Armed Islamic Group, which claimed responsibility for many of these killings, has since declared that it is imposing the "death penalty" on all local radio and television journalists. Between May 1993 and February 1995, a total of 33 journalists had been murdered by fundamentalist extremists in Algeria.

In Rwanda, 14 reporters and editors were killed during the year in what evidence indicates were also intentional murders of well-known local journalists. A further five such cases remain under investigation by CPJ staff researchers. The genocidal massacres of 1994 claimed the lives of at least another 30 Rwandan journalists, but there is no clear causal link between these deaths and the victims' professions.

In Tajikistan, four journalists were murdered by unidentified gunmen in incidents that CPJ believes were deliberate political killings. Those deaths bring to 27 the number of Tajik journalists known to have been slain since 1992.

Three Cambodian reporters were murdered by unidentified assailants in what CPJ researchers found to be the first deliberate killings of journalists since Cambodia's emergence as a new democracy. Pakistan, in two related killings, also witnessed its first documented murders of working journalists in many years.

In an especially disturbing development, two Russian investigative reporters were killed in apparent retaliation for their work. One was investigating Moscow's criminal underworld; the other a story on corruption in the military.

A reporter and editor for two opposition-linked journals in Zaire were murdered in separate incidents last year. In Turkey, a pro-Kurdish reporter and a left-wing newspaper editor were murdered in circumstances that strongly suggested political motives.

Other journalists murdered last year include a BBC correspondent in Afghanistan; an Iranian reporter in Mostar; a Brazilian small-town newspaper publisher; a Burundian broadcast journalist; a Colombian talk-show host; a Guatemalan radio news director; a German free-lancer in Kurdish-controlled northern Iraq; and the editor of a weekly newsmagazine in Cuernavaca, Mexico.

The 72 confirmed cases of journalists killed as a direct result of their profession is the largest number ever documented by CPJ. But the real number is undoubtedly higher.

In 1993, 64 journalists were killed on the job; 10 of these cases, however, were not confirmed until 1994. Reports of journalists killed in the line of duty are investigated by CPJ staff researchers, who verify that the victims were employed in news-gathering and were killed as a direct consequence of their work.

CPJ researchers are currently investigating 13 other murders—five in Rwanda, two in Mexico, two in Russia, and one each in Belarus, Bosnia, Colombia and Madagascar—that also may have been targeted political killings. It has not yet been possible in these cases to establish a direct link between the crime and the victim's profession, but many of their colleagues are convinced such a link exists. We have asked the appropriate national authorities to investigate these homicides promptly and thoroughly, and to bring those responsible to justice.

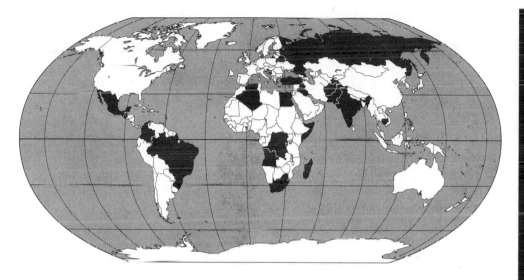

Countries Where Journalists were Killed in 1994

Afghanistan

CONFIRMED: **1**

Mirwais Jalil, *BBC Worldwide*
Date of Death: July 29, 1994
Place of Death: Near Kabul
Confirmed

Jalil, a reporter for the BBC's Pashto- and Persian-language services, was kidnapped and murdered near Kabul. Jalil was abducted by five masked men while returning from an interview with Hezb-i-Islami party leader and renegade Prime Minister Gulbuddin Hekmatyar. His body was found the following morning, with at least 20 bullet wounds to his head and chest.

Algeria

CONFIRMED: **19**

Olivier Quemener, *Free lancer*
Date of Death: February 1, 1994
Place of Death: Algiers
Confirmed

Quemener, a French free-lance television journalist, was shot dead while shooting video footage in the Casbah section of Algiers.

Abdelkader Hireche, *ENTV*
Date of Death: February 28, 1994
Place of Death: Algiers
Confirmed

Hireche, a journalist with Algerian Television (ENTV), was shot and killed in an eastern suburb of Algiers by three men bearing automatic weapons.

Mohamed Hassaine,
Alger Républicain
Date of Death: March 1, 1994
Place of Death: Blida
Confirmed

Hassaine, a correspondent for the daily *Alger Républicain*, was taken from his home in Larbatache in the Blida region. His body was later found decapitated.

Hassan Benaouda, *ENTV*
Date of Death: March 12, 1994
Place of Death: Algiers
Confirmed

Benaouda, a journalist with Algerian Television (ENTV), was shot in the head on March 5 by a group of armed assailants in the Casbah section of Algiers. He died of his wounds one week later.

Yahia Djamel Benzaghou,
   Prime Minister's press department
Date of Death: March 19, 1994
Place of Death: Algiers
Confirmed

Benzaghou, a journalist with the Prime Minister's press department, was gunned down in Bab El Oued, Algiers, where he lived.

Madjid Yacef, *L'Hebdo Libéré*
Date of Death: March 20, 1994
Place of Death: Algiers
Confirmed

Men armed with automatic weapons and disguised as policemen raided the Algiers offices of the independent French-language weekly *L'Hebdo Libéré* and opened fire on those inside the composing room, killing photojournalist Madjid Yacef and a driver with the paper and wounding several others.

Mohamed Meceffeuk, *Détective*
Date of Death: April 13, 1994
Place of Death: Near Chlef
Confirmed

Meceffeuk, a journalist with the weekly magazine *Détective* was shot and killed about 35 kilometers outside the town of Chlef.

Ferhat Cherkit, *El Moudjahid*
Date of Death: June 7, 1994
Place of Death: Algiers
Confirmed

Cherkit, adjunct editor in chief of the National Liberation Front (FLN) daily *El Moudjahid*, was shot and killed in downtown Algiers, not far from the paper's headquarters.

Yasmina Drici, *Le Soir d'Algérie*
Date of Death: July 10, 1994
Place of Death: Algiers
Confirmed

Men disguised in police uniforms stopped Drici, a proofreader for *Le Soir d'Algérie*, and a friend as they were driving in a suburb of Algiers. The men released her friend, but decided not to release Drici after they found her press card. Police found Drici's body the next day. Her throat had been slit.

Mohamed Lamine Legoui, *APS*
Date of Death: July 21, 1994
Place of Death: M'Sila
Confirmed

Unidentified gunmen shot and killed Legoui, a correspondent with the Algerian Press Service (APS), outside his home in Bou-Saada, in the M'Sila region.

Mouloud Barroudi, *ANAF*
Date of Death: September 25, 1994
Place of Death: Algiers
Confirmed

The body of Barroudi, a cameraman with the National Agency of Filmed News (ANAF), was found stabbed to death near his home, west of Algiers.

Smail Sbaghdi, *APS*
Date of Death: September 25, 1994
Place of Death: Algiers
Confirmed

Sbaghdi, a reporter with the official Algerian Press Service (APS), was killed in Algiers when gunmen opened fire on the taxi in which he was a passenger.

Lahcene Bensaadallah, *El Irshad*
Date of Death: October 12, 1994
Place of Death: Algiers
Confirmed

Bensaadallah, director of *El Irshad*, a publication affiliated with the moderate Islamist party Hamas, was shot and killed outside his home in Badr, a neighborhood in Algiers.

Tayeb Bouterfif, *Algerian Radio*
Date of Death: October 16, 1994
Place of Death: South of Algiers
Confirmed

Bouterfif, who worked for the government's Berber-language radio station, was fatally shot outside his home, south of Algiers.

Farah Ziane, *Révolution Africaine*
Date of Death: October 20, 1994
Place of Death: Blida
Confirmed

Ziane, editor of the National Liberation Front (FLN) weekly *Révolution Africaine*, was shot and killed outside his home in Blida, south of Algiers.

Mohamed Salah Benachour, *APS*
Date of Death: October 27, 1994
Place of Death: Boufarik
Confirmed

Benachour, a reporter for the Algerian Press Service (APS) was shot and killed in Boufarik, south of Algiers, as he was returning from work.

Ahmed Issaad, *ENTV*
Nasseredine Lekhal, *El Massa*
Date of Death: November 30, 1994
Place of Death: Boufarik
Confirmed

Issaad, a reporter for Algerian Television (ENTV), and Lekhal, a reporter for the state-owned Arabic-language daily *El Massa*, were killed in Boufarik, about 30 kilometers south of Algiers. They were among five residents of Boufarik whom gunmen killed in a raid on the neighborhood. The journalists were forced out of their homes, then shot and beheaded.

Saïd Mekbel, *Le Matin*
Date of Death: December 4, 1994
Place of Death: Algiers
Confirmed

Mekbel, editor in chief of the independent French-language daily *Le Matin*, was shot in the head on Dec. 3 by unknown assailants as he ate in a restaurant near his paper's offices in downtown Algiers. He went into a coma and died of his wounds the next morning.

Angola

CONFIRMED: **1**
Artur Gilela, *Angolan*
   National Radio
Date of Death: June 16, 1994
Place of Death: Kuito
Confirmed

Gilela, a radio sound engineer with Angolan National Radio (RNA) was killed covering heavy fighting in Kuito between government forces and rebels of the National Union for the Total Independence of Angola (UNITA).

Belarus

UNDER CPJ INVESTIGATION: **1**

Alexander Chulanov, *Belarus National Television*
Date of Death: March 1, 1994
Place of Death: Minsk
Under CPJ Investigation

Chulanov, sports correspondent for Belarus National Television was found dead in his apartment in Minsk. He was killed by a blow to the head with a heavy object. Local sources told CPJ he may have been murdered for filming Russian and Belarussian racketeers in Poland.

Bosnia-Herzegovina

CONFIRMED: **6**

Dario D'Angelo, *RAI-TV*
Marco Luchetta, *RAI-TV*
Alessandro Otta, *RAI-TV*
Date of Death: January 28, 1994
Place of Death: Near Mostar
Confirmed

D'Angelo, Luchetta and Otta, all Italian journalists working for RAI-TV, were killed by mortar fire from the Bosnian Croats as they were entering Mostar in their car. They were going to film a documentary about children orphaned by war.

Brian Brinton, *Free-lancer*
Francis Tomasic, *Free-lancer*
Date of Death: May 1, 1994
Place of Death: Near Mostar
Confirmed

Brinton, a free-lance photographer from the United States, and Tomasic, a free-lance journalist acting as a translator for William Vollman of *Spin* magazine, were killed by road mines en route to Mostar.

Mohammed Hussein Navab, *Keyhan*
Date of Death: August 30, 1994
Place of Death: Mostar
Confirmed

Navab, a correspondent for the Tehran daily *Keyhan*, disappeared on Aug. 28, and his body was discovered on Sept. 5. A coroner determined that he died on Aug. 30. A fact-finding mission sent to Mostar by the Iranian government concluded that Navab was abducted and killed by Croat militiamen.

UNDER CPJ INVESTIGATION: **1**

Risto Djogo, *Bosnian-Serb Television*
Date of Death: September 1994
Place of Death: Bosnia
Under CPJ Investigation

Djogo, the director of Bosnian-Serb Television in Pale, was last seen on Sept. 10 near the border between Muslim-led Bosnia and Serbian-controlled Bosnia. His body was later found in a lake. An official autopsy concluded that his death was an accident, but colleagues suspect he was murdered. Djogo was a Serbian nationalist who ridiculed Muslims on his news show. He had also criticized Serbian President Slobodan Milosevic for cutting off support for the Bosnian Serbs.

Brazil

CONFIRMED: **1**

Joao Alberto Ferreira Souto, *Jornal Do Estado*
Date of Death: February 19, 1994
Place of Death: Vitória da Conquista
Confirmed

Souto, owner of *Jornal do Estado* in Vitória da Conquista, was shot dead by unidentified gunmen outside his home. He was an outpoken critic of politicians and government officials.

Burundi

CONFIRMED: **1**

Alexis Bandyatuyaga,
*National Radio and Television of
Burundi (RTNB)*
Date of Death: September 15, 1994
Place of Death: Burundi
Confirmed

Bandyatuyaga, a journalist with the National Radio and Television of Burundi (RTNB), was killed by Burundian army soldiers. Bandyatuyaga had received death threats from an army unit after he reported, in July, about army atrocities in the central part of the country.

Cambodia

CONFIRMED: **3**

Tou Chhom Mongkol, *Antarakum*
Date of Death: June 11, 1994
Place of Death: Phnom Penh
Confirmed

Mongkol, editor in chief of the Khmer-language biweekly *Antarakum*, succumbed to head injuries on June 11, one day after police found him lying unconscious on a Phnom Penh thoroughfare. Prior to Mongkol's death, *Antarakum* had carried a number of articles charging government and military officials with corruption, and its offices had been the target of a grenade attack in March.

Nun Chan,
Samleng Yuvachun Khmer
Date of Death: September 6, 1994
Place of Death: Phnom Penh
Confirmed

Nun Chan, editor in chief of *Samleng Yuvachun Khmer,* was shot and killed by two unidentified gunmen in central Phnom Penh. Nun had received several official warnings and anonymous death threats for his coverage of government corruption earlier in the year.

Chan Dara, *Koh Santepheap*
Date of Death: December 8, 1994
Place of Death: Kompong Cham
Confirmed

Dara, a reporter for the Khmer-language newspaper *Koh Santepheap*, was fatally shot while leaving a restaurant in the northeastern province of Kompong Cham. Dara had reportedly received threats from local officials who thought Dara was writing articles for *Preap Norm Sar,* an opposition newspaper that had reported on corruption in the region. Later in the month a high ranking army officer was arrested and charged with the murder.

Colombia

CONFIRMED: **1**

Jesus Medina Parra
Date of Death: January 28, 1994
Place of Death: Cucuta
Confirmed

Medina Parra, a journalist with a local radio station in conflict-ridden Cucuta, was killed on his way to work when an unidentified gunman shot him three times in the head before escaping on a motorcycle. Medina Parra hosted a morning show during which listeners would call in to complain about government corruption.

UNDER CPJ INVESTIGATION: **1**

Martin Eduardo Munera, *Radio Reloj
(Radio Caracol network)*
Date of Death: September 3, 1994
Place of Death: Medellín
Under CPJ Investigation

Munera, a broadcaster with Radio Reloj, a subsidiary of Caracol Radio Network, and vice president of the network's workers' union was killed while walking to a bus station in the city of Medellín. He was stabbed in the neck with a syringe apparently containing cyanide.

Journalists Killed in 1994

273

Egypt

CONFIRMED: **1**

Labib Ibrahim, *Egyptian Television*
Date of Death: September 17, 1994
Place of Death: Near Qena
Confirmed

Ibrahim, a camerman for Egyptian Television on assignment for UNICEF, was killed when gunmen attacked a convoy of UNICEF employees and Egyptian police as they were driving from Luxor to Qena in southern Egypt. Al-Gamaa al-Islamiyyah (the Islamic Group) claimed responsibility for the attack.

Guatemala

CONFIRMED: **1**

Victor Hugo Lopez Escobar,
   Radio Progreso
Date of Death: September 12, 1994
Place of Death: Guatemala City
Confirmed

Lopez, director of a news program on Radio Progreso, was gunned down by unidentified assailants as he emerged from his car in downtown Guatemala City.

India

CONFIRMED: **1**

Ghulam Muhammad Lone,
   Free-lancer
Date of Death: August 29, 1994
Place of Death: Near Srinagar
Confirmed

A group of masked gunmen fatally shot Lone and his 7-year-old son in their home in Kangan, Kashmir. Lone, a newspaper salesmen and free-lance journalist who contributed to several publications, including the English-language *Greater Kashmir,* had reportedly received death threats from a security agent for his coverage of troop movements in Kashmir. Srinagar police attributed the killing to Kashmiri separatists.

Iraq

CONFIRMED: **1**

Lissy Schmidt, *Free-lancer*
Date of Death: April 3, 1994
Place of Death: Sulaymaniyah
Confirmed

Schmidt, a German free-lance journalist who filed with Agence France-Presse (AFP) and the German newspapers *Frankfurter Rundschau* and *Der Tagesspiegel,* and a friend were shot and killed when gunmen opened fire on their car outside the city of Sulaymaniyah in the Kurdish-controlled area of northern Iraq.

Madagascar

UNDER CPJ INVESTIGATION: **1**

Victor Randrianirina, *Malagasy*
   National Radio
Date of Death: August 23, 1994
Place of Death: Madagascar
Under CPJ Investigation

Randrianirina, a journalist with Malagasy National Radio (RNM) died nearly a week after he was admitted to the hospital in a coma. He was severely injured by unknown assailants on Aug. 17 and never regained consciousness. A month prior to the attack he had broadcast a report from the south of Madagascar on sapphire trafficking. The report indicated Mafia involvement in the trafficking, and provided names of some of those said to be implicated. An ongoing government investigation still has not identified the assailants.

Mexico

CONFIRMED: **1**

Jorge Martín Dorantes, *El Crucero*
Date of Death: June 6, 1994
Place of Death: Morelos
Confirmed

Unknown assailants shot and killed Martín Dorantes, editor of the weekly *El Crucero*, published in Cuernavaca, Morelos. He was a known critic of local government officials. No one has been arrested for the murder.

UNDER CPJ INVESTIGATION. **2**

Enrique Peralta Torres,
La Union de Morelos
Date of Death: July 6, 1994
Place of Death: Morelos
Under CPJ Investigation

Peralta Torres, a reporter with *La Union de Morelos* and the second journalist from the region to be killed in less than a month, died from multiple shot wounds. He reportedly identified his assassin, a business associate who has since fled the country.

Jose Luis Rojas,
La Union de Morelos
Date of Death: July 11, 1994
Place of Death: Morelos
Under CPJ Investigation

Luis Rojas, a prominent reporter for *La Union de Morelos,* was found strangled to death on July 13. He was the second journalist from the paper killed in less than a week. The coroner reported that he had probably been killed two days earlier.

Pakistan

CONFIRMED: **2**

Mohammad Salahuddin, *Takbeer*
Date of Death: December 4, 1994
Place of Death: Karachi
Confirmed

Salahuddin, editor of the Urdu-language weekly *Takbeer,* was fatally shot by two unidentified gunmen on a motorcycle. The assailants ambushed him outside the paper's offices. In his editorials he was very critical of the Muhajir Quami Movement (MQM), a Karachi-based party supported by many Muslim migrants from India.

Mohammad Samdani Warsi,
Parcham
Date of Death: December 6, 1994
Place of Death: Karachi
Confirmed

Samdani, business manager of the Urdu-language daily *Parcham*, was shot and killed by unknown gunmen at the newspaper's office. The assailants were looking for *Parcham*'s editor, but turned on Samdani when they failed to find their original target. The paper's editorial policy supports the Muhajir Quami Movement (MQM).

Russia

CONFIRMED: **4**

Yuri Soltis, *Interfax*
Date of Death: June 12, 1994
Place of Death: Moscow
Confirmed

Soltis, a crime reporter for the independent news agency Interfax, was found beaten to death at a train station in the Stroitel district on the outskirts of Moscow. Soltis' colleagues in Moscow told CPJ that they believe the reporter's murder is linked to his investigation of Russia's criminal underworld.

Dmitry Kholodov,
Moscovski Komsomolets
Date of Death: October 17, 1994
Place of Death: Moscow
Confirmed

Kholodov, an investigative reporter for the *Moskovski Komsomolets*, was killed in a bomb blast at the newspaper's offices. Kholodov, who had been investigating Mafia connections with the military, was killed when he opened a briefcase he had been led to believe contained secret documents exposing military corruption.

Cynthia Elbaum,
Free-lance photographer
Date of Death: December 22, 1994
Place of Death: Grozny, Chechnya
Confirmed

Elbaum, an American free-lance photographer was killed during a Russian air raid over Grozny, capital of the breakaway republic of Chechnya.

Vladimir Zhitarenko,
Krasnaya Zvezda
Date of Death: December 31, 1994
Place of Death: Grozny, Chechnya
Confirmed

Zhitarenko, a correspondent for the Russian armed forces daily *Krasnaya Zvezda*, was hit by two bullets as he stepped out of an armoured personnel carrier on a front-line near the Chechen capital of Grozny. He died of his wounds on New Year's Day.

UNDER CPJ INVESTIGATION: **2**
Sergei Dubov, *Vsyo Dlya Vas, Novoye Vremya, International* and *Moscow Business Week*
Date of Death: February 1, 1994
Place of Death: Moscow
Under CPJ Investigation

Dubov, publisher of several newspapers and magazines *(Vsyo Dlya Vas, Novoye Vremya, International* and *Moscow Business Week)* was shot dead in front of his house. He was killed by a single bullet fired by an assailant who was standing in a telephone booth.

Andrei Aizderdzis, *Who's Who*
Date of Death: April 26, 1994
Place of Death: Near Moscow
Under CPJ Investigation

Aizderdzis, publisher of the weekly newspaper *Who's Who* and a member of the Russian State Duma was killed by a shotgun blast to the throat as he returned to his home in the Moscow suburb of Khimki. Russian lawmakers believe the slaying stems from the publication in *Who's Who* of the names of 266 organized crime figures.

Rwanda

CONFIRMED: **15**
André Kameya, *Rwanda Rushya*
Date of Death: April-June, 1994
Place of Death: Rwanda
Confirmed

Kameya, editor in chief of the newspaper *Rwanda Rushya* and an official of the opposition Liberal Party (PL), was killed with his wife and son. Kameya had been imprisoned and threatened with death under the Habyarimana regime on several occasions since 1991.

Winifrida Mukamana, *Reba Videwo*
Date of Death: April 7, 1994
Place of Death: Kigali
Confirmed

Mukamana, an editor at the video production company Reba Videwo, was killed by the military in Remera, near Kigali's airport, on the first day of the massacres.

Eudès Nshimiryo, *TV Rwanda*
Date of Death: April 7, 1994
Place of Death: Kigali
Confirmed

Nshimiryo, a director with the state-run TV Rwanda, was killed at home in Nyamirambo, Kigali, on the first day of the massacres. Soldiers came to his home while he was entertaining guests, some of whom were Tutsi. The soldiers attacked the guests, and Nshimiryo attempted to come to their defense by showing the soldiers his press card. He was killed immediately.

Aloys Nyimbuzi, *L'Observateur*
Date of Death: April 7, 1994
Place of Death: Kigali
Confirmed

Nyimbuzi, a journalist with the opposition paper *L'Observateur,* was killed at his home in Gikondo, Kigali, on the first day of the massacres.

Gilbert Munana, *Le Flambeau*
Date of Death: April 8, 1994
Place of Death: Kigali
Confirmed

Munana, a journalist on the opposition newspaper *Le Flambeau,* was killed by militiamen in Gikondo, Kigali, on the second day of the massacres.

Tharcisse Rubwiriza, *Orinfor*
Date of Death: April 8 or 9, 1994
Place of Death: Kigali
Confirmed

Rubwiriza, a journalist in the radio section of the official information department Orinfor, was killed at his home in Gikondo, Kigali, on April 8 or 9. Rubwiriza ran a popular Sunday morning radio program where he reviewed a cross-section of the week's newspapers, and discussed opposition views.

Gratien Karambizi, *Imbaga*
Date of Death: April 9, 1994
Place of Death: Kigali
Confirmed

Karambizi, a journalist on the opposition paper *Imbaga*, was killed at his home in Kimisayara, Kigali. Two of his children were killed with him. He had been detained for six weeks in 1991.

Vincent Rwabukwizi, *Kanguku*
Date of Death: April 10-12, 1994
Place of Death: Kigali
Confirmed

Rwabukwizi, director of the opposition newspaper *Kanguku,* was shot dead by the military between April 10 and April 12, in front of his home in Nyamirambo, Kigali. He was considered to be close to the rebel Rwandan Patriotic Front (FPR). Rwabukwizi had a long history of persecution by the government for his work as a journalist, including a 15-year jail term imposed in 1990, of which he served 10 months. Within a month of his release, he was detained again for a further four months. He was freed in September 1991, but was constantly harassed, and at times went into hiding.

Obed Bazimaziki, *Le Flambeau*
Date of Death: April 11, 1994
Place of Death: Kigali
Confirmed

Bazimaziki, a journalist with the opposition paper *Le Flambeau,* was killed near his home in Nyakabanda, Kigali. He had been detained by the government in 1991.

277

Charles Bideri-Munyangabe,
Le Messager
Date of Death: April 11, 1994
Place of Death: Kigali
Confirmed

Bideri-Munyangabe, a journalist with *Le Messager,* was killed in Nyakabanda, at the same time as his colleague Obed Bazimaziki.

Marcellin Kayiranga, *Kanguka*
Date of Death: April 22, 1994
Place of Death: Kigali
Confirmed

Kayiranga, an editor for the opposition newspaper *Kanguka,* was thrown into the latrine at his cousin's home, in Muhima, Kigali, and killed. In 1993, Kayiranga had gone into hiding for several weeks after learning that state security agents were searching for him.

Charles Karinganire, *Le Flambeau*
Date of Death: April 24, 1994
Place of Death: Kigali
Confirmed

Karinganire, a journalist on the opposition paper *Le Flambeau,* was killed at home by soldiers who butchered him with machetes, cutting him into pieces in front of his young brother. Karinganire had been detained for over two months in 1991.

Emmanuel-Damien Rukondo,
Rubyiruko-Rubanda
Date of Death: April 24, 1994
Place of Death: Kigali
Confirmed

Rukondo, a free-lance journalist for *Rubyiruko-Rubanda* and president of the Association of Newspaper Owners, was killed in Centre Saint-Paul, in Kiyovu, Kigali. He was forced to get into the back of a truck and was paraded naked around the neighborhood before being killed and cut up into pieces.

Anastase Seruvumba, *Imbaga*
Date of Death: April 29, 1994
Place of Death: Rwanda
Confirmed

Seruvumba, a journalist with the opposition paper *Imbaga,* was killed after having been denounced. He had returned to Rwanda in January 1994, after two years of study in Switzerland. He also worked for *Kinyamateka* newspaper.

Vénant Ntawucikayenda,
TV Rwanda
Date of Death: May 10, 1994
Place of Death: Kigali
Confirmed

Ntawucikayenda, a cameraman for state-run TV Rwanda, was killed in a bomb blast at the TV station.

UNDER CPJ INVESTIGATION: **5**

Théotime Kamanayo, *Kiberinka*
Date of Death: April-June 1994
Place of Death: Kigali
Under CPJ Investigation

Kamanayo, a journalist with the opposition paper *Kiberinka,* was killed at his home in Mumena, Kigali, by members of a militia. In 1992, Kamanayo and three colleagues had been harassed by the government and had temporarily gone into hiding.

Jeanne d'Arc Mukamusoni, *Le Soleil*
Date of Death: April-June 1994
Place of Death: Kigali
Under CPJ Investigation

Mukamusoni, director of the opposition newspaper *Le Soleil,* which was close to the Social Democrat Party (PSD), was killed by militiamen at a checkpoint in Nyakabanda as she tried to flee Kigali.

Ignace Ruhatana, *Kanyarwanda*
Date of Death: April-June 1994
Place of Death: Kigali
Under CPJ Investigation

Ruhatana, editor in chief of the journal *Kanyarwanda* and an official of the human rights organization by the same name, was killed in his home district of Nyakabanda by a soldier of the Rwandan Armed Forces. In 1993, he was attacked and injured by armed men who tried to take documents belonging to Kanyarwanda from him.

Alfonoe Rutsindura,
Amakuruki i Butare
Date of Death: April-June 1994
Place of Death: Butare
Under CPJ Investigation

Rutsindura, editor in chief of *Amakuruki i Butare* and a contributor to the intellectual journal *Dialogue*, was killed by militiamen was he was returning to his home in Butare. His wife, children and parents were also murdered. In 1990, Rutsindura had been detained for six months for reporting on massacres of students in Butare.

Vincent Shabakaka, *Kiberinka*
Date of Death: April-June 1994
Place of Death: Kigali
Under CPJ Investigation

Shabakaka, a journalist on the Kigali-based newspaper *Kiberinka*, was killed by militiamen in Nyamirambo, at the home of his neighbors. In 1992, he and several colleagues from the paper were threatened and had gone into hiding, fearing arrest.

Somalia
CONFIRMED: **3**
Ilaria Alpi, *RAI-3 television*
Miran Krovatin, *RAI-3 television*
Date of Death: March 20, 1994
Place of Death: Mogadishu
Confirmed

Alpi, an Italian journalist, and Krovatin, a Slovakian cameraman, on assigment for the Italian state television station RAI-3, were killed when men armed with machine guns opened fire on their pickup truck outside the Italian embassy.

Pierre Anceaux,
CARITAS-Switzerland
Date of Death: August 31, 1994
Date of Death: Baidoa
Confirmed

Anceaux, a Swiss journalist on assigment with the charity group CARITAS-Switzerland, was shot and killed in a CARITAS-run refugee camp in Baidoa, southwest of Mogadishu. Armed men in a jeep fired at Anceaux as he was interviewing a Somali woman. CARITAS shut down its operations in Somalia after Anceaux was killed.

South Africa
CONFIRMED: **2**
Abdul Shariff, *Free-lancer*
Date of Death: January 9, 1994
Place of Death:
Katlehong Township
Confirmed

Shariff, a free-lance photographer on assignment for the Associated Press (AP), was killed in crossfire while covering an African National Congress (ANC) tour in the township of Katlehong. He died of a bullet wound to the chest.

Ken Oosterbroek, *The Star*
Date of Death: April 18, 1994
Place of Death: Thokoza
Confirmed

Oosterbroek, chief photographer for Johannesburg's *The Star* newspaper, was shot and killed while covering a gun battle between Inkatha-supporting hostel-dwellers and the National Peacekeeping Force (NPKF) in the township of Thokoza, 11 days before South Africa's first democratic election.

Tajikistan

CONFIRMED: **4**

Olim Abdulov,
  Tajikistan State Television
Date of Death: May 16, 1994
Place of Death: Near Dushanbe
Confirmed

Abdulov, a staff member of Tajikistan State Television, was shot and killed by unknown persons near Dushanbe.

Khushvakht Haydarsho, *Jumhuriyat*
Date of Death: May 18, 1994
Place of Death: Dushanbe
Confirmed

Haydarsho, secretary of the editorial board of the Tajik-language government newspaper *Jumhuriyat*, was shot dead near his home in Dushanbe. Local journalists believe his murder is connected to a series of articles he published on "the criminal and political mafia" in Tajikistan.

Davlatali Rakhmonaliev,
  Tajikistan State Television
Date of Death: August 18, 1994
Place of Death: Dushanbe
Confirmed

Rakhmonaliev, director of programming at the national television station, was fatally shot in front of his home in Dushanbe. He was reported to have close ties to the pro-Communist government.

Khamidjon Khakimov, *Khaksuz*
Date of Death: November 18, 1994
Place of Death: Dushanbe
Confirmed

Khakimov, editor of the Uzbek-language newspaper *Khaksuz*, was shot in the head in Dushanbe and died overnight. He was a prominent member of Tajikistan's Uzbek minority.

Turkey

CONFIRMED: **2**

Nazim Babaoglu, *Özgür Gündem*
Date of Death: March 12, 1994
Place of Death: Near Urfa
Confirmed

Babaoglu, Urfa correspondent for the pro-Kurdish daily *Özgür Gündem*, disappeared in Siverek, a small town near Urfa. He had traveled there to follow up on a news tip from a colleague, who later denied phoning him. Babaoglu is presumed dead.

Erol Akgün, *Devrimci Çözüm*
Date of Death: September 8, 1994
Place of Death: Near Istanbul
Confirmed

Akgün, editor in chief of the left-wing weekly *Devrimci Çözüm*, was killed by unidentified assailants as he left his home in Gebze, near Istanbul. His colleagues at the paper believe he was killed by a rival left-wing faction because of his role as the weekly's editor.

Zaire

CONFIRMED: **2**

Pierre Kabeya, *Kin-Matin*
Date of Death: June 8
Place of Death: Kinshasa
Confirmed

Kabeya, a reporter for the opposition weekly *Kin-Matin*, was found dead on June 9 near Loana military camp in the Kintambo district of Kinshasa. A copy of *Kin-Matin* had been placed near his body. His death may have been linked to an article he filed on a 1991 trial in which security forces were implicated in the 1990 attack on the Lumbumbashi University campus in which several students lost their lives.

Adolphe Missamba Ndengi Kavula,
Nsemo
Date of Death: November 12, 1994
Place of Death: Kasangulu
Confirmed

Kavula, editor in chief and owner of the opposition newspaper *Nsemo* and a prominent member of the Union for Democracy and Social Progress (UDPS), was kidnapped on Oct. 28 by a group of men thought to be from the presidential militia. Ten days later, he was found barely alive in a field on his farm outside Kasangulu, 30 kilometers from Kinshasa. He appeared to have been badly tortured. He died in a Kinshasa clinic on Nov. 12. An autopsy was not performed, but medical tests indicated that he may have been injected with a toxic substance. The Zairian authorities claimed that Kavula's death was a suicide.

Journalists Receive
1994 Press Freedom Awards

THE INTERNATIONAL PRESS FREEDOM AWARDS are given annually by CPJ to journalists from around the world who have courageously provided independent news coverage and viewpoints under difficult circumstances. To defend press freedom, award winners have risked arrest, imprisonment, violence against themselves and their families, and even death.

The 1994 Awards were presented on Nov. 9 in New York City to the following individuals:

Iqbal Athas, is one of Sri Lanka's leading military reporters and is associate editor of *The Sunday Leader*, a new, independent broadsheet based in the Sri Lankan capital of Colombo. Athas' unbiased coverage of the Sri Lankan army's wars with the Liberation Tigers of Tamil Eelam (LTTE) and other insurgent groups has frequently angered both the military and their adversaries. In 1993, in the face of death threats to him and his family, Athas reported on the failures of two army offensives against ethnic Tamil guerrillas. His exposure of the army's staggering losses played a key role in prompting the resignation of Sri Lanka's army commander. National Public Radio correspondent Maria Hinojosa, the award presenter, recounted how Athas told her "what kept him going was knowing that there were several good men, men in the army he was exposing, who he believed would stand up for him and protect him. Even in the face of fear and hatred and corrupted power, Iqbal Athas can still see the goodness in humanity, still believe in his fellow man to do the right thing. Isn't that one of the most important characteristics a journalist should have?"

Aziz Nesin, until recently the front page columnist for the leftist newspaper *Aydinlik*, is the grand old man of independent journalism in Turkey. A journalist and author, the 79-year-old Nesin writes what he believes and has been a constant advocate of free expression, despite continuous government harassment and a price on his head. During a 1993 literary festival in Sivas, a mob demanding his death attacked and burned down the hotel where Nesin was staying. Though he managed to escape with minor injuries, 37 others died. That same year, Nesin had planned to publish Salman Rushdie's controversial *Satanic Verses*. Publishers rejected Nesin's plans, but *Aydinlik* ran 13 excerpts. An angry mob raided the paper's office, damaging several presses, and the government has launched more than 30 trials against the publication for articles published since May 1993. Nesin's is a "voice of freedom for Turkey and the world," said awards presenter Barbara Walters of ABC News. "He writes and continues to speak because he feels fundamentalism is not just a problem in Turkey but is a threat that looms over all nations."

Yndamiro Restano, a 46-year-old former radio journalist, has been serving a 10-year jail term in Cuba since 1992 for organizing Harmony Movement (MAR), a popular, nonviolent movement for Cuba's transition to democratic socialism. *Esquire* Editor in Chief Edward Kosner, the awards presenter, noted that "Restano is one of the few journalists imprisoned in our hemisphere, but the Castro regime denies him even that distinction. Cubans claim Restano isn't a journalist at all but a social agitator." In June 1991, Restano was beaten and detained on his way to the trial of two Cuban doctors accused of taking part in a plot to kill President Fidel Castro. His house was searched by state security, Restano was put under surveillance, and on Dec. 20, 1991, he was arrested. He was tried and convicted of rebellion in May 1992, after top officials accused him of planning economic sabotage. A founding member of the Cuban Association of Independent Journalists (APIC), which represents journalists dismissed for political reasons, Restano is an Amnesty International Prisoner of Conscience and an honorary member of PEN International. He has been promised freedom if he agrees to leave Cuba, but Restano has said he will stay behind bars until he is set free in his homeland.

Daisy Li Yuet-wah has worked to ensure that China upholds press freedom in Hong Kong after 1997. The former chair of the Hong Kong Journalists Association (HKJA) and currently vice chair of its executive committee, Li led the HKJA campaign to reform 17 largely arcane British colonial laws, which the Chinese government could invoke to justify press restrictions after it gains sovereignty in the region. The laws include those that govern official secrets, emergency regulations and public order—grounds Beijing commonly cites when detaining dissident writers and foreign correspondents. Li, who is currently the assignment editor for *Ming Pao*, also mobilized local and international support for Xi Yang, *Ming Pao's* Beijing correspondent, who was arrested in 1993 by Chinese security officers and sentenced in May 1994 to 12 years in prison for allegedly leaking state banking secrets. Presenting the award by satellite, CNN's Peter Arnett said, "This award honors Daisy Li and her colleagues, and enlists our help in ensuring that the great free trade city of Hong Kong will also continue to have a great free press."

In memory of the staff journalists of *Navidi Vakhsh* and all Tajik journalists who have been killed in the line of duty, CPJ posthumously presented its International Press Freedom Award in 1994. Perhaps nothing reflects the recent state of events in Tajikistan better than the fate of *Navidi Vakhsh*, a Tajik-language newspaper in the impoverished Khatlon region, 100 miles south of the capital of Dushanbe. Four *Navidi Vakhsh* staff journalists were murdered between June 1993 and September 1993. CPJ interviews with local journalists, foreign diplomats and exiled opposition sources indicate that the People's Front, a paramilitary group that has become a part of Tajikistan's state security apparatus, was responsible for most, if not all, of these killings. Amid the murder of its staff members and the banning of all independent print and broadcast media, *Navidi Vakhsh* ceased publication. **Saidjonol Fakhriddinov** was killed in June 1993; his body was found on the streets of Dushanbe. **Sharofuddin Kosimov** was abducted in June or July 1993 by members of the People's Front, according to his colleagues' accounts. His body was discovered and identified by family members. **Pirimkul Sattori** was killed in Kurgan-Tyube in the summer of 1993 by members of the People's Front. Tajik journalists say he was murdered in retaliation for a speech in which he criticized the current government. **Kishvaroy Sharifova** disappeared in the fall of 1993 and is presumed dead. "The murder of reporters is, of course, not the whole story," said presenter David Remnick of *The New Yorker*. "It's the symptom, the sign of a disaster too often overlooked. I hope the memory of these reporters one day becomes a sign of the beginning of decency in Tajikistan."

George Soros, the Hungarian-born founder of the Open Society Fund and the Soros Foundations in Hungary and the Soviet Union, was given CPJ's 1994 Burton Benjamin Memorial Award in honor of his dedication to freedom of the press and his philanthropic work. He now has a network of foundations operating in 24 countries throughout Central and Eastern Europe, as well as South Africa and the United States. These foundations are helping to build the infrastructure and institutions of an open society through the support of a variety of educational, cultural and economic restructuring activities. Soros is also the founder of The Central European University in Budapest and Prague. Established in 1990, the University offers postgraduate programs in history, economics, political science, art history and the social sciences, and serves as the centerpiece of Soros' educational initiatives in Eastern Europe. Presenting the award was Ted Turner, chairman and president of Turner Broadcasting System and CPJ's 1993 honoree.

International Press Freedom Award Winners 1991–1993

1991

Pius Njawe, *Le Messager,* Cameroon
Wang Juntao and Chen Ziming, *Economics Weekly*, China
Bill Foley and Cary Vaughan, United States
Tatyana Mitkova, *TSN,* former Soviet Union
Byron Barrera, *La Epoca*, Guatemala

1992

David Kaplan, *ABC News*
Muhammad Al-Saqr, *Al-Qabas*, Kuwait
Sony Esteus, *Radio Tropic FM*, Haiti
Gwendolyn Lister, *The Namibian*, Namibia
Thepchai Yong, *The Nation*, Thailand

1993

Omar Belhouchet, *El Watan*, Algeria
Doan Viet Hoat, *Freedom Forum*, Vietnam
Nosa Igiebor, *Tell* magazine, Nigeria
Veran Matic, *Radio B92*, Belgrade
Ricardo Uceda, *Si*, Peru

Burton Benjamin Memorial Award

1991

Walter Cronkite, *CBS News*

1992

Katherine Graham, *The Washington Post Company*

1993

R.E. Turner, *Turner Broadcasting System Inc.*

Facts About the Organization and Its Activities

The Committee to Protect Journalists is a nonpartisan, nonprofit organization founded in 1981 to monitor abuses against the press and promote press freedom around the world.

How did CPJ get started?

A group of American correspondents created CPJ in response to the often brutal treatment of their foreign colleagues by authoritarian governments and other enemies of independent journalism.

Who runs CPJ?

CPJ has a professional staff of 14 at its New York headquarters, including an area specialist for each major world region. The Committee's activities are directed by a 30-member board of prominent American journalists.

How is CPJ funded?

CPJ depends on private donations from journalists, news organizations and independent foundations. CPJ accepts no government funding.

The press is powerful; why does it need protection?

On average, at least one journalist gets killed every week somewhere in the world. Scores of journalists are imprisoned every year because of what they have reported. Hundreds more are routinely subjected to physical attack, illegal detention, spurious legal action and threats against their lives.

How does CPJ "protect" journalists?

CPJ investigates and publicizes abuses against the press and acts on behalf of imprisoned and threatened journalists. Staff experts organize international protest campaigns, arrange emergency legal counsel, lead fact-finding missions, and find threatened journalists safe refuge abroad. CPJ advises local press groups on how to document violations and mobilize international support. CPJ publishes articles and news releases, special reports, a quarterly newsletter and the most comprehensive annual report on attacks against the press around the world. CPJ makes sure that no one can violate the rights of journalists with impunity.

Where does CPJ get its information?

Through its own reporting. CPJ has full-time program coordinators monitoring the press in the Americas, Asia, the Middle East, Africa, and Europe. They track developments through their own independent research and firsthand contacts in the field, including reports from other journalists. CPJ shares information on breaking cases with other press freedom organizations worldwide through the International Freedom of Expression Exchange (IFEX), a global e-mail network.

When would journalists call upon CPJ?

• When they or colleagues get in trouble. CPJ has developed a vast network of media and government contacts and can intervene any time a journalist is endangered.

287

- When traveling on assignment. CPJ is in regular contact with local journalists around the world and is happy to put them in touch with each other. CPJ also can brief correspondents on upcoming assignments.
- When covering the news. Attacks against the press are news, and they often serve as the first signal of a crackdown on all freedoms. CPJ is uniquely situated to provide journalists with information and insight into press conditions around the world.
- When becoming a member. A basic membership costs only $35 and each donation helps assure that CPJ will be there to defend you or a colleague if the need arises. Members receive CPJ's quarterly newsletter, *Dangerous Assignments*, and a discount on other publications.

Ways to Help CPJ

	Journalists	**Everyone**
Become a Member *Starting at $35*	Show your support for your colleagues and stay informed about press conditions by becoming a member of CPJ. Gift memberships are also available.	Show your support for freedom of the press and stay informed about press conditions by becoming a member of CPJ. Gift memberships are also available.
Buy CPJ's Publications *Members receive a 50% discount*	CPJ's reports on press conditions and safety manuals for journalists are an invaluable tool for reporters. Buy them for your newsrooms and help defray the cost of this important service.	CPJ's reports on press conditions around the world shed light on emerging political developments. They are essential reading for anyone interested in freedom of expression or human rights.
Attend the International Press Freedom Awards Dinner *November 1995* *New York City*	The International Press Freedom Awards Dinner honors the struggle of journalists who risk their lives to report the news. It is a major gathering of journalists and media companies, and it raises more than half of CPJ's operating funds. Show your support for freedom of the press by attending this important event.	The International Press Freedom Awards Dinner honors the struggle of journalists who risk their lives to report the news. It is a major gathering of journalists and media companies, and it raises more than half of CPJ's operating funds. Show your support for freedom of the press by attending this important event.
Provide Information on Cases	Whenever a colleague or news organization is threatened, harassed or attacked, we need reliable information fast.	We need information from as many sources as possible. If you have information about a journalist or news organization being threatened, harassed or attacked, contact CPJ immediately.
Support our Campaigns	Letters from journalists in support of their colleagues under attack do make a difference. Stay on top of current cases by subscribing to CPJ's quarterly newsletter, *Dangerous Assignments*, and by accessing the Human Rights Gopher on the Internet, where CPJ files many of its action alerts and reports. Call CPJ for details.	There is strength in numbers. Letters of protest from the business community concerning the cases CPJ is working on adds to the international pressure applied by news organizations and human rights groups. Stay on top of current cases by subscribing to CPJ's quarterly newsletter *Dangerous Assignments*, and by accessing the Human Rights Gopher on the Internet, where CPJ files many of its action alerts and reports. Call CPJ for details.
News Coverage and Letters to the Editor	Freedom of the press is a barometer of social and political upheaval. Coverage of the problems faced by independent journalists in developing countries is the best way of furthering the cause of press freedom worldwide.	Write letters to the editor of your local news organization, expressing your concern for the cases that CPJ is working on.

Ways to Help CPJ

	News Organizations	**Companies**
Become a Corporate Member *Starting at $1,000*	CPJ works on behalf of journalists everywhere. Your organization's membership sends a powerful message that journalists everywhere are looking out for the rights of their colleagues.	Companies rely on the up-to-the-minute information that news organizations provide. And news organizations rely on advertising revenue. This close working relationship makes freedom of the press vitally important to all businesses. Your company's membership contribution is a symbolic message that says, "Freedom of the press is everybody's business."
Buy CPJ's Publications *Members receive a 50% discount*	CPJ's reports on press conditions and safety manuals for journalists are invaluable tools for reporters. Buy them for your newsrooms and help defray the cost of this important service.	CPJ's reports on press conditions around the world shed light on emerging political developments. This information can be extremely useful for international businesses.
Support our Membership Campaign	Encourage your employees to become members of CPJ by distributing our membership materials at work. Your company can also match employee contributions to CPJ.	Encourage your employees to become members of CPJ by distributing our membership materials at work. Your company can also match employee contributions to CPJ.
Buy a table at the International Press Freedom Awards Dinner *November 1995* *New York City*	The International Press Freedom Awards Dinner honors the struggle of journalists who risk their lives to report the news. It is a major gathering of media companies and journalists, and it raises more than half of CPJ's operating funds. Show your company's commitment to CPJ's work by purchasing a table for 1995.	The International Press Freedom Awards Dinner honors the struggle of journalists who risk their lives to report the news. It is a major gathering of media companies and journalists, and it raises more than half of CPJ's operating funds. Show your company's commitment to CPJ's work by purchasing a table for 1995.
Donate products and services	CPJ is well-known for its solid research. You can help keep us informed by joining the many news organizations around the world that donate their newspapers, magazines, wire services and other information services.	Your company can keep our costs down by providing products and services we need, such as publicity, graphic design, advertising, long-distance telephone, printing, travel, video, photography, computers, software, cameras and office furniture.

CPJ Publications

All members receive a 50 percent discount off the cost of publications. Visa, Mastercard, American Express, check and money orders are accepted. To order any titles listed below, please call (212) 465-1004 (x115).

Attacks on the Press, $30

A comprehensive annual survey of attacks against journalists and news organizations around the world.
1994 Edition, Preface by John Seigenthaler
1993 Edition, Preface by Charlayne Hunter-Gault
1992 Edition, Preface by Terry Anderson

Dangerous Assignments Quarterly, $10

CPJ's newsletter focuses on international press conditions and attacks on the press. Free to members.

Silenced: The Unsolved Murders
of Immigrant Journalists in the United States, (1976-1993), $10

A study of journalists killed in the United States reveals that when foreign-born journalists are murdered, their cases are rarely solved. DECEMBER1994 [SOLD OUT]

Journalists' Survivial Guide:
The Former Yugoslavia, $10

This easy-to-carry booklet provides advice from journalists for journalists on everything from where to get flak jackets, insurance and rental cars to tips on avoiding sniper fire in Sarajevo. It includes a list of phone numbers for U.N. and other relief agencies in the area, as well as organizations to call when making travel plans or in case of emergency. NOVEMBER 1994.

Don't Force Us to Lie, $20

The Struggle of Chinese Journalists in the Reform Era
A detailed study of the determined efforts of Chinese journalists to speak and write freely throughout the 1980s and early 1990s. With a foreword by Dan Rather and contributions by China scholar Anne Thurston, this book is one of the most comprehensive accounts available of how journalism works in the world's most populous country. JANUARY 1993

In the Censor's Shadow, $10

Journalism in Suharto's Indonesia
A comprehensive account of media repression in Indonesia despite the government's avowed policy of openness. It includes eyewitness accounts by two American reporters of the Army massacre in Dili, East Timor. NOVEMBER 1991

The Soviet Media's Year of Decision, $10

Pulitzer Prize-winning journalist Hedrick Smith analyzes the press in Gorbachev's Soviet Union and events leading up to the attempted coup of August 1991. This report includes a comprehensive guide to media organizations, primarily in Russia. SEPTEMBER 1991

Dangerous Assignments, $10

A Study Guide
Designed to stimulate classroom discussion of press freedom issues, *Dangerous Assignments* describes the dangers that reporters face in Latin America, Southeast Asia, and Africa. Also available is a companion 60-minute television documentary featuring U.S. network anchors. FALL 1991

Journalism Under Occupation, $20

Israel's Regulation of the Palestinian Press
In this report, CPJ and Article 19 argue that the control Israel exercises over the Palestinian press goes well beyond what might be justified to avert clear threats to security. OCTOBER 1988

Donors

The Committee to Protect Journalists gratefully acknowledges the news organizations, foundations, companies and individuals whose contributions make our work possible. In 1994, over $1.1 million in gifts and grants allowed CPJ to work on all of the cases listed in this volume of *Attacks on the Press*. To find out how you or your company can help, please see pages 289-290.

$50,000 and above
The Ford Foundation
The Joyce Mertz Gilmore Foundation
The Robert McCormick Tribune Foundation

$25,000-$49,999
Capital Cities/ABC, Inc.
CBS
The Hearst Corporation
The John S. and James L. Knight Foundation
The John D. and Catherine T. MacArthur Foundation
The John Roderick MacArthur Foundation
The Menemsha Fund
NBC, Inc.
The New York Times
The Samuel I. Newhouse Foundation
News Corporation Ltd.
The Scherman Foundation
Time Warner, Inc.

$10,000-$24,999
Allen & Company
Franz and Marcia Allina
The Chicago Tribune Foundation
The Coca-Cola Company
Dow Jones & Company, Inc.
The Freedom Forum
Goldman, Sachs & Co.
Johnson & Johnson
The New Yorker
Open Society Institute
Dan Rather
Rogers & Wells
Soros Fund Management

Marlo Thomas and Phil Donahue
Time Magazine
Viacom International, Inc.
The Washington Post Company

$5,000-$9,999
Advertising Age
American Lawyer Media, L.P./Court TV
AT&T Foundation
Baker & Hostetler
New York *Daily News*
Debevoise & Plimpton
The Discovery Channel
ESPN
Harper's Magazine
Mrs. Henry J. Heinz, II
K-III Magazine Corporation
Morgan Stanley & Co.
New York Newsday
Newsweek
NYNEX Corporation
Ogilvy Adams & Rinehart
People Magazine
Random House Trade Division
Reebok Foundation
Reuters America, Inc.
Mr. and Mrs. William Ruane
Times Mirror Company
Turner Broadcasting System, Inc.
TV Guide
Twentieth Century Fox Film Corporation
USA Today
Weil, Gotshal & Manges
William Zabel

$1,000-$4,999

Mr. and Mrs. Louis Begley
Mr. and Mrs. Robert L. Bernstein
BIIC Communications, Inc.
The Boston Globe
Benjamin Bradlee and Sally Quinn
Calmers Publishing Company
Cox Newspapers
Cowles Media Foundation
Mr. and Mrs. Richard Clurman
Helen K. Copley
Mrs. Jan Cowles
Alan Dresher
Edelman PR Worldwide
Lewis M. Edmonds
Osborn and Inger Elliott
Paul J. Elston
Katherine Fanning
Samuel N. Friedman
James C. Goodale
Alice Gottesman
Richard Grand-Jean and Christine Doudna
Mr. and Mrs. Gustave M. Hauser
James F. Hoge
The Horowitz Family Fund
Joseph Kingsbury-Smith
Gary E. Knell, Esq.
Knight-Ridder, Inc.
Joan Konner
Lazard Freres & Co.
Richard Leibner
Lexis/Nexis
Life Magazine
Robert MacNeil
David Marash
Kati Marton

Mr. and Mrs. Emanuel Massing
Robert McGuire
Geraldine Fabrikant Mertz
  and Robert T. Mertz
The Miami Herald
Judith Moses
Victor Navasky
Newhouse Newspapers
The Newspaper Guild
The New York Review of Books
Victor Niederhoffer
Donald A. Pels
Playboy
Mr. and Mrs. David Rockefeller
Carolyn Roehm
Andrew A. Rooney
Robert D. Sack, Esq.
Gerald Schonfeld
Scudder, Stevens & Clark
Sidney Sheldon
Gay and Nan Talese
Seymour Topping
A. Robert Towbin
Mr. and Mrs. Garry Trudeau
Enzo Viscusi
WABC-TV, Inc.
Jann S. Wenner
Michael and Zena Wiener

IN-KIND SERVICES

The Associated Press
Leadership Directories, Inc.
Lexis/Nexis
New York Newsday
Reuters America Inc.
Time Inc.

CONTRIBUTING NEWS ORGANIZATIONS

Advertising Age
American Lawyer Media, L.P./Court TV
The Associated Press
BHC Communications, Inc.
The Boston Globe
Cahners Publishing Company
Capital Cities/ABC, Inc.
CBS
The Chicago Tribune
Cowles Media Foundation
Cox Newspapers
New York *Daily News*
The Democrat and Chronicle/Times Union
The Discovery Channel
Dow Jones & Company, Inc.
ESPN
The Freedom Forum
Harper's Magazine
The Hearst Corporation
K-III Magazine Corporation
Knight-Ridder, Inc.
Lexis/Nexis
Life Magazine
The Miami Herald
NBC, Inc.
New York Newsday

The New York Review of Books
The New York Times
The New Yorker
Newhouse Newspapers
News Corporation Ltd.
The Newspaper Guild
Newsweek
People Magazine
The Philadelphia Inquirer
Playboy
Random House Trade Division
Reuters America Inc.
Rolling Stone
San Jose Mercury News
Time Magazine
Time Warner Inc.
Times Mirror Company
Turner Broadcasting System, Inc.
TV Guide
Twentieth Century Fox Film Corporation
USA Today & *USA Today International*
Variety Magazine
Viacom International Inc.
WABC-TV, Inc.
The Washington Post Company

Staff

William A. Orme, Jr.
Executive Director
(212) 465-9344 x102
E-Mail: orme@cpj.igc.apc.org

Program Coordinators
Avner Gidron
Director of Research and Coordinator,
Middle East and North Africa
(212) 465-9344 x105
E-Mail: middleeast@cpj.igc.apc.org

Ana Arana
Americas
(212) 465-9344 x106
E-Mail: latinamerica@cpj.igc.apc.org

Jennifer Pogrund
Africa
(212) 465-9344 x103
E-Mail: africa@cpj.igc.apc.org

Vikram Parekh
Asia
(212) 465-9344 x109
E-Mail: asia@cpj.igc.apc.org

Leonid Zagalsky
Central Europe (including the republics
of the former Soviet Union)
(212) 465-9344 x104
E-Mail: europe@cpj.igc.apc.org

Research Associates
Yalman Onaran
Turkey and The Balkans
(212) 465-9344 x101
E-Mail: turkey@cpj.igc.apc.org

Mira Gajević
Americas
(212) 465-9344, x117
E-Mail: mgajevic@cpj.igc.apc.org

Development
Todd Wiener
Director of Development
(212) 465-9344 x113
E-Mail: twiener@cpj.igc.apc.org

Kari Corwin
Membership and Event Coordinator
(212) 465-9344 x107
E-Mail: kcorwin@cpj.igc.apc.org

Publications
Jeanne Sahadi
Director of Publications
(212) 465-9344 x108
E-Mail: editor@cpj.igc.apc.org

Administration
Sunsh Stein
Business Manager
(212) 465-9344 x116
E-Mail: sstein@cpj.igc.apc.org

Nicole Cordrey
Administrative Assistant
(212) 465-9344 x115
E-Mail: ncordrey@cpj.igc.apc.org

Fiona Dunne
Administrative Assistant
(212) 465-9344 x100
E-Mail: fdunne@cpj.igc.apc.org

Board of Directors

How to Report an Attack on the Press

CPJ needs accurate, detailed information in order to document abuses of press freedom and effectively help journalists in trouble. CPJ corroborates the information and takes appropriate action on behalf of the journalists and news organizations involved.

What to report:

Journalists who are:
- Missing
- Killed
- Arrested or kidnapped
- Wounded
- Assaulted
- Threatened
- Harassed
- Wrongfully expelled
- Wrongfully sued for libel or defamation
- Denied credentials
- Censored

News organizations that have been:
- Attacked, raided or illegally searched
- Closed by force
- Wrongfully sued for libel or defamation
- Censored
- Materials confiscated or damaged
- Editions confiscated or transmissions jammed

Information Needed:

CPJ needs accurate, detailed information about:
- Journalists and news organizations involved
- Date and circumstances of incident
- Background information

Who to call:
Anyone with information about an attack on the press should call CPJ:

Call collect if necessary.
(212) 465-1004

Or send us a fax at:
(212) 465-9568

Africa: Jennifer Pogrund
(212) 465-9344 x103
E-Mail: africa@cpj.igc.apc.org

Americas: Ana Arana
(212) 465-9344 x106
E-Mail: latinamerica@cpj.igc.apc.org

Asia: Vikram Parekh
(212) 465-9344 x109
E-Mail: asia@cpj.igc.apc.org

Central Europe (including the republics of the former Soviet Union): Leonid Zagalsky
(212) 465-9344 x104
E-Mail: europe@cpj.igc.apc.org

Middle East and North Africa: Avner Gidron
(212) 465-9344 x105
E-Mail: middleeast@cpj.igc.apc.org

What happens next:

Depending on the case, CPJ will:
- Confirm the report.
- Pressure authorities to respond.
- Notify human rights groups and press organizations around the world: *IFEX, Article 19, Amnesty International, Reporters Sans Frontières, PEN, International Federation of Journalists, Human Rights Watch and others.*
- Increase public awareness through the press.
- Publish advisories to warn other journalists about potential dangers.
- Send a fact-finding mission to investigate.

Becoming a CPJ Member

**CPJ helps journalists fight •Wrongful Imprisonment •Assaults •Harassment •Censorship
Your membership includes a subscription to CPJ's newsletter, _Dangerous Assignments_,
and a 50 percent discount on all other CPJ publications.**

"CPJ often is the only thing keeping a journalist alive,
the only thing that offers hope of release from prison or persecution."
Terry Anderson

Member Profile

I want to join as a:
[ ] Member $35
[ ] Student........................$15
[ ] Contributor...............$100
[ ] Supporter..................$500
[ ] Benefactor..............$1,000

I work as a:
[ ] Reporter
[ ] Photographer
[ ] Editor/Producer
[ ] Publisher
[ ] Other:

Name

Company

Address

City   State   Zip

Work Phone   Home Phone

Fax   E-Mail

PAYMENT INFORMATION

[ ] Visa   [ ] Mastercard   [ ] American Express   [ ] Check Enclosed

Card Number   Expiration Date

Name On Card   Amount to Charge

Signature
                                    All contributions are tax-deductible

---

330 Seventh Avenue, 12th Floor, New York, NY 10001, USA
(212) 465-1004 • Fax: (212) 465-9568 • E-Mail: cpj@igc.apc.org

Index of Countries